The Executive's Guide to New Food Safety Laws

*How the Food Safety Modernization Act
Impacts Your Business*

James T. O'Reilly
Shannon G. May

ASPATORE

Project Manager, Kristen Lindeman; edited by Eddie Fournier; proofread by Melanie Zimmerman

ISBN 978-0-314-27572-1

For corrections, updates, comments, or any other inquiries, please e-mail TLR.AspatoreEditorial@thomson.com.

First Printing, 2011
10 9 8 7 6 5 4 3 2 1

Mat #41154257

ASPATORE

Aspatore Books, a Thomson Reuters business, exclusively publishes C-Level executives (CEO, CFO, CTO, CMO, Partner) from the world's most respected companies and law firms. C-Level Business Intelligence™, as conceptualized and developed by Aspatore Books, provides professionals of all levels with proven business intelligence from industry insiders—direct and unfiltered insight from those who know it best—as opposed to third-party accounts offered by unknown authors and analysts. Aspatore Books is committed to publishing an innovative line of business and legal books, those which lay forth principles and offer insights that, when employed, can have a direct financial impact on the reader's business objectives, whatever they may be. In essence, Aspatore publishes critical tools for all business professionals.

Dedication

This book is dedicated to George M. Burditt, the gentle giant for whom food safety law has been an abiding passion and inspiration for half a century, with thanks from the many whom he mentored and inspired.

CONTENTS

Preface 9

Chapter 1: Introduction and Background of the New Act 11

Chapter 2: Required Safety Plans for Food Facilities 23

Chapter 3: Safety Standards, Testing, and Precautions 61

Chapter 4: Food Defense Obligations 97

Chapter 5: Certification of Imported Food Compliance 107

Chapter 6: Food Importers and Verification Duties 143

Chapter 7: Registration of Food Facilities 163

Chapter 8: Requirements for Tracing and Recordkeeping
of Food Shipments 189

Chapter 9: FDA Inspections of Facilities and Records
at Food Facilities in the United States and Foreign Nations 223

Chapter 10: Enforcement Tools: Recalls, Detention, and Penalties 273

Chapter 11: Costs and Fees 313

Chapter 12: International Trade Constraints
on FDA Import Controls 333

Chapter 13: Impacts on Existing Food Registry and Controls 349

Chapter 14: Employee Concerns and Whistleblower Risks 357

Chapter 15: Dietary Supplements and Other Provisions 369

Chapter 16: Organizing a Food Business for Compliance 381

Appendix: Final Text of the Statute 389

Topical Index by Chapter 563

About the Author 575

Preface

Rising from the dead isn't easy. The story of Lazarus in the Bible has been repeatedly cited, as friends of the 2010 food safety legislation have tried to explain how such a complex bill survived the harshly toxic environment of Senate and House political wrangling in the turbulent final year of the 111th Congress. It took a miracle amid a crowd of doubters for the original Lazarus to be brought back from the dead. Likewise, it took a series of last-minute legislative compromises and high-risk deals for the food safety legislation to endure, despite repeated claims that the bill was "dead." A favorite headline along the way came from lawyer/raconteur Bill Marler of Seattle, that if food safety were left to the sole control of the dominant party in the 2012 Congress, "Food safety would be toast." The final bill passed the House on the last night just before the Christmas break, at the very end of a tumultuous lame-duck session. Despite the timing, it was no Christmas gift. David Weigel of *Slate* magazine made the cynical observation: "It's a Christmas miracle, if the key characteristics of Christmas are self-interest and fatigue." Whatever the legislators' motivations, the compromise bill passed, and now the task for you is to deal with the law's requirements.

Our goal is to make this complex law understandable by not writing the conventional boring law textbook. The authors hope you will find this text a useful reference for the expensive implementation process, which is likely to consume several years of further wrangling and discontent. The evolution will perhaps lead to further legislative debates over funding, as well as to improvement of the sometimes odd compromise arrangements, like the "275-mile radius" exception for farmers who are selling food without complying with a full set of safety requirements. Fans of local food might not have had 275 miles within their concept of "local," but that was the Montana senator's compromise wording. The final bill lost key features of the House-passed 2009 version, like quarantine powers and user fees for all facilities, but the bill effects positive changes overall.

The authors express appreciation for the insights of the numerous industry and consumer advocates and journalists who have shared their perspectives during the grueling process of adoption. For reasons of discretion, these sources' names won't appear here, but the contents of this book reflect the benefits of their many suggestions and insights. Professor Joel Hoffman offered invaluable suggestions, which were gratefully accepted.

Professor O'Reilly wishes to thank his student research assistants at the University of Cincinnati College of Law, especially Jenna Washatka, Catherine Terrell, and Chad Thompson, and he greatly appreciates his family's encouragement from Carol, Jessie, and C.B. Ms. May wishes to thank her family and her professional colleagues for their encouragement of her efforts to complete this project.

The authors welcome feedback for future editions, via Professor O'Reilly at the College of Law, University of Cincinnati, Cincinnati, OH 45221-0040.

James O'Reilly and Shannon May
February 2011

1

Introduction and Background
of the New Act

Is Imported Food a Significant Part of the US Economy?

From 1997 to 2007, US imports of agricultural and seafood products increased by 94 percent, from $43 billion in 1997 to $83.6 billion in 2007.[1] Fifteen percent of food consumed annually in the United States is imported, although for some foods, such as seafood and produce, imported food makes up a far greater percentage. More than 60 percent of the fruit and vegetables consumed in the United States are imported.[2]

How Does the FDA Manage Imported Food Safety Oversight?

The Food and Drug Administration (FDA) exercises less oversight over imported food than domestically produced food.[3] The FDA only inspects a very small percentage of food being imported into the United States. Since

---

[1] Geoffrey S. Becker, CRS Report for Congress, *U.S. Food and Agricultural Imports: Safeguards and Selected Issues* 1 (2009) [hereinafter *Safeguards and Selected Issues*].

[2] U.S. Gen. Accounting Office, *Food Safety: Agencies Need to Address Gaps in Enforcement and Collaboration to Enhance Safety of Imported Food* 1 (2009) [hereinafter *Agencies Need to Address Gaps in Enforcement and Collaboration to Enhance Safety of Imported Food*].

[3] *See* U.S. GEN. ACCOUNTING OFFICE, FEDERAL OVERSIGHT OF FOOD SAFETY, *FDA Has Provided Few Details on the Resources and Strategies Needed to Implement Its Food Protection Plan* 8 (2008) [hereinafter *FDA Has Provided Few Details on the Resources and Strategies Needed to Implement Its Food Protection Plan*]; U.S. GEN. ACCOUNTING OFFICE, FEDERAL OVERSIGHT OF FOOD SAFETY, *Fundamental Restructuring Is Needed to Address Fragmentation and Overlap* 7 (2004) [hereinafter *Fundamental Restructuring Is Needed to Address Fragmentation and Overlap*].

1997, the FDA has physically examined just over 1 percent of imported foods.[4] In addition, much of the food entering the United States is ready to be eaten, unlike in years past when further processing was often required. Thus, an increasing percentage of the US food supply is escaping the FDA's more stringent domestic authority.[5]

Why Are International Food Handling Issues Impactful for US Food Consumers?

Because of the shift to imported sources of ready-to-eat foods, consumers' diets are becoming more dependent on other countries' methods of food production. Since the scope and opportunity for adulteration increases as food trade and food processing expands, it is not a surprise that foodborne sicknesses are regular occurrences.[6] Although the food supply in the United States is one of the safest in the world, the Centers for Disease Control and Prevention estimates that foodborne illnesses cause approximately 76 million illnesses a year, resulting in 325,000 hospitalizations and 5,000 deaths.[7]

How Have Imported Food Problems Affected Perceptions?

Foodborne illnesses not only cost consumers in medical bills, loss of wages, and sometimes loss of life, but they also result in lost profits to food companies. Nearly half of consumers questioned in a poll conducted by the Consumer Reports National Research Center in 2008 said their confidence in food safety in the United States had decreased. Eighty-one percent of

---

[4] Becker, *Safeguards and Selected Issues, supra* note 1, at 4-5; *see also Agencies Need to Address Gaps in Enforcement and Collaboration to Enhance Safety of Imported Food, supra* note 2, at 49 (for 2006-2008 figures).
[5] *See* U.S. Gen. Accounting Office, *Food Safety: Selected Countries' Systems Can Offer Insights into Ensuring Import Safety and Responding to Foodborne Illness* 1 (2008).
[6] *See* Kristin Choo, *Hungry for Change: The Feds Consider a Steady Diet of Stronger Regulation to Help Fix the U.S. Food Safety Network,* ABA JOURNAL, Sept. 2009; Neal Fortin, Address at the University of Wisconsin Food Import Safety: Systems, Infrastructure, and Governance Conference (May 27, 2009) (discussing the impact of the trade and processing on the safety of food).
[7] Paul S. Mead, et al., *Food Related Illness and Death in the United States,* Centers for Disease Control and Prevention, available at www.cdc.gov/ncidod/eid/vol5no5/mead.htm.

those polled were concerned with the safety of imported foods.[8] Companies are not immune to their customers' concerns; to make a profit, companies need consumers to feel confident in the safety of their products.

How Does US Food Law Operate as a Government Function?

Food safety law in the United States is not a strategically organized body of law, but is instead a Byzantine-like structure of various laws adopted similarly to this one—as a reaction to public awareness of foodborne illnesses and in response to economic concerns.[9] Modern-day food safety law in the United States started with the passage of the Pure Food and Drug Act of 1906. Separate laws for meats and poultry came later; the 1938 comprehensive change to food safety was the last major change, though alterations of various food powers and provisions occurred in 1954, 1958, 1990, 1997, and 2007.

How Do FDA and USDA Jurisdiction Interact?

The existence of a dual-track system—one for meat, poultry, and eggs, and one for all other food—has been criticized for decades. The Food Safety Inspection Service (FSIS), which is part of the US Department of Agriculture (USDA),[10] shares supervision of food oversight with the FDA.

The 2010 Act specifically exempts from all provisions of the bill the food products and facilities that are regulated by the USDA under the Federal Meat Inspection Act, Poultry Products Inspection Act, and Egg Products Inspection Act.[11] For political reasons, the constituents supporting meat companies made certain that the bills that became the Act do not change the existing jurisdictional division between the FDA and the FSIS.[12] As a result, the Act primarily affects FDA administration, although it is expected that the FDA would do as the 2010 Act directed, and FDA food regulators

---

[8] *Consumer Reports Poll: Two-thirds of Americans Want the FDA to Inspect Domestic and Foreign Food Supply Once a Month*, FOOD AND DRUG LAW WEEKLY, Nov. 28, 2008.

[9] See *Fundamental Restructuring Is Needed to Address Fragmentation and Overlap, supra* note 3; Food Safety Working Group, Executive Office of the President, *Food Safety Working Group Key Findings* (2009), www.foodsafetyworkinggroup.gov/FSWG_Key_Findings.pdf.

[10] *See* Becker, *The Federal Food Safety System, supra* note 1.

[11] H.R. 2749, 111th Cong. § 5 (as passed by House of Representatives, July 29, 2009).

[12] H.R. 2749, 111th Cong. § 4 (as passed by House of Representatives, July 29, 2009).

will work in conjunction with other agencies to achieve the required rules and guidances authorized by the Act.[13]

To the average consumer, the boundaries of the two agencies' jurisdictions are not only complex and nebulous, but also at odds with everyday distinctions among food groups. The FSIS regulates the production, nutritional standards, and labeling of domestic and imported meat, poultry, and some egg products.[14] The FDA is responsible for the safety of all imported and domestic food products sold in interstate commerce that do not fall under the jurisdiction of the FSIS. This includes produce, dairy products, nuts, grains, juice, most seafood, processed foods, eggs, and some meat products.[15] The statutory division of responsibility between the FDA and the FSIS is defined by existing laws, but the fine details of plant and import jurisdiction are determined by memoranda of understanding.[16]

How Is the FDA's Food Safety Import Authority Expressed?

It has long been established that imported goods are treated differently than domestically produced goods.[17] Congress's power is exclusive and absolute in foreign commerce and thus in the field of importation.[18] An article of food being imported or offered for import is to be refused if it "appears from the examination of such samples or otherwise" that it is adulterated,

---

[13] H.R. 2479, Hearing on Food Safety Enhancement Act of 2009, Before the Subcommittee on Health of the H. Committee on Energy and Commerce, 111th Cong. 9 (2009) [hereinafter Hearing on Food Safety Enhancement Act of 2009] (Prepared Statement by Margaret A. Hamburg, Commissioner of U.S. Food and Drug Administration, Department of Health and Human Services, Rockville, MD).

[14] Federal Meat Inspection Act of 1906, 21 U.S.C. §§ 601 et. seq.; Poultry Products Inspection Act of 1957, 21 U.S.C. §§ 451 et. seq.; Egg Products Inspection Act, 21 U.S.C. §§ 1031 et. seq. While it does have sole jurisdiction over the most commonly sold meat and poultry varieties, the FSIS shares jurisdiction with the FDA over other animals, including buffalo, antelope, reindeer, elk, migratory waterfowl, game birds, and rabbits. Agricultural Marketing Act of 1946, 7 U.S.C. § 1621; Geoffrey S. Becker, CRS Report for Congress, *Meat and Poultry Inspection: Background and Selected Issues* 2 (2009).

[15] See Becker, *The Federal Food Safety System, supra* note 1. The FSIS and the FDA also share jurisdiction over eggs. The FSIS is responsible for the safety of frozen and dried egg products and for the safe disposition of damaged and dirty eggs. The FDA is responsible for shell eggs sold in stores and used in restaurants. Egg Products Inspection Act, 21 U.S.C. §§ 1031 et. seq.

[16] *See,* e.g., Food and Drug Administration, *Investigations Operations Manual* 3.2.1.4. (2009), available at www.fda.gov/ICECI/Inspections/IOM/default.htm.

[17] *See Continental Seafoods Inc. v. Schweiker,* 674 F.2d 38, 41 (D.C. Cir. 1982).

[18] *See Buttfield v. Stranahan,* 192 U.S. 470, 496 (1904).

misbranded, or in violation of the law.[19] This standard gives the FDA wide deference in determining whether food should be admitted into the United States.[20] Courts defer to the FDA's decision to bar an import, and only overturn if the decision is unconstitutional, arbitrary, or capricious, a finding courts have been unlikely to conclude.[21]

Although imported foods are subject to more exacting legal standards, in practice the FDA exercises less oversight over imported food than it does over domestically produced food. Part of the reason for this is lack of financial resources. Although the FDA is responsible for approximately 79 percent of US food supply, it currently receives only 40 percent of the total federal food budget.[22] In addition, the FDA does not have as broad authority over imported foods as it does over domestically produced foods. Current legislation is unclear on whether there is legal authority for foreign inspections.[23] Foreign inspections have been rare and are usually only in response to a safety concern and only then with the permission of the foreign government.[24] In 2008, for example, the FDA conducted inspections at 153 of the estimated 189,000 foreign food facilities.[25]

What Did the FDA Seek in the New Legislation?

The FDA did not obtain all the powers it had sought. The bill that originated in the House represented the larger request of powers sought by the FDA. FDA Commissioner Hamburg at the Subcommittee on Health hearing on June 3, 2009, expressed the FDA's preference for the House bill's penalty of adulteration, stating:

---

[19] 21 U.S.C. § 381(a) (2009).

[20] *See Sugarman v. Forbragd,* 405 F.2d 1189 (9th Cir. 1968), *cert. den* (1969) 395 US 960; *Goodwin v. United States,* 371 F. Supp. 433, 436 (S.D. Cal. 1972).

[21] *See* 21 C.F.R. 10.45(d) (2009); *Sugarman v. Forbragd,* 405 F.2d 1189 (9th Cir. 1968), *cert. den* (1969) 395 US 960.

[22] *Fundamental Restructuring Is Needed to Address Fragmentation and Overlap, supra* note 3, at 8.

[23] Hearing to Review Current Issues in Food Safety: Hearing Before the H. Committee on Agriculture, 111th Cong. 124 (2009) [hereinafter Hearing to Review Current Issues in Food Safety] (Prepared Statement of Michael R. Taylor, J.D. Senior Advisor to the Commissioner, U.S. Food and Drug Administration, Department of Health and Human Services, Rockville, MD).

[24] Becker, *Safeguards and Selected Issues, supra* note 1, at 5.

[25] *Agencies Need to Address Gaps in Enforcement and Collaboration to Enhance Safety of Imported Food, supra* note 2, at 16.

The [House] draft legislation recognizes the importance of modernizing FDA's efforts to protect the safety of the food supply. Sections 102, 103, and 104 provide that the failure to comply with preventive controls, the food safety plan requirement, performance standards, or safety standards for produce would deem the food adulterated. An adulterated food is subject to seizure, condemnation, and forfeiture, and also may be refused admission when offered for import into the United States.[26]

On July 16, after the House bill had been reported by the House Committee, Michael Taylor, the senior advisor to the FDA Commissioner, testified at a Hearing to Review Current Issues in Food Safety at the House Agriculture Committee, saying:

The Working Group noted the need to modernize the food safety statutes to provide key tools that both FDA and USDA need to keep food safe. At FDA, the new statutory tools that we need, broadly speaking, include enhanced ability to require science-based preventive controls for food safety at food facilities; enhanced ability to establish and enforce performance standards that ensure the proper implementation of preventive controls; better tools to foster compliance with science-based standards, including enhanced inspection and access to basic food safety records; and, finally, new tools to strengthen FDA's ability to oversee food imports. H.R. 2749, the bill we are focusing on today, addresses all of these authorities.[27]

---

[26] Hearing on Food Safety Enhancement Act of 2009, *supra* note 23, at 4-5 (Prepared Statement by Margaret A. Hamburg, Commissioner of U.S. Food and Drug Administration, Department of Health and Human Services, Rockville, MD).

[27] Hearing to Review Current Issues in Food Safety, *supra* note 23, at 124-25 (Prepared Statement of Michael R. Taylor, J.D. Senior Advisor to the Commissioner, U.S. Food and Drug Administration, Department of Health and Human Services, Rockville, MD).

What Studies Have Led to the 2010 Legislative Change?

Recent years have seen a clamoring for reform of food safety law. A number of advocacy groups have offered proposals.[28] A series of executive reports have highlighted food safety concerns and proposed widespread reform.[29] In January 2007, the Government Accountability Office designated the federal oversight of food safety as a high-risk area for the first time.[30] Much of the emphasis for reform has focused on providing further authority to the FDA. Since the foods the FDA regulates are responsible for two-thirds of all foodborne illnesses, some commentators think the emphasis is well directed.[31]

In July 2007, the Bush administration established an Interagency Working Group on Import Safety to analyze import safety practices and suggest improvements.[32] In November 2007, the working group issued its report. Its overall emphasis was on prevention, calling for a:

> transition from an outdated "snapshot" approach to import safety, in which decisions are made at the border, to a cost-effective, prevention-focused "video" model that identifies and targets critical points in the import life cycle where the risk of the product is greatest, and then verifies the safety of products at those important points.[33]

---

[28] Caroline Smith DeWaal and David W. Plunkett, Center for Science in the Public Interest, *Building a Modern Food Safety System for FDA Regulated Foods* (2009); Hearing on "How Do We Fix Our Ailing Food System?" Before the Subcommittee on Health of the H. Committee on Energy and Commerce 111th Cong. (Mar. 11, 2009) (Statement by Wouldiam K. Hubbard, Advisor to the Alliance for a Stronger FDA) (discussing the group's concerns and suggestions).

[29] *Agencies Need to Address Gaps in Enforcement and Collaboration to Enhance Safety of Imported Food, supra* note 2; U.S. Gen. Accounting Office, *Federal Oversight of Food Safety: High-Risk Designation Can Bring Needed Attention to Fragmented System* (2007) [hereinafter *High-Risk Designation Can Bring Needed Attention to Fragmented System*]; *Steps Should Be Taken to Reduce Overlapping Inspections and Related Activities, supra* note 20; *Fundamental Restructuring Is Needed to Address Fragmentation and Overlap, supra* note 3; *Federal Efforts to Ensure Imported Food Safety Are Inconsistent and Unreliable, infra* note 52.

[30] *High-Risk Designation Can Bring Needed Attention to Fragmented System, infra* note 70.

[31] Caroline Smith DeWaal, *From Hand to Mouth, infra* note 16.

[32] Exec. Order No. 13,439, 72 Fed. Reg. 40,053 (July 20, 2007).

[33] Interagency Working Group on Import Safety, *Action Plan for Import Safety: A Roadmap for Continual Improvement*, Report to the President 4 (2007).

The FDA's own Food Protection Plan, also released in late 2007, paralleled the broader report and laid out a threefold food safety strategy of prevention, intervention, and response.[34] In issuing the Food Protection Plan, the FDA envisioned vast changes to its administration and requested legislative action to provide it statutory authority to accomplish its plan. Specifically the FDA wanted authority to require preventive controls for high-risk foods, to implement more frequent registration requirements, to require fees from specific facilities, to accredit independent third parties to evaluate compliance, to implement certification programs, to refuse imports from facilities that delay, limit, or deny FDA inspection access, to implement mandatory recalls, and to provide the FDA increased access to food records during an emergency.[35]

There were at least a dozen food safety bills introduced in the 110th Congress, each addressing some aspect of import safety.[36] Numerous hearings focused on reviewing and improving the current food safety administration.[37] The passage of the Food and Drug Administration Amendments Act of 2007 added new requirements to current programs, but no comprehensive food safety legislation passed in the 110th Congress.[38]

Why Did Food Import Legislation Move in the 2009–2010 Congress?

Shortly into his term, President Obama organized a new working group, chaired by the Secretaries of Health and Human Services (HHS) and the USDA, and composed of a handful of food-related agencies including the FDA, for the purpose of advising on improving the food safety of the United States.[39] FDA Commissioner Margaret Hamburg took up this challenge by signaling a shift in agency approach, from passive and hamstrung by lack of resources and authority, to a proactive, strong FDA.

---

[34] *See* Department of Health and Human Services, Food and Drug Administration, *Food Protection Plan: An Integrated Strategy for Protecting the Nation's Food Supply* (2007).
[35] *Id.*
[36] *See* Becker, *Safeguards and Selected Issues, supra* note 1, at 21.
[37] *See* Caroline Smith DeWaal and David W. Plunkett, *infra* note 69, Appx. A.
[38] *See* Geoffrey S. Becker, CRS Report for Congress, *Food Safety: Selected Issues and Bills in the 111th Congress* 3, 20 (2009) [hereinafter *Selected Issues and Bills in the 111th Congress*].
[39] Gardiner Harris, *President Promises to Bolster Food Safety*, N.Y. TIMES, Mar. 14, 2009, at A24; *Food Safety Working Group Key Findings, supra* note 14.

Indicative of significant change, Commissioner Hamburg said the FDA would no longer send multiple letters to noncompliant companies, but would instead limit the internal review of warning letters, and in some egregious cases may consider immediate action even without a formal warning letter.[40] The early part of the 111th Congress saw the introduction of a number of bills designed to change food safety administration. Each bill differed somewhat in approach, but a clear pattern emerged: the proposals sought to replace the reactive approach in use at the FDA by envisioning a preventative, risk-based approach.[41]

How Was Passage of the Legislation Achieved?

The Senate barely passed its modified form of S. 510 on a late Sunday evening during the lame-duck session of the 111th Congress in 2010, and the House barely agreed to the modified text as part of H.R. 3082, the December extension of federal agency appropriations into 2011. Each of the passages of the legislation came after multiple separate declarations of the "death" of the bill; the "cliffhanger" results were a story of persistent efforts and extraordinary lobbying compromises under great time pressure.

The original text of S. 510 was introduced in the Senate by Senator Richard Durbin of Illinois on March 3, 2009, and referred to the Senate HELP Committee. The HELP Committee held a hearing on October 22, 2009, on the topic of the proposed food safety legislation, and held a mark-up session on the bill on November 18, 2009, where it received bipartisan support and was approved by a unanimous voice vote in the committee.[42]

Although S. 510 and H.R. 2749 had similar provisions, there were significant differences. The most dramatic difference was S. 510's exclusion of user fees and several enforcement tools. S. 510 had no registration fee provision. FDA Commissioner Margaret Hamburg had specifically stated that registration fees are necessary to the funding of the FDA's activities, so

---

[40] Helena Bottemiller, *FDA: Hamburg Outlines Tougher Food Safety Enforcement*, FOOD SAFETY NEWS, Aug. 10, 2009, www.foodsafetynews.com/2009/08/fda-hamburg-outlines-tougher-food-safety-enforcement.

[41] Becker, *Selected Issues and Bills in the 111th Congress*, *infra* note 79.

[42] Bottemiller, *Food Safety Bill Clears Senate Committee*, *infra* note 10; Helena Bottemiller, *Senate Holds Hearing on Food Safety Reform*, FOOD SAFETY NEWS, www.foodsafetynews.com/2009/10/senate-takes-up-food-safety-reform/.

the exclusion of user fees in the final bill was a major deviation from the FDA's previous requests.[43] H.R. 2749's $500 yearly registration fee would have gone towards defraying the costs of food safety activities. The exclusion of user fees in the Senate bill, however, has been one reason the Senate bill had enjoyed broad, bipartisan support.[44] Senator Tom Harkin, the chairman of the Senate HELP Committee, had declined to rule out the addition of user fees, stating that he wanted to wait until the Congressional Budget Office made an estimate that the costs of the bill can be covered through appropriations alone. However, late realizations of the unconstitutionality of tax provisions originating in the Senate left little time for any user fees, whether directed toward imported food or domestic food.[45]

A second important difference from the H.R. 2749 was S. 510's hesitancy to use food tracing systems, much less active than the House-passed legislation. The final S. 510 requires that three pilot programs be conducted on the feasibility and utility of a tracing system, and then allows the FDA three years to propose a rule.[46] H.R. 2749 only requires one pilot program and allows the FDA only one year to propose a rule.[47]

What Implementation Steps Must Be Taken?

After the January 2011 signing by President Obama, FDA staff received some powers immediately, but the use of many new FDA authorities will be dependent upon the adoption of implementing regulations. Staffing with new agency personnel to actually carry out the new sets of responsibilities in 2011–2013, on the schedule set by the Act, will depend on the FDA receiving an increase in newly appropriated domestic budget funds. This new money is needed, since the industry successfully eliminated the user fees provision of the Act that the House expected would have paid for the

---

[43] Hearing on the FDA Food Safety Modernization Act of 2009, Before the S. Committee on Health, Education, Labor, and Pensions, 111th Cong. 9 (Oct. 22, 2009) (Prepared Statement by Margaret A. Hamburg, Commissioner of U.S. Food and Drug Administration, Department of Health and Human Services, Rockville, MD).

[44] *Fears Over Trade Linger After Senate Committee Reports Food Safety Bill*, INSIDE HEALTH POLICY, Nov. 25, 2009.

[45] *See* Baker, *infra* note 168.

[46] *See* S. 510, 111th Cong. § 204 (as reported by the S. Heath, Education, Labor, and Pensions Committee on Nov. 18, 2009).

[47] *See* H.R. 2749 § 107, 111th Cong. (as passed by House of Representatives, July 29, 2009).

new responsibilities. Soon after passage, the 112th Congress began, and several of the more conservative House members told the media that they would not provide the full funding that the FDA anticipated would be needed.

2

Required Safety Plans
for Food Facilities

What Do Managers Need to Know?

Most food facilities, except for smaller farms covered by special exemptions, will have to satisfy an important new set of regulatory requirements. In briefest terms, "Don't ship food from a plant if you can't be sure the food is safe." While this section of the 2010 law seems like a paperwork burden, the real burden is the stop-shipment command if the company no longer is certain of the food's safety. Operating a plant that is out of compliance is a "prohibited act" that can be punished whether or not the actual food products are "adulterated."

Revisiting the older plans and process diagrams for a plant is a minor part of the cost of the new law. The larger cost will be documenting the food hazards that might occur and implementing a set of controls that prevent the harm. The big economic bite will come from a plant's uncertainty about its controls; if the plant is not sure the food is not adulterated, it must stop shipping until the food safety measures are under control.

Risks for the food manager come in two types: regulatory and liability. Upon inspection at the plant, the risk of not having an adequate set of the FDA-required plans could interrupt shipments, until and unless the controls and preventing systems are fully functional. Further, the risk from injuries caused by contaminants inside a plant or within the food may be a significant source of liability, if the newly required plans will show a trial court or jury that the company knew of this food safety risk, and yet had failed to prevent that risk from occurring.

The FDA's focus in requiring these plans is on adulteration (contamination, glass or other foreign materials in the food, infectious or toxic conditions in the food, etc.) and on proper allergen warnings. Three actions are key to the food company's success: analyze the risk that might exist with this food; put in place a set of preventive controls for plant operations, ingredients, and materials; and monitor/document the activities performed to meet these objectives.

Signing off on the company's food safety plan is significant, a "teachable moment." The chief executive officer is legally accountable if the company violates the law. Under the 2010 amendment, failure of the company to follow its own food safety plan is a violation of the law. The prudent chief executive officer will meet, read, ask questions, schedule updates, discuss this with the board's audit committee, and otherwise stay in tune with food safety. Ignorance is not a legal excuse anymore.

A "sleeper" provision will catch many plant managers unaware. Before, and not after, a significant process change is made, new Section 418(i) requires documentation in the file of a new analysis of potential risks. It will be easy for the FDA to impose civil penalties on a food plant that makes process changes but overlooks the new legal obligation to have the reanalysis done "before" the change is implemented.

What if the controls don't work? New Section 418(e) requires the food company to stop shipping and make the corrections needed. Note the standard:If you cannot be certain that the controls will work and the risk will not happen, you must stop shipping. A facility manager who ignores the "out of control" conditions is risking recalls, civil penalties, and possible criminal prosecution if food injuries result.

What Is the Requirement for Food Safety Plans?

The Senate bill created two tracks of safety analysis and planning, one for raw agricultural crops and one for all others.

Section 419 applies to fruit, vegetables, nuts, and other "raw agricultural commodities," and the safety plans required of such foods are known as "standards for produce safety." Banana plantations, orange groves, almond processors, and others will develop safety plans that adhere to FDA-developed standards for produce safety. These safety plans are discussed in Chapter 3.

Section 418 "hazard analysis" commands apply to foods that are not "raw agricultural commodities." Qualified facilities, which include very small businesses and facilities that in the three previous years sold the majority of their food directly to "qualified end-users" and have an average yearly value of the food sold of less than $500,000, are exempt from being required to have food safety plans.

Companies subject to Section 418 will have to write a plan that "documents and describes that procedures used by the facility to comply with the requirements of this section, including analyzing…hazards…and identifying the preventive controls…to address those hazards." Additionally, the company will have to maintain any required records alongside this written plan. The company must make these documents "promptly available" to an FDA agent upon oral or written request.[48]

What Must Be in the Plans?

The new law requires in new Section 18(h) that the facility's written food safety plan must include[49] the hazard analysis for the food and any later re-analysis,[50] and the preventive controls being implemented under new Section 418, including those to address hazards identified by the FDA.[51]

What Is the Process for Hazard Analysis?

Under the Senate bill, the "hazard analysis" terms in Section 418 for the great majority of foods will require the food company to do three things.

---

[48] S. 510 § 103, 111th Cong. (as reported by the Senate HELP Committee, Nov. 18, 2009).
[49] 21 U.S.C. 350g.
[50] This is the analysis conducted as required under 21 U.S.C. 350g, new section 418 of the amended FD&C Act.
[51] The preventive controls will include measures to avoid adulteration and to prevent hazards from occurring within the plant. 21 U.S.C. 350g(c).

These build upon decades of experience with agricultural HACCP ("hazard analysis of critical control points") programs for the reduction of the predictable sources of food contamination.

First, the food company must "evaluate the hazards that could affect food manufactured, processed, packed, or held by such facility." The FDA requires evaluation of "known or reasonably foreseeable hazards that may be associated with the facility." These hazards include "biological, chemical, physical, and radiological hazards, natural toxins, pesticides, drug residues, decomposition, parasites, allergens, and unapproved food and color additives." Terrorism considerations also must be considered. A written analysis must be made for each hazard.

Second, the company must "identify and implement preventive controls to significantly minimize or prevent the occurrence of such hazards and provide assurances that such food is not adulterated…or misbranded."

Third, the company must "monitor the performance of those controls, and maintain records of this monitoring as a matter of routine practice." This will provide "assurance" that the goals will be met and the controls will reduce risks.[52]

What Are These Food "Preventive Controls"?

The hazards are to be identified, listed, planned for, and avoided by adopting a new set of controls that will prevent the hazard. The term "preventive controls" means "those risk-based, reasonably appropriate procedures, practices, and processes that a *person knowledgeable* about the safe manufacturing, processing, packing, or holding of food *would employ* to significantly minimize or prevent the hazards identified under the hazard analysis…and that are consistent with the *current scientific understanding of safe food* manufacturing, processing, packing, or holding at the time of the analysis"[53] (emphasis supplied). The phrasing will require the FDA to have some objective basis in both industry and science in order to live up to the caliber of evidence that Congress—via the ubiquitous industry lobbyists— has set as the norm for such controls. During the rulemaking process, it is

---

[52] S. 510 § 103, 111th Cong. (as reported by the Senate HELP Committee, Nov. 18, 2009).
[53] 21 U.S.C. 350g(c).

inevitable that industry will pressure the FDA against certain innovative approaches the FDA favors, arguing for a less rigid "state-of-the-art" level of adequate controls. However, Congress included the "person knowledgeable" standard to maximize the FDA's freedom of action. This curious statutory phrasing, referring to a reasonable expert standard, is an interesting parallel to the federal statutory language for "general recognition of safety"[54] and "current good manufacturing practices." It means the FDA gets a great deal of deference from the courts if a company challenges the FDA's view of what steps should be taken. The FDA will probably use advisory committees to validate its view of what "persons knowledgeable" would do.

Under the new law, these mandatory controls included in each facility's plan will include some familiar topical programs already in place in many facilities:

(A) Sanitation procedures for food contact surfaces and utensils and food-contact surfaces of equipment.

(B) Supervisor, manager, and employee hygiene training.

(C) An environmental monitoring program to verify the effectiveness of pathogen controls in processes where a food is exposed to a potential contaminant in the environment.[55]

(D) A food allergen control program.

(E) A recall plan.

(F) Good Manufacturing Practices (GMPs).

(G) Supplier verification activities.[56]

Under the proposed House version of the legislation, "preventive controls" would have included:

- sanitation procedures and practices;
- supervisor, manager, and employee hygiene training;

---

[54] 21 U.S.C. 321(p), and see James O'Reilly, GRAS Roots, FDLI Monograph Series, fdli.org (2009).

[55] The language "in processes where a food is exposed to a potential contaminant in the environment" was added by the bill as reported by the Senate Committee.

[56] 21 U.S.C. 350g(a).

- process controls;
- allergen control programs;
- good manufacturing practices;
- verification procedures, practices, and processes for suppliers and incoming ingredients.[57]

Can Alternative Controls Be Permitted?

The Senate bill did not consider the opportunity for alternative preventive controls, but does require that the FDA provide flexibility in the regulations, specifically in the instance of small businesses.[58]

Under the House version that was not adopted, the FDA would have been required to allow a facility to implement an alternative preventive control than one established by the FDA, as long as the owner, operator, or agent could present to the FDA "information sufficient to demonstrate that the alternative control effectively addresses the hazard."[59] However, this allowance of alternatives would not be permitted for preventive controls in regard to sanitation procedures and practices; supervisor, manager, and employee hygiene training; and good manufacturing practices. The FDA would have retained the discretion on specific choices in these fields. One representative noted in a House floor statement that the alternative control provision gave "flexibility" to food facilities.[60] In practice, the FDA will grant some and deny some; the trade associations for each food class will probably make a collective presentation.

---

[57] H.R. 2749 § 102, 111th Cong. (as engrossed by House of Representatives, July 30, 2009).
[58] S. 510 § 106, 111th Cong. (as reported by the Senate HELP Committee, Nov. 18, 2009).
[59] The bill as introduced by the House did not include a provision allowing a facility to implement alternative preventive controls than ones established by the Secretary. This was adopted by a voice vote after the Chairmen offered a manager's amendment during the mark-up by the House Committee. According to the Committee report, the "manager's amendment clarifies that the Secretary must permit the use of alternative preventive controls which have sufficiently demonstrated to effectively address the hazard." H.R. Rep. No. 111-234, at 57 (2009); compare H.R. 2749 § 102, 111th Cong. (as reported by the House Committee on Energy and Commerce, June 17, 2009) with H.R. 2749 § 102, 111th Cong. (as introduced in House of Representatives, June 8, 2009).
[60] 155 Cong. Rec. H9009 (daily ed. July 29, 2009) (statement of Rep. Shimkus).

How Will Implementation Be Done?

A company must monitor the preventive controls to determine if the controls are effective in significantly minimizing or preventing hazards and in preventing the food "manufactured, processed, packed, or held" by the company from being adulterated or misbranded. If the monitoring indicates that the preventive controls are ineffective such that the food is adulterated under Section 402 or misbranded under Section 403(w), the company must stop shipping the food and engage in corrective actions.[61]

How Will Verification Be Done?

The 2010 legislation requires the facility owner, operator, or agent in charge to verify that:

- The preventive controls are adequate to control the hazards.
- The company is conducting monitoring.
- The company is making appropriate decisions about corrective actions.
- The preventive controls are "effectively and significantly minimizing or preventing the occurrence of identified hazards, including through the use of environmental and product testing programs and other appropriate means."
- The company periodically reanalyzes the hazard analysis.

When introduced, this section did not specifically require testing as a component of hazard analysis and preventive controls. In the bill as reported by the Senate Committee, a provision was added to the list of standards that must be verified, requiring that "the preventive controls…are effectively and significantly minimizing or preventing the occurrence of identified hazards, including through the use of environmental and product testing programs and other appropriate means." This amendment to the bill was likely in response to the Make Our Food Safe Coalition, which had specifically urged that the bill include language requiring the FDA to issue rules for testing food for contamination. The amendment did not go as far

---

[61] S. 510 § 103, 111th Cong. (as reported by the Senate HELP Committee, Nov. 18, 2009).

as the coalition and the Center for Science in the Public Interest had urged in requiring the mandatory reporting of positive test results.[62]

Do food ingredient suppliers continue to meet the food company's standards? How many pallets or container loads were rejected? The company is required to document a periodic reanalysis of the plan to ensure the plan is "still relevant to the raw materials, conditions and processes in the facility, and new and emerging threats."

The House bill, not adopted, would have required controls that have been "validated as scientifically and technically sound," such that if the preventive controls are implemented, the hazards "will be prevented, eliminated, or reduced to an acceptable level."[63]

What "Sleeper" Provision Will Catch Managers Unaware That Additional Analysis Had Been Needed?

Little noticed in the law is a small sentence in Section 418(i): re-analysis of the risk assessment for a food facility must be conducted and placed into the FDA-inspectable file at the food company *before* a change in food operations can occur.[64] This is a departure from past practice, a century of the entrepreneur's freedom to make changes but subject to later government enforcement action. This sends a more robust government message of supervision and regulation.

To be more specific, each time the food facility makes a change (e.g., in baking or cleaning or in applying nano-particles of spice, "if the change

---

[62] Compare S. 510 § 103, 111th Cong. (as reported by the Senate HELP Committee, Nov. 18, 2009) with S. 510 § 103, 111th Cong. (as introduced in Senate, Mar. 3, 2009). Helena Bottemiller, *Food Safety Storm: Victims off to Senate*, FOOD SAFETY NEWS, Oct. 7, 2009, www.foodsafetynews.com/2009/10/nyt-sets-off-food-safety-storm-as-victims-head-to-senate-1.

[63] The bill as reported out by the House Committee required the owner, operator, or agent of a facility to ensure that preventive controls have been validated "as adequate to control the hazards identified" under a hazard analysis. The bill as engrossed by the House changed this language to require the preventive controls be validated "as scientifically and technically sound so that, if such system is implemented, the hazards identified…will be prevented, eliminated, or reduced to an acceptable level." Compare H.R. 2749 § 102, 111th Cong. (as engrossed by House of Representatives, July 30, 2009) with H.R. 2749 § 102, 111th Cong. (as reported by the House Committee on Energy and Commerce, June 17, 2009).

[64] 21 U.S.C. 350g(i), adopted as sec. 418 of the FD&C Act in Pub.L. 111-353 (2010).

creates a reasonable potential for a new hazard or a significant increase in a previously identified hazard," then must be a re-analysis of the existing risk plans before the change is made.

Revisions must be made no less frequently than once every three years. The re-analysis "shall be completed and additional preventive controls needed to address the hazard identified, if any, shall be implemented *before* the change in activities at the facility is operative" (emphasis added).[65] Federal FDA pre-approval of a food plant change is not required, but the law expressly commands that the analysis of risks be amended, prior to making the change.

This is a vulnerability that those training plant management teams must emphasize. It is a violation of the 2010 law for a food plant to make a "significant" change without updating the paperwork of the hazard analysis first, before the change. Since the great majority of surveyed managers of US food plants did not know that, since 2007, updated reports to the FDA had already been required when changes occurred,[66] there may also be ignorance of this express statutory command.

This will be overlooked until caught by the inspector or the company's audit teams. One can predict from past experience with food inspections that plants will continue to make process changes as needed. Managers of food plants will probably ignore the duty to update hazard analysis; the regulatory inspection reports and warning letters, and perhaps even civil penalties, will flow from plant operators ignoring or being unaware of the new requirements.

Educating line managers about regulatory commands that are seen as being counterintuitive behavior will require some careful planning by prudent management teams. "Before we can reduce heat for the cooking of our mushroom soup, we should document in the file that we do not expect this to increase microbial conditions for growth of microbes."

---

[65] 21 U.S.C. 350g(i). This provision was changed by the bill reported by the Senate Committee to require the reanalysis before the change is "operative," as opposed to before the change is "commenced," as was the language in the bill as introduced. S. 510 § 103, 111th Cong. (as reported by the Senate HELP Committee, Nov. 18, 2009).

[66] HHS Inspector General Report, FDA's Food Facility Registry, Report 02-08-00060 (Dec. 2009), available on web at www.hhs.gov/oig.

Are Records Required to Be Kept?

Yes. The facility operator is required to maintain records documenting the monitoring of the preventive controls, retaining them for at least two years. The results of tests performed as a component of hazard analysis and preventive controls must be maintained with the other required records. Records must disclose those instances of nonconformance that were material to food safety, the results of testing and other verification, instances when corrective actions were implemented, and the efficacy of preventive controls and corrective actions.

What Standards Apply to These Analysis and Control Activities?

Within eighteen months of enactment of the Act, the FDA must promulgate "science-based minimum standards for conducting a hazard analysis, documenting hazards, implementing preventive controls, and documenting the implementation of the preventive controls."[67] Prior to promulgating regulations, the FDA must review regulatory programs in existence to make sure the program under this section is "consistent, to the extent practicable, with applicable domestic and internationally-recognized standards in existence on such date." The bill is clear that the FDA is not given the authority to apply "specific technologies, practices, or critical controls to an individual facility." The FDA is required to issue a guidance document related to complying with the regulations promulgated for hazard analysis and preventive controls.[68]

What Sites Are Exempted?

One of the most controversial aspects of the final months before passage was Montana Senator Tester's desire to exclude from the requirements smaller farm-based food operations. This resulted in an exemption of the hazard analysis provision for what is known under the Act as "qualified facilities." Qualified facilities are either "very small businesses," to be

---

[67] The bill as introduced in the Senate did not provide a time by when the regulations "to establish science-based minimum standards" for hazard analysis and preventive controls were to be promulgated. The bill as reported by the Senate Committee added a provision requiring the Secretary to promulgate these regulations within eighteen months of enactment of the bill.

[68] S. 510 § 103, 111th Cong. (as reported by the Senate HELP Committee, Nov. 18, 2009).

defined by regulations, or facilities that in the three previous years sold the majority of their food directly to "qualified end-users" and have an average yearly value of the food sold of less than $500,000. Qualified end-users are consumers or restaurants or retail food establishments that sell directly to consumers and are located in the same state as the qualified facility or are located no further than 275 miles from the qualified facility. Thus, a facility with an average monetary value of food sold of less than $500,000 that sells the majority of its food directly to consumers is not subject to the same hazard analysis requirements established under the Act. Further, a facility with an average monetary value of food sold of less than $500,000 is similarly exempt from the section if it sells the majority of its food to establishments selling directly to consumers and the establishments are located either within the same state as the facility or no further than 275 miles away from the facility. Such qualified facilities still must "demonstrate that the owner, operator, or agent in charge of the facility has identified potential hazards associated with the food being produced, is implementing preventive controls to address the hazards, and is monitoring the preventive control to ensure that such controls are effective," or must present documentation showing compliance with state, local, or county food safety laws and any other documentation required by the FDA, which is to be established by guidance within one year of the enactment of the Act. If an outbreak occurs associated with the qualified facility, the FDA may withdraw the exemption.

The final Section 418 requirements[69] also exclude facilities solely engaged in the production of food for animals other than man;[70] sites for the storage of raw agricultural commodities (other than fruits and vegetables) intended for further distribution or processing; and sites for storage of packaged goods not exposed to the environment.[71] These exclusions are the result of strong lobbying on behalf of these industries.

---

[69] 21 U.S.C. 350g.

[70] The House bill would have allowed the FDA to take into account differences between food intended for humans and food intended for animals in implementing these standards.

[71] This provision was not included in the bill as introduced in the Senate. The bill as reported by the Senate Committee amended the provision allowing the FDA to exempt or modify how the hazard analysis and preventive control section applies to certain facilities and foods, by adding "the storage of raw agricultural commodities (other than fruits and vegetables) intended for further distribution or processing" to the list of foods.

Those food plants previously subject to, and currently in compliance with, special government rules for seafood, juice, and low-acid canned food plants are also not subject to the new planning rules. Provisions were added to the bill as reported by the Senate Committee stating that the section does not apply to facilities making dietary supplements or alcohol.[72] As mentioned previously, this section does not apply to a facility subject to Section 419, on produce standards.[73]

When Does This Requirement Begin to Affect Food Facilities?

The plans and standards requirements of this section will not take effect for eighteen months after the date of enactment for larger facilities, and for two and three years, respectively, for small businesses and very small businesses. The FDA must provide for flexibility in the regulations, specifically in the instance of small businesses. A provision was added to the bill as reported by the Senate Committee requiring the FDA to define the term "small business" and "very small business" within ninety days of the enactment of the Act. This addition was the result of small-business groups lobbying for more clarity in the bill.[74]

How Are Existing HACCP Obligations Impacted?

Not at all. Both the House and Senate bills stated that this section does not affect the applicability of any HACCP requirements placed on facilities by other legislation.[75]

How Are the FDA Requirements for Plans and Standards Enforced?

It will be a "prohibited act," punishable under 21 U.S.C. 331, for a company to manufacture, process, pack, or hold food to be sold in the United States that is not in compliance with this section.[76] Under the House bill (not adopted), food would be "adulterated" and subject to enforcement action if it was "manufactured, processed, packed, transported, or held under

---

[72] S. 510 § 103, 111th Cong. (as reported by the Senate HELP Committee, Nov. 18, 2009).
[73] Id.
[74] Compare S. 510 § 103, 111th Cong. (as reported by the Senate HELP Committee, Nov. 18, 2009) with S. 510 § 103, 111th Cong. (as introduced in Senate, Mar. 3, 2009).
[75] 21 U.S.C. 350g(j).
[76] S. 510 § 103, 111th Cong. (as reported by the Senate HELP Committee, Nov. 18, 2009).

conditions that do not meet the requirements" in a facility that does not meet the requirements for hazard analysis and preventive controls.[77] As with other standards under pre-existing food law, the FDA can impose penalties upon the failure to meet a particular paperwork standard. The FDA need not show any actual contamination of the food or the site. This result may seem harsh, but it is the chosen vehicle to raise food- processing standards, after the inadequacies exposed by the 2008–2009 peanut product recalls that form the backdrop for the 2010 legislation.

What Effect Will International Standards Have?

Prior to promulgating regulations to carry out this section, the FDA must review regulatory programs in existence to make sure the program under this section is "consistent, to the extent practicable, with applicable domestic and internationally-recognized standards in existence on such date."[78] A separate section of the law expresses the intent of Congress not to interfere with existing international treaty obligations. Under the House bill (not adopted), the FDA would have been required to issue guidance or promulgate regulations to establish science-based performance standards for implementing a food safety plan. In doing so, the FDA was to consider international standards to ensure consistency to the extent "practicable and appropriate."[79] Chapter 12 in this book describes international trade requirements under the World Trade Organization systems, and these "sanitation" norms should be considered. The FDA could choose to be more stringent in food safety, if it wished, than the World Health Organization or the Food and Agricluture Organization or any other international body.

What Happens if a Facility Fails to Meet Its Own Safety Plan?

This is something new: conviction of *not meeting a standard that you yourself have set.* Safety plans for a food facility can and will be used against the firm that drafts them. The FDA can seize food products, bring injunction suits,

---

[77] H.R. 2749 § 102, 111th Cong. (as engrossed by House of Representatives, July 30, 2009).
[78] S. 510 § 103, 111th Cong. (as reported by the Senate HELP Committee, Nov. 18, 2009).
[79] This provision was not included in the bill as introduced in the House, but was added in the bill as reported out by the House Committee. Compare H.R. 2749 § 102, 111th Cong. (as reported by the House Committee on Energy and Commerce, June 17, 2009) with H.R. 2749 § 102, 111th Cong. (as introduced in House of Representatives, June 8, 2009).

or use other enforcement powers under its "adulteration" authorities, if a facility does not meet its own safety plan. Some veterans of the FDA regulatory scene will find this scary, while others will hold it to be a natural extension of modern business accountability practices for sound management of quality.

Facilities must draft their food safety plans with an awareness that once they make the commitment, the failure to meet the plan can produce an enforcement case. Under the House bill that was not adopted, food that is "manufactured, processed, packed, transported, or held" under conditions that do not meet the requirements for a food safety plan under this provision would have been considered "adulterated."[80] The final text of the Act reaches the same conclusion by making it a prohibited act to operate "not in compliance with Section 418."[81]

This is a big vulnerability for managers of food facilities that launch an ambitious safety plan without actually committing to meeting the terms of their plan. Since 1906, the FDA could punish dirty facilities. Since 1938, the FDA could punish facilities that do not meet FDA-set Good Manufacturing Practices. But after 2010, the FDA can now punish facilities that do not meet plans that the firms have set for themselves.

What Would the Unadopted House Bill Have Done?

The House bill was not adopted, but it is instructive about Congressional intent. That bill had different provisions. Under Section 418 of the House-proposed version of the legislation, any food facility that is required to register with the FDA, as most have been since the 2002 bioterrorism defense statutory changes, would be required to develop and implement a written food safety plan before introducing or delivering for introduction food into interstate commerce. Further, the owner, operator, or agent of a facility would have had to evaluate whether, in the absence of preventive controls, there are "hazards reasonably likely to occur" that could affect the "safety, wholesomeness, or sanitation of the food manufactured, processed, packed, transported, or held by the facility."[82] A hazard that would have

---

[80] H.R. 2749 § 102, 111th Cong. (as engrossed by House of Representatives, July 30, 2009).
[81] 21 U.S.C. 331(uu).
[82] H.R. 2749 § 102, 111th Cong. (as engrossed by House of Representatives, July 30, 2009).

been considered reasonably likely to occur was one for which a prudent person "would establish controls because experience, illness data, scientific reports, or other information provides a basis to conclude that there is a reasonable possibility that the hazard will occur in the type of food being manufactured, processed, pack, transported, or held in the absence of the controls."[83]

The House bill would have required that the owner, operator, or agent of a facility identify the hazards by analyzing whether there are any "biological, chemical, physical, and radiological hazards, natural toxins, pesticides, drug residues, filth, decomposition, parasites, allergens, and unapproved food and color additives; and hazards that occur naturally or that may be unintentionally introduced."[84]

The FDA would have been required to identify, by regulation or guidance, "hazards that are reasonably likely to occur in the absence of preventive controls."[85] To complete a hazard analysis, the owner, operator, or agent of a facility would have had to describe the hazards identified through the internal hazard identification process and those hazards identified through regulations or guidance by the FDA.[86]

After identifying the hazards, the owner, operator, or agent of a facility would have had to "identify and implement effective preventive controls to prevent, eliminate, or reduce to acceptable levels the occurrence of any hazards identified in the hazard analysis." These preventive controls could have been established by the FDA through regulation or guidance "for specific product types to prevent unintentional contamination throughout the supply chain."

The House bill that was not adopted would also have required the plans to include

1. Verification activities for the preventive controls, including:
    - Validation that the system of controls, if implemented, will prevent, eliminate, or reduce to an acceptable level the identified hazards

---

[83] *Id.*
[84] *Id.*
[85] *Id.*
[86] *Id.*

- Review of monitoring and corrective action records
- Procedures for determining whether the system of controls as implemented is effectively preventing, eliminating, or reducing to an acceptable level the occurrence of identified hazards
- Including the use of environmental and product testing programs

2. Description of the facility's record-keeping procedures
3. Description of the facility's procedures for the recall of articles of food, whether voluntarily or when required
4. Description of the facility's procedures for tracing the distribution history of articles of food, whether voluntarily or when required[87]
5. Description of the facility's procedures to ensure a safe and secure supply chain for the ingredients or components used in making the food manufactured, processed, packed, transported, or held by such facility
6. Description of the facility's procedures to implement the science-based performance standards required by new Section 419[88]

Industry opponents would accept the bare minimum but were able to drop from the bill many of the House-passed requirements of the plans.

What Was the Pre-2010 Situation?

The prior situation was entirely "libertarian"—no explicit government requirement for plans existed. The closest analogy would be food good manufacturing practice rules that dated back to 1986.[89] The rules spoke very generically of "adequate" sanitation and "appropriate" quality control.[90] The planning process occurs, in practice, in the great majority of food processing facilities, but the new legislation is a quantum leap forward over the prior law ("forward" depending, of course, on one's view of regulation as a protection of health).

---

[87] This ties in to the amended law's expansion of recall powers. See Chapter 10.
[88] 21 U.S.C. 350h, *see* H.R. 2749 § 102, 111th Cong. (as engrossed by House of Representatives, July 30, 2009).
[89] FDA, Final Rules, 51 Fed. Reg. 24475 (June 19, 1986).
[90] 21 C.F.R. 110.80.

In the past, the FDA did not have the power to punish a firm for making a change to its food processing methods without first making a change to its hazard analysis documentation.[91] That was then, and this is now. Prudent food company managers will be educated and will educate their teams.

How Did the FDA Respond to the Section?

FDA Commissioner Hamburg testified at the Senate HELP Committee hearing on October 22, 2009, that:

> Section 103 of S. 510 outlines requirements for conducting a hazard analysis and implementing risk-based controls. This authority is an essential component of a modern food safety system. However, the effectiveness of this provision would be greatly strengthened if it deemed food that is in violation of this section as "adulterated," as in the House bill. As currently drafted, S. 510 addresses enforcement via the creation of a prohibited act. Creation of a prohibited act would support an injunction but would not provide a legal basis, for example, for a seizure, administrative detention (as amended by the legislation), or refusal of admission of imported food from a facility that is not in compliance with the requirements. We encourage this Committee to include an effective enforcement mechanism, as provided in the comparable section of H.R. 2749. That would make this section consistent with most other enforcement mechanisms in the Federal Food, Drug, and Cosmetic Act.[92]

The bill as reported out by the Senate Committee did not address Commissioner Hamburg's concern. A violation of Section 103 remains a prohibited act.

---

[91] 21 U.S.C. 350g(i).

[92] Hearing on Keeping America's Families Safe: Reforming the Food Safety System, S. Committee on Health, Education, Labor, and Pensions, 111th Cong. 8, Oct. 22, 2009 (Testimony of FDA Commissioner Hamburg).

How Did Industry Respond To This New Requirement?

A representative for the Food Marketing Institute testified at the Senate HELP Committee hearing on October 22, 2009:

> We support the requirement that every registered food facility design, conduct and maintain an evaluation of food safety risks in their business that identifies potential sources of contamination, identifies appropriate food safety controls, and documents those controls in a food safety plan. The correct development and use of a food safety plan goes a long way toward developing a culture within the company that is critical to ensuring food safety. We commend the legislation for recognizing the low-risk nature of warehouse facilities that store packaged food that is not exposed to the environment by allowing the Secretary to modify the requirements for these facilities.
>
> At Publix, the food safety systems designed in our manufacturing operations have redundant food safety control processes. This begins with ingredient suppliers. Prior to producing new product, the food safety requirements and ingredient controls are verified. Pre-requisite food safety programs along with cleaning and sanitation elements lead into the Hazard Analysis and Critical Control Points (HACCP) food safety system. We recognize the importance of a quality-first food safety system and understand that food safety is everyone's mutual responsibility.[93]

The Make Our Food Safe Coalition called for S. 510 to be amended to include and issue rules for a testing and reporting requirement for all food

---

[93] Hearing on Keeping America's Families Safe: Reforming the Food Safety System, S. Committee on Health, Education, Labor, and Pensions, 111th Cong. 4-5, Oct. 22, 2009 (Testimony of Michael Roberson, Director of Corporate Quality Assurance, Publix Super Markets Inc. on behalf of the Food Marketing Institute).

processors.[94] Caroline Smith DeWaal, director of the Center for Science in the Public Interest, testified at the Senate HELP hearing on October 22, 2009:

> In order for a system based on preventive controls to be truly effective, food companies must be required to test for the types of contamination most common in their (or similar) products to determine whether their systems are actually working. We recommend that you strengthen the testing and reporting requirements of S. 510 by adopting requirements that:
>
> • A facility conduct testing as a verification step in its preventive control plan; and
> • Facilities report promptly to FDA any positive results from its testing program.[95]

Senator Enzi asked DeWaal about her testimony in regard to facilities being required to report positive results to the FDA, saying he did not want to discourage testing, but that he did not want the FDA overwhelmed with testing results. DeWaal responded that the key to mandatory reporting is efficient technology that can sift through results and decide which should be followed up on.[96]

The Grocery Manufacturers Association testified at the House Committee on Energy and Commerce's Subcommittee on Health hearing on Food

---

[94] *The Senate Must Pass Strong FDA Food Safety Legislation This Year*, Make Our Food Safe Coalition, Dec. 1, 2009, www.makeourfoodsafe.org/tools/assets/files/PDF-Senate-Fall-Fact-Sheet.pdf; Helena Bottemiller, *Senate Schedules Markup of S. 510*, FOOD SAFETY NEWS, Nov. 11, 2009, www.foodsafetynews.com/2009/11/senate-schedules-markup-of-s-510.

[95] Hearing on Keeping America's Families Safe: Reforming the Food Safety System, S. Committee on Health, Education, Labor, and Pensions, 111th Cong. 8 Oct. 22, 2009 (Testimony of Caroline Smith DeWaal, Director of the Center for Science in the Public Interest, testimony supported by Center for Foodborne Illness Research and Prevention, Consumer Federation of America, Consumers Union, Food and Water Watch, National Consumers League, Safe Tables Our Priority, and Trust for America's Health).

[96] Hearing on Keeping America's Families Safe: Reforming the Food Safety System, S. Committee on Health, Education, Labor, and Pensions, 111th Cong. Oct. 22, 2009 (Oral Testimony of Caroline Smith DeWaal, Director of the Center for Science in the Public Interest).

Safety Enhancement Act of 2009.[97] The association specifically urged that H.R. 2749 include provisions on hazard analysis and food safety plan requirements, to require "every food manufacturer to conduct a hazard analysis that identifies potential sources of contamination. This would be another way to raise the bar to assure everyone is following the same regulations."[98]

A representative of the Food Marketing Institute, a trade association that represents food retailers and wholesalers, testified at the House Energy and Commerce Committee's Subcommittee on Health hearing on food safety on June 3, 2009, stating that the institute:

> support[s] the requirement that every registered food facility conduct a risk assessment and implement and maintain a validated food safety plan and identify potential resources of contamination and appropriate food safety controls and document those controls that would prevent, eliminate, and reduce potential hazards.
>
> Adherence to food safety plans goes a long way towards developing a culture within a company that is critical to ensuring food safety.[99]

Some changes made to the House bill section during the drafting of the legislation appear to have directly resulted from the Agriculture Committee's work with the House Committee to resolve concerns about the bill's effect on farms.[100] Specific groups, including the Representatives of the Farm Bureau Federation, the American Meat Institute, the National

---

[97] Hearing on Food Safety Enhancement Act of 2009, Before the Subcommittee on Health of the H. Committee on Energy and Commerce, 111th Cong. (2009) [hereinafter Hearing on Food Safety Enhancement Act of 2009] (Prepared Statement by Pamela G. Bailey, President of the Grocery Manufacturers Association).

[98] *See* April Terreri, *Will New FDA Penalties Break your Bank?* FOOD LOGISTICS, Sept. 2009, at 26.

[99] Hearing on Food Safety Enhancement Act of 2009, Before the Subcommittee on Health of the H. Committee on Energy and Commerce, 111th Cong. 149 (2009) [hereinafter Hearing on Food Safety Enhancement Act of 2009] (Statement of Mike Ambrosio, Food Marketing Institute, in Preliminary Transcript).

[100] Jerry Hagstrom, *Peterson Seeks Tweaks in Pending Food Safety Legislation,* NATIONAL JOURNAL'S CONGRESS DAILY, July 17, 2009.

Cattlemen's Beef Association, and the National Farmers Union, had contacted the Agriculture Committee with their concerns about the bill's requirement for food safety plans, among other things.[101] When the bill was introduced, this section did not include a provision allowing the FDA to exempt or modify how the requirements apply to certain facilities, such as was later added, allowing the FDA to exempt or modify how the requirements apply to facilities that solely engage in "the production of food for animals," "the storage of packaged goods that are not exposed to the environment," or "the storage of raw agricultural commodities for further distribution or processing." Nor was a provision included allowing the FDA to take into account differences between food intended for humans and food intended for animals in implementing this section. These provisions were added in the bill as reported out by the House Committee.[102]

Text of the Law as Adopted

SEC. 103. HAZARD ANALYSIS AND RISK-BASED PREVENTIVE CONTROLS.

(a) In General.--Chapter IV (21 U.S.C. 341 et seq.) is amended by adding at the end the following:

"SEC. 418. HAZARD ANALYSIS AND RISK-BASED PREVENTIVE CONTROLS.

"(a) In General.--The owner, operator, or agent in charge of a facility shall, in accordance with this section, evaluate the hazards that could affect food manufactured, processed, packed, or held by such facility, identify and implement preventive controls to significantly minimize or prevent the occurrence of such hazards and provide assurances that such food is not adulterated under section 402 or misbranded under section 403(w), monitor the performance of those controls, and maintain records of this monitoring as a matter of routine practice.

---

[101] Annie Johnson, *Chairman Wants No New Feds on the Farm*, CQ POLITICS, July 16, 2009, www.cqpolitics.com/wmspage.cfm?docID=news-000003168449.
[102] Compare H.R. 2749 § 102, 111th Cong. (as reported by the House Committee on Energy and Commerce, June 17, 2009) with H.R. 2749 § 102, 111th Cong. (as introduced in House of Representatives, June 8, 2009).

"(b) Hazard Analysis.--The owner, operator, or agent in charge of a facility shall--

> *"(1) identify and evaluate known or reasonably foreseeable hazards that may be associated with the facility, including--*

>> *"(A) biological, chemical, physical, and radiological hazards, natural toxins, pesticides, drug residues, decomposition, parasites, allergens, and unapproved food and color additives; and*

>> *"(B) hazards that occur naturally, or may be unintentionally introduced; and*

> *"(2) identify and evaluate hazards that may be intentionally introduced, including by acts of terrorism; and*

> *"(3) develop a written analysis of the hazards.*

"(c) Preventive Controls.--The owner, operator, or agent in charge of a facility shall identify and implement preventive controls, including at critical control points, if any, to provide assurances that--

> *"(1) hazards identified in the hazard analysis conducted under subsection (b)(1) will be significantly minimized or prevented;*

> *"(2) any hazards identified in the hazard analysis conducted under subsection (b)(2) will be significantly minimized or prevented and addressed, consistent with section 420, as applicable; and*

> *"(3) the food manufactured, processed, packed, or held by such facility will not be adulterated under section 402 or misbranded under section 403(w).*

"(d) Monitoring of Effectiveness.--The owner, operator, or agent in charge of a facility shall monitor the effectiveness of the preventive controls implemented under subsection (c) to provide assurances that the outcomes described in subsection (c) shall be achieved.

"(e) Corrective Actions.--The owner, operator, or agent in charge of a facility shall establish procedures to ensure that, if the preventive controls implemented under subsection (c) are not properly implemented or are found to be ineffective--

"(1) appropriate action is taken to reduce the likelihood of recurrence of the implementation failure;

"(2) all affected food is evaluated for safety; and

"(3) all affected food is prevented from entering into commerce if the owner, operator or agent in charge of such facility cannot ensure that the affected food is not adulterated under section 402 or misbranded under section 403(w).

"(f) Verification.--The owner, operator, or agent in charge of a facility's "(1) the preventive controls implemented under subsection (c) are adequate to control the hazards identified under subsection (b);

"(2) the owner, operator, or agent is conducting monitoring in accordance with subsection (d);

"(3) the owner, operator, or agent is making appropriate decisions about corrective actions taken under subsection (e);

"(4) the preventive controls implemented under subsection (c) are effectively and significantly minimizing or preventing the occurrence of identified hazards, including through the use of environmental and product testing programs and other appropriate means; and

"(5) there is documented, periodic reanalysis of the plan under subsection (i) to ensure that the plan is still relevant to the raw materials, conditions and processes in the facility, and new and emerging threats.

"(g) Recordkeeping.--The owner, operator, or agent in charge of a facility shall maintain, for not less than 2 years, records documenting the monitoring of the preventive controls implemented under subsection (c), instances of nonconformance material to food safety, the results of testing and other

appropriate means of verification under subsection (f)(4), instances when corrective actions were implemented, and the efficacy of preventive controls and corrective actions.

"(h) Written Plan and Documentation.--The owner, operator, or agent in charge of a facility shall prepare a written plan that documents and describes the procedures used by the facility to comply with the requirements of this section, including analyzing the hazards under subsection (b) and identifying the preventive controls adopted under subsection (c) to address those hazards. Such written plan, together with the documentation described in subsection (g), shall be made promptly available to a duly authorized representative of the Secretary upon oral or written request.

"(i) Requirement To Reanalyze.--The owner, operator, or agent in charge of a facility shall conduct a reanalysis under subsection (b) whenever a significant change is made in the activities conducted at a facility operated by such owner, operator, or agent if the change creates a reasonable potential for a new hazard or a significant increase in a previously identified hazard or not less frequently than once every 3 years, whichever is earlier. Such reanalysis shall be completed and additional preventive controls needed to address the hazard identified, if any, shall be implemented before the change in activities at the facility is operative. Such owner, operator, or agent shall revise the written plan required under subsection (h) if such a significant change is made or document the basis for the conclusion that no additional or revised preventive controls are needed. The Secretary may require a reanalysis under this section to respond to new hazards and developments in scientific understanding, including, as appropriate, results from the Department of Homeland Security biological, chemical, radiological, or other terrorism risk assessment.

"(j) Exemption for Seafood, Juice, and Low-acid Canned Food Facilities Subject to HACCP.--

> *"(1) IN GENERAL.--This section shall not apply to a facility if the owner, operator, or agent in charge of such facility is required to comply with, and is in compliance with, 1 of the following standards and regulations with respect to such facility:*

"(A) The Seafood Hazard Analysis Critical Control Points Program of the Food and Drug Administration.

"(B) The Juice Hazard Analysis Critical Control Points Program of the Food and Drug Administration.

"(C) The Thermally Processed Low-Acid Foods Packaged in Hermetically Sealed Containers standards of the Food and Drug Administration (or any successor standards).

"(2) APPLICABILITY.--The exemption under paragraph (1)(C) shall apply only with respect to microbiological hazards that are regulated under the standards for Thermally Processed Low-Acid Foods Packaged in Hermetically Sealed Containers under part 113 of chapter 21, Code of Federal Regulations (or any successor regulations).

"(k) Exception for Activities of Facilities Subject to Section 419.--This section shall not apply to activities of a facility that are subject to section 419.

"(l) Modified Requirements for Qualified Facilities.--

"(1) QUALIFIED FACILITIES.--

"(A) IN GENERAL.--A facility is a qualified facility for purposes of this subsection if the facility meets the conditions under subparagraph (B) or (C).

"(B) VERY SMALL BUSINESS.--A facility is a qualified facility under this subparagraph--

"(i) if the facility, including any subsidiary or affiliate of the facility, is, collectively, a very small business (as defined in the regulations promulgated under subsection (n)); and

"(ii) in the case where the facility is a subsidiary or affiliate of an entity, if such subsidiaries or affiliates, are, collectively, a very small business (as so defined).

"(C) LIMITED ANNUAL MONETARY VALUE OF SALES.--

"(i) IN GENERAL.--A facility is a qualified facility under this subparagraph if clause (ii) applies--

"(I) to the facility, including any subsidiary or affiliate of the facility, collectively; and

"(II) to the subsidiaries or affiliates, collectively, of any entity of which the facility is a subsidiary or affiliate.

"(ii) AVERAGE ANNUAL MONETARY VALUE.--This clause applies if--

"(I) during the 3-year period preceding the applicable calendar year, the average annual monetary value of the food manufactured, processed, packed, or held at such facility (or the collective average annual monetary value of such food at any subsidiary or affiliate, as described in clause (i)) that is sold directly to qualified end-users during such period exceeded the average annual monetary value of the food manufactured, processed, packed, or held at such facility (or the collective average annual monetary value of such food at any subsidiary or affiliate, as so described) sold by such facility (or collectively by any such subsidiary or affiliate) to all other purchasers during such period; and

> *"(II) the average annual monetary value of all food sold by such facility (or the collective average annual monetary value of such food sold by any subsidiary or affiliate, as described in clause (i)) during such period was less than $500,000, adjusted for inflation.*

"(2) EXEMPTION.--A qualified facility--

> *"(A) shall not be subject to the requirements under subsections (a) through (i) and subsection (n) in an applicable calendar year; and*

> *"(B) shall submit to the Secretary--*

>> *"(i)(I) documentation that demonstrates that the owner, operator, or agent in charge of the facility has identified potential hazards associated with the food being produced, is implementing preventive controls to address the hazards, and is monitoring the preventive controls to ensure that such controls are effective; or*

>>> *"(II) documentation (which may include licenses, inspection reports, certificates, permits, credentials, certification by an appropriate agency (such as a State department of agriculture), or other evidence of oversight), as specified by the Secretary, that the facility is in compliance with State, local, county, or other applicable non-Federal food safety law; and*

>> *"(ii) documentation, as specified by the Secretary in a guidance document issued not later than 1 year after the date of enactment of this section,*

that the facility is a qualified facility under paragraph (1)(B) or (1)(C).

"(3) WITHDRAWAL; RULE OF CONSTRUCTION.--

"(A) IN GENERAL.--In the event of an active investigation of a foodborne illness outbreak that is directly linked to a qualified facility subject to an exemption under this subsection, or if the Secretary determines that it is necessary to protect the public health and prevent or mitigate a foodborne illness outbreak based on conduct or conditions associated with a qualified facility that are material to the safety of the food manufactured, processed, packed, or held at such facility, the Secretary may withdraw the exemption provided to such facility under this subsection.

"(B) RULE OF CONSTRUCTION.--Nothing in this subsection shall be construed to expand or limit the inspection authority of the Secretary.

"(4) DEFINITIONS.--In this subsection:

"(A) AFFILIATE.--The term 'affiliate' means any facility that controls, is controlled by, or is under common control with another facility.

"(B) QUALIFIED END-USER.--The term 'qualified end-user', with respect to a food, means--

"(i) the consumer of the food; or

"(ii) a restaurant or retail food establishment (as those terms are defined by the Secretary for purposes of section 415) that--

"(I) is located--

"*(aa) in the same State as the qualified facility that sold the food to such restaurant or establishment; or*

"*(bb) not more than 275 miles from such facility; and*

"*(II) is purchasing the food for sale directly to consumers at such restaurant or retail food establishment.*

"*(C) CONSUMER.--For purposes of subparagraph (B), the term 'consumer' does not include a business.*

"*(D) SUBSIDIARY.--The term 'subsidiary' means any company which is owned or controlled directly or indirectly by another company.*

"*(5) STUDY.--*

"*(A) IN GENERAL.--The Secretary, in consultation with the Secretary of Agriculture, shall conduct a study of the food processing sector regulated by the Secretary to determine--*

"*(i) the distribution of food production by type and size of operation, including monetary value of food sold;*

"*(ii) the proportion of food produced by each type and size of operation;*

"*(iii) the number and types of food facilities co-located on farms, including the number and proportion by commodity and by manufacturing or processing activity;*

"*(iv) the incidence of foodborne illness originating from each size and type of operation and the type of food facilities for which no reported or known hazard exists; and*

"*(v) the effect on foodborne illness risk associated with commingling, processing, transporting, and storing food and raw agricultural commodities, including differences in risk based on the scale and duration of such activities.*

"*(B) SIZE.--The results of the study conducted under subparagraph (A) shall include the information necessary to enable the Secretary to define the terms 'small business' and 'very small business', for purposes of promulgating the regulation under subsection (n). In defining such terms, the Secretary shall include consideration of harvestable acres, income, the number of employees, and the volume of food harvested.*

"*(C) SUBMISSION OF REPORT.--Not later than 18 months after the date of enactment the FDA Food Safety Modernization Act, the Secretary shall submit to Congress a report that describes the results of the study conducted under subparagraph (A).*

"*(6) NO PREEMPTION.--Nothing in this subsection preempts State, local, county, or other non-Federal law regarding the safe production of food. Compliance with this subsection shall not relieve any person from liability at common law or under State statutory law.*

"*(7) NOTIFICATION TO CONSUMERS.--*

"*(A) IN GENERAL.--A qualified facility that is exempt from the requirements under subsections (a) through (i) and subsection (n) and does not prepare documentation under paragraph (2)(B)(i)(I) shall--*

"(i) with respect to a food for which a food packaging label is required by the Secretary under any other provision of this Act, include prominently and conspicuously on such label the name and business address of the facility where the food was manufactured or processed; or

"(ii) with respect to a food for which a food packaging label is not required by the Secretary under any other provisions of this Act, prominently and conspicuously display, at the point of purchase, the name and business address of the facility where the food was manufactured or processed, on a label, poster, sign, placard, or documents delivered contemporaneously with the food in the normal course of business, or, in the case of Internet sales, in an electronic notice.

"(B) NO ADDITIONAL LABEL.--Subparagraph (A) does not provide authority to the Secretary to require a label that is in addition to any label required under any other provision of this Act.

"(m) Authority With Respect to Certain Facilities.--The Secretary may, by regulation, exempt or modify the requirements for compliance under this section with respect to facilities that are solely engaged in the production of food for animals other than man, the storage of raw agricultural commodities (other than fruits and vegetables) intended for further distribution or processing, or the storage of packaged foods that are not exposed to the environment.

"(n) Regulations.--

"(1) IN GENERAL.--Not later than 18 months after the date of enactment of the FDA Food Safety Modernization Act, the Secretary shall promulgate regulations--

"(A) to establish science-based minimum standards for conducting a hazard analysis, documenting hazards, implementing preventive controls, and documenting the implementation of the preventive controls under this section; and

"(B) to define, for purposes of this section, the terms 'small business' and 'very small business', taking into consideration the study described in subsection (l)(5).

"(2) COORDINATION.--In promulgating the regulations under paragraph (1)(A), with regard to hazards that may be intentionally introduced, including by acts of terrorism, the Secretary shall coordinate with the Secretary of Homeland Security, as appropriate.

"(3) CONTENT.--The regulations promulgated under paragraph (1)(A) shall--

"(A) provide sufficient flexibility to be practicable for all sizes and types of facilities, including small businesses such as a small food processing facility co-located on a farm;

"(B) comply with chapter 35 of title 44, United States Code (commonly known as the 'Paperwork Reduction Act'), with special attention to minimizing the burden (as defined in section 3502(2) of such Act) on the facility, and collection of information (as defined in section 3502(3) of such Act), associated with such regulations;

"(C) acknowledge differences in risk and minimize, as appropriate, the number of separate standards that apply to separate foods; and

"(D) not require a facility to hire a consultant or other third party to identify, implement, certify, or audit preventative controls, except in the case of negotiated enforcement resolutions that may require such a consultant or third party.

"(4) RULE OF CONSTRUCTION.--Nothing in this subsection shall be construed to provide the Secretary with the authority to prescribe specific technologies, practices, or critical controls for an individual facility.

"(5) REVIEW.--In promulgating the regulations under paragraph (1)(A), the Secretary shall review regulatory hazard analysis and preventive control programs in existence on the date of enactment of the FDA Food Safety Modernization Act, including the Grade 'A' Pasteurized Milk Ordinance to ensure that such regulations are consistent, to the extent practicable, with applicable domestic and internationally-recognized standards in existence on such date.

"(o) Definitions.--For purposes of this section:

"(1) CRITICAL CONTROL POINT.--The term 'critical control point' means a point, step, or procedure in a food process at which control can be applied and is essential to prevent or eliminate a food safety hazard or reduce such hazard to an acceptable level.

"(2) FACILITY.--The term 'facility' means a domestic facility or a foreign facility that is required to register under section 415.

"(3) PREVENTIVE CONTROLS.--The term 'preventive controls' means those risk-based, reasonably appropriate procedures, practices, and processes that a person knowledgeable about the safe manufacturing, processing, packing, or holding of food would employ to significantly minimize or prevent the hazards identified under the hazard analysis conducted under subsection (b) and that are consistent with the current scientific understanding of safe food manufacturing, processing, packing, or holding at the time of the analysis. Those procedures, practices, and processes may include the following:

"(A) Sanitation procedures for food contact surfaces and utensils and food-contact surfaces of equipment.

"(B) Supervisor, manager, and employee hygiene training.

"(C) An environmental monitoring program to verify the effectiveness of pathogen controls in processes where a food is exposed to a potential contaminant in the environment.

"(D) A food allergen control program.

"(E) A recall plan.

"(F) Current Good Manufacturing Practices (cGMPs) under part 110 of title 21, Code of Federal Regulations (or any successor regulations).

"(G) Supplier verification activities that relate to the safety of food.".

(b) Guidance Document.--The Secretary shall issue a guidance document related to the regulations promulgated under subsection (b)(1) with respect to the hazard analysis and preventive controls under section 418 of the Federal Food, Drug, and Cosmetic Act (as added by subsection (a)).

(c) Rulemaking.--

(1) PROPOSED RULEMAKING.--

(A) IN GENERAL.--Not later than 9 months after the date of enactment of this Act, the Secretary of Health and Human Services (referred to in this subsection as the "Secretary") shall publish a notice of proposed rulemaking in the Federal Register to promulgate regulations with respect to--

(i) activities that constitute on-farm packing or holding of food that is not grown, raised, or consumed on such farm or another farm under the same ownership for purposes of section 415 of the Federal Food, Drug, and Cosmetic Act (21 U.S.C. 350d), as amended by this Act; and

(ii) activities that constitute on-farm manufacturing or processing of food that is not consumed on that farm or on *another farm under common ownership for purposes of such section 415.*

(B) CLARIFICATION.--The rulemaking described under subparagraph (A) shall enhance the implementation of such section 415 and clarify the activities that are included as part of the definition of the term "facility" under such section 415. Nothing in this Act authorizes the Secretary to modify the definition of the term "facility" under such section.

(C) SCIENCE-BASED RISK ANALYSIS.--In promulgating regulations under subparagraph (A), the Secretary shall conduct a science-based risk analysis of--

(i) specific types of on-farm packing or holding of food that is not grown, raised, or consumed on such farm or another farm under the same ownership, as such packing and holding relates to specific foods; and

(ii) specific on-farm manufacturing and processing activities as such activities relate to specific foods that are not consumed on that farm or on another farm under common ownership.

(D) AUTHORITY WITH RESPECT TO CERTAIN FACILITIES.--

(i) IN GENERAL.--In promulgating the regulations under subparagraph (A), the Secretary shall consider the results of the science-based risk analysis conducted under subparagraph (C), and shall exempt certain facilities from the requirements in section 418 of the Federal Food, Drug, and Cosmetic Act (as added by this section), including hazard analysis and preventive controls, and the mandatory inspection frequency in section 421 of such Act (as added by section 201), or modify the requirements in such sections 418 or 421, as the Secretary determines appropriate, if such facilities are engaged only in specific types of on-farm

manufacturing, processing, packing, or holding activities that the Secretary determines to be low risk involving specific foods the Secretary determines to be low risk.

(ii) LIMITATION.--The exemptions or modifications under clause (i) shall not include an exemption from the requirement to register under section 415 of the Federal Food, Drug, and Cosmetic Act (21 U.S.C. 350d), as amended by this Act, if applicable, and shall apply only to small businesses and very small businesses, as defined in the regulation promulgated under section 418(n) of the Federal Food, Drug, and Cosmetic Act (as added under subsection (a)).

(2) FINAL REGULATIONS.--Not later than 9 months after the close of the comment period for the proposed rulemaking under paragraph (1), the Secretary shall adopt final rules with respect to--

(A) activities that constitute on-farm packing or holding of food that is not grown, raised, or consumed on such farm or another farm under the same ownership for purposes of section 415 of the Federal Food, Drug, and Cosmetic Act (21 U.S.C. 350d), as amended by this Act;

(B) activities that constitute on-farm manufacturing or processing of food that is not consumed on that farm or on another farm under common ownership for purposes of such section 415; and shall verify that—

(C) the requirements under sections 418 and 421 of the Federal Food, Drug, and Cosmetic Act, as added by this Act, from which the Secretary may issue exemptions or modifications of the requirements for certain types of facilities.

(d) Small Entity Compliance Policy Guide.--Not later than 180 days after the issuance of the regulations promulgated under subsection (n) of section 418 of the Federal Food, Drug, and Cosmetic Act (as added by subsection (a)), the Secretary shall issue a small

entity compliance policy guide setting forth in plain language the requirements of such section 418 and this section to assist small entities in complying with the hazard analysis and other activities required under such section 418 and this section.

(e) Prohibited Acts.--Section 301 (21 U.S.C. 331) is amended by adding at the end the following:

> "(uu) The operation of a facility that manufactures, processes, packs, or holds food for sale in the United States if the owner, operator, or agent in charge of such facility is not in compliance with section 418.".

(f) No Effect on HACCP Authorities.--Nothing in the amendments made by this section limits the authority of the Secretary under the Federal Food, Drug, and Cosmetic Act (21 U.S.C. 301 et seq.) or the Public Health Service Act (42 U.S.C. 201 et seq.) to revise, issue, or enforce Hazard Analysis Critical Control programs and the Thermally Processed Low-Acid Foods Packaged in Hermetically Sealed Containers standards.

(g) Dietary Supplements.--Nothing in the amendments made by this section shall apply to any facility with regard to the manufacturing, processing, packing, or holding of a dietary supplement that is in compliance with the requirements of sections 402(g)(2) and 761 of the Federal Food, Drug, and Cosmetic Act (21 U.S.C. 342(g)(2), 379aa-1).

(h) Updating Guidance Relating to Fish and Fisheries Products Hazards and Controls.--The Secretary shall, not later than 180 days after the date of enactment of this Act, update the Fish and Fisheries Products Hazards and Control Guidance to take into account advances in technology that have occurred since the previous publication of such Guidance by the Secretary.

(i) Effective Dates.--

> (1) GENERAL RULE.--The amendments made by this section shall take effect 18 months after the date of enactment of this Act.

> (2) FLEXIBILITY FOR SMALL BUSINESSES.--Notwithstanding paragraph (1)--

(A) the amendments made by this section shall apply to a small business (as defined in the regulations promulgated under section 418(n) of the Federal Food, Drug, and Cosmetic Act (as added by this section)) beginning on the date that is 6 months after the effective date of such regulations; and

(B) the amendments made by this section shall apply to a very small business (as defined in such regulations) beginning on the date that is 18 months after the effective date of such regulations.

3

Safety Standards, Testing, and Precautions

What Do Managers Need To Know?

Within a set of limitations and constraints, the FDA has been given the power to fix and enforce new limits on contaminants and other problem substances in foods. The FDA is now empowered to set "performance standards" for foods to be identified by the FDA to protect against the most significant foodborne contaminants. Separately, the FDA is empowered to set "standards for produce safety" that apply only to fruits, vegetables, and mixes of fruits and vegetables determined to be "raw agricultural commodities." The standards under these two sections are separate.

Section 419, which sets standards for produce safety, drew extensive debate and lobbying efforts since the food that does not meet the new FDA standard will either need a variance, in the FDA's discretion to give one, or must be withheld from the US food marketplace. Much of the debate among lobbying forces dealt with how to prevent contamination while keeping costs down for the food processors. Most controversial was the amendment by Montana Senator Jon Tester that exempts certain small farms.[103] Section 419 seems to concede more flexibility for the industry than the FDA had sought, but ultimately the new law has the potential to bring up the quality levels of all significant producers. If a particular food is subject to a final and enforceable standard, a variance can be requested. The

---

[103] Pub.L. 111-353, adding new §418(l)(4)(B)(ii)(I)(bb).

FDA has a great deal of discretion in granting, denying, or withdrawing a variance that might, for example, allow 15 percent more flies and fly parts in butter during a very wet season, compared to "normal" butter. The burden is on the food company to show the FDA that the food made or shipped under that variance is not more likely to have serious adverse health effects. Interesting proofs will be presented, not all of which will be found by the FDA to be legitimate for excusing lower-quality foods.

For the section on performance standards, the final compromise allows the FDA to set "contaminant-specific and science-based" guidance documents or regulations that may require testing and may set limits.

Higher compliance costs are inevitable, regardless of how the FDA writes the implementing rules. Non-US food producers will have the expensive chore of complying with more stringent norms as well as with greater paperwork burdens. Depending on the successful adaptation of electronic coding and accountability systems, and the costs of expert US food consultants, this program may be extremely costly for a developing country's food exporters. Small margins of profit in food distribution make it more likely that costs are going to be shifted to the food consumer, not absorbed entirely by the food processors, growers, or sellers.

Performance Standards

What Will Be Required?

The FDA must identify the most significant foodborne contaminants and, based on a biennial review and "when appropriate to reduce the risk of serious illness or death to humans or animals or prevent adulteration of food...or to prevent the spread of communicable disease," must issue "contaminant-specific and science-based guidance documents, action levels, or regulations."[104] The biennial review will require the FDA to "review and evaluate relevant health data and other relevant information, including toxicological and epidemiological studies and analyses."[105]

---

[104] Pub.L. 111-353 §104(b).
[105] *Id.* at § 104(a).

What Foods Will Be Covered?

Congress left the decision of what food will be subject to performance standards up to FDA discretion, with some direction. The FDA is not required to establish standards for all food categories, but is required to establish standards for foods and food classes that the FDA determines are appropriate, based on the review required by this legislation. For example, peanut shelling, roasting, and cleaning will be a candidate for rules that exclude salmonella, after tens of millions of dollars were expended on recalls from a poorly cleaned Georgia plant that disseminated peanut paste to many producers of flavored products. The FDA realizes that each of the many food categories will argue that their class of food needs no mandatory standard. Congress has given the FDA discretion to select which foods are subject to standards.

What Requirements Will the FDA Rules Include?

The Act does not specify what form and content the FDA rules should include. The FDA may decide whether it will issue the rules through guidance documents, action levels, or regulations. The bill does make clear that the rules "shall apply to products or product classes and shall not be written to be facility-specific."[106] The legislation as it had been passed by the House did not set a firm deadline for the FDA to issue standards, but would have required they be set "as soon as practicable."[107] Risk reviews must be done at least every two years.

What Did Congress Intend?

Congress has indicated that performance standards will play a pivotal role in maintaining the safety of food. According to the chair of an important House committee that oversees the FDA, "Performance standards form the backbone for monitoring the effectiveness of process control systems and identifying the foods at greatest risk."[108]

---

[106] *Id.* at § 104(b)(3).

[107] H.R. 2749 § 103, 111th Cong. (as engrossed by House of Representatives, July 30, 2009).

[108] 155 Cong. Rec. H9009 (daily ed. July 29, 2009) (statement of Rep. DeLauro).

According to Representative Dingell, this section would provide the FDA with "clear authority to issue and require manufacturers to meet strong, enforceable performance standards to ensure the safety of different types of food."[109] Although the Senate reduced the explicit powers for the FDA, these House provisions will be considered when the final regulations are written.

Standards for Produce Safety

What Categories of Foods Can Be Subjected to Standards for Produce Safety?

This section will apply to "fruits and vegetables, including specific mixes or categories of fruits and vegetables, that are raw agricultural commodities for which the Secretary has determined that [safety] standards minimize the risk of serious adverse health consequences or death."[110] This section does not apply to a production facility, like a factory that is already separately subject to new Section 418 added by the 2010 Act, which imposes requirements on hazard analysis and risk-based preventive controls.[111]

In the House bill that was not adopted, that version would have specifically required the establishment of science-based standards for "raw agricultural commodities (1) that are a fruit, vegetable, nut, or fungus; and (2) for which the FDA has determined that such standards are reasonably necessary to minimize the risk of serious adverse health consequences or death to humans or animals."[112] For example, lettuce and peppers have had contamination issues; the peanut recalls reached about 1,300 distinct products nationwide; mushroom recalls have occurred for toxic effects in some past cases; and rhubarb's natural oxalic acid can be a problem with excessive consumption. Note that the grain company lobbyists were careful

---

[109] 155 Cong. Rec. H9157 (daily ed. July 30, 2009) (statement of Rep. Dingell).

[110] Id., §105, adding new §419(a)(1)(A).

[111] Id., 419(h).

[112] H.R. 2749 § 104, 111th Cong. (as engrossed by House of Representatives, July 30, 2009). The bill as reported out by the House Committee did not include fruit and vegetables among the commodities the Secretary is to establish standards for, and did not require the Secretary to establish the regulations in consultation with the Secretary of Agriculture. Compare H.R. 2749 § 104, 111th Cong. (as engrossed by House of Representatives, July 30, 2009) with H.R. 2749 § 104, 111th Cong. (as reported by the House Committee on Energy and Commerce, June 17, 2009).

to exclude their foods from coverage. Even though the House version was not the same as the final version, rulemaking debates often cite to the early versions of a new law as generalized indicators of the congressional intent.

The FDA will set safety standards, in coordination with the USDA and "representative of State departments of agriculture (including with regard to the national organic program)." The FDA is required to publish a notice of proposed rulemaking to establish science-based minimum standards for the safe production and harvesting of those types of fruits and vegetables that are raw agricultural commodities, for which the Secretary has determined that such standards minimize the risk of serious adverse health consequences or death.[113] Note the key terms: (1) raw crop standards must be based on science, and (2) the goal is to reduce serious risks by enforcing higher safety norms than had been the case in the past.

What Requirements Must the FDA Rule-Writing Process Follow?

The Act as adopted empowers the FDA to adopt food safety regulations that may establish the procedures, processes, and practices the FDA determines to be reasonably necessary to prevent intentional or unintentional acts of contamination by biological, chemical, and physical hazards and "to provide reasonable assurances" that such commodities are not adulterated.[114]

The FDA is to publish notice of proposed rulemaking for this section within one year of the enactment of the Act, and is to conduct at least three public meetings in diverse geographic locations to provide for an opportunity for public comment.[115]

The proposed rules are to:

> (A) provide sufficient flexibility to be applicable to various
> types of entities engaged in the production and harvesting
> of raw agricultural commodities, including small businesses

---

[113] Pub.L. 111-353, adding new §419(a)(1)(A).
[114] Pub.L. 111-353, adding new 419(c)(1)(A), and see H.R. 2749 § 104, 111th Cong. (as engrossed by House of Representatives, July 30, 2009).
[115] *Id.* at 419(a)(2).

and entities that sell directly to consumers, and be appropriate to the scale and diversity of the production and harvesting of such commodities;

(B) include, with respect to growing, harvesting, sorting, packing, and storage operations, minimum standards related to soil amendments, hygiene, packaging, temperature controls, animals in the growing area, and water;

(C) consider hazards that occur naturally, may be unintentionally introduced, or may be intentionally introduced, including by acts of terrorism;

(D) take into consideration, consistent with ensuring enforceable public health protection, conservation and environmental practice standards and policies established by Federal natural resource conservation, wildlife conservation, and environmental agencies; and

(E) in the case of production that is certified organic, not include any requirements that conflict with or duplicate the requirements of the national organic program established under the Organic Foods Production Act of 1990 (7 U.S.C. 6501 et seq.), while providing for public health protection consistent with the requirements of [this Act].[116]

The language laying out the contents of the proposed rulemaking was altered to include provisions stating that the rulemaking shall "provide sufficient flexibility to be applicable to various types of entities engaged in the production and harvesting of raw agricultural commodities, including small business and entities that sell directly to consumers, and be appropriate to the scale and diversity of the production and harvesting of such commodities." [117]

---

[116] *Id.* at 419(a)(3).
[117] *Id.* at 419(a)(3)(A).

How Will the New Standards for Produce Safety Be Set?

Standards will be set by the FDA issuance of several new regulations. The FDA is to prioritize implementing regulations for fruits and vegetables that have a history of foodborne illness outbreaks. Within a year after the comment period closes, the FDA must adopt final regulations for "minimum standards" for fruits and vegetables that the FDA "has determined that such standards minimize the risk of serious adverse health consequences or death." The regulations must:

> (A) provide for coordination of education and enforcement activities by State and local officials, as designated by the Governors of the respective States or the appropriate elected State official as recognized by State statute; and

> (B) include a description of the variance process under subsection (c) and the types of permissible variances the Secretary may grant.

Within one year of this Act being enacted, the FDA must publish "updated good agricultural practices and guidance for the safe production and harvesting of specific types of fresh produce."[118] In doing so, the FDA must consult with the USDA, representatives of state departments of agriculture, and, as added by the bill reported by the Senate Committee, "farmer representatives, and various types of entities engaged in the production and harvesting of fruits and vegetables that are raw agricultural commodities, including small businesses."[119]

Additionally, the provision on food standards guidance was altered to require that the FDA, before issuing guidance, must conduct no fewer than three public meetings in diverse locations as part of an effort to conduct education and outreach regarding the guidance (published under this section) for persons in different regions who are involved in the production and harvesting of fruits and vegetables that are raw agricultural commodities, including persons that sell directly to consumers and farmer

---

[118] *Id.* 419(e)(1).
[119] *Id.* 419(e)(1).

representatives.[120] The use of good agricultural practices with input from the various voices in the food industry was something that small and diverse producers strongly urged.[121]

In issuing the regulations, the FDA must allow a reasonable period of time for compliance, taking into account small businesses' ability to comply.[122] If the FDA chooses to follow the House language in adopting its rules, in addition to the requirements of the final Act, the FDA could consider issues like wildlife habitat, conservation practices, watershed protection efforts, and organic production methods.[123] "Guidance" is a quicker process than rulemaking. A guidance can be rewritten in several weeks to de-list a particular program that failed to catch the contamination. This section has no effect on already existing HACCP requirements that are in effect for USDA and some FDA facilities.

What Is the Enforcement Aspect of the Standards Requirement?

The Act as passed does not contain an enforcement mechanism that is different from the existing food adulteration powers held by the FDA.[124] Under the former House bill, food that has been "manufactured, processed, packed transported or held under conditions" that do not comply with the performance standards set by the FDA would be considered adulterated.[125] The case law decisions clearly show that the actual proof of contamination in a shipment of food is not required, where the food came from a plant that did not comply with good manufacturing practice rules.[126] The 2010 legislation passed by the House would have raised this one more step—not

---

[120] *Id.* 419(e)(2). Compare S. 510 § 105, 111th Cong. (as reported by the Senate HELP Committee, Nov. 18, 2009) with S. 510 § 105, 111th Cong. (as introduced in Senate, Mar. 3, 2009).

[121] Cookson Beecher, *Small Growers Concerned About FDA Reform*, FOOD SAFETY NEWS, Nov. 25, 2009, www.foodsafetynews.com/2009/11/small-growers-concerned-about-fda-reform/index.html?p=2.

[122] Pub.L. 111-353, adding new 419(a)(3).

[123] The bill as introduced in the House did not require the Secretary to consider the impact on small-scale and diversified farms in establishing the standards. This provision was added by the House Committee. Compare H.R. 2749 § 104, 111th Cong. (as reported by the House Committee on Energy and Commerce, June 17, 2009) with H.R. 2749 § 104, 111th Cong. (as introduced in House of Representatives, June 8, 2009).

[124] 21 U.S.C. 342, 331.

[125] H.R. 2749 § 103, 111th Cong. (as engrossed by House of Representatives, July 30, 2009).

[126] *See e.g. U.S. v Certified Grocers Co-op*, 546 F.2d 1308 (7th Cir., 1976).

just generic rules[127] on facility cleanliness on carrot processing lines, but actual performance standards for each step of the carrot's "life" on its way to the consumer. Enforcement action could have been taken against the firm that failed to follow the new standards.

How Will Variances Be Managed by the FDA?

Congress recognized the existence of a need for state or other national governments to be able to make requests for the FDA to grant waivers or exceptions. The standard the FDA must apply to the grant of a waiver is whether the state or foreign country can demonstrate "that the variance does not increase the likelihood that the food for which the variance is requested will be adulterated under Section 402, and that the variance provides the same level of public health protection as the requirements of the regulations adopted under" requirement for standards for produce safety.[128] In other words, equivalence of safety of the food (with and without variance) is the test to be met.[129] The request is to be made in writing to the FDA.

It should be noted that facitlies subject to requirement for hazard analysis under Section 418 are not subject to standards for produce safety.

What Background Data Supported Adopting Safety Standards for Produce and Certain Other Raw Agricultural Commodities?

Consumer Reports released a study in February 2010 showing that in an analysis of packaged leafy greens, nearly 40 percent of the samples contained bacteria indicating poor sanitation, at levels that industry consultants deem unacceptable. Consumers Union, the nonprofit publisher of *Consumer Reports*, urged the Senate to quickly pass S. 510. Dr. Michael Hansen, the senior scientist at Consumers Union, said, "The Senate should act immediately to pass pending FDA food safety reform legislation that requires the agency to set performance standards as well as develop safety standards for the growing or processing of fresh produce. FDA should also formally declare that certain pathogenic bacteria—such as E. coli O157:H7,

---

[127] 21 C.F.R. 110.
[128] Pub.L. 111-353, adding new §419(c)(1)(F).
[129] *Id.* 419(c)(2).

Salmonella, and Listeria—be considered adulterants when found in salad greens."[130]

What Models Exist for Safety Standards?

The FDA has set economic standards for certain foods for decades under its old 1938 "food standards" authority.[131] But the establishment of federal standards to enhance safety is just one of many federal efforts following a rulemaking process that already exists at the FDA[132], and rulemaking like this is well understood in several product categories.[133] There are familiar models: automobile safety standards, aircraft parts certification and airworthiness directives, and others already have this type of system in place. The FDA has experience in setting safety norms for drugs and food additive materials, so the 2010 law will give the FDA a series of tasks for which it is well equipped.

What Costs Will Result?

The 2010 legislation imposes very significant new expense items for those in the food industry supply chain. But costs of implementation and daily compliance are passed along to the food consumer, as they are to car buyers and airplane purchasers for comparable standards.

The highly visible problems of noncompliance with the new standards could pose a significant increase in risk to the brand reputation or consumer confidence for domestic food suppliers. They are an even greater risk to continued ability for foreign food firms to export to US customers. The ability to stringently remain below the level of contaminants included in the content of the final binding rules or guidance documents is critical to the feasibility of continued sale of foreign foods into the US market.

---

[130] *Consumer Reports: Packaged Salad Can Contain High Levels of Bacteria, Consumers Union Urges FDA to Set Performance Standards for Greens*, Consumers Union, Feb. 2, 2010, www.consumersunion.org/pub/core_food_safety/015723.html; Ben Moscovitch, *Consumer Group Highlights Lettuce Risk to Urge Food Safety Bill Passage*, INSIDE HEALTH POLICY, Feb. 25, 2010.

[131] 21 U.S.C. 341.

[132] 21 C.F.R. 10.

[133] *See* James O'Reilly, *Administrative Rulemaking* (West 2d Ed. 2010).

Publicly traded firms have another layer of concern. It is important to note that the news media and FDA compliance officials may utilize web postings of reported noncompliance by food firms. This web listing, like warning letters for drug makers, is very "newsworthy" and may affect the stock market's perceptions about publicly traded food company stocks.

What Intermediary Entities Will Prosper from the New Law?

Those entities that perform safety tests on samples of foods, and those that consult with food companies, will prosper. The creation of standards increases the business available to technical laboratory intermediaries, several of whom, like the international lab network Intertek, have lab testing facilities in foreign nations as well as in the United States.[134] Laboratory operators' obligations to report findings of risk in their client's products have yet to be defined in statutory form. Prudent managers will note that whistleblowers who reveal the safety concerns are shielded from firing or other adverse action.[135]

How Does This Law Relate To the Existing Reportable Foods Registry?

Chapter 13 addresses this earlier legislative requirement, adopted in 2007. Even in the short time since, the climate for business "crisis management" in foods has changed. The FDA had been dependent on belatedly tracking outbreaks of foodborne illness, or "catching" foreign food safety violators by analysis of food cargo samples taken at ports of entry. Now firms must create analysis, planning, and certification systems. The 2007 law had required food firms to self-report their most serious risk problems in the processing and handling of raw foods.[136] Noncompliance is a prohibited act under current law.[137] After 2010, when a standard exists and the food fails a test under that standard, there is more basis for asserting a legal duty to notify the FDA.

---

[134] Pub.L. 111-353 §202.
[135] Pub. L. 111-353 §402.
[136] 21 U.S.C. 350f.
[137] 21 U.S.C. 331(mm).

This statute builds upon the 2007 legislation that created a "Reportable Foods Registry."[138] The 2009 FDA final rules implementing the registry, combined with the expanded recall requirements of the 2010 legislation, must be included in any calculus of risk handling by a food company. Nondisclosure of bad news, such as the Georgia peanut processor's case of allegedly ignoring a salmonella report before deaths occurred, may be pursued by the FDA as a criminal offense in some circumstances.

What Should Prudent Companies Recognize about Regulatory Requirements on Their Suppliers?

Food safety regulation is no longer a game of "catch and release." The importing firm, the foreign food supplier, the foreign lab that certifies the foods, the accrediting body that certifies the labs, and the retailer are all vulnerable to legal penalties and court actions, if the quality of the food substantially fails to meet standards. Perhaps "it takes a village" to assure safety. Congress recognizes in the new law that multiple participants in the food process must be responsible, not simply the final shipper to consumers. The public protection for food safety no longer will be only the official government employees, the FDA inspector, the Customs inspector, and the local or state health inspector. The industry participants and service providers are "all in this together," and false or inaccurate actions will be subject to punishments.

What Is the Consequence for Foods That Don't Meet a Standard?

If a standard exists and you learn that the foods will not meet that standard, it is safest to mulch or landfill the food rather than selling it. The 2010 law makes it a prohibited act to not comply with a standard adopted under this section. In enforcing this section, the FDA "may coordinate" with the USDA and, "as appropriate," coordinate with state authorities.[139] Repeat shipment of food that does not meet the standards just compounds the likelihood of increasingly severe penalties.

---

[138] Pub.L. 110-85 §1005.
[139] S. 510 § 105, 111th Cong. (as reported by the Senate HELP Committee, Nov. 18, 2009).

What Was the Response from the FDA?

FDA Commissioner Hamburg testified at the Senate HELP Committee hearing on October 22, 2009, that:

> Section 105, which authorizes mandatory safety standards for fresh produce, addresses enforcement via the creation of a prohibited act. As explained above, this means that FDA may not seize or refuse admission of fresh produce because it is not in compliance with the requirements. Section 105 provides important authorities that will help prevent foodborne illnesses only if the standards are effectively implemented and enforced; therefore, it is essential to have effective tools for enforcing these requirements.[140]

Commissioner Hamburg's concern was not addressed by the bill as reported by the Senate Committee, and a violation of Section 105 remains a prohibited act.

Why Is the "Prohibited Act" Difference from "Adulteration" Significant?

There is a nuance in the use of "prohibited acts" contrasted to "adulterated" status. The House bill had been slightly different: a food that is "grown, harvested, processed, packed, sorted, transported, or held under conditions" that does not comply with this section would have been considered adulterated if the House bill had become law.[141]

Note that the actual conditions of the shipment of food (e.g., level of contaminants) will be compared to the wording of the final FDA rule that creates the standard. The food company loses if the FDA has written the standard very tightly, or if the conditions objectively applied show that this company is out of compliance. Note, also, that this tightens the constraints

---

[140] Hearing on Keeping America's Families Safe: Reforming the Food Safety System, S. Committee on Health, Education, Labor, and Pensions, 111th Cong. 8, Oct. 22, 2009 (Testimony of FDA Commissioner Hamburg).

[141] H.R. 2749 § 105, 111th Cong. (as engrossed by House of Representatives, July 30, 2009).

on factories processing food. Part 110 of the existing FDA rules[142] has already compelled the food maker to be compliant with several generic safety and recordkeeping requirements ("good manufacturing practices"). The new legislation sharply increases standard setting and tighter safety controls. It is now an extra level of violations—the food standard sets a bar, and food that does not meet that norm should not be marketed.

What Limits Would Have Been Imposed by the House Bill?

The final Act reflects the Senate compromises, but there is often a value to understanding the meaning of a provision by considering what the House had passed—a view of intent of some members but not of the final text. On the House floor, Representative John Dingell attempted to assuage the concerns about impact of this section, by saying:

> FDA is prohibited from imposing safety standards unless it determines those standards are "reasonably necessary to minimize the risk of serious adverse health consequences or death," a very, very high standard that they have to meet. This will ensure protection of the concerns of organic farmers and that they are taken into consideration before issuing standards.[143]

According to the House Report, the amended language clarified the produce standards by establishing "that the FDA should issue standards only for the riskiest types of products."[144] Multiple representatives on the House floor stated that grain and related commodities are exempt from produce standards.[145] The language favoring grain appeased members of the House Agriculture Committee. According to Representative Peterson:

> We did have some concerns in the Agriculture Committee that we engaged in some discussions and negotiations with Mr. Dingell and others on the staff of the Energy and

---

[142] 21 C.F.R.110.
[143] 155 Cong. Rec. H9157 (daily ed. July 30, 2009) (statement of Rep. Dingell).
[144] H. Rept. 111-234, 111th Cong. 1st Sess. (2009).
[145] 155 Cong. Rec. H9133 (daily ed. July 30, 2009) (statement of Rep. Moran); 155 Cong. Rec. H9157 (daily ed. July 30, 2009) (statement of Rep. Shimkus).

Commerce Committee on, and we think we have further improved the bill in terms of how it relates to agriculture. We were able to clarify things in terms of livestock and grain farmers that there was some concern about the language, so that we cleared up some things in terms of performance standards and record keeping. As the bill came out of Energy and Commerce, there were concerns registered by some of the farm groups. Some of them even indicated they might oppose it. But at this point, because of the changes that have been made, we now have groups that in the past had some concerns, they are now either neutral or supporting this bill. The United Fresh Fruit and Vegetable Group, Western Growers, the American Farm Bureau, National Association of Wheat Growers, the Cattlemen Beef Association, Turkey Federation, Chicken Council, Pork Producers, Corn Growers, Soybean Association, Rice Federation, American Food Industry Association, United Egg Producers, the American Sheep Industry, the Wheat Growers and the Barley Growers, are now either supporting the legislation or are neutral on the legislation.[146]

What Input Did Congress Receive about These Issues?

The United Fresh Produce Association had urged that language be added to the section allowing for flexibility in how the rules are applied to the various production methods.[147] After her oral statement at the Senate hearing on October 22, Commissioner Hamburg noted, in response to a question about organic farming, that there is a "diverse array of agricultural types and conditions that exists in our country." She thought the bill took this into consideration and said the FDA is attempting to protect diverse agricultural

---

[146] 155 Cong. Rec. H9160 (daily ed. July 30, 2009) (statement of Rep. Peterson).

[147] Compare S. 510 § 105, 111th Cong. (as reported by the Senate HELP Committee, Nov. 18, 2009) with S. 510 § 105, 111th Cong. (as introduced in Senate, Mar. 3, 2009); Hearing on Keeping America's Families Safe: Reforming the Food Safety System, S. Committee on Health, Education, Labor, and Pensions, 111th Cong. 3-4, Oct. 22, 2009 (Testimony of Thomas Stenzel, President and CEO of United Fresh Produce Association).

techniques by trying to "work flexibility into any guidance and rulemaking...so that we can have a system that works for everyone and ultimately works for the consumer in terms of safety."[148]

"Packing" was added to the list of activities that will be subject to proposed rulemaking. This was likely in response to the letter from the National Organic Coalition, the National Farmers Union, the Organic Trade Association, and a number of other national, regional, and local food and agricultural groups just prior to mark-up, in which the groups had specifically stated, "FDA should be instructed to create standards for holding, sorting, packing, processing, and transporting and not just growing and harvesting of raw fruits and vegetables."[149]

In regard to organic, small, and diverse producers, the provision on proposed rulemaking was altered to require that the rulemaking shall:

> take into consideration, consistent with ensuring enforceable public health protection, conservation and environmental practice standards and policies established by Federal natural resource conservation, wildlife conservation, and environmental agencies; and in the case of production that is certified organic, not include any requirements that conflict with or duplicate the requirements of the national organic program established under the Organic Foods Production Act of 1990 (7 U.S.C. 6501 et seq.), while providing for public health protection consistent with the requirements of this Act.

These additions were specifically suggested by the letter from the National Organic Coalition, the National Farmers Union, the Organic Trade

---

[148] Hearing on Keeping America's Families Safe: Reforming the Food Safety System, S. Committee on Health, Education, Labor, and Pensions, 111th Cong. 6, Oct. 22, 2009 (Testimony of FDA Commissioner Hamburg).

[149] Compare S. 510 § 105, 111th Cong. (as reported by the Senate HELP Committee, Nov. 18, 2009) with S. 510 § 105, 111th Cong. (as introduced in Senate, Mar. 3, 2009); Letter on Senate Food Safety Bill (S. 510) to members of Senate HELP Committee, National Sustainable Agriculture Coalition, Nov. 16, 2009, http://sustainableagriculture.net/wp-content/uploads/2008/08/Letter-to-HELP-on-S-510-11-16-092.pdf.

Association, and a number of other national, regional, and local food and agricultural groups just prior to mark-up.[150]

A representative for the Food Marketing Institute testified at the Senate HELP Committee hearing on October 22, 2009:

> We support directing FDA, in consultation with USDA and state departments of agriculture, to establish science-based standards for the safe production and harvesting of fruits and vegetables. Publix expects all suppliers of fresh produce to maintain strong food safety compliance programs to address the management of Good Agricultural Practices (GAPs) and minimize the microbial hazards associated with fruits and vegetables. Recent industry best practices guidance has been developed for fresh leafy greens, melons, and tomatoes. We support these collaborative efforts to improve food safety associated with fresh produce and believe standards can be designed that can be implemented on any size farm.[151]

Thomas Stenzel, president and chief executive officer of the United Fresh Produce Association, testified at the Senate HELP Committee hearing on October 22, 2009:

> • <u>Must allow for a commodity-specific approach, based on the best available science.</u> We believe produce safety standards must allow for commodity-specific food safety practices based on the best available science. In a highly diverse industry that is more aptly described as hundreds of different commodity industries, one size clearly does

---

[150] Compare S. 510 § 105, 111th Cong. (as reported by the Senate HELP Committee, Nov. 18, 2009) with S. 510 § 105, 111th Cong. (as introduced in Senate, Mar. 3, 2009); Letter on Senate Food Safety Bill (S. 510) to members of Senate HELP Committee, National Sustainable Agriculture Coalition, Nov. 16, 2009, http://sustainableagriculture.net/wp-content/uploads/2008/08/Letter-to-HELP-on-S-510-11-16-092.pdf.

[151] Hearing on Keeping America's Families Safe: Reforming the Food Safety System, S. Committee on Health, Education, Labor, and Pensions, 111th Cong. 5, Oct. 22, 2009 (Testimony of Michael Roberson, Director of Corporate Quality Assurance, Publix Super Markets Inc. on behalf of the Food Marketing Institute).

not fit all. For example, the food safety requirements of products grown close to the ground in contact with soil are far different from those grown on vines or trees. And, the large majority of produce commodities have never been linked to a foodborne disease. In fact, a recent FDA federal register notice confirms that five produce commodities have been associated with 80 percent of all foodborne disease outbreaks in the past 10 years, and that is where we must direct our resources.

• In addition, government and industry alike must be careful that broad strokes do not result in requirements that should not apply to specific commodities, and do nothing to enhance safety. Taking a general approach would be far too easy to add regulatory costs and burdens to sectors where those requirements are unneeded, without doing anything to enhance safety where most critical. Finally, as part of this commodity specific approach, FDA must develop a rule-making procedure that establishes risk and science-based regulations for the production, handling and distribution of those types of fruits and vegetables for which the Secretary determines such standards are necessary to minimize the risk of microbial illness.

• <u>Must be consistent and applicable to the identified commodity or commodity sector, no matter where grown or packaged in the United States, or imported into the country.</u> We believe produce safety standards must be consistent for an individual produce commodity grown anywhere in the United States, or imported into this country. Consumers must have the confidence that safety standards are met no matter where the commodity is grown or processed. Because of the variation in our industry's growing and harvesting practices in different climates and regions, flexibility is very appropriate and necessary. For example, some production areas use deep wells for irrigation while others use river water supplied from dams. Some farms use sprinkler irrigation, others use a drip system laid along the ground, and still others use water in the furrows between rows of produce. But the common factor must be that all uses of water for irrigation must meet safety standards that protect the product. That must be true whether the produce is grown in California, Florida, Wisconsin or Mexico.

- Must be federally mandated with sufficient federal oversight of compliance in order to be most credible to consumers. We believe achieving consistent produce safety standards across the industry requires strong federal government oversight and responsibility in order to be most credible to consumers and equitable to producers. We believe that the U.S. Food and Drug Administration, which is the public health agency charged by law with ensuring the safety of the nation's produce supply, must determine appropriate nationwide safety standards in an open and transparent process, with full input from the states, industry, academia, consumers and all stakeholders. We are strong advocates for food safety standards based on sound science and a clear consensus of expert stakeholders.

- In turn, it is important for FDA to work with its partners at the USDA and state departments of agriculture to ensure compliance with produce safety standards. We do not see a need for thousands of new FDA inspectors moved from processing plants to farms and fields, but rather a close working relationship with the USDA that understand agricultural production and can better monitor and assure compliance with FDA rules.[152]

In a joint letter to the Senate HELP Committee with the National Organic Coalition, the National Farmers Union, the Organic Trade Association, and

---

[152] Hearing on Keeping America's Families Safe: Reforming the Food Safety System, S. Committee on Health, Education, Labor, and Pensions, 111th Cong. 3-4, Oct. 22, 2009 (Testimony of Thomas Stenzel, President and CEO of United Fresh Produce Association).

a number of other national, regional, and local food and agricultural groups just prior to mark-up, the groups urged that the:

> FDA should be instructed to create standards for holding, sorting, packing, processing, and transporting and not just growing and harvesting of raw fruits and vegetables. To guarantee that its standards do not unwittingly result in diminishing food safety, FDA's produce standards and Good Agricultural Practices guidance should:
>
> • Be consistent with conservation and environmental practice standards established by other federal agencies and promote diverse cropping systems which mitigate the spread of pathogens. Conservation measure such as perennial forage, buffer strips, and grasses filter out contamination in overland water flows from livestock feedlots, loafing yards, pastures, and manure storage areas. It is imperative that new food safety standards encourage farmers to maintain and develop enhanced conservation system practices rather than penalize them for doing so. It is also imperative that the government deliver a consistent message to farmers and not force the farmer to choose between irreconcilable directives from different agencies.
>
> • Be consistent between food safety standards and certified organic farming production methods and requirements. FDA and USDA should coordinate to establish the standards relevant to certified organic production. Special consideration for certified organic farms and ranches should be made so that new food safety standards and their enforcement are not duplicative with those already in place through the Organic Food Production Act of 1990 and do not act as a barrier to organic production and organic conversion. Again, the government needs to deliver a consistent message and not a conflicting one.

- Prioritize mixed fruits or vegetables or specific processes that have been consistently associated with food-borne illnesses. In most of the recent outbreaks of food borne illness, the main source of the problem was centralized co-mingling, processing and distribution, not growing and harvesting. For instance, fresh cut, ready-to-eat packaged fruits and vegetables pose a far greater risk than whole produce and should thus be a primary target of standards developed for raw commodities.[153]

An early 2010 report by the Food Safety Project at Georgetown University highlighted the concern about increased regulations on growing produce. According to the group, a study of the Central Coast region of California indicated that:

> growers report yielding to tremendous pressure from auditors, inspectors, and other food safety professionals to change .on-farm management practices in ways that not only generate uncertain food safety benefits, but also create serious environmental consequences.
>
> Environmental concerns include reduction of water quality, removal of wetland, riparian and other habitat, and elimination of wildlife on and near farm land.

The Food Safety Project noted that although the study had been conducted on a limited area, the study's findings should be of concern in moving forward with increased regulations on fruit and vegetable farming.[154]

Tom Stenzel, president of the United Fresh Produce Association, a trade association representing growers, packers, shippers, fresh-cut processors,

---

[153] Compare S. 510 § 105, 111th Cong. (as reported by the Senate HELP Committee, Nov. 18, 2009) with S. 510 § 105, 111th Cong. (as introduced in Senate, Mar. 3, 2009); Letter on Senate Food Safety Bill (S. 510) to members of Senate HELP Committee, National Sustainable Agriculture Coalition, Nov. 16, 2009, http://sustainableagriculture.net/wp-content/uploads/2008/08/Letter-to-HELP-on-S-510-11-16-092.pdf.

[154] *Co-Managing for Food Safety and Ecological Health in California's Central Coast Region,* Produce Safety Project, Feb. 17, 2010, www.producesafetyproject.org/admin/assets/files/Summary-TNC.pdf.

distributors, and marketers of fresh fruits and vegetables, testified at the House Energy and Commerce Committee's Subcommittee on Health hearing on food safety on June 3, 2009:

> First, we strongly support the bill's intent in Sections 104 and 419A for FDA to focus on maximizing public health by implementing regulatory standards for those specific raw agricultural commodities that it believes are most critical. The FDA has estimated that only five commodities have been associated with 80 percent of all produce related foodborne disease outbreaks in the past 10 years, and that is where we must direct our resources. In a highly diverse industry that is more aptly described as hundreds of different commodity industries, one size clearly does not fit all. For example, the food safety requirements of products grown close to the ground in contact with soil are far different from those grown on vines or trees.

> We support Congress specifying that FDA have broad authority to regulate any produce commodities it determines necessary, but with the clear mandate to develop rulemaking that focuses resources for maximum public health benefit on those types of raw agricultural commodities for which the Secretary determines such standards are necessary to minimize the risk of serious adverse health consequences.

> We also recommend that Section 104 strengthen its support for eventual FDA regulatory standards, recognizing that such regulations must set the "most appropriate" standards for safety, not "minimum" standards.

> Finally, we recommend that Section 104 strengthen its support for collaboration between HHS and the U.S. Department of Agriculture and state agencies in all areas of education, research and enforcement with regard to produce. It is important to bring the broadest knowledge

and resource base possible to assist all stakeholders in understanding, implementing and complying with FDA-set public health standards.[155]

Following Stenzel's testimony, Representative Shimkus remarked that he too believed "appropriate standards" would be the better language in the bill instead of "minimum standards," and asked Stenzel to elaborate. Stenzel added:

> I don't think we should be using such terms as minimum or expecting minimum standards. We should have the agency write the standards that are most appropriate that all producers should follow. I can tell you this: that as soon as we have minimum standards, the first thing that is going to happen is someone is going to say that is not good enough. So if we are going to go down this path, let us make sure the agency writes the most appropriate standards.[156]

The final draft of the House bill provision seemed to have been largely influenced by the above testimony. In the initial draft as introduced into the House, the FDA would have been required to establish regulations for "science-based standards for the safe growing, harvesting, packing, sorting, transporting, and holding of [certain] raw agricultural commodities." Among other things, the regulations could "include, with respect to growing, harvesting, packing, sorting, transporting, and storage operations, minimum standards for safety as the [FDA] determines to be reasonably necessary." As noted above, the president of United Fresh Produce Association, a prominent produce trade association, and Representative Shimkus objected to this language of minimum standards. In the final draft as passed by the House, the FDA is required to establish regulations for

---

[155] Hearing on Food Safety Enhancement Act of 2009, Before the Subcommittee on Health of the H. Committee on Energy and Commerce, 111th Cong. 3 (2009) [hereinafter Hearing on Food Safety Enhancement Act of 2009] (Prepared Statement of Tom Stenzel, President of United Fresh Produce Association).

[156] Hearing on Food Safety Enhancement Act of 2009, Before the Subcommittee on Health of the H. Committee on Energy and Commerce, 111th Cong. 188 (2009) [hereinafter Hearing on Food Safety Enhancement Act of 2009] (Statement of Tom Stenzel, President of United Fresh Produce Association in Preliminary Transcript).

"scientific and risk-based food safety standards for the growing, harvesting, processing, packing, sorting, transporting, and holding of those types of [certain] raw agricultural commodities," and the regulations can "include, with respect to growing, harvesting, processing, packing, sorting, transporting, and storage operations, standards for safety as the [FDA] determines to be reasonably necessary."[157]

Furthermore, Stenzel's call for increased collaboration across agencies and with a variety of stakeholders appear to have influenced the drafting of the section. A provision was added in the bill as reported out by the House Committee allowing the FDA to work with other government agencies, universities, private entities, and others that work directly with farms to provide for coordination of education and training. Although the bill as reported out by the House Committee did include a provision requiring the FDA to work with the Secretary of Agriculture on compliance activities, it did not require the Secretary to work with the Secretary of Agriculture on establishing the standards and in efforts to educate relevant industry players. The bill as engrossed by the House added this requirement. Ultimately, it was the Senate, not the House, whose version became the Act.

What Was the Response from Trade Associations and Consumer Groups?

Caroline Smith DeWaal, director of food safety at the Center for Science in the Public Interest, testified at the House Energy and Commerce Committee's Subcommittee on Health hearing on food safety on June 3, 2009:

> FDA's ability to set performance standards for the most serious hazards and to require food processors to meet those standards is essential to ensure that food is produced in a sanitary manner that limits the likelihood of disease-causing contamination. When I talk to safety experts from industry, I am frequently told the biggest challenge is

---

[157] Compare H.R. 2749 § 104, 111th Cong. (as reported by the House Committee on Energy and Commerce, June 17, 2009) with H.R. 2749 § 104, 111th Cong. (as engrossed by House of Representatives, July 30, 2009).

deciding what the best measures to evaluate a HACCP system are. But an FDA-established performance standard helps eliminate the guess work for the companies and provides a level playing field for similar products. Section 103 addresses this need by requiring FDA to review epidemiological data, identify significant contaminants, and issue performance standards that minimize, prevent or eliminate the hazard. While we would like to see a more structured program at FDA for reviewing and issuing performance standards, we believe the language in the bill is the minimum necessary and we urge the committee not to weaken it.[158]

The language in Section 103 of the House bill was not weakened by further amendments. In fact, more prescriptive language was added to the section further defining how the FDA will implement a system of performance standards. A provision was added requiring the FDA to establish science-based performance standards as appropriate for contaminants already identified, and to publish in the Federal Register a list of foodborne contaminants that have the largest effect on public health in the United States. Additionally, an amendment authorizes the FDA to "make recommendations to industry for conducting product sampling."[159] But the House version was not adopted.

Text of the Law as Adopted

SEC. 104. PERFORMANCE STANDARDS.

(a) In General.--The Secretary shall, in coordination with the Secretary of Agriculture, not less frequently than every 2 years, review and evaluate relevant health data and other relevant information, including from toxicological and epidemiological studies and analyses, current Good Manufacturing Practices issued by the Secretary relating to food,

---

[158] Hearing on Food Safety Enhancement Act of 2009, Before the Subcommittee on Health of the H. Committee on Energy and Commerce, 111th Cong. 5 (2009) [hereinafter Hearing on Food Safety Enhancement Act of 2009] (Prepared Statement of Caroline Smith DeWaal, Director of Food Safety at the Center for Science in the Public Interest).
[159] H.R. 2749 § 103, 111th Cong. (as engrossed by House of Representatives, July 30, 2009).

and relevant recommendations of relevant advisory committees, including the Food Advisory Committee, to determine the most significant foodborne contaminants.

(b) Guidance Documents and Regulations.--Based on the review and evaluation conducted under subsection (a), and when appropriate to reduce the risk of serious illness or death to humans or animals or to prevent adulteration of the food under section 402 of the Federal Food, Drug, or Cosmetic Act (21 U.S.C. 342) or to prevent the spread by food of communicable disease under section 361 of the Public Health Service Act (42 U.S.C. 264), the Secretary shall issue contaminant-specific and science-based guidance documents, including guidance documents regarding action levels, or regulations. Such guidance, including guidance regarding action levels, or regulations--

(1) shall apply to products or product classes;

(2) shall, where appropriate, differentiate between food for human consumption and food intended for consumption by animals other than humans; and

(3) shall not be written to be facility-specific.

(c) No Duplication of Efforts.--The Secretary shall coordinate with the Secretary of Agriculture to avoid issuing duplicative guidance on the same contaminants.

(d) Review.--The Secretary shall periodically review and revise, as appropriate, the guidance documents, including guidance documents regarding action levels, or regulations promulgated under this section.

SEC. 105. STANDARDS FOR PRODUCE SAFETY.

(a) In General.--Chapter IV (21 U.S.C. 341 et seq.), as amended by section 103, is amended by adding at the end the following:

"SEC. 419. STANDARDS FOR PRODUCE SAFETY.

"(a) Proposed Rulemaking.--

"(1) IN GENERAL.--

"*(A) RULEMAKING.--Not later than 1 year after the date of enactment of the FDA Food Safety Modernization Act, the Secretary, in coordination with the Secretary of Agriculture and representatives of State departments of agriculture (including with regard to the national organic program* established under the Organic Foods Production *Act of 1990), and in consultation with the Secretary of Homeland Security, shall publish a notice of proposed rulemaking to establish science-based minimum standards for the safe production and harvesting of those types of fruits and vegetables, including specific mixes or categories of fruits and vegetables, that are raw agricultural commodities for which the Secretary has determined that such standards minimize the risk of serious adverse health consequences or death.*

"*(B) DETERMINATION BY SECRETARY.-- With respect to small businesses and very small businesses (as such terms are defined in the regulation promulgated under subparagraph (A)) that produce and harvest those types of fruits and vegetables that are raw agricultural commodities that the Secretary has determined are low risk and do not present a risk of serious adverse health consequences or death, the Secretary may determine not to include production and harvesting of such fruits and vegetables in such rulemaking, or may modify the applicable requirements of regulations promulgated pursuant to this section.*

"*(2) PUBLIC INPUT.--During the comment period on the notice of proposed rulemaking under paragraph (1), the Secretary shall conduct not less than 3 public meetings in diverse geographical areas of the United States to provide persons in different regions an opportunity to comment.*

"*(3) CONTENT.--The proposed rulemaking under paragraph (1) shall--*

"(A) provide sufficient flexibility to be applicable to various types of entities engaged in the production and harvesting of fruits and vegetables that are raw agricultural commodities, including small businesses and entities that sell directly to consumers, and be appropriate to the scale and diversity of the production and harvesting of such commodities;

"(B) include, with respect to growing, harvesting, sorting, packing, and storage operations, science-based minimum standards related to soil amendments, hygiene, packaging, temperature controls, animals in the growing area, and water;

"(C) consider hazards that occur naturally, may be unintentionally introduced, or may be intentionally introduced, including by acts of terrorism;

"(D) take into consideration, consistent with ensuring enforceable public health protection, conservation and environmental practice standards and policies established by Federal natural resource conservation, wildlife conservation, and environmental agencies;

"(E) in the case of production that is certified organic, not include any requirements that conflict with or duplicate the requirements of the national organic program established under the Organic Foods Production Act of 1990, while providing the same level of public health protection as the requirements under guidance documents, including guidance documents regarding action levels, and regulations under the FDA Food Safety Modernization Act; and

"(F) define, for purposes of this section, the terms 'small business' and 'very small business'

"(4) PRIORITIZATION.--The Secretary shall prioritize the implementation of the regulations under this section for specific fruits and vegetables that are raw agricultural commodities based on known risks which may include a history and severity of foodborne illness outbreaks.

"(b) Final Regulation.--

> *"(1) IN GENERAL.--Not later than 1 year after the close of the comment period for the proposed rulemaking under subsection (a), the Secretary shall adopt a final regulation to provide for minimum science-based standards for those types of fruits and vegetables, including specific mixes or categories of fruits or vegetables, that are raw agricultural commodities, based on known safety risks, which may include a history of foodborne illness outbreaks.*

> *"(2) FINAL REGULATION.--The final regulation shall--*

> > *"(A) provide for coordination of education and enforcement activities by State and local officials, as designated by the Governors of the respective States or the appropriate elected State official as recognized by State statute; and*

> > *"(B) include a description of the variance process under subsection (c) and the types of permissible variances the Secretary may grant.*

> *"(3) FLEXIBILITY FOR SMALL BUSINESSES.-- Notwithstanding paragraph (1)--*

> > *"(A) the regulations promulgated under this section shall apply to a small business (as defined in the regulation promulgated under subsection (a)(1)) after the date that is 1 year after the effective date of the final regulation under paragraph (1); and*

> > *"(B) the regulations promulgated under this section shall apply to a very small business (as defined in the regulation promulgated under subsection (a)(1)) after the date that is 2 years after the effective date of the final regulation under paragraph (1).*

"(c) Criteria.--

> *"(1) IN GENERAL.--The regulations adopted under subsection (b) shall--*
>
> > *"(A) set forth those procedures, processes, and practices that the Secretary determines to minimize the risk of serious adverse health consequences or death, including procedures, processes, and practices that the Secretary determines to be reasonably necessary to prevent the introduction of known or reasonably foreseeable biological, chemical, and physical hazards, including hazards that occur naturally, may be unintentionally introduced, or may be intentionally introduced, including by acts of terrorism, into fruits and vegetables, including specific mixes or categories of fruits and vegetables, that are raw agricultural commodities and to provide reasonable assurances that the produce is not adulterated under section 402;*
> >
> > *"(B) provide sufficient flexibility to be practicable for all sizes and types of businesses, including small businesses such as a small food processing facility co-located on a farm;*
> >
> > *"(C) comply with chapter 35 of title 44, United States Code (commonly known as the 'Paperwork Reduction Act'), with special attention to minimizing the burden (as defined in section 3502(2) of such Act) on the business, and collection of information (as defined in section 3502(3) of such Act), associated with such regulations;*
> >
> > *"(D) acknowledge differences in risk and minimize, as appropriate, the number of separate standards that apply to separate foods; and*
> >
> > *"(E) not require a business to hire a consultant or other third party to identify, implement, certify, compliance with these procedures, processes, and practices, except in the case*

of negotiated enforcement resolutions that may require such a consultant or third party; and

"(F) permit States and foreign countries from which food is imported into the United States to request from the Secretary variances from the requirements of the regulations, subject to paragraph (2), where the State or foreign country determines that the variance is necessary in light of local growing conditions and that the procedures, processes, and practices to be followed under the variance are reasonably likely to ensure that the produce is not adulterated under section 402 and to provide the same level of public health protection as the requirements of the regulations adopted under subsection (b).

"(2) VARIANCES.--

    "(A) REQUESTS FOR VARIANCES.--A State or foreign country from which food is imported into the United States may in writing request a variance from the Secretary. Such request shall describe the variance requested and present information demonstrating that the variance does not increase the likelihood that the food for which the variance is requested will be adulterated under section 402, and that the variance provides the same level of public health protection as the requirements of the regulations adopted under subsection (b). The Secretary shall review such requests in a reasonable timeframe.

    "(B) APPROVAL OF VARIANCES.--The Secretary may approve a variance in whole or in part, as appropriate, and may specify the scope of applicability of a variance to other similarly situated persons.

    "(C) DENIAL OF VARIANCES.--The Secretary may deny a variance request if the Secretary determines that such variance is not reasonably likely to ensure that the food is not adulterated under section 402 and is not reasonably

likely to provide the same level of public health protection as the requirements of the regulation adopted under subsection (b). The Secretary shall notify the person requesting such variance of the reasons for the denial.

"(D) MODIFICATION OR REVOCATION OF A VARIANCE.--The Secretary, after notice and an opportunity for a hearing, may modify or revoke a variance if the Secretary determines that such variance is not reasonably likely to ensure that the food is not adulterated under section 402 and is not reasonably likely to provide the same level of public health protection as the requirements of the regulations adopted under subsection (b).

"(d) Enforcement.--The Secretary may coordinate with the Secretary of Agriculture and, as appropriate, shall contract and coordinate with the agency or department designated by the Governor of each State to perform activities to ensure compliance with this section.

"(e) Guidance.--

"(1) IN GENERAL.--Not later than 1 year after the date of enactment of the FDA Food Safety Modernization Act, the Secretary shall publish, after consultation with the Secretary of Agriculture, representatives of State departments of agriculture, farmer representatives, and various types of entities engaged in the production and harvesting or importing of fruits and vegetables that are raw agricultural commodities, including small businesses, updated good agricultural practices and guidance for the safe production and harvesting of specific types of fresh produce under this section.

"(2) PUBLIC MEETINGS.--The Secretary shall conduct not fewer than 3 public meetings in diverse geographical areas of the United States as part of an effort to conduct education and outreach regarding the guidance described in paragraph (1) for persons in different regions who are involved in the production and harvesting of fruits and vegetables that are raw agricultural commodities, including

persons that sell directly to consumers and farmer representatives, and for importers of fruits and vegetables that are raw agricultural commodities.

"(3) PAPERWORK REDUCTION.--The Secretary shall ensure that any updated guidance under this section will--

"(A) provide sufficient flexibility to be practicable for all sizes and types of facilities, including small businesses such as a small food processing facility co-located on a farm; and

"(B) acknowledge differences in risk and minimize, as appropriate, the number of separate standards that apply to separate foods.

"(f) Exemption for Direct Farm Marketing.--

"(1) IN GENERAL.--A farm shall be exempt from the requirements under this section in a calendar year if--

"(A) during the previous 3-year period, the average annual monetary value of the food sold by such farm directly to qualified end-users during such period exceeded the average annual monetary value of the food sold by such farm to all other buyers during such period; and

"(B) the average annual monetary value of all food sold during such period was less than $500,000, adjusted for inflation.

"(2) NOTIFICATION TO CONSUMERS.--

"(A) IN GENERAL.--A farm that is exempt from the requirements under this section shall--

"(i) with respect to a food for which a food packaging label is required by the Secretary under any other provision of this Act, include prominently and conspicuously on such label the name and business address of the farm where the produce was grown; or

"(ii) with respect to a food for which a food packaging label is not required by the Secretary under any other provision of this Act, prominently and conspicuously display, at the point of purchase, the name and business address of the farm where the produce was grown, on a label, poster, sign, placard, or documents delivered contemporaneously with the food in the normal course of business, or, in the case of Internet sales, in an electronic notice.

"(B) NO ADDITIONAL LABEL.--Subparagraph (A) does not provide authority to the Secretary to require a label that is in addition to any label required under any other provision of this Act.

"(3) WITHDRAWAL; RULE OF CONSTRUCTION.--

"(A) IN GENERAL.--In the event of an active investigation of a foodborne illness outbreak that is directly linked to a farm subject to an exemption under this subsection, or if the Secretary determines that it is necessary to protect the public health and prevent or mitigate a foodborne illness outbreak based on conduct or conditions associated with a farm that are material to the safety of the food produced or harvested at such farm, the Secretary may withdraw the exemption provided to such farm under this subsection.

"(B) RULE OF CONSTRUCTION.--Nothing in this subsection shall be construed to expand or limit the inspection authority of the Secretary.

"*(4) DEFINITIONS.--*

"*(A) QUALIFIED END-USER.--In this subsection, the term 'qualified end-user', with respect to a food means--*

"*(i) the consumer of the food; or*

"*(ii) a restaurant or retail food establishment (as those terms are defined by the Secretary for purposes of section 415) that is located--*

"*(I) in the same State as the farm that produced the food; or*

"*(II) not more than 275 miles from such farm.*

"*(B) CONSUMER.--For purposes of subparagraph (A), the term 'consumer' does not include a business.*

"*(5) NO PREEMPTION.--Nothing in this subsection preempts State, local, county, or other non-Federal law regarding the safe production, harvesting, holding, transportation, and sale of fresh fruits and vegetables. Compliance with this subsection shall not relieve any person from liability at common law or under State statutory law.*

"*(6) LIMITATION OF EFFECT.--Nothing in this subsection shall prevent the Secretary from exercising any authority granted in the other sections of this Act.*

"*(g) Clarification.--This section shall not apply to produce that is produced by an individual for personal consumption.*

"*(h) Exception for Activities of Facilities Subject to Section 418.--This section shall not apply to activities of a facility that are subject to section 418.*".

(b) Small Entity Compliance Policy Guide.--Not later than 180 days after the issuance of regulations under section 419 of the Federal Food, Drug, and Cosmetic Act (as added

by subsection (a)), the Secretary of Health and Human Services shall issue a small entity compliance policy guide setting forth in plain language the requirements of such section 419 and to assist small entities in complying with standards for safe production and harvesting and other activities required under such section.

(c) Prohibited Acts.--Section 301 (21 U.S.C. 331), as amended by section 103, is amended by adding at the end the following:

"(vv) The failure to comply with the requirements under section 419.".

(d) No Effect on HACCP Authorities.--Nothing in the amendments made by this section limits the authority of the Secretary under the Federal Food, Drug, and Cosmetic Act (21 U.S.C. 301 et seq.) or the Public Health Service Act (42 U.S.C. 201 et seq.) to revise, issue, or enforce product and category-specific regulations, such as the Seafood Hazard Analysis Critical Controls Points Program, the Juice Hazard Analysis Critical Control Program, and the Thermally Processed Low-Acid Foods Packaged in Hermetically Sealed Containers standards.

4

Food Defense Obligations

Terrorist attacks through food contamination are a concern to the FDA. Risks of an attack through imported foods are of special concern. The FDA, Customs, and Homeland Security will cooperate on a strategy for dealing with this set of risks. For food producers, this item will become important once the FDA develops a broad food defense strategy and a narrower plan to protect against intentional contamination, as Congress ordered the FDA to do through the 2010 legislation.

How Does the 2010 Legislation Act Against Food Terrorism?

A person who purposefully contaminates food, regardless of the motive, is a criminal whose actions, through legislative empowerment, the FDA hopes to foresee and have the repercussions avoided. The FDA is given new powers by the 2010 legislation, and will use that authority through rules that tighten practices at food processing and holding facilities. Unlike the House bill, which would have required owners, operators, and agents of a facility to develop and implement a detailed written food defense plan, in accordance with prescribed parameters, to prevent intentional contamination, the 2010 Act only requires that the FDA develop plans to prevent intentional adulteration within high-risk foods, and develop a broad food defense strategy. To protect against intentional contamination of high-risk foods, the FDA will develop strategies for identifying high-risk food and may, as the House bill stipulated, require that companies introducing such high-risk foods to US commerce implement security measures to avoid intentional adulteration.

What Food Producers Are to Be Regulated Under the Plan to Protect Against Intentional Adulteration?

The FDA will be selective. The regulations will apply only if the food is one for which the FDA "has identified clear vulnerabilities (including short shelf-life or susceptibility to intentional contamination at critical control points)" and that is in bulk or batch form, prior to being packaged for the final consumer, and "for which there is a high risk of intentional contamination, as determined by the [FDA], that could cause serious adverse health consequences or death to humans or animals." The 2010 legislation does not specify the rules that will apply to such foods, but instead entrusts the FDA to specify "science-based mitigation strategies or measures to prepare and protect the food supply chain at specific vulnerable points" that would apply to such foods. The rules must specify how the food operator can determine whether the law's protective measure requirements are applicable.[160]

The failure to comply with this section will be considered a prohibited act under 21 U.S.C. 331. This section does not apply to farms, except those farms that produce milk.

How Will the FDA Develop a Plan to Protect Against Intentional Adulteration?

In developing a plan to protect against intentional adulteration both through the usage of regulations and guidance documents, the FDA will gather information by "conduct[ing] vulnerability assessments of the food system." The FDA must "consider the best available understanding of uncertainties, risks, costs, and benefits associated with guarding against intentional adulteration at vulnerable points." Further, the FDA is required to "determine the types of science-based mitigation strategies or measures that are necessary to protect against the intentional adulteration of food."[161]

The FDA will develop regulations for high-risk foods no later than eighteen months after the date of enactment of this act, and will do so in consultation with the USDA.

---

[160] 21 U.S.C. 350i(d).
[161] 21 U.S.C. 350i(c).

Within one year of enactment of the Act, HHS, in consultation with Homeland Security and the USDA, is to develop guidance documents for food companies to explain mitigation strategies and measures to guard against adulteration. These guidance documents must include a model assessment, include examples of mitigation strategies and measures, and detail situations when these mitigation strategies and measures are appropriate.[162]

What Is the New Requirement for a National Agriculture and Food Defense Strategy?

Within one year of the enactment of the Act, the FDA, in coordination with the USDA and Homeland Security, must submit to Congress a national agriculture and food defense strategy. Thereafter, these plans must be revised and submitted to Congress every four years. The strategy must focus on a holistic set of goals specified by Congress, which include to prepare for, detect, respond to, and recover from contamination in food. The national agriculture and food defense strategy need not be publicly disclosed.

Text of the Law as Adopted

SEC. 106. PROTECTION AGAINST INTENTIONAL ADULTERATION.

(a) In General- Chapter IV (21 U.S.C. 341 et seq.), as amended by section 105, is amended by adding at the end the following:

"SEC. 420. PROTECTION AGAINST INTENTIONAL ADULTERATION.

    "(a) Determinations-

        "(1) IN GENERAL- The Secretary shall--

            "(A) conduct a vulnerability assessment of the food system, including by consideration of the Department of Homeland

---

[162] S. 510 § 106, 111th Cong. (as reported by the Senate HELP Committee, Nov. 18, 2009).

Security biological, chemical, radiological, or other terrorism risk assessments;

"(B) consider the best available understanding of uncertainties, risks, costs, and benefits associated with guarding against intentional adulteration of food at vulnerable points; and

"(C) determine the types of science-based mitigation strategies or measures that are necessary to protect against the intentional adulteration of food.

"(2) LIMITED DISTRIBUTION- In the interest of national security, the Secretary, in consultation with the Secretary of Homeland Security, may determine the time, manner, and form in which determinations made under paragraph (1) are made publicly available.

"(b) Regulations- Not later than 18 months after the date of enactment of the FDA Food Safety Modernization Act, the Secretary, in coordination with the Secretary of Homeland Security and in consultation with the Secretary of Agriculture, shall promulgate regulations to protect against the intentional adulteration of food subject to this Act. Such regulations shall--

"(1) specify how a person shall assess whether the person is required to implement mitigation strategies or measures intended to protect against the intentional adulteration of food; and

"(2) ` specify appropriate science-based mitigation strategies or measures to prepare and protect the food supply chain at specific vulnerable points, as appropriate.

"(c) Applicability- Regulations promulgated under subsection (b) shall apply only to food for which there is a high risk of intentional contamination, as determined by the Secretary, in consultation with the Secretary of Homeland Security, under subsection (a), that could cause serious adverse health consequences or death to humans or animals and shall include those foods--

"*(1) for which the Secretary has identified clear vulnerabilities (including short shelf-life or susceptibility to intentional contamination at critical control points); and*

"*(2) in bulk or batch form, prior to being packaged for the final consumer.*

"*(d) Exception- This section shall not apply to farms, except for those that produce milk.*

"*(e) Definition- For purposes of this section, the term 'farm' has the meaning given that term in section 1.227 of title 21, Code of Federal Regulations (or any successor regulation).'.*

(b) Guidance Documents-

(1) IN GENERAL- Not later than 1 year after the date of enactment of this Act, the Secretary of Health and Human Services, in consultation with the Secretary of Homeland Security and the Secretary of Agriculture, shall issue guidance documents related to protection against the intentional adulteration of food, including mitigation strategies or measures to guard against such adulteration as required under section 420 of the Federal Food, Drug, and Cosmetic Act, as added by subsection (a).

(2) CONTENT- The guidance documents issued under paragraph (1) shall--

(A) include a model assessment for a person to use under subsection (b)(1) of section 420 of the Federal Food, Drug, and Cosmetic Act, as added by subsection (a);

(B) include examples of mitigation strategies or measures described in subsection (b)(2) of such section; and

(C) specify situations in which the examples of mitigation strategies or measures described in subsection (b)(2) of such section are appropriate.

(3) LIMITED DISTRIBUTION- In the interest of national security, the Secretary of Health and Human Services, in consultation with the Secretary of Homeland Security, may determine the time, manner, and form in which the guidance documents issued under paragraph (1) are made public, including by releasing such documents to targeted audiences.

(c) Periodic Review- The Secretary of Health and Human Services shall periodically review and, as appropriate, update the regulations under section 420(b) of the Federal Food, Drug, and Cosmetic Act, as added by subsection (a), and the guidance documents under subsection (b).

(d) Prohibited Acts- Section 301 (21 U.S.C. 331 et seq.), as amended by section 105, is amended by adding at the end the following:

"(ww) The failure to comply with section 420.'.

SEC. 108. NATIONAL AGRICULTURE AND FOOD DEFENSE STRATEGY.

(a) Development and Submission of Strategy-

(1) IN GENERAL- Not later than 1 year after the date of enactment of this Act, the Secretary of Health and Human Services and the Secretary of Agriculture, in coordination with the Secretary of Homeland Security, shall prepare and transmit to the relevant committees of Congress, and make publicly available on the Internet Web sites of the Department of Health and Human Services and the Department of Agriculture, the National Agriculture and Food Defense Strategy.

(2) IMPLEMENTATION PLAN- The strategy shall include an implementation plan for use by the Secretaries described under paragraph (1) in carrying out the strategy.

(3) RESEARCH- The strategy shall include a coordinated research agenda for use by the Secretaries described under paragraph (1) in conducting research to support the goals and activities described in paragraphs (1) and (2) of subsection (b).

(4) REVISIONS- Not later than 4 years after the date on which the strategy is submitted to the relevant committees of Congress under paragraph (1), and not less frequently than every 4 years thereafter, the Secretary of Health and Human Services and the Secretary of Agriculture, in coordination with the Secretary of Homeland Security, shall revise and submit to the relevant committees of Congress the strategy.

(5) CONSISTENCY WITH EXISTING PLANS- The strategy described in paragraph (1) shall be consistent with--

(A) the National Incident Management System;

(B) the National Response Framework;

(C) the National Infrastructure Protection Plan;

(D) the National Preparedness Goals; and

(E) other relevant national strategies.

(b) Components-

(1) IN GENERAL- The strategy shall include a description of the process to be used by the Department of Health and Human Services, the Department of Agriculture, and the Department of Homeland Security--

(A) to achieve each goal described in paragraph (2); and

(B) to evaluate the progress made by Federal, State, local, and tribal governments towards the achievement of each goal described in paragraph (2).

(2) GOALS- The strategy shall include a description of the process to be used by the Department of Health and Human Services, the Department of Agriculture, and the Department of Homeland Security to achieve the following goals:

(A) PREPAREDNESS GOAL- Enhance the preparedness of the agriculture and food system by--

  (i) conducting vulnerability assessments of the agriculture and food system;

  (ii) mitigating vulnerabilities of the system;

  (iii) improving communication and training relating to the system;

  (iv) developing and conducting exercises to test decontamination and disposal plans;

  (v) developing modeling tools to improve event consequence assessment and decision support; and

  (vi) preparing risk communication tools and enhancing public awareness through outreach.

(B) DETECTION GOAL- Improve agriculture and food system detection capabilities by--

  (i) identifying contamination in food products at the earliest possible time; and

  (ii) conducting surveillance to prevent the spread of diseases.

(C) EMERGENCY RESPONSE GOAL- Ensure an efficient response to agriculture and food emergencies by--

  (i) immediately investigating animal disease outbreaks and suspected food contamination;

  (ii) preventing additional human illnesses;

  (iii) organizing, training, and equipping animal, plant, and food emergency response teams of--

(I) the Federal Government; and

(II) State, local, and tribal governments;

(iv) designing, developing, and evaluating training and exercises carried out under agriculture and food defense plans; and

(v) ensuring consistent and organized risk communication to the public by--

(I) the Federal Government;

(II) State, local, and tribal governments; and

(III) the private sector.

(D) RECOVERY GOAL- Secure agriculture and food production after an agriculture or food emergency by--

(i) working with the private sector to develop business recovery plans to rapidly resume agriculture, food production, and international trade;

(ii) conducting exercises of the plans described in subparagraph (C) with the goal of long-term recovery results;

(iii) rapidly removing, and effectively disposing of--

(I) contaminated agriculture and food products; and

(II) infected plants and animals; and

(iv) decontaminating and restoring areas affected by an agriculture or food emergency.

(3) EVALUATION- The Secretary, in coordination with the Secretary of Agriculture and the Secretary of Homeland Security, shall--

> *(A) develop metrics to measure progress for the evaluation process described in paragraph (1)(B); and*

> *(B) report on the progress measured in subparagraph (A) as part of the National Agriculture and Food Defense strategy described in subsection (a)(1).*

(c) Limited Distribution- In the interest of national security, the Secretary of Health and Human Services and the Secretary of Agriculture, in coordination with the Secretary of Homeland Security, may determine the manner and format in which the National Agriculture and Food Defense strategy established under this section is made publicly available on the Internet Web sites of the Department of Health and Human Services, the Department of Homeland Security, and the Department of Agriculture, as described in subsection (a)(1).

5

Certification of Imported Food Compliance

What Do Managers Need To Know?

You should change your methods of selecting, reviewing, and importing food from non-US sources, to avoid problems with the 2010 law's much more stringent requirements. Create a paperwork system that records the information about the food, its certifications of compliance, and so on. Problems inevitably occur, so use documentation to be able to show future inspectors that any problem with the food you sold was the fault of another entity, despite your doing all that reasonably could have been done. Be prepared to deal with new intermediaries, some governmental and some private, who will be auditing the quality of the food grown and processed for your company in its country of origin. And be careful what you, as the responsible manager, sign or certify, in person or electronically.

What Affect Will Certification Provisions Have on Food Companies?

The FDA may require, as a condition of granting entry to the United States, that a food offered for import "provide a certification or such other assurances as the Secretary determines appropriate that the article of food complies with some or all applicable requirements of this Act, as specified by the Secretary."[163] This is a significant new power for the FDA and a process that will add time and cost complications for the supply chain of food companies. It makes you accountable, and increases your vulnerability,

---

[163] 21 U.S.C. 381(q).

thereby inducing you to be an additional safety monitor over your foreign and US suppliers.

Importers may want to volunteer for certification as a way to speed up clearance by the FDA of food shipments through the borders. An eligible entity must apply for annual recertification by an accredited third-party auditor or audit agent if the entity "intends to participate in voluntary qualified importer program." The FDA now has explicit power to demand that, before food enters the United States from a foreign facility, a qualified certifying entity must provide "certification" that the food complies with US food law. Companies involved with importing food will find this to be either a blessing or a curse. Additional work will be required to have the company's shipments certified by another national government, or by a technical laboratory service. National governments, foreign private entities, and multinational lab companies will be participants in the overall movement of food into the United States. Your company may have had an excellent record on your own, but there now may be requirements that apply to all bananas, peanuts, lettuce, granola, and other items that require you to deal with these additional players.

Note that the third-party system of certification cannot be automatic. There must be a "regulatory audit" of the food shipper or of a shipment of food, before the third-party issues the certification.[164]

The operational concern with these third-party certifications is that the paperwork increases exponentially as the certifier needs to protect itself. The resulting problems of testing, recording, reporting, and paying for the certification may be more difficult to unravel than a pre-2010 scenario of a routine out-of-specification test result on a food shipment.

Who Can Give a Certification?

Certifying entities will be "an agency or a representative of the government of the country from which the article of food at issue originated, as designated by the Secretary; or such other persons or…accredited [third-party auditors] to provide such certification or assurance."

---

[164] Pub.L. 111-353, §307, adding new 808(c)(1)(C) (2010). [Note: The 808 series cited herein is likely to be codified as 21 U.S.C. 388 by the Revisor of Statutes in 2011.]

An accreditation body or, in the event of direct accreditation, the FDA can accredit a foreign government or an agency of a foreign government to be an accredited third-party auditor. Prior to accreditation, the accreditation body or the FDA must "perform such reviews and audits of food safety programs, systems, and standards of the government as the Secretary deems necessary…to determine that the foreign government is capable of adequately ensuring that eligible entities or foods certified by such government or agency meet the requirements of this Act with respect to food manufactured, processed, packed, or held for import into the United States."

An accreditation body or, in the event of direct accreditation, the FDA can also accredit "a foreign cooperative that aggregates the products of growers or processors, or any other third party that the Secretary determines appropriate to be an accredited third-party auditor." Prior to accreditation, the accreditation body or the FDA must "perform such reviews and audits of the training and qualifications of audit agents used by that cooperative or party and conduct such reviews of internal systems and such other investigation of the cooperative or party as the Secretary deems necessary…to determine that each eligible entity certified by the cooperative or party has systems and standards in use to ensure that such entity or food meets the requirements of this Act."

No third-party auditor may be accredited unless it "agrees to issue a written and, as appropriate, electronic certification…to accompany each food shipment for import into the United States from an eligible entity, subject to requirements set forth by the Secretary." The FDA will use certification information to determine the eligibility of an importer to participate in the voluntary qualified importer program.[165] Further, the FDA will consider this information, along with information regarding involvement in the voluntary qualified importer program to target inspections.

How Will Conflicts of Interest Be Controlled?

The legislation provides detailed restrictions on third-party auditors and audit agents. Third-party auditors may "not be owned, managed, or

---

[165] S. 510 § 307, 111th Cong.

controlled by any person that owns or operates an eligible entity to be certified by such auditor," and "in carrying out audits of eligible entities under this section, [a third-party auditor must] have procedures to ensure against the use of any officer or employee of such auditor that has a financial conflict of interest regarding an eligible entity to be certified by such auditor," and annually disclose to the FDA its efforts to comply with such requirements. An audit agent may "not own or operate an eligible entity to be certified by such agent," "in carrying out audits of eligible entities under this section, [an audit agent must] have procedures to ensure that such agent does not have a financial conflict of interest regarding an eligible entity to be certified by such agent," and annually disclose to the FDA its efforts to comply with such requirements.

Within eighteen months of the enactment of this Act, the FDA must promulgate regulations "to ensure that there are protections against conflicts of interest between an accredited third-party auditor and the eligible entity to be certified by such auditor or audited by such audit agent." These regulations must include:

> (i) requiring that audits performed under this section be unannounced;

> (ii) a structure to decrease the potential for conflicts of interest, including timing and public disclosure, for fees paid by eligible entities to accredited third-party auditors or audit agents; and

> (iii) appropriate limits on financial affiliations between an accredited third-party auditor or audit agents of such auditor and any person that owns or operates an eligible entity to be certified by such auditor[166]

The FDA must establish a publicly available list of accreditation bodies and accredited third-party auditors and audit agents.[167]

---

[166] S. 510 § 308, 111th Cong. (as reported by the Senate HELP Committee, Nov. 18, 2009).
[167] Id.

How Will the FDA Evaluate Accreditation Bodies and Entities That Certify Imports?

By 2012, the FDA must establish a system for recognizing accreditation bodies that accredit third-party auditors. Congress anticipated the possibility that the FDA may face difficulties in quickly establishing such a system, and added a provision that allows the FDA to directly accredit third-party auditors if, by two years after the enactment of this Act, the FDA has not recognized any accreditation bodies.[168] Accreditation bodies must submit to the FDA a list of all accredited third-party auditors and audit agents it accredits. If an accreditation body is not in compliance with the requirements of this section, the FDA will revoke the recognition of the accreditation body.[169] The Senate added a provision requiring that the FDA establish procedures to reinstate the recognition of an accreditation body if the revocation was inappropriate or the accreditation body meets the requirements.

Accreditation bodies will have to ensure that any third-party auditor and its audit agents meets the model standards developed by the FDA. The FDA must develop model standards within eighteen months of enactment. In developing model standards for accreditation bodies to use, the FDA will include audit report requirements and look to standards in place "to avoid unnecessary duplication of efforts and costs."[170]

The FDA must "periodically, or at least once every four years, reevaluate the accreditation bodies," "periodically, or at least once every four years, evaluate the performance of each accredited third-party auditor, through the review of regulatory audit reports by such auditors, the compliance history as available of eligible entities certified by such auditors and audit agents, and any other measures deemed necessary by the Secretary," "at any time, conduct an onsite audit of any eligible entity certified by an accredited third-party auditor, with or without the auditor or audit agent present," and may take any other measures "deemed necessary by the Secretary."[171]

---

[168] S. 510 § 307, 111th Cong.

[169] *Id.*

[170] *Id.*

[171] S. 510 § 308, 111th Cong.

When Is Revocation or Withdrawal of Accreditation Possible?

If the FDA revokes recognition of an accreditation body, it may also withdraw accreditation from any third-party auditors accredited by that accreditation body.

The FDA will withdraw the accreditation of a third-party auditor if a food from the entity facility certified by such third-party auditor is "linked to an outbreak of foodborne illness that has a reasonable probability of causing serious adverse health consequences or death in humans or animals." It should be noted that a safety mechanism was built into the provision as passed by the Senate to allow the FDA to waive withdrawal if the FDA conducts an investigation of the outbreak, and is satisfied with the safety level after a review of steps that had been taken by the third-party auditor. Accreditation will also be withdrawn "following an evaluation and finding by the Secretary that the third-party auditor no longer meets the requirements for accreditation" or "following a refusal to allow United States officials to conduct such audits and investigations as may be necessary to ensure continued compliance with the requirements set forth in this section."[172]

The FDA is required to establish procedures to reinstate accreditation for third-party auditors if adequate grounds for revocation no longer exist and where the accreditation of the third-party auditor is revoked because the accreditation of the accreditation body is revoked.

How Will Audits Come to the FDA?

An accredited third-party auditor or audit agent must prepare an audit report for an audit within forty-five days of conducting an audit in a form and manner established by the FDA, and which must include:

> (i) the identity of the persons at the audited eligible entity responsible for compliance with food safety requirements;

> (ii) the dates of the audit;

---

[172] *Id.*

(iii) the scope of the audit; and

(iv) any other information required by the Secretary that relates to or may influence an assessment of compliance with this Act.

The FDA may require submission of these reports and any other documents required as part of the audit process at any time following an accreditation. This authority does not allow the FDA to obtain access to "any report or other documents resulting from a consultative audit by the accredited third-party auditor or audit agent, except that the Secretary may access the results of a consultative audit in accordance with [its authority to inspect records]."[173]

The FDA must establish a method, similar to the method used by the Department of Agriculture, by which the FDA assesses fees on the third-party auditors and audit agents for the purpose of reimbursing the FDA for the work performed to administer the accreditation system. The fee system must be revenue-neutral.[174]

The earlier House version of the section gave the FDA more inspection authority. To determine whether an accreditation body continues to meet the standards set by the FDA or whether a certification should be accepted from a qualified certifying entity, the FDA could have observed the on-site audits conducted by an accreditation body of qualified certifying entities, or the FDA could have, upon request and upon presentation of credentials, conducted on-site audits of facilities certified by a qualified certifying entity, including accessing, copying, and verifying any related records "at reasonable times and within reasonable limits and in a reasonable manner."[175]

---

[173] S. 510 § 307, 111th Cong.
[174] *Id.*
[175] This provision was not in the bill as reported out by the House Committee and as introduced in the House. Compare H.R. 2749 § 109, 111th Cong. (as engrossed by House of Representatives, July 30, 2009) with H.R. 2749 § 109, 111th Cong. (as reported by the House Committee on Energy and Commerce, June 17, 2009).

How Will the FDA Make the Decision That an Imported Food Needs a Certification?

Certification will be based on the following factors:

(A) known safety risks associated with the food;

(B) known food safety risks associated with the country, territory, or region of origin of the food;

(C) a finding by the Secretary, supported by scientific, risk-based evidence, that--

(i) the food safety programs, systems, and standards in the country, territory, or region of origin of the food are inadequate to ensure that the article of food is as safe as a similar article of food that is manufactured, processed, packed, or held in the United States in accordance with the requirements of this Act; and

(ii) the certification would assist the Secretary in determining whether to refuse or admit the article of food under subsection (a); and

(D) information submitted to the Secretary in accordance with the [mandate on the Secretary to assess the food safety programs, systems, and standards of foreign regions, countries, and territories] [176]

Cumulatively, the effect of Congress giving the FDA so much discretion is that courts will be very reluctant to hear a complaint that the FDA should not require certification of a particular imported food. If the dispute is between an entity operated by a nation and the FDA, the nation is more likely to bring the dispute in a World Trade Organization panel hearing than in a federal district court in the United States.

---

[176] These factors were not included when introduced in the Senate, but were added by the bill as passed by the Senate.

The Senate bill as introduced stated that the certification program was to be used for "designated food imported from countries with which the Food and Drug Administration has an agreement to establish a certification program." This was eliminated when it was passed in the Senate, suggesting that the certification will not only be used for food coming from countries with which the FDA has an agreement, but used for foods that the FDA determines should require certification based on the above-mentioned factors.

What Are the Consequences of Foreign Corruption Allegations?

Notice the interplay involved when the FDA is induced to rely on an intermediary for the safety review of a food company's foreign supply chain. The food may be fine, but you may have relied on an intermediary who has trouble because of its laxity in awarding certification. Once the certifier has problems, the companies who are its customers will have major problems. All of the customers of a lab or other certifier are at risk if there are significant failings the certifier should have detected.

What could go wrong with the food company's inspection and certification by an intermediary entity such as a small nation's health ministry? Corporate and in-house attorneys for US food companies are already very sensitive to the US Justice Department prosecution of Foreign Corrupt Practices Act crimes, when companies are accused of paying bribes for other nations' officials to release products or approve shipments.

If the agent of their national government or the accredited third-party certifier had been bribed by someone producing or selling food in that nation, the US company that contracted for those services is at some risk. The FDA might learn from news media about foreign investigations of corruption, from competitors, or from whistleblower employees, and if the FDA has doubts about the certifications, many food shipments in the pipeline to the United States may be put at risk. Notice that it is a prohibited act to have a false certification whether or not the food is "adulterated." This is not an idle threat, but a new reality of the international sourcing of food products, which will inevitably draw much closer scrutiny after the 2010 law.

What Are the Consequences of Not Complying with the New Imported Food Certification Requirement?

Food that is subject to, but not in compliance with the certification requirement will be denied entry to the United States. The FDA already has power to refuse admission to food that has not given the pre-shipment notification, a system that has been in place since 2003.[177] Further, the FDA may refuse any certification or assurance it determines is not valid or reliable.

If, during an audit of a company, a third-party auditor or an audit agent "discovers a condition that could cause or contribute to a serious risk to the public health," the audit agent is required to immediately contact the FDA and inform it of "the identification of the eligible entity subject to the audit" and "such condition." In other words, when food is found to be contaminated, the FDA must be told. If the contamination is hidden and the FDA is not informed, a later discovery of the contaminant will result in charges against the foreign facility and against the certifier.

An eligible entity must apply for annual recertification by an accredited third-party auditor if the entity "intends to participate in voluntary qualified importer program under section 806" or if the entity is required to "provide to the Secretary a certification under section 801(q) for any food from such entity."[178]

What Else Must the FDA Be Told by the Importer?

At the time of the import's transmitting of the prior notice of food importation, an obligation that has been in use since 2003,[179] the FDA must be given notice of the certification, if any, and must be told if the shipment of food has been refused entry by any other nation.[180]

Can the FDA Waive the Need for Certifications?

Certification is not required for all foods. The FDA may make its own determination, based on factors established by Congress, as to whether

---

[177] 21 C.F.R. 1.279.
[178] S. 510 § 308, 111th Cong.
[179] 21 U.S.C. 381(m); 21 C.F.R. 1.279.
[180] 21 U.S.C. 381(m)(1), as amended by Pub.L. 111-353 §304 (2010).

certification is required.[181] Certification would only be required if food safety programs within the region, country, territory, or region of origin of the food are inadequate to ensure that the article of food is as safe as a similar article of food that is manufactured, processed, packed, or held in the United States. Note the discretion the FDA has with the term "as safe." Judges are unlikely to ever override that discretion if the FDA were challenged for a particular decision. However, the 2010 legislation does state that if the FDA finds the "food safety programs, systems, and standards in a foreign region, country, or territory" inadequate to guarantee that food coming from such areas is safe, the FDA is to establish a procedure by which the foreign region, country, or territory is to communicate with the FDA regarding controls put in place that ensure food is safe. This places a burden on the foreign region, country, or territory to show that the food exported from such countries into the United States is safe.

The earlier versions of the legislation were "opt out" formats with certification as the norm, and the FDA would have been required to establish a protocol by which "a country or territory may demonstrate that its government controls are adequate to ensure that…food exported from its territory to the United States is safe."[182] If a country may so demonstrate, then no certification would have been required.[183] The final text of the Act makes the FDA more fully discretionary in choosing when it will require certifications.

Can the FDA Continue to Use Its Import Enforcement Powers?

Yes. The legislation expressly says that certification or delegated powers do not limit the FDA's authority to inspect facilities. A slight change was made to the wording of the section on import certifications. In the bill as introduced in the Senate, there was a provision stating that the increase on the authority of the FDA provided by this section did not limit the FDA's authority "to conduct random inspections of imported food." In the bill as reported by the Senate Committee, the word "random" was removed from

---

[181] 21 U.S.C. 381(q)(1) is stated as an FDA option, "may require…certification."

[182] H.R. 2749 § 109, 111th Cong. (as engrossed by House of Representatives, July 30, 2009).

[183] This provision was not in the bill as reported out by the House Committee and as introduced in the House. Compare H.R. 2749 § 109, 111th Cong. (as engrossed by House of Representatives, July 30, 2009) with H.R. 2749 § 109, 111th Cong. (as reported by the House Committee on Energy and Commerce, June 17, 2009).

the clause.[184] This might have been in response to the Food Marketing Institute's testimony that unannounced inspections would not be as useful when for the purposes of certification. This change does not fully address the Food Marketing Institute's concern, but eliminating the word "random" does pose the question of whether the section limits the FDA's ability to engage in random inspections.[185]

What Form Will the Certification Take?

The FDA will promulgate a final rule with a format for submissions. The certification or assurances "may be provided in the form of shipment-specific certificates, a listing of certified entities, or in such other form" as the FDA may specify. It will probably be required to be electronically submitted along with the existing requirement for an electronic "prior notification" filing.[186]

The earlier bill as reported out by the House Committee and as introduced in the House had stated the "certification shall include such information as the Secretary may specify, and may be provided in the form of a shipment-specific certificate, a listing of certified facilities or other entities, or in such other forms as the Secretary may specify."[187] Congress intended for the form of the certification to be decided at the discretion of the FDA.

How Will Electronic Submissions Work?

Certifications will be submitted electronically, probably building upon the existing FDA system for pre-shipment notification of incoming foods.[188] This e-mail format may pose a logistical problem for smaller companies in more remote nations that use older paper systems. The FDA may use its discretion to allow alternative mechanisms.

---

[184] Compare S. 510 § 303, 111th Cong. (as reported by the Senate HELP Committee, Nov. 18, 2009) with S. 510 § 303, 111th Cong. (as introduced in Senate, Mar. 3, 2009).
[185] Hearing on Keeping America's Families Safe: Reforming the Food Safety System, S. Committee on Health, Education, Labor, and Pensions, 111th Cong. 7, Oct. 22, 2009 (Testimony of Michael Roberson, Director of Corporate Quality Assurance, Publix Super Markets Inc. on behalf of the Food Marketing Institute).
[186] 21 C.F.R. 1.279.
[187] Compare H.R. 2749 § 109, 111th Cong. (as engrossed by House of Representatives, July 30, 2009) with H.R. 2749 § 109, 111th Cong. (as reported by the House Committee on Energy and Commerce, June 17, 2009).
[188] 21 C.F.R. 1.279.

When Does Certification Begin?

The 2010 Act does not specify when certification begins. However, the bill does include certain timelines for aspects of the certification program. The FDA must establish the recognition system for accreditation bodies and third-party auditors within two years of enactment. The FDA must develop the model accreditation standards within eighteen months of enactment. Further, within eighteen months of enactment, the FDA must promulgate regulations on the prohibition of conflicts of interest among third-party auditors and entities.

How Does the Bill Require the FDA to Help Non-U.S. Governments?

Within two years of the enactment of the bill, the FDA is to "develop a comprehensive plan to expand the technical, scientific, and regulatory capacity of foreign governments, and their respective food industries, from which foods are exported to the United States." In doing so, the FDA must consult with "the Secretary of Agriculture, Secretary of State, Secretary of the Treasury, the Secretary of Homeland Security, the United States Trade Representative, and the Secretary of Commerce, representatives of the food industry, appropriate foreign government officials, nongovernmental organizations that represent the interests of consumers, and other stakeholders." The plan is to include:

(1) Recommendations for bilateral and multilateral arrangements and agreements, including provisions to provide for responsibility of exporting countries to ensure the safety of food.

(2) Provisions for secure electronic data sharing.

(3) Provisions for mutual recognition of inspection reports.

(4) Training of foreign governments and food producers on United States requirements for safe food.

(5) Recommendations on whether and how to harmonize requirements under the Codex Alimentarius.

(6) Provisions for the multilateral acceptance of laboratory methods and detection techniques.[189]

---

[189] S. 510 § 306, 111th Cong. (as reported by the Senate HELP Committee, Nov. 18, 2009).

Does the Legislation Require the FDA to Establish Foreign Offices?

In consultation with the Secretary of State and the US Trade Representative, the FDA is to establish FDA offices in foreign countries "to provide assistance to the appropriate governmental entities of such countries with respect to measures to provide for the safety of articles of food and other products regulated by the Food and Drug Administration exported by such country to the United States, including by directly conducting risk-based inspections of such articles and supporting such inspections by such governmental entity."

The bill as introduced in the Senate was more prescriptive in the section of foreign offices of the FDA than the bill as reported by the Senate Committee. According to the bill as introduced, by October 10, 2010, the FDA was to open not less than five offices in foreign countries. The bill reported by the Senate Committee eliminated the deadline and made no requirements as to the number of FDA offices needed to be opened in foreign countries.[190]

How Did Trade Associations React To the Drafting of the Bill?

A representative for the Food Marketing Institute testified at the Senate HELP Committee hearing on October 22, 2009:

> *Sec. 306. Building Capacity of Foreign Governments with Respect to Food*
>
> All food in the United States must meet the same high standards for safety, regardless of where the food was produced. Nonetheless, not all countries have the same standards for food production as exist in the United States. Accordingly, we commend S. 510 for including a provision that requires FDA to develop a plan within 2 years of the bill's enactment to assist foreign governments in building their technical, scientific and regulatory capacity.

---

[190] Compare S. 510 § 309, 111th Cong. (as reported by the Senate HELP Committee, Nov. 18, 2009) with S. 510 § 309, 111th Cong. (as introduced in Senate, Mar. 3, 2009).

Sec. 308. Accreditation of Third-Auditors and Audit Agents

Properly constructed accredited third party certification programs provide rigorous, objective evaluations of a food producer's safety programs. Although these programs cannot replace government oversight, certification from an accredited third party can provide some assurance that the certified company has received extensive and objective scrutiny for compliance with food safety standards that often exceed the legal requirements.

We support the legislation's recognition of certification by accredited third party auditors, but we would encourage that the Committee further amend this section to ensure that all terminology is consistent with internationally recognized language and terms. We also support the use of certification programs in the assessment of risk that FDA must perform in allocating its enforcement resources. Specifically, accredited third party certification programs are appropriate tools for use in both the Voluntary Qualified Importer Program (Section 306) and in the Import Certification Program (Section 303).

However, these programs should not replace government oversight or attempt to deputize private-sector auditors as an enforcement arm of the federal government. As an example, we are concerned with the provision that audits be "unannounced"—the same manner that a government inspection is conducted. Audits performed under an accredited third party certification program are different than a "snapshot-in-time" governmental inspection. During a third party certification audit, the auditor is watching and observing how the company manages safety as a part of its regular operations. It is a thorough rigorous assessment of the systems that are in place. Even announced, a company cannot just "cover up" fundamental procedural flaws.

Most audits involve two parts: (1) a "desk" audit which is a review of all of the plant's documentation, written food safety plans, risk and hazard assessments, etc. and (2) an onsite evaluation. These two audits, together help, to verify compliance with federal food safety standards and internationally recognized best practices. Announcing the audit ensures that the necessary people and documents will be available to the auditing company's auditors at the appropriate time and place.[191]

Tom Stenzel, president of the United Fresh Produce Association, a trade association representing growers, packers, shippers, fresh-cut processors, distributors, and marketers of fresh fruits and vegetables, testified at the House Energy and Commerce Committee's Subcommittee on Health hearing on food safety on June 3, 2009:

> In Section 201, we support the bill's intent to require importers to register with FDA, and comply with good importer practices. The committee should make clear that this is the standard protocol for importing foods, and that the limitations and further restrictions contained in Section 109 provide extreme authorities to be used by FDA only when "required to minimize the risk of severe adverse health consequences." Should FDA issue blanket condemnations of entire countries or commodity groups, we are concerned that the certification procedures of Section 109 would be impossible to achieve, and thus offer no real means of meeting acceptable import status regardless of the safety of such foods.
>
> Section 109 should require a standard for implementation only when such restrictions are necessary to minimize the risk of severe adverse health consequences, and thus allow the Secretary to determine whether to refuse to admit such article.[192]

---

[191] Hearing on Keeping America's Families Safe: Reforming the Food Safety System, S. Committee on Health, Education, Labor, and Pensions, 111th Cong. 7, Oct. 22, 2009 (Testimony of Michael Roberson, Director of Corporate Quality Assurance, Publix Super Markets Inc. on behalf of the Food Marketing Institute).

[192] Hearing on Food Safety Enhancement Act of 2009, Before the Subcommittee on Health of the H. Committee on Energy and Commerce, 111th Cong. 4 (2009) [hereinafter Hearing on Food Safety Enhancement Act of 2009] (Prepared Statement of Tom Stenzel, President of United Fresh Produce Association).

Although the House Committee did not go so far as to include in the House bill that certification should only be used when "required to minimize the risk of severe adverse health consequences," the House Committee did narrow instances that certification should be required. When the bill was introduced, the section stated that the FDA *must* require certification of certain foods, including foods "that could pose a significant risk to health, [where] certification would assist the Secretary in determining whether such article poses such risk." In the bill as passed by the House, the language was changed to *allow* the FDA to require certification of certain foods, including foods "for which there is scientific evidence that there is a particular risk associated with the food that presents a threat of serious adverse health consequences or death, [where] the Secretary finds that certification would assist the Secretary in determining whether to refuse to admit such article under subsection."[193]

What Did Consumer Organizations Seek in This Law?

The Make Our Food Safe Coalition called for S. 510 to be amended:

> to give the FDA the power to accredit governments or independent certifiers who can verify that foods being exported here meet US standards for safety. This would better protect Americans from foreign countries and facilities that have a history of poor food safety practices. S. 510 should also establish a dedicated corps of foreign inspectors who could be dispatched to any country, and not just static foreign offices in a handful of countries.[194]

Caroline Smith DeWaal, director of the Center for Science in the Public Interest, testified at the Senate HELP Committee hearing on October 22, 2009, that:

---

[193] Compare H.R. 2749 § 109, 111th Cong. (as engrossed by House of Representatives, July 30, 2009) with H.R. 2749 § 109, 111th Cong. (as reported by the House Committee on Energy and Commerce, June 17, 2009).

[194] *The Senate Must Pass Strong FDA Food Safety Legislation This Year*, Make Our Food Safe Coalition, Dec. 1, 2009, www.makeourfoodsafe.org/tools/assets/files/PDF-Senate-Fall-Fact-Sheet.pdf.

We generally support the language in S. 510 on imports, which provides for certification of food facilities that import food products. The language should be strengthened by:

- Requiring government-to-government certification for high-risk foods;
- Clarifying that FDA has the principle responsibility for accrediting the import programs of foreign governments;
- Clarifying that private accrediting bodies must be under strict FDA oversight, and FDA should be notified of all actions they take regarding the agents they accredit; and
- Adding language requiring FDA to set up a system for determining whether standards for imported produce are at least equal to standards applicable to such commodities produced in the United States.[195]

Senator Harkin questioned DeWaal about the suggestion for government-to-government certification for high-risk foods. He asked about the situation of when the FDA decides it cannot certify the other government; can a facility within the country be certified on a facility-by-facility basis, he asked. DeWaal said the bill did provide for the situation where a government could not be certified. The bill provides for independent certifying agents that just serve the role of certifying an entity in a foreign country. She noted that this is an important new concept that is already in use in the food industry, including by the Food Marketing Institute, and that by including this provision in the bill, the FDA would be adopting something already in the private sector to help them in this area of imports.

---

[195] Hearing on Keeping America's Families Safe: Reforming the Food Safety System, S. Committee on Health, Education, Labor, and Pensions, 111th Cong. 8 Oct. 22, 2009 (Testimony of Caroline Smith DeWaal, Director of the Center for Science in the Public Interest, testimony supported by Center for Foodborne Illness Research and Prevention, Consumer Federation of America, Consumers Union, Food and Water Watch, National Consumers League, Safe Tables Our Priority, and Trust for America's Health).

As an aside, DeWaal brought up a provision on the accreditation body within the import section, saying that the way it is laid out complicates the section and is not something within the House bill. DeWaal noted that she believes the drafters of the bill did not intend for it, but according to the Senate bill an accreditation body gets between the US government and a foreign government in assuring that the foreign government can certify. She thought this language needed to be clarified.[196] It should be noted that this language (at 308(c)(1)(a)) was not modified to the extent the Center for Science in the Public Interest requested, that the bill clarify "that FDA has the principle responsibility for accrediting the import programs of foreign governments." However, the bill as reported by the Senate Committee did refine the section on accreditation of third-party auditors and audit agents, by adding a provision allowing the FDA, in the event that the FDA has not identified and recognized an accreditation body within one year of the enactment of the bill, to directly accredit third-party auditors and audit agents, which would include foreign governments.[197]

Text of the Law as Adopted

SEC. 303. AUTHORITY TO REQUIRE IMPORT CERTIFICATIONS FOR FOOD.

(a) In General.--Section 801(a) (21 U.S.C. 381(a)) is amended by inserting after the third sentence the following: "With respect to an article of food, if importation of such food is subject to, but not compliant with, the requirement under subsection (q) that such food be accompanied by a certification or other assurance that the food meets applicable requirements of this Act, then such article shall be refused admission.".

(b) Addition of Certification Requirement.--Section 801 (21 U.S.C. 381) is amended by adding at the end the following new subsection:

---

[196] Hearing on Keeping America's Families Safe: Reforming the Food Safety System, S. Committee on Health, Education, Labor, and Pensions, 111th Cong. Oct. 22, 2009 (Oral Testimony of Caroline Smith DeWaal, Director of the Center for Science in the Public Interest).

[197] Compare S. 510 § 308, 111th Cong. (as reported by the Senate HELP Committee, Nov. 18, 2009) with S. 510 § 308, 111th Cong. (as introduced in Senate, Mar. 3, 2009).

"(q) Certifications Concerning Imported Foods.--

"(1) IN GENERAL.--The Secretary may require, as a condition of granting admission to an article of food imported or offered for import into the United States, that an entity described in paragraph (3) provide a certification, or such other assurances as the Secretary determines appropriate, that the article of food complies with applicable requirements of this Act. Such certification or assurances may be provided in the form of shipment-specific certificates, a listing of certified facilities that manufacture, process, pack, or hold such food, or in such other form as the Secretary may specify.

"(2) FACTORS TO BE CONSIDERED IN REQUIRING CERTIFICATION.--The Secretary shall base the determination that an article of food is required to have a certification described in paragraph (1) on the risk of the food, including--

"(A) known safety risks associated with the food;

"(B) known food safety risks associated with the country, territory, or region of origin of the food;

"(C) a finding by the Secretary, supported by scientific, risk-based evidence, that--

"(i) the food safety programs, systems, and standards in the country, territory, or region of origin of the food are inadequate to ensure that the article of food is as safe as a similar article of food that is manufactured, processed, packed, or held in the United States in accordance with the requirements of this Act; and

"(ii) the certification would assist the Secretary in determining whether to refuse or admit the article of food under subsection (a); and

"*(D) information submitted to the Secretary in accordance with the process established in paragraph (7).*

"*(3) CERTIFYING ENTITIES.--For purposes of paragraph (1), entities that shall provide the certification or assurances described in such paragraph are--*

"*(A) an agency or a representative of the government of the country from which the article of food at issue originated, as designated by the Secretary; or*

"*(B) such other persons or entities accredited pursuant to section 808 to provide such certification or assurance.*

"*(4) RENEWAL AND REFUSAL OF CERTIFICATIONS.--The Secretary may--*

"*(A) require that any certification or other assurance provided by an entity specified in paragraph (2) be renewed by such entity at such times as the Secretary determines appropriate; and*

"*(B) refuse to accept any certification or assurance if the Secretary determines that such certification or assurance is not valid or reliable.*

"*(5) ELECTRONIC SUBMISSION.--The Secretary shall provide for the electronic submission of certifications under this subsection.*

"*(6) FALSE STATEMENTS.--Any statement or representation made by an entity described in paragraph (2) to the Secretary shall be subject to section 1001 of title 18, United States Code.*

"*(7) ASSESSMENT OF FOOD SAFETY PROGRAMS, SYSTEMS, AND STANDARDS.--If the Secretary determines that the food safety programs, systems, and standards in a foreign region, country, or territory are inadequate to ensure that an article of food is as safe as a similar article of food that is manufactured, processed, packed, or held in the United States in accordance with the requirements of this Act, the Secretary shall, to the extent practicable, identify such inadequacies and establish a process by which the foreign region, country, or territory may inform the Secretary of improvements made to such food safety program, system, or standard and demonstrate that those controls are adequate to ensure that an article of food is as safe as a similar article of food that is manufactured, processed, packed, or held in the United States in accordance with the requirements of this Act.".*

(c) Conforming Technical Amendment.--Section 801(b) (21 U.S.C. 381(b)) is amended in the second sentence by striking "with respect to an article included within the provision of the fourth sentence of subsection (a)" and inserting "with respect to an article described in subsection (a) relating to the requirements of sections 760 or 761,".

(d) No Limit on Authority.--Nothing in the amendments made by this section shall limit the authority of the Secretary to conduct inspections of imported food or to take such other steps as the Secretary deems appropriate to determine the admissibility of imported food.

SEC. 307. ACCREDITATION OF THIRD-PARTY AUDITORS.

Chapter VIII (21 U.S.C. 381 et seq.), as amended by section 306, is amended by adding at the end the following:

"SEC. 808. ACCREDITATION OF THIRD-PARTY AUDITORS.

"(a) Definitions.--In this section:

"(1) AUDIT AGENT.--The term 'audit agent' means an individual who is an employee or agent of an accredited third-party auditor and, although not individually accredited, is qualified to conduct food safety audits on behalf of an accredited third-party auditor.

"(2) ACCREDITATION BODY.--The term 'accreditation body' means an authority that performs accreditation of third-party auditors.

"(3) THIRD-PARTY AUDITOR.--The term 'third-party auditor' means a foreign government, agency of a foreign government, foreign cooperative, or any other third party, as the Secretary determines appropriate in accordance with the model standards described in subsection (b)(2), that is eligible to be considered for accreditation to conduct food safety audits to certify that eligible entities meet the applicable requirements of this section. A third-party auditor may be a single individual. A third-party auditor may employ or use audit agents to help conduct consultative and regulatory audits.

"(4) ACCREDITED THIRD-PARTY AUDITOR.--The term 'accredited third-party auditor' means a third-party auditor accredited by an accreditation body to conduct audits of eligible entities to certify that such eligible entities meet the applicable requirements of this section. An accredited third-party auditor may be an individual who conducts food safety audits to certify that eligible entities meet the applicable requirements of this section.

"(5) CONSULTATIVE AUDIT.--The term 'consultative audit' means an audit of an eligible entity--

> *"(A) to determine whether such entity is in compliance with the provisions of this Act and with applicable industry standards and practices; and*

> *"(B) the results of which are for internal purposes only.*

"(6) ELIGIBLE ENTITY.--The term 'eligible entity' means a foreign entity, including a foreign facility registered under section 415, in the food import supply chain that chooses to be audited by an accredited third-party auditor or the audit agent of such accredited third-party auditor.

"*(7) REGULATORY AUDIT.--The term 'regulatory audit' means an audit of an eligible entity--*

"*(A) to determine whether such entity is in compliance with the provisions of this Act; and*

"*(B) the results of which determine--*

"*(i) whether an article of food manufactured, processed, packed, or held by such entity is eligible to receive a food certification under section 801(q); or*

"*(ii) whether a facility is eligible to receive a facility certification under section 806(a) for purposes of participating in the program under section 806.*

"*(b) Accreditation System.--*

"*(1) ACCREDITATION BODIES.--*

"*(A) RECOGNITION OF ACCREDITATION BODIES.--*

"*(i) IN GENERAL.--Not later than 2 years after the date of enactment of the FDA Food Safety Modernization Act, the Secretary shall establish a system for the recognition of accreditation bodies that accredit third-party auditors to certify that eligible entities meet the applicable requirements of this section.*

"*(ii) DIRECT ACCREDITATION.--If, by the date that is 2 years after the date of establishment of the system described in clause (i), the Secretary has not identified and recognized an accreditation body to meet the requirements of this section, the Secretary may directly accredit third-party auditors.*

"(B) NOTIFICATION.--Each accreditation body recognized by the Secretary shall submit to the Secretary a list of all accredited third-party auditors accredited by such body and the audit agents of such auditors.

"(C) REVOCATION OF RECOGNITION AS AN ACCREDITATION BODY.--The Secretary shall promptly revoke the recognition of any accreditation body found not to be in compliance with the requirements of this section.

"(D) REINSTATEMENT.--The Secretary shall establish procedures to reinstate recognition of an accreditation body if the Secretary determines, based on evidence presented by such accreditation body, that revocation was inappropriate or that the body meets the requirements for recognition under this section.

"(2) MODEL ACCREDITATION STANDARDS.--Not later than 18 months after the date of enactment of the FDA Food Safety Modernization Act, the Secretary shall develop model standards, including requirements for regulatory audit reports, and each recognized accreditation body shall ensure that third-party auditors and audit agents of such auditors meet such standards in order to qualify such third-party auditors as accredited third-party auditors under this section. In developing the model standards, the Secretary shall look to standards in place on the date of the enactment of this section for guidance, to avoid unnecessary duplication of efforts and costs.

"(c) Third-party Auditors.--

"(1) REQUIREMENTS FOR ACCREDITATION AS A THIRD-PARTY AUDITOR.--

"*(A) FOREIGN GOVERNMENTS.--Prior to accrediting a foreign government or an agency of a foreign government as an accredited third-party auditor, the accreditation body (or, in the case of direct accreditation under subsection (b)(1)(A)(ii), the Secretary) shall perform such reviews and audits of food safety programs, systems, and standards of the government or agency of the government as the Secretary deems necessary, including requirements under the model standards developed under subsection (b)(2), to determine that the foreign government or agency of the foreign government is capable of adequately ensuring that eligible entities or foods certified by such government or agency meet the requirements of this Act with respect to food manufactured, processed, packed, or held for import into the United States.*

"*(B) FOREIGN COOPERATIVES AND OTHER THIRD PARTIES.--Prior to accrediting a foreign cooperative that aggregates the products of growers or processors, or any other third party to be an accredited third-party auditor, the accreditation body (or, in the case of direct accreditation under subsection (b)(1)(A)(ii), the Secretary) shall perform such reviews and audits of the training and qualifications of audit agents used by that cooperative or party and conduct such reviews of internal systems and such other investigation of the cooperative or party as the Secretary deems necessary, including requirements under the model standards developed under subsection (b)(2), to determine that each eligible entity certified by the cooperative or party has systems and standards in use to ensure that such entity or food meets the requirements of this Act.*

"*(2) REQUIREMENT TO ISSUE CERTIFICATION OF ELIGIBLE ENTITIES OR FOODS.--*

"*(A) IN GENERAL.--An accreditation body (or, in the case of direct accreditation under subsection (b)(1)(A)(ii), the Secretary) may not accredit a third-party auditor unless such third-party auditor agrees to issue a written and, as appropriate, electronic food certification, described in section 801(q), or facility certification under section 806(a), as appropriate, to accompany each food shipment for import into the United States from an eligible entity, subject to requirements set forth by the Secretary. Such written or electronic certification may be included with other documentation regarding such food shipment. The Secretary shall consider certifications under section 801(q) and participation in the voluntary qualified importer program described in section 806 when targeting inspection resources under section 421.*

"(B) PURPOSE OF CERTIFICATION.--The Secretary shall use certification provided by accredited third-party auditors to--

> *"(i) determine, in conjunction with any other assurances the Secretary may require under section 801(q), whether a food satisfies the requirements of such section; and*

> *"(ii) determine whether a facility is eligible to be a facility from which food may be offered for import under the voluntary qualified importer program under section 806.*

"(C) REQUIREMENTS FOR ISSUING CERTIFICATION.--

> *"(i) IN GENERAL.--An accredited third-party auditor shall issue a food certification under section 801(q) or a facility certification described under subparagraph (B) only after conducting a regulatory audit and such other activities that may be necessary to establish compliance with the requirements of such sections.*

"(ii) PROVISION OF CERTIFICATION.-- Only an accredited third-party auditor or the Secretary may provide a facility certification under section 806(a). Only those parties described in 801(q)(3) or the Secretary may provide a food certification under 301(q).

"(3) AUDIT REPORT SUBMISSION REQUIREMENTS.--

"(A) REQUIREMENTS IN GENERAL.--As a condition of accreditation, not later than 45 days after conducting an audit, an accredited third-party auditor or audit agent of such auditor shall prepare, and, in the case of a regulatory audit, submit, the audit report for each audit conducted, in a form and manner designated by the Secretary, which shall include--

"(i) the identity of the persons at the audited eligible entity responsible for compliance with food safety requirements;

"(ii) the dates of the audit;

"(iii) the scope of the audit; and

"(iv) any other information required by the Secretary that relates to or may influence an assessment of compliance with this Act.

"(B) RECORDS.--Following any accreditation of a third-party auditor, the Secretary may, at any time, require the accredited third-party auditor to submit to the Secretary an onsite audit report and such other reports or documents required as part of the audit process, for any eligible entity certified by the third-party auditor or audit agent of such auditor. Such report may include documentation that the eligible entity is in compliance with any applicable registration requirements.

"*(C)   LIMITATION.--The   requirement   under subparagraph (B) shall not include any report or other documents resulting from a consultative audit by the accredited third-party auditor, except that the Secretary may access the results of a consultative audit in accordance with section 414.*

"*(4) REQUIREMENTS OF ACCREDITED THIRD-PARTY AUDITORS AND AUDIT AGENTS OF SUCH AUDITORS.--*

"*(A) RISKS TO PUBLIC HEALTH.--If, at any time during an audit, an accredited third-party auditor or audit agent of such auditor discovers a condition that could cause or contribute to a serious risk to the public health, such auditor shall immediately notify the Secretary of--*

"*(i) the identification of the eligible entity subject to the audit; and*

"*(ii) such condition.*

"*(B) TYPES OF AUDITS.--An accredited third-party auditor or audit agent of such auditor may perform consultative and regulatory audits of eligible entities.*

"*(C) LIMITATIONS.--*

"*(i) IN GENERAL.--An accredited third party auditor may not perform a regulatory audit of an eligible entity if such agent has performed a consultative audit or a regulatory audit of such eligible entity during the previous 13-month period.*

"*(ii) WAIVER.--The Secretary may waive the application of clause (i) if the Secretary determines that there is insufficient access to accredited third-party auditors in a country or region.*

"(5) CONFLICTS OF INTEREST.--

    "(A) THIRD-PARTY AUDITORS.--An accredited third-party auditor shall--

        "(i) not be owned, managed, or controlled by any person that owns or operates an eligible entity to be certified by such auditor;

        "(ii) in carrying out audits of eligible entities under this section, have procedures to ensure against the use of any officer or employee of such auditor that has a financial conflict of interest regarding an eligible entity to be certified by such auditor; and

        "(iii) annually make available to the Secretary disclosures of the extent to which such auditor and the officers and employees of such auditor have maintained compliance with clauses (i) and (ii) relating to financial conflicts of interest.

    "(B) AUDIT AGENTS.--An audit agent shall--

        "(i) not own or operate an eligible entity to be audited by such agent;

        "(ii) in carrying out audits of eligible entities under this section, have procedures to ensure that such agent does not have a financial conflict of interest regarding an eligible entity to be audited by such agent; and

        "(iii) annually make available to the Secretary disclosures of the extent to which such agent has maintained compliance with clauses (i) and (ii) relating to financial conflicts of interest.

"(C) REGULATIONS.--The Secretary shall promulgate regulations not later than 18 months after the date of enactment of the FDA Food Safety Modernization Act to implement this section and to ensure that there are protections against conflicts of interest between an accredited third-party auditor and the eligible entity to be certified by such auditor or audited by such audit agent. Such regulations shall include--

"(i) requiring that audits performed under this section be unannounced;

"(ii) a structure to decrease the potential for conflicts of interest, including timing and public disclosure, for fees paid by eligible entities to accredited third-party auditors; and

"(iii) appropriate limits on financial affiliations between an accredited third-party auditor or audit agents of such auditor and any person that owns or operates an eligible entity to be certified by such auditor, as described in subparagraphs (A) and (B).

"(6) WITHDRAWAL OF ACCREDITATION.--

"(A) IN GENERAL.--The Secretary shall withdraw accreditation from an accredited third-party auditor--

"(i) if food certified under section 801(q) or from a facility certified under paragraph (2)(B) by such third-party auditor is linked to an outbreak of foodborne illness that has a reasonable probability of causing serious adverse health consequences or death in humans or animals;

"(ii) following an evaluation and finding by the Secretary that the third-party auditor no longer meets the requirements for accreditation; or

"(iii) following a refusal to allow United States officials to conduct such audits and investigations as may be necessary to ensure continued compliance with the requirements set forth in this section.

"(B)   ADDITIONAL   BASIS   FOR WITHDRAWAL OF ACCREDITATION.--The Secretary may withdraw accreditation from an accredited third-party auditor in the case that such third-party auditor is accredited by an accreditation body for which recognition as an accreditation body under subsection (b)(1)(C) is revoked, if the Secretary determines that there is good cause for the withdrawal.

"(C) EXCEPTION.--The Secretary may waive the application of subparagraph (A)(i) if the Secretary--

"(i) conducts an investigation of the material facts related to the outbreak of human or animal illness; and

"(ii) reviews the steps or actions taken by the third party auditor to justify the certification and determines that the accredited third-party auditor satisfied the requirements under section 801(q) of certifying the food, or the requirements under paragraph (2)(B) of certifying the entity.

"(7) REACCREDITATION.--The Secretary shall establish procedures to reinstate the accreditation of a third-party auditor for which accreditation has been withdrawn under paragraph (6)--

"*(A) if the Secretary determines, based on evidence presented, that the third-party auditor satisfies the requirements of this section and adequate grounds for revocation no longer exist; and*

"*(B) in the case of a third-party auditor accredited by an accreditation body for which recognition as an accreditation body under subsection (b)(1)(C) is revoked--*

"*(i) if the third-party auditor becomes accredited not later than 1 year after revocation of accreditation under paragraph (6)(A), through direct accreditation under subsection (b)(1)(A)(ii) or by an accreditation body in good standing; or*

"*(ii) under such conditions as the Secretary may require for a third-party auditor under paragraph (6)(B).*

"*(8) NEUTRALIZING COSTS.--The Secretary shall establish by regulation a reimbursement (user fee) program, similar to the method described in section 203(h) of the Agriculture Marketing Act of 1946, by which the Secretary assesses fees and requires accredited third-party auditors and audit agents to reimburse the Food and Drug Administration for the work performed to establish and administer the accreditation system under this section. The Secretary shall make operating this program revenue-neutral and shall not generate surplus revenue from such a reimbursement mechanism. Fees authorized under this paragraph shall be collected and available for obligation only to the extent and in the amount provided in advance in appropriation Acts. Such fees are authorized to remain available until expended.*

"*(d) Recertification of Eligible Entities.--An eligible entity shall apply for annual recertification by an accredited third-party auditor if such entity--*

"*(1) intends to participate in voluntary qualified importer program under section 806; or*

"(2) is required to provide to the Secretary a certification under section 801(q) for any food from such entity.

"(e) False Statements.--Any statement or representation made--

"(1) by an employee or agent of an eligible entity to an accredited third-party auditor or audit agent; or

"(2) by an accredited third-party auditor to the Secretary,

shall be subject to section 1001 of title 18, United States Code.

"(f) Monitoring.--To ensure compliance with the requirements of this section, the Secretary shall--

"(1) periodically, or at least once every 4 years, reevaluate the accreditation bodies described in subsection (b)(1);

"(2) periodically, or at least once every 4 years, evaluate the performance of each accredited third-party auditor, through the review of regulatory audit reports by such auditors, the compliance history as available of eligible entities certified by such auditors, and any other measures deemed necessary by the Secretary;

"(3) at any time, conduct an onsite audit of any eligible entity certified by an accredited third-party auditor, with or without the auditor present; and

"(4) take any other measures deemed necessary by the Secretary.

"(g) Publicly Available Registry.--The Secretary shall establish a publicly available registry of accreditation bodies and of accredited third-party auditors, including the name of, contact information for, and other information deemed necessary by the Secretary about such bodies and auditors.

"(h) Limitations.--

    "(1) NO EFFECT ON SECTION 704 INSPECTIONS.-- The audits performed under this section shall not be considered inspections under section 704.

    "(2) NO EFFECT ON INSPECTION AUTHORITY.-- Nothing in this section affects the authority of the Secretary to inspect any eligible entity pursuant to this Act.".

6

Food Importers and
Verification Duties

What Do Managers Need To Know?

The importers of foods and food ingredients will bear a considerable weight of new regulatory paperwork under the Act. Foreign supplier food safety "verification" is the primary obligation for importers.[198] While the more stringent proposals for registration were defeated by the lobbying efforts of importers, the 2010 requirements will impose more documentation and submission obligations than had existed under prior law. Budgeting for more staff positions in FDA field offices, if Congress provides the funds,[199] will also make importers more likely to be inspected and more likely to have their shipments detained. Importers will be encouraged by the new voluntary qualified importer provisions of the law to volunteer for faster entry.[200] In return for more advance paperwork, shipments of food will be more likely to have an expedited passage through US Customs.

---

[198] 21 U.S.C. 385(a).

[199] "Rep. Jack Kingston of Georgia, the ranking GOP member on the appropriations subcommittee that oversees the FDA, said the number of cases of food-borne illnesses in the country does not justify the $1.4 billion the new law is estimated to cost over the first five years. 'I would not identify it as something that will necessarily be zeroed out, but it is quite possible it will be scaled back if it is significant overreach,' said Kingston, who is likely to become chairman of the subcommittee when Republicans assume control of the House in January." Lyndsey Layton, *Food Safety Overhaul Faces Obstacles*, WASHINGTON POST (Dec. 24, 2010).

[200] Pub.L. 111-353, adopting 21 U.S.C. 386 (2010).

How Is the Process of Sampling and Holding Import Shipments Conducted?

The 2010 amendments add considerably to the paperwork obligations of food importers and the customs brokers who work for them as agents. The existing requirement for an electronic advance notification of food imports remains in place.[201] The same process for sample-related inquiries remains in place: if the FDA learns of the import and decides to take a sample of an imported food, it must give notice to the importer. If the sampling demonstrates a potential problem with the food, the importer is served with a notice of detention and hearing.[202] The food is held and cannot be moved.[203] At the informal hearing held at the local FDA office, the importer may try to demonstrate that the shipment is in compliance, or may request to recondition the item to comply with FDA standards, a process that is entirely at the discretion of the FDA.[204] If an article of food is found to not comply or cannot be brought into compliance with the Food, Drug, and Cosmetic Act (FDCA), the FDA must destroy the food, if it is not re-exported within ninety days after the item was refused entry.[205]

In some instances, the FDA may decide to sample and inspect a shipment after it has been conditionally released to the importer.[206] If the importer does not redeliver the shipment, Customs can institute proceedings to obtain the liquidated damages provided for in the bond.[207] The 2010 legislation does not change the inspection process, but instead increases the burden on food importers to demonstrate compliance with US food safety laws through the use of a foreign supplier verification system.[208]

---

[201] 21 C.F.R. 1.277.

[202] 21 U.S.C. 381.

[203] 21 C.F.R. 1.377 et seq.

[204] 21 C.F.R. § 1.94(a) (2009); *See* GAO, *Food Safety: Agencies Need to Address Gaps in Enforcement and Collaboration to Enhance Safety of Imported Food* 55-56 (2009) [hereinafter *Agencies Need to Address Gaps in Enforcement and Collaboration to Enhance Safety of Imported Food*].

[205] 21 U.S.C. § 381(A) (2009).

[206] *See* GAO, *Food Safety: Agencies Need to Address Gaps in Enforcement and Collaboration to Enhance Safety of Imported Food* 18 (2009) [hereinafter *Agencies Need to Address Gaps in Enforcement and Collaboration to Enhance Safety of Imported Food*].

[207] 21 U.S.C. § 381(b) (2009).

[208] 21 U.S.C. 385.

What Problems Did the Pre-2010 Import System Have?

Before delving into the new Foreign Supplier Verification System and the Voluntary Qualified Importer Program, it is worth discussing the problems of the pre-2010 import system that Congress hopes to alleviate through the new legislation. The pre-2010 FDA practice has been criticized for its emphasis on reacting to unsafe foods that arrive and are selected for sampling at ports of entry, as opposed to preventing unsafe food from ever arriving in the United States. The food distribution chain is a long one, and the pre-2010 import system did little to protect against the safety of a food item being jeopardized as it made its way along what are often extended distribution chains. As food moves from production to the point of sale, it may change hands a number of times. First, it is produced, grown, or manufactured. This first step alone might involve multiple ingredients from many different suppliers. If the food is produced in a foreign country, perhaps the original producer or a separate importer will decide to export the food into the United States. A broker in the United States will then prepare the import documents and oversee moving the shipment through Customs. At some point along the way, the food may be temporarily placed in a warehouse. From there, distributors and wholesalers may purchase and transport the food to a retailer, at which point it will finally be sold to consumers.[209] All of these points along the distribution chain increase the opportunity for contamination.

Since the passage of the 2002 legislation known as the Public Health Security and Bioterrorism Preparedness and Response Act of 2002, all food importers are required to provide the FDA advance notice of any shipment of human or animal food imported or offered for import into the United States.[210] This provision was enacted to facilitate the FDA in allocating resources for inspecting and sampling articles of food. If a food shipment arrives at a port of entry and there has not been prior notice, the food shipment would not be admitted entry, nor returned to the importer.[211]

---

[209] *See Food Supply Chain Handbook*, Grocery Manufacturer Association 4-6 (2008), www.gmabrands.com/publications/GMA_SupplyChain2.pdf.

[210] Public Health Security and Bioterrorism Preparedness and Response Act of 2002 (Bioterrorism Act), Public Law 107-188, § 306, 116 Stat. 594 (codified at 21 U.S.C. § 381(m)).

[211] GAO, *Food Safety: Agencies Need to Address Gaps in Enforcement and Collaboration to Enhance Safety of Imported Food* 12 (2009) [hereinafter *Agencies Need to Address Gaps in Enforcement and Collaboration to Enhance Safety of Imported Food*].

Most of these situations are negotiated with FDA import specialists on the specifics of each case.

The FDA works with the US Customs and Border Protection of the Department of Homeland Security to screen the entry documents of imported food and determine whether it should sample and examine an entry. However, lapses in communication between the two agencies sometimes allow unsafe food to enter the United States. Although the FDA should have prior notice of the shipment of food before it arrives through the Bioterrorism Act, it does not receive notification from Customs once the shipment does in fact arrive.[212] If the shipment clears Customs' inspection process, it is conditionally released, and the importer is required to post a bond, which stipulates that the importer is to return the goods should the FDA want to sample or inspect.[213] In practice, this mechanism enables importers to sometimes move food items into US commerce without the FDA's prior approval.[214]

The FDA seeks to use its central databases to guide inspectors in deciding which food shipments to inspect, by informing inspectors of problems and violative trends specific to certain importers, manufacturers, or commodities. But an FDA study found that much of the information that would have been helpful in determining whether a food should be admitted, such as past violations and laboratory results, has not been passed along to inspectors because of inefficiencies and lack of organization. As a result, inspectors utilize their own discretion to determine which foods should be sampled and inspected.[215] The results are inconsistent enforcement actions, in which the same types of food are treated differently depending on the port of entry and the inspector making the decision.[216]

---

[212] *See* GAO, *Food Safety: Agencies Need to Address Gaps in Enforcement and Collaboration to Enhance Safety of Imported Food* 18 (2009) [hereinafter *Agencies Need to Address Gaps in Enforcement and Collaboration to Enhance Safety of Imported Food*].
[213] 21 U.S.C. § 381(B) (2009).
[214] *See* GAO, *Food Safety: Agencies Need to Address Gaps in Enforcement and Collaboration to Enhance Safety of Imported Food* 18 (2009) [hereinafter *Agencies Need to Address Gaps in Enforcement and Collaboration to Enhance Safety of Imported Food*].
[215] *See* U.S. Gen. Accounting Office, *Federal Efforts to Ensure Imported Food Safety Are Inconsistent and Unreliable* 5-7 (1998) [hereinafter *Federal Efforts to Ensure Imported Food Safety Are Inconsistent and Unreliable*].
[216] *See* John R. Fleder, *Imported Products: The FDA Is Not Fooling Around*, FDLI UPDATES (Jan./Feb. 2009).

Inspecting food shipments at ports of entry has shown to be ineffective at halting the movement of imported contaminated food into US commerce. An overworked FDA field office employee makes decisions about admissibility based on the limited information provided to them on their computer screen, decisions not based on risk factors such as how the food was grown, produced, and handled.[217] The current system allows an importer to remain in control over a shipment throughout the entire inspection process, and can serve to encourage importers to treat the payment of a bond as a cost of doing business.[218] Liquidated damages for erroneously releasing food into commercial channels are rarely recovered by the Customs Service.[219]

In 1998, the Government Accountability Office reported that a Customs surveillance operation demonstrated that 40 percent of imported food shipments the FDA found to be in violation of food safety standards were never redelivered to Customs upon request. It is presumed that these foods were sold to US consumers.[220] Recognizing that current legislation does not support a comprehensive approach, the FDA has recently begun engaging in various agency-initiated methods to ensure the safety of imported foods.[221] In September 2009, the FDA implemented a new pilot program, called the Predictive Risk-Based Evaluation for Dynamic Import Compliance Targeting (PREDICT). The database gives a numerical risk score that is determined for every importer, by analyzing set criteria such as the country of origin, the violative history, and the result of past laboratory tests. This numerical risk score is passed on to inspectors through an automated system. This is an improvement over the current system, which requires that FDA inspectors manually look up background information on

---

[217] See *Protecting American Consumers Every Step of the Way: A Strategic Framework for Continual Improvement in Import Safety*, Report to the President, Interagency Working Group on Import Safety 7-10 (2007).

[218] See GAO, *Food Safety: Agencies Need to Address Gaps in Enforcement and Collaboration to Enhance Safety of Imported Food* 21 (2009) [hereinafter *Agencies Need to Address Gaps in Enforcement and Collaboration to Enhance Safety of Imported Food*].

[219] GAO, *Federal Efforts to Ensure Imported Food Safety Are Inconsistent and Unreliable* 8-9 (1998) [hereinafter *Federal Efforts to Ensure Imported Food Safety Are Inconsistent and Unreliable*].

[220] U.S. Gen. Accounting Office, *Food Safety and Security: Fundamental Changes Needed to Ensure Safe Food* 7 (2001).

[221] See Linda R. Horton, *FDA at the International Level* 705-06, *in* FOOD AND DRUG LAW REGULATION (David G. Adams, *et al.*) (2008).

an importer and make a more subjective decision. Preliminary data on the PREDICT system indicates that it is more effective in targeting shipments that pose a more dangerous threat to the safety of US consumers, thereby increasing the efficiency of an inspector's work.[222]

How Will Foreign Supplier Verification Be Implemented?

The 2010 legislation creates the Foreign Supplier Verification System, which mandates that food imports must have a verification program in place when the food is received at the US port of entry, and it is a violation to bring in a shipment of food for which there is no foreign supplier verification in place.[223]

The responsibility is placed on the US food importer, or the US agent of the foreign food company, to be able to provide adequate assurances that the "processes and procedures, including reasonably appropriate risk-based preventive controls" applicable to a food are able to "provide the same level of public health protection as those required under section 418 or section 419."[224] The key words are "same level," so that the US food producer who has to comply with safety plan or hazard assessment rules is not at a disadvantage.[225] The content of the verification plans may include "monitoring records for shipments, lot-by-lot certification of compliance, annual on-site inspections, checking the hazard analysis and risk-based preventive control plan of the foreign supplier, and periodically testing and sampling shipments."[226] The purpose of the verification program is to verify that the food imported is produced in compliance with the requirements of Section 418 or Section 419, as appropriate, and is not adulterated under Section 402 or misbranded under Section 403(w).[227]

Within one year of enactment, the FDA will publish guidance to help importers comply with the Foreign Supplier Verification Program.

---

[222] GAO, *Food Safety: Agencies Need to Address Gaps in Enforcement and Collaboration to Enhance Safety of Imported Food* 33-36 (2009) [hereinafter *Agencies Need to Address Gaps in Enforcement and Collaboration to Enhance Safety of Imported Food*].
[223] Pub.L. 111-353, Title III sec. 305, adopting new 21 U.S.C. 385.
[224] Pub. L. 111-353, Title III sec. 301, adopting new 21 U.S.C. 385(c)(2).
[225] 21 U.S.C. 385(c)(2)(A)(ii).
[226] Id. at 21 U.S.C. 385(c)(4).
[227] *Id.* at 21 U.S.C. 385(c)(2).

Additionally, within one year of enactment, the FDA must establish rules for the content of the Foreign Supplier Verification Program, including providing for regulations adequate to provide that the imported food is produced in compliance with the requirements of Section 418 or Section 419 and is not adulterated under Section 402 or misbranded under Section 403(w).[228] Further, the regulations must include any other requirements the FDA finds necessary to ensure that imported food is as safe as food produced and sold within the United States.

A person required to comply with this section must maintain records related to the Foreign Supplier Verification Program for no less than two years.

Importing or offering for import "a food if the importer (as defined in section 805) does not have in place a foreign supplier verification program in compliance with such section 805" is a prohibited act under 21 U.S.C. 331.[229]

The amendments under this section will go into effect two years from the date of enactment of this Act.[230]

Is the Foreign Supplier Program Confidential?

No. The FDA is required to periodically publish on its website the names of the importers who are participating in the Foreign Supplier Verification Program.

What Is the Voluntary Qualified Importer Program?

The 2010 legislation calls for the FDA, in consultation with Homeland Security, to create a system that would provide for expedited entry of food that is in compliance with the Voluntary Qualified Importer Program.[231] The FDA must establish this system no later than eighteen months from the date of enactment and must issue a guidance document related to participation in, revocation of, reinstatement in, and compliance with such

---

[228] *Id.* at 21 U.S.C. 385(a)(1).
[229] 21 U.S.C. 331(zz).
[230] S. 510 § 301, 111th Cong. (as reported by the Senate HELP Committee, Nov. 18, 2009).
[231] Pub.L. 111-353 adding 21 U.S.C. §386(a).

program. An importer is defined as a "person that brings food, or causes food to be brought, from a foreign country into the customs territory of the United States."[232]

Participation in this system is not mandatory for importers, but it is a system importers can request to participate in for the purpose of obtaining expedited entry for food items. In determining whether to issue certification to a facility, the FDA will consider the following factors:[233]

> (1) The known safety risks of the food to be imported.
>
> (2) The compliance history of foreign suppliers used by the importer, as appropriate.
>
> (3) The capability of the regulatory system of the country of export to ensure compliance with United States food safety standards for a designated food.
>
> (4) The compliance of the importer with the requirements of [the Foreign Supplier Verification System].
>
> (5) The recordkeeping, testing, inspections and audits of facilities, traceability of articles of food, temperature controls, and sourcing practices of the importer.
>
> (6) The potential risk for intentional adulteration of the food.
>
> (7) Any other factor that the Secretary determines appropriate.

The FDA must reevaluate each importer qualified under this program at least every three years.[234] The FDA will revoke the "qualified importer status" of any importer not in compliance with the criteria.[235]

Are Regulatory Risks Greater for Food Importers?

Yes. The 2010 legislation puts into place more exacting standards on importers than regular facilities.[236] Certification also introduces an element

---

[232] 21 U.S.C. 386(g).
[233] 21 U.S.C. 386(d).
[234] 21 U.S.C. 386(e).
[235] *Id.*; *see* S. 510 § 302, 111th Cong. (as reported by the Senate HELP Committee, Nov. 18, 2009).

of uncertainty. The final Act does not require use of a unique facility identifier specific to the facility, or for importers and custom brokers, specific to the principal place of business for which the person is registering.

What Records Should Importers Retain for FDA Inspection?

A person required to comply with the Foreign Supplier Verification Program must maintain records for no less than two years.[237] Further, it should be noted that the 2002 legislation had implemented new recordkeeping requirements for those in food importation, provisions that had never been required previously.[238] Under the Act, manufacturers, processors, and receivers of imported food must keep records of the "immediate previous sources and the immediate subsequent recipients of food." Records must be maintained for at least two years.[239] A 2009 federal study revealed that this recordkeeping provision has not received anywhere near universal compliance. Out of 118 food facilities questioned in the study, 59 percent of the facilities (70 facilities) were not in compliance with the traceability requirement. One quarter of the facilities questioned was not even aware of the FDA's recordkeeping requirements.[240]

How Did the FDA Respond?

FDA Commissioner Hamburg testified at the Senate HELP Committee hearing on October 22, 2009, that:

> section 301 (Foreign Supplier Verification Program) will provide FDA with important information about importers and require that they verify for each supplier that food is not adulterated and is in compliance with allergen labeling

---

[236] 21 U.S.C. 385(c), Pub.L. 111-353, §303, and see H.R. 2749 § 204, 111th Cong. (as engrossed by House of Representatives, July 30, 2009).

[237] 21 U.S.C. 385(d).

[238] *See* GAO, *Overseeing the U.S. Food Supply: Steps Should Be Taken to Reduce Overlapping Inspections and Related Activities* 4 (2005) [hereinafter *Steps Should Be Taken to Reduce Overlapping Inspections and Related Activities*].

[239] Bioterrorism Act, Public Law 107-188, § 306, 116 Stat. 594 (codified at 21 U.S.C. § 350c).

[240] Department of Health and Human Services, *Traceability in the Food Supply Chain* 12-17 (2009) [hereinafter *Traceability in the Food Supply Chain*].

requirements, preventive control requirements, and safety standards for produce. These requirements are enforced by a prohibited act and refusal of entry. These new requirements will help reduce risks to consumers from potentially harmful products by requiring importers to take appropriate steps to protect product safety.[241]

Commissioner Hamburg discussed the importer registration provision at the House Energy and Commerce Committee's Subcommittee on Health hearing on food safety on June 3, 2009, saying:

> Well, the importer fee refers to fees on the individuals or the companies that are serving as the link between foods that are grown, processed, manufactured overseas and being brought into the United States to be distributed to consumers here. And so they are not necessarily representing a given manufacturer, but it is a very important function because it is that bridge between what is happening on the international scene and what is coming into this country for use.[242]

What Proposed Requirements for Importers Were Not Adopted?

Currently importers are not required to register with the FDA.[243] The House bill would have required registration of importers and custom brokers, and each food importer would have been required to pay a $500 annual fee, with increases to be adjusted with inflation, and to obtain a

---

[241] Hearing on Keeping America's Families Safe: Reforming the Food Safety System, S. Committee on Health, Education, Labor, and Pensions, 111th Cong. 6, Oct. 22, 2009 (Testimony of FDA Commissioner Hamburg).

[242] Hearing on Food Safety Enhancement Act of 2009, Before the Subcommittee on Health of the H. Committee on Energy and Commerce, 111th Cong. 138 (2009) [hereinafter Hearing on Food Safety Enhancement Act of 2009] (Statement of FDA Commissioner Hamburg in Preliminary Transcript).

[243] Hearing on Food Safety Enhancement Act of 2009, Before the Subcommittee on Health of the H. Committee on Energy and Commerce, 111th Cong. 5 (2009) [hereinafter Hearing on Food Safety Enhancement Act of 2009] (Prepared Statement by Margaret A. Hamburg, Commissioner of FDA, HHS, Rockville, MD).

unique facility identifier.[244] The House proposed that "good importer practices" be established through regulations, in consultation with Customs.[245] The purpose of good importer practices would have been to fill the gap shown by the Chinese melamine scandals of 2007–2009. Finding the suspect food after its entry into US commerce is quite difficult. The new power would have ensured that the importer is able to trace, withhold, and recall any food that is not in compliance with US food safety laws. Future laws may impose these requirements.

What Did Trade Associations Say?

A number of groups, including the American Wholesale Marketers Association, the International Foodservice Distributors Association, and the International Warehouse Logistics Association, voiced concerns that Congress is too unfamiliar with food industry logistics to draft comprehensive food safety reform whereby the burdens are placed on the right players.[246] Under H.R. 2749, most of the players involved in the long path that food may travel will have to register and pay the $500 yearly fee. This will include manufacturers, some farms, warehouses, distributors, importers, and customs brokers.[247] According to Anne Holloway, vice president of government affairs for the American Wholesale Marketers Association, "Our members already operate on a very slim profit margin and with the current economic downturn, these additional costs will be tough on our members."

---

[244] The bill as introduced in the House did not set the exact fee amount for importers, but instead left it for the Secretary to determine. Compare H.R. 2749 § 204 111th Cong. (as reported by the House Committee on Energy and Commerce) with H.R. 2749 § 205 111th Cong. (as introduced in House of Representatives, June 8, 2009).

[245] The bill as reported by the House Committee on Energy and Commerce did not leave good importer practices to the Secretary to promulgate, but instead simply detailed that: "Good importer practices shall include the verification of good manufacturing practices and preventive controls of the importer's foreign suppliers, as applicable." Compare H.R. 2749 § 204, 111th Cong. (as engrossed by House of Representatives, July 30, 2009) with H.R. 2749 § 204 111th Cong. (as reported by the House Committee on Energy and Commerce, passed by House of Representatives, June 17, 2009).

[246] *See* April Terreri, *Will New FDA Penalties Break Your Bank?* FOOD LOGISTICS, Sept. 2009, at 26.

[247] *See* April Terreri, *Will New FDA Penalties Break Your Bank?* FOOD LOGISTICS, Sept. 2009, at 26.

A representative for the Food Marketing Institute testified at the Senate HELP Committee hearing on October 22, 2009:

Sec. 301. Foreign Supplier Verification Program

> Food retailers are extremely reliant on imports as our customers demand a wide range of products—such as fresh produce—regardless of the season. However, importers play a mutually important role to import product into our country with the assurance that it is safe. At Publix, we only source food from suppliers that are able to meet our strict requirements for food safety and product quality. For Publix branded products, this includes an in-depth review of total quality systems through audits and evaluations. We believe that food safety supplier verification activities will further assist to mitigate food safety risks associated with imported foods.

Sec. 302. Voluntary Qualified Importer Program

> We believe it is appropriate to establish systems to encourage the use of additional measures of assurance by importers and foreign producers. We support the use of incentives to encourage food producers to take steps beyond those that are required by law to ensure the safety of the food supply and the use of a variety of factors to determine the risk posed by different foods. [248]

Tom Stenzel, president of the United Fresh Produce Association, a trade association representing growers, packers, shippers, fresh-cut processors, distributors, and marketers of fresh fruits and vegetables, testified at the House Energy and Commerce Committee's Subcommittee on Health hearing on food safety on June 3, 2009:

---

[248] Hearing on Keeping America's Families Safe: Reforming the Food Safety System, S. Committee on Health, Education, Labor, and Pensions, 111th Cong. 7, Oct. 22, 2009 (Testimony of Michael Roberson, Director of Corporate Quality Assurance, Publix Super Markets Inc. on behalf of the Food Marketing Institute).

In Section 201, we support the bill's intent to require importers to register with FDA, and comply with good importer practices… [W]ith regard to imports, we support the concept of the Safe and Secure Food Importation Program in Section 113, and urge that the bill require FDA to implement such a program with a direction that it "shall" be implemented rather than "may" be implemented. This program is a critical component of a secure food importing system that can both assure safety while meeting the volume demands for safe foods moving quickly through well established and rigorous channels in global commerce.[249]

Although Stenzel encouraged the House to require the FDA to establish a safe and secure food importation program, the language in the bill remained the same. The FDA "may establish by regulation or guidance in coordination with the Commissioner responsible for Customs and Border Protection a program that facilitates the movement of food through the importation process."[250]

A letter sent by the National Customs Brokers and Forwarders Association of America just prior to the mark-up of H.R. 2749 appears to have encouraged the House to back down on the requirements placed on customs brokers in the House bill. Association president Mary Jo Muoio expressed, "'These provisions surfaced only last week [and] were proceeded by no consultation with our industry."[251] When the bill was introduced in the House, the bill subjected both custom brokers and filers to a yearly fee to be determined by the FDA. The fee was dropped because of a voice vote after the chairmen offered a manager's amendment during the mark-up by

---

[249] Hearing on Food Safety Enhancement Act of 2009, Before the Subcommittee on Health of the H. Committee on Energy and Commerce, 111th Cong. 4 (2009) [hereinafter Hearing on Food Safety Enhancement Act of 2009] (Prepared Statement of Tom Stenzel, President of United Fresh Produce Association).

[250] Compare H.R. 2749 § 113, 111th Cong. (as engrossed by House of Representatives, July 30, 2009) with H.R. 2749 § 113, 111th Cong. (as reported by the House Committee on Energy and Commerce, June 17, 2009).

[251] *Dingell's Food Safety Bill Gives Some a Bad Taste*, NATIONAL JOURNAL'S HILL BRIEFS, June 10, 2009.

the House Committee.[252] Waxman clarified that customs brokers do have to register with the FDA but are not required to pay a yearly fee and are not subject to good importer practices. He said this was in response to concerns that it would be duplicative to require customs brokers to register with the FDA when they are already required to register with Customs.[253] Also dropped from the bill was a provision subjecting the registration of a custom broker to suspension for a violation of the FDCA, or for a knowing or repeated making of an inaccurate or incomplete statement or for submission of information relating to food.[254] In the final text of the Act, issues of registration numbers and customs brokers were assigned to a study and were not made mandatory.

Text of the Law as Adopted

SEC. 301. FOREIGN SUPPLIER VERIFICATION PROGRAM.

(a) In General- Chapter VIII (21 U.S.C. 381 et seq.) is amended by adding at the end the following:

"SEC. 805. FOREIGN SUPPLIER VERIFICATION PROGRAM.

"(a) In General-

> *"(1) VERIFICATION REQUIREMENT- Except as provided under subsections (e) and (f), each importer shall perform risk-based foreign supplier verification activities for the purpose of verifying that the food imported by the importer or agent of an importer is--*

---

[252] H.R. Rep. No. 111-234, at 58 (2009); compare H.R. 2749 § 205, 111th Cong. (as reported by the House Committee on Energy and Commerce) with H.R. 2749 § 205, 111th Cong. (as introduced in House of Representatives, June 8, 2009).

[253] Amy Tsui, *House Commerce Committee Passes Food Safety Bill, Including Import Provisions*, 26 INTL TRADE REPORTER 845 (2009).

[254] Compare H.R. 2749 § 205, 111th Cong. (as engrossed by House of Representatives, July 30, 2009) with H.R. 2749 § 205 111th Cong. (as reported by the House Committee on Energy and Commerce, June 17, 2009).

"(A) produced in compliance with the requirements of section 418 or section 419, as appropriate; and

"(B) is not adulterated under section 402 or misbranded under section 403(w).

"(2) IMPORTER DEFINED- For purposes of this section, the term 'importer' means, with respect to an article of food--

"(A) the United States owner or consignee of the article of food at the time of entry of such article into the United States; or

"(B) in the case when there is no United States owner or consignee as described in subparagraph (A), the United States agent or representative of a foreign owner or consignee of the article of food at the time of entry of such article into the United States.

"(b) Guidance- Not later than 1 year after the date of enactment of the FDA Food Safety Modernization Act, the Secretary shall issue guidance to assist importers in developing foreign supplier verification programs.

"(c) Regulations-

"(1) IN GENERAL- Not later than 1 year after the date of enactment of the FDA Food Safety Modernization Act, the Secretary shall promulgate regulations to provide for the content of the foreign supplier verification program established under subsection (a).

"(2) REQUIREMENTS- The regulations promulgated under paragraph (1)--

"(A) shall require that the foreign supplier verification program of each importer be adequate to provide assurances that each foreign supplier to the importer produces the imported food in compliance with--

"(i) processes and procedures, including reasonably appropriate risk-based preventive controls, that provide the same level of public health protection as those required under section 418 or section 419 (taking into consideration variances granted under section 419), as appropriate; and

"(ii) section 402 and section 403(w).

"(B) shall include such other requirements as the Secretary deems necessary and appropriate to verify that food imported into the United States is as safe as food produced and sold within the United States.

"(3) CONSIDERATIONS- In promulgating regulations under this subsection, the Secretary shall, as appropriate, take into account differences among importers and types of imported foods, including based on the level of risk posed by the imported food.

"(4) ACTIVITIES- Verification activities under a foreign supplier verification program under this section may include monitoring records for shipments, lot-by-lot certification of compliance, annual on-site inspections, checking the hazard analysis and risk-based preventive control plan of the foreign supplier, and periodically testing and sampling shipments.

"(d) Record Maintenance and Access- Records of an importer related to a foreign supplier verification program shall be maintained for a period of not less than 2 years and shall be made available promptly to a duly authorized representative of the Secretary upon request.

"(e) Exemption of Seafood, Juice, and Low-acid Canned Food Facilities in Compliance With HACCP- This section shall not apply to a facility if the owner, operator, or agent in charge of such facility is required to comply with, and is in compliance with, 1 of the following standards and regulations with respect to such facility:

"(1) The Seafood Hazard Analysis Critical Control Points Program of the Food and Drug Administration.

"(2) The Juice Hazard Analysis Critical Control Points Program of the Food and Drug Administration.

"(3) The Thermally Processed Low-Acid Foods Packaged in Hermetically Sealed Containers standards of the Food and Drug Administration (or any successor standards).

The exemption under paragraph (3) shall apply only with respect to microbiological hazards that are regulated under the standards for Thermally Processed Low-Acid Foods Packaged in Hermetically Sealed Containers under part 113 of chapter 21, Code of Federal Regulations (or any successor regulations).

"(f) Additional Exemptions- The Secretary, by notice published in the Federal Register, shall establish an exemption from the requirements of this section for articles of food imported in small quantities for research and evaluation purposes or for personal consumption, provided that such foods are not intended for retail sale and are not sold or distributed to the public.

"(g) Publication of List of Participants- The Secretary shall publish and maintain on the Internet Web site of the Food and Drug Administration a current list that includes the name of, location of, and other information deemed necessary by the Secretary about, importers participating under this section.'.

(b) Prohibited Act- Section 301 (21 U.S.C. 331), as amended by section 211, is amended by adding at the end the following:

"(zz) The importation or offering for importation of a food if the importer (as defined in section 805) does not have in place a foreign supplier verification program in compliance with such section 805.'.

(c) Imports- Section 801(a) (21 U.S.C. 381(a)) is amended by adding 'or the importer (as defined in section 805) is in violation of such section 805' after 'or in violation of section 505'.

(d) Effective Date- The amendments made by this section shall take effect 2 years after the date of enactment of this Act.

SEC. 302. VOLUNTARY QUALIFIED IMPORTER PROGRAM.

Chapter VIII (21 U.S.C. 381 et seq.), as amended by section 301, is amended by adding at the end the following:

"SEC. 806. VOLUNTARY QUALIFIED IMPORTER PROGRAM.

"(a) In General- Beginning not later than 18 months after the date of enactment of the FDA Food Safety Modernization Act, the Secretary shall--

"(1) establish a program, in consultation with the Secretary of Homeland Security--

"(A) to provide for the expedited review and importation of food offered for importation by importers who have voluntarily agreed to participate in such program; and

"(B) consistent with section 808, establish a process for the issuance of a facility certification to accompany food offered for importation by importers who have voluntarily agreed to participate in such program; and

"(2) issue a guidance document related to participation in, revocation of such participation in, reinstatement in, and compliance with, such program.

"(b) Voluntary Participation- An importer may request the Secretary to provide for the expedited review and importation of designated foods in accordance with the program established by the Secretary under subsection (a).

"(c) Notice of Intent To Participate- An importer that intends to participate in the program under this section in a fiscal year shall submit a notice and application to the Secretary of such intent at the time and in a manner established by the Secretary.

"(d) Eligibility- Eligibility shall be limited to an importer offering food for importation from a facility that has a certification described in subsection (a). In reviewing the applications and making determinations on such applications, the Secretary shall consider the risk of the food to be imported based on factors, such as the following:

"(1) The known safety risks of the food to be imported.

"(2) The compliance history of foreign suppliers used by the importer, as appropriate.

"(3) The capability of the regulatory system of the country of export to ensure compliance with United States food safety standards for a designated food.

"(4) The compliance of the importer with the requirements of section 805.

"(5) The recordkeeping, testing, inspections and audits of facilities, traceability of articles of food, temperature controls, and sourcing practices of the importer.

"(6) The potential risk for intentional adulteration of the food.

"(7) Any other factor that the Secretary determines appropriate.

"(e) Review and Revocation- Any importer qualified by the Secretary in accordance with the eligibility criteria set forth in this section shall be reevaluated not less often than once every 3 years and the Secretary shall promptly revoke the qualified importer status of any importer found not to be in compliance with such criteria.

"(f) False Statements- Any statement or representation made by an importer to the Secretary shall be subject to section 1001 of title 18, United States Code.

"(g) Definition- For purposes of this section, the term 'importer' means the person that brings food, or causes food to be brought, from a foreign country into the customs territory of the United States.'.

7

Registration of Food Facilities

What Will Managers Need to Know?

The 2010 legislation imposes new aspects to the existing registration requirements. It does not add fees for registration of facilities. This chapter addresses the new requirements for domestic and foreign food facilities. The purposes of registration are simple: "Cut off food contamination problems at their source" was the cry of advocates for these registration provisions. Getting corrective action at the source requires knowledge about the source's location, food type, and other vital statistics.

The focus is to be on safety of growing, processing, and handling food at the food production facility. Both the FDA and the US food distribution industry recognized that they could not possibly afford the equipment and skilled inspectors to inspect enough of the flood of foreign and domestic food shipments. There are not enough inspectors to intercept the various health or safety problems of food that has already been shipped. Congress had a choice. By choosing to reach back into the food production cycle and demand closer scrutiny of the food grower and manufacturer, and of the importing agents, the new Act attempts to control the quality of the conditions at the site from which the food begins its journey. With these additional registration efforts, the food safety advocates expected that they could foster a safer food supply. Congress agreed; time will tell.

How Will Expanded Facility Site Registration Operate?

The existing 2002 law's registrations continue in force, with some modifications and a new enforcement power. During an initial registration period, and every even-numbered year thereafter in the autumn of even-numbered years, each food facility must file a registration with the FDA.[255] Information about the food produced there, the company responsible, the US contact person's name and e-mail address, and other information can be included in the new FDA requirements. The registration must include an assurance that the FDA is allowed to inspect the food facility "in the times and in the manner permitted by this Act."[256]

Food facility registration is an existing requirement, not a new one.[257] The 2002 law[258] adopted after anthrax bioterrorism required registration as a means of tracing poisoned foods. It should be noted that even under pre-2010 requirements, the FDA has been unable to verify the initial registrations of all foreign facilities or whether foreign facilities comply with the requirement to update their registrations if changes are made in the food products.[259] More than half of the food plants sampled by the Inspector General were unaware that updating of registrations was required.[260]

What Facilities Are Exempted or Excluded?

All food facilities are subject to the registration requirements. The House bill, which was not enacted, would have exempted specific categories of food companies.

What If the Company Fails to Register a Site?

If foreign, its food from that facility will be stopped at the US port of entry. The registration numbers are a mandatory part of the "prior notice" paperwork for imports of food products.[261]

---

[255] 21 U.S.C. 350d(a)(3).
[256] S. 510 § 102, 111th Cong. (as reported by the Senate HELP Committee, Nov. 18, 2009).
[257] 21 U.S.C. 350d.
[258] Pub.L. 107-188(2002).
[259] HHS Office of Inspector General, FDA's Food Facility Registry (Dec. 2009), on web at www.oig.hhs.gov/oei/reports/oei-02-08-00060.pdf.
[260] HHS Office of Inspector General, FDA's Food Facility Registry (Dec. 2009), on web at www.oig.hhs.gov/oei/reports/oei-02-08-00060.pdf.
[261] 21 U.S.C. 381(m). The FDA specifically asserted the site registration number is required on the prior notice submission, as a precondition to importation, 73 Fed. Reg. 66350 (Nov. 7, 2008).

What Will Lead To Suspension of Registration or Shutting Down a Site?

The FDA wanted Congress to grant authority to bar the movement of food from unsafe facilities. Detention powers, discussed in Chapter 10, and the traditional seizure[262] and injunction[263] powers take time to implement. In the worst cases, inspections will produce an initial finding by the FDA that the site is so unclean or so potentially subject to contamination that registration must be suspended. After a series of amendments reduced the FDA's requested authority, the standard in new Section 415[264] was set by Congress at a level very comparable to the 2007 amendments' Reportable Food Registry.[265] Now the site registration will be suspended if the FDA finds the food has "a reasonable probability of causing serious adverse health consequences or death to humans or animals" from the conditions at the site.[266] Suspension of the company's ability to have its food shipped interstate or entered into the United States results,[267] so suspension of a food facility registration is a very stiff penalty. Industry lobbying produced an unusual delegation; only the person serving as Commissioner may sign or authorize the suspension (and not the local FDA officials who usually make such decisions).[268]

What Is the New Legal Standard for Suspension of Plant Operations?

The FDA may suspend the registration of a facility for a violation of the FDCA "that could result in serious adverse health consequences or death to humans and animals."

The decision to suspend registration and shut down a food plant asks two alternate questions, answers to either one of which justifies suspension.[269] Did food manufactured, processed, packed, received, or held by this facility

---

[262] 21 U.S.C. 334.
[263] 21 U.S.C. 332. The temporary restraining order option is discussed in 1 James O'Reilly, *Food & Drug Administration* ch. 7 (3d Ed. 2010 Supp.).
[264] 21 U.S.C. 350d(b)(1).
[265] 21 U.S.C. 350f(a)(2).
[266] 21 U.S.C. 350d.
[267] 21 U.S.C. 350d(b)(4).
[268] 21 U.S.C. 350d.
[269] 21 U.S.C. 350d(b).

have a "reasonable probability of causing serious adverse health consequences or death to humans or animals"? If yes, did this facility create, cause, or was otherwise responsible for such reasonable probability? Or, did this facility have "reason to know of, such reasonable probability" of causing serious adverse health consequences or death to humans or animals, but still went ahead and packed, received, or held such food?

Virtually all cases will be in the first category. To get enough evidence to shut down a plant under the second option, the FDA would have to obtain e-mails, admissions, witnesses, or other inside sources about what risk information the company knew at the time it ignored the probable harm and shipped the food. So, assume a peanut plant shipped peanut butter with salmonella that caused deaths. The FDA could suspend registration immediately without notice, by serving a suspension order.[270] Or assume a plant employee called the FDA and said the boss was ignoring lab results showing salmonella. If credible, that would be "reason to know," and suspension could result. (The worker is protected from retaliation under Section 402 of the 2010 Act; see Chapter 14.)

What Can the Company Do to Fight a Suspension?

Not much. The order of suspension comes without notice.[271] The plant is shut down, and the food it shipped is subject to recall or seizure. Managers of the company can expect to complain about the suspension immediately, so the food industry lobbyists put a very urgent response time of two days into the 2010 statutory language on suspension for the requirement for an informal hearing.[272] The FDA then has an indefinite time to decide whether the suspension is really necessary.

If it is determined that the suspension should be maintained, the facility may "submit a corrective action plan to demonstrate how the registrant plans to correct the conditions found." The FDA has up to fourteen days to review such a plan, but has discretion to take longer, "such other time period as determined by the Secretary."

---

[270] 21 U.S.C. 350d(b)(1).
[271] 21 U.S.C. 350d(b).
[272] 21 U.S.C. 350d(b)(2).

What One Individual Can Decide To Undo a Suspension?

The food industry lobbyists made a significant overreach when requesting wording for this provision of the Senate bill, an error they may regret. To hold back industry fears of aggressive local FDA enforcement, the lobbyists for industry requested from Senate staff and won a restricted delegation, a statutory clause that only the Commissioner of the FDA can decide on imposing or removing a food registrant's suspension.[273] This barring of normal delegation of power is unusual, an intriguing twist that may be regretted later by the actual defenders of a facility far away from Washington.

The sponsors of the House bill included language that sought to take power away from local FDA managers, apparently reflecting larger food industry members' desire to centralize all settlement negotiations in Washington. The House bill provided that the authority to suspend or cancel a registration may not be delegated "to any officer or employee other than the Commissioner of Food and Drugs, the Principal Deputy Commissioner, the Associate Commissioner for Regulatory Affairs, or the Director for the Center for Food Safety and Applied Nutrition, of the Food and Drug Administration."[274] In this provision, headquarters approval of the action by one of four people would have been required, making the decision unlike other sanctions under other laws, which FDA district directors can impose. In one respect, this was rationalized by a desire for tighter centralized control of decisions to shut down a facility, to prevent too rapid an FDA decision. But in reality, it reflects the industry's expectation of its greater ability to leverage its influence with Washington executives, when a local FDA official is acting hostile to the particular facility or its local representatives.

The language in the Senate bill as introduced would have allowed "officials" to make those decisions.[275] The bill was amended in the Senate process to

---

[273] 21 U.S.C. 350d(b)(7).

[274] H.R. 2749 § 101, 111th Cong. (as engrossed by House of Representatives, July 30, 2009). This provision was not included in the bill as introduced in the House, but was added by the bill reported out by the House Committee. Compare H.R. 2749 § 101, 111th Cong. (as reported by the House Committee on Energy and Commerce, June 17, 2009) with H.R. 2749 § 101, 111th Cong. (as introduced in House of Representatives, June 8, 2009).

[275] S. 510 § 102, 111th Cong. (as reported by the Senate HELP Committee, Nov. 18, 2009).

go even further, to allow only the Commissioner to have the authority to make a determination on (1) the suspension of a facility's registration and (2) the work needed to remediate the bad conditions found at the facility.[276] This victory for industry will get rather awkward in practice.

The food plant operator "registrant" was given a right to an informal hearing. Under FDA administrative procedures since the 1970s, informal hearings do not involve the presence of the Commissioner.[277] So the person whom the industry lobbying designated as the sole decision-maker will never be at the "informal hearing" about the facility, as a result of this new delegation clause. Expectations of success are few. Even with quick delivery to the FDA district office of terrific exhibits, fine lab work, and honest testimony of renowned experts, all seeking to overcome the suspension, the company can't win a favorable decision in the local informal hearing, because the industry lobbying for the bill wanted suspension decisions centralized.

Time is on the side of the FDA. The facility is closed, and the suspect food cannot enter interstate commerce. The company presents its best case to reopen. Then the paperwork will have to go from the field staff that holds the hearing, through its chain of command, to headquarters. Because a question of public safety was initially involved, FDA middle managers are not likely to rush to undo a safety-related decision that their ultimate boss, the Commissioner, had already made. By contrast, the internal speed of an FDA field manager's claim of a serious public health problem with food is likely to move the pro-suspension paperwork across the Commissioner's desk much faster than the subsequent paperwork dealing with a corporate plea for reopening the facility to resume shipping food.

As a result, a suspension (once the FDA decides to impose it) will be faster to put on than to take off. The two-day deadline for the FDA to offer an informal hearing does not mean the Commissioner himself or herself would conduct the hearing. The Act could have said so, but did not. Instead, there may be a week or more before the non-delegable decision to remove a suspension comes back to the desk of the Commissioner.

---

[276] 21 U.S.C. 350d(b)(7).
[277] 21 C.F.R. 10.

The company may need more time to prepare its defense. While the bill as introduced specified that an informal hearing on a suspension had to be held within two business days of the suspension, the bill as reported by the Senate Committee was amended to allow the Secretary and the registrant the opportunity to agree upon a different time period by which the hearing would be held. (The company will not be given notice that the FDA chief counsel is preparing a temporary restraining order application, as the government usually seeks such orders *ex parte* from the federal district court where the facility or the importing company is located.)

Suspension orders need not be announced in advance. The food company will know that it had a bad outcome to its most recent FDA food inspection, but it won't know whether or when the order of suspension is coming. As soon as the suspension order is received and the shipment of food halts, the company will feel pressure to begin negotiating the corrective plan for removal of the suspension immediately.

The Commissioner has discretionary power, so it would be useless for the plant operator to rush to court without "exhausting administrative remedies." The food company will come to understand that the removal of suspension takes much longer than the company desires, because only one person, the Commissioner, can vacate the suspension, as discussed above. So the delegation clause makes a suspension "easy to put on, but hard to take off."

The FDA Commissioner has been given broad discretion to vacate a suspension, based on a later inspection or adequate corrective measures or at the request of the owner, operator, or agent of the facility, once the violation is corrected. So a court action seeking mandamus would not be available.

When Will This Registration Requirement Go Into Effect?

The bill as introduced did not include a provision stating when the registration requirement would apply, because many food facilities already have registered under the 2003 legislation. But that law did not have a suspension power. The bill as reported by the Senate Committee was amended to subject facilities to the suspension provision on the earlier of two dates: "the date on which the Secretary issues regulations [for the suspension provision]; or 180 days after the date of enactment of the FDA Food Safety Modernization Act" [May 29, 2011].[278] Within 180 days of the issuance of regulations, the FDA must issue guidance for small entity compliance.

What Use Will Be Made of the Facility Registration Number?

The FDA has used registration numbers on import food notifications for years. The FDA proposed to impose a mandatory registration number on all facilities, to improve tracing of contamination causes. Industry efforts to kill a provision that required a unique numerical system were successful; the Government Accountability Office must study costs and benefits of establishing a facility-specific unique identifier.[279] The study will consider established "unique" identifier systems and compatibility with existing systems utilized by Customs.[280]

Currently, when an importer registers with Customs at the time of import, the importer receives an identification number. That number is passed on to the FDA by Customs, and the FDA creates its own identifying number for the importer. An importer may have received multiple identifying numbers over the course of multiple import entries because of minor changes in information when the importer registers a new shipment. For

---

[278] Compare S. 510 § 102, 111th Cong. (as reported by the Senate HELP Committee, Nov. 18, 2009) with S. 510 § 102, 111th Cong. (as introduced in Senate, Mar. 3, 2009).

[279] The bill as reported out by the House Committee did not include a provision requiring the FDA to consult with Customs. Requiring the FDA to work with Customs was added by the amendment in the nature of a substitute to be considered as adopted. H.R. Rep. 111-235, at 2-3 (2009); compare H.R. 2749 § 206, 111th Cong. (as engrossed by House of Representatives, July 30, 2009) with H.R. 2749 § 206 111th Cong. (as reported by the House Committee on Energy and Commerce, passed by House of Representatives, June 17, 2009). When the bill was introduced in the House, the provision required that in the absence of the FDA establishing a unique identifier system by guidance, a Dunn & Bradstreet Universal Numbering System was to be used for the unique identifier system. Compare H.R. 2749 § 206, 111th Cong. (as reported by the House Committee on Energy and Commerce) with H.R. 2749 § 206, 111th Cong. (as introduced in House of Representatives, June 8, 2009).

[280] Prior to the bill as engrossed by the House, this section did not include a provision requiring the FDA to take into account other established unique identifier systems. Compare H.R. 2749 § 206, 111th Cong. (as engrossed by House of Representatives, July 30, 2009) with H.R. 2749 § 206 111th Cong. (as reported by the House Committee on Energy and Commerce, passed by House of Representatives, June 17, 2009).

example, if an importer provides a business address in a slightly different form from its previous registration, the computer will not recognize that the importer already has an identifying number, and the importer will receive a new number. One importing firm was found to have seventy-five identifying numbers.[281] This proliferation in identifying numbers makes it harder for the FDA to keep a record of an importer's historical performance of importing safe food. If the study on this issue is deemed to be fruitful, the FDA will ask again for that authority in later legislation.

Will a Fee Be Collected for Each Registration?

No. Former Section 415(c) did not establish a fee for the earlier sets of facility registrations. The House bill, not adopted into law, had proposed a $500 fee for each registration, beginning in fiscal year 2010. A person who owns or operates multiple facilities would not have had to pay more than $175,000 in registration fees in a single year. Opposition in the Senate killed that fee. So, as Chapter 11 relates, no fees are charged.

How Does the Coverage of Foreign Sites Under the Duty to Register Help U.S. Food Firms?

For the US food executive, adoption of this requirement is generally a net benefit, but with some costs. It levels the playing field, since the foreign-source food producers will be subjected to the same controls as the domestic producers. The US food sites already have registrations with state health or food inspection entities, and the larger sites are already well known to the FDA's district offices. The pre-2010 formalities of registration varied, but the reality is that the food-producing sites inside the United States are known, and the regulator who wishes to find a site could check with US Department of Agriculture Agricultural Marketing Service farm records, FDA district office site inspection records, state food inspection agencies, or local food safety inspectors. That regulator would have enjoyed an easier time finding the sites and food sources, under the House-proposed unique identifier number, if and when the centralized database is up and running. The creation of the central database will speed the FDA response to food crises.

---

[281] GAO, *Food Safety: Agencies Need to Address Gaps in Enforcement and Collaboration to Enhance Safety of Imported Food* 21-22 (2009) [hereinafter *Agencies Need to Address Gaps in Enforcement and Collaboration to Enhance Safety of Imported Food*].

The significant problems to be avoided are the inevitable lag time of communicating a new set of expectations to non-US food entities. These international aspects pose a threat to business continuity for firms that do not have a solid "compliance network" in place. The anticipated problems for plant-level or grower-level sites may delay implementation.[282] These issues include the bureaucratic chores of writing definitions, transmitting the guidance and rules, adopting standardized data entry, filling in and submitting the electronic forms, updating as changes occur, accounting internally for fee payment collections, and so on. These are administrative "back office" hassles that should be surmountable, with trade association, embassy, and farm bureau cooperation.

Far more difficult will be the multi-language, multicultural coordination of each food supplier nation's data collection effort. We assume the US food market continues to be attractive to shippers from Zanzibar to Andorra, despite the additional hassles. One way to implement this portion of the new law would be for national grower organizations and national food entities to bring their constituents into awareness of the new requirements. Each nation will have obligations to educate and coordinate among its growers, processors, and food handlers. Then the FDA will have to enter each of the data points into its system, making for a very challenging information technology requirement.

For the best quality sites, the FDA will expect that ideals of sanitation and food safety will be part of their existing "company culture." Getting other producers up to that level will be part of the international coordination challenge the FDA will face as this section is rolled out.

What Were the Key Controversies in 2009–2010 Drafting?

The registration fee amount and the fee exceptions were the most significant area of dispute during the legislative process. Congressional maneuvering by the various food lobbying teams resulted in elimination of the facility registration fee the House offered.

---

[282] 21 U.S.C. 350d(b)(5); the electronic-only submission requirement is postponed until Dec. 21, 2015, id. at (b)(5)(B).

Registration is an early step of a longer-term process for FDA oversight. Focusing in on site-level food safety improvements at each registered site will be next. For example, a sanitation problem with plant water supplies would be addressed after an inspector evaluates the cause of a liquid contaminant in a beverage. The FDA has amassed a large amount of experience with contaminant sources and pathways. The FDA now has employees stationed in other nations, and the 2010 Act will authorize it to send more.[283] Registered sites for exporting food to the United States will be subjected to more frequent inspections; some portion of the facilities will be found to be deficient. Site problems may be identified when the FDA seeks the source of food contamination. If the actual source of the E. Coli can be identified, the FDA will be in a position to limit the scope of the import alert or conduct a targeted product recall in a limited manner.[284]

What Did the FDA Seek To Gain from These New Powers in the 2010 Legislation?

FDA Commissioner Margaret Hamburg told the House Subcommittee on Health hearing on June 3, 2009, that:

> The draft bill also recognizes the importance of providing FDA with improved access to information. Section 101 requires facilities to register annually, deems products of nonregistered facilities misbranded and consequently prohibits their sale, and allows FDA to modify the food categories that firms provide during registration. These measures will help ensure that the Agency has accurate information about who is making food for American consumers.
>
> . . .
>
> The requirements in this section of the bill represent significant enhancements to FDA's authorities with respect to imported products. At present, importers and brokers are not required to register with FDA. These

---

[283] Pub.L. 111-353 §308.
[284] S. 510 § 102, 111th Cong. (as reported by the Senate HELP Committee, Nov. 18, 2009).

changes will reduce risks to consumers from potentially harmful products by requiring importers to take appropriate steps to protect product safety, and by allowing FDA to take action against importers who do not implement appropriate measures to ensure the safety of the products they import.[285]

How Did Trade Associations Respond?

In a joint letter to the Senate HELP Committee, signed by the National Organic Coalition, the National Farmers Union, the Organic Trade Association, and a number of other national, regional, and local food and agricultural groups just prior to mark-up, the groups urged that:

> A thoughtful and enforceable definition of farm "facilities" will be critical to the Food Safety Modernization Act's effectiveness at decreasing food-borne illness. We propose the bill direct FDA to conduct a formal public notice and comment rulemaking process to revise regulations with respect to what constitutes on-farm manufacturing or processing. In sharp contrast to the current rule enacted to satisfy the narrower considerations of the Bioterrorism Act, this new rule should be established in the context of the pending comprehensive food safety act and should be informed by risk-based analysis of specific activities as they relate to specific foods and distribution systems.

> We also propose that a two track system based on the size and type of a farm's production is the best way to assure the safety of the food system. Farms whose three-year average annual market value of agricultural production is less than $1,000,000, do not co-mingle product, and are not involved in high risk processing activities, should not be classified as facilities but instead tracked to participation in training and technical assistance programs to assist them to develop food

---

[285] Hearing on Food Safety Enhancement Act of 2009, Before the Subcommittee on Health of the H. Committee on Energy and Commerce, 111th Cong. 5 (2009) [hereinafter Hearing on Food Safety Enhancement Act of 2009] (Prepared Statement by Margaret A. Hamburg, Commissioner of FDA, HHS, Rockville, MD).

safety plans. We believe this two track system will result in far better real world food safety outcomes, at less cost, and with less popular opposition, than the one-size-fits-all approach in the bill as introduced.

Under current FDA regulations, which S. 510 does not propose to alter and which H R 2749 as passed would codify into law, any farm is defined as a facility if it either co-mingles products from several farms or does any one of a very wide variety of activities to prepare the product for market including washing, cooling, trimming, labeling, or packaging. These farms, regardless of size or type of production, would be subject to FDA registration, preventive controls, inspections, and, if the House were to prevail, would also be paying special taxes. While current bioterrorism regulations and the pending House food safety bill provide an outright exemption if the farm "facility" direct markets more than 50 percent of the processed food to consumers, this is an inappropriate policy approach. We believe current rules are not only very difficult to enforce, but needlessly overreach and do not result in appreciably improving the safety of the food supply. Instead, their net result instead would be to stave off the growth of value-added agriculture serving the increasing consumer demand for high quality, fresh and local product, doing real harm to family farm survival, rural community economic development, and improved nutrition and food access.[286]

The groups' concerns were not addressed by any amendments to S. 510. Unlike the House bill, the Senate bill did not alter the definition of a facility.

The amendment also added a provision stating that the authority to suspend or cancel a registration may not be delegated by the Secretary "to any officer or employee other than the Commissioner of Food and Drugs, the Principal Deputy Commissioner, the Associate Commissioner for Regulatory Affairs,

---

[286] Letter on Senate Food Safety Bill (S. 510) to members of Senate HELP Committee, National Sustainable Agriculture Coalition, Nov. 16, 2009, http://sustainableagriculture.net/wp-content/uploads/2008/08/Letter-to-HELP-on-S-510-11-16-092.pdf.

or the Director for the Center for Food Safety and Applied Nutrition, of the Food and Drug Administration."[287]

Did the Pre-2010 System Have Problems?

Yes. Tracking backward from illness to source is essential to preventing further consumer illnesses, but it was quite deficient. Federal law since 2002 has required any facility, whether domestic or foreign, that engages in manufacturing, processing, packing, or holding food for consumption in the United States to register with the FDA. In its registration, the facility is to state its name, address, trade name, and the general food category it produces.

If an article of food is being imported or offered for import into the United States by a foreign facility that has not registered with the FDA, the article must be held at the port of entry until the foreign facility registers with the FDA. The facility is not allowed to post a bond that would allow it to import the article prior to registration.[288]

The facility is to notify the FDA on a timely basis if there are any changes to the information provided in its registration.[289] The purpose of the 2002 food legislation was to require food facilities to register so that food recalls could be facilitated, but major gaps exist in the system for registration.

The system has not achieved the original intent. A 2006 FDA survey found that 18.5 percent of information in the database for certain sampled facilities was incorrect.[290] In a government sampling of 130 food sites, five sites were unaware of FDA registration requirements, and more than half of the food facility managers in a sample interviewed by federal auditors were unaware of the updating required for FDA registrations.[291] The news media was critical of the flaws in that system.[292] Due to a high number of foreign facilities and a

---

[287] Compare H.R. 2749 § 101, 111th Cong. (as reported by the House Committee on Energy and Commerce, June 17, 2009) with H.R. 2749 § 101, 111th Cong. (as introduced in House of Representatives, June 8, 2009).

[288] 21 U.S.C. § 381(l) (2009).

[289] 21 U.S.C. § 350d (2009).

[290] HHS Office of Inspector General Report, www.oig.hhs.gov/oei/reports/oei-02-08-00060.pdf, at page 7 (2008).

[291] HHS Office of Inspector General Report, www.oig.hhs.gov/oei/reports/oei-02-08-00060.pdf.

[292] Editorial, *The 76 Million Food Victims*, NEW YORK TIMES A30 (Dec. 20, 2009).

lack of resources, the FDA has been unable to verify either the initial registrations of all foreign facilities, or that foreign facilities comply with the requirement to update their registrations if changes are made in the food produced. As a result, the FDA is working to enlist third-party organizations to visit foreign facilities to verify registration information.[293]

So the 2010 legislation toughens enforcement and makes the system more demanding on the food company. A 2009 federal study found a need for further improvements, some of which are addressed in the 2010 Act.

Matters Debated But Not Adopted

These form part of the history, but not the final content of the 2010 legislation.

Facility Site Registration

The House bill contained three sections on registration that focused on expanding registration coverage, deterring failure to register, and affecting those involved in the food industry. An enforcement case for "misbranding" food could have been brought by the FDA against a firm that has manufactured, processed, packed, or held food in a facility that was subject to, but did not comply with, the registration requirements.[294]

Section 101 of the House bill would have modified the 2002 registration requirements, which require a one-time no-charge registration, to require that all facilities that engage in manufacturing, processing, packing, or holding of food, for the purpose of consumption in the United States or for the purpose of exporting from the United States, renew their registration annually and pay a $500 yearly fee, an amount that will be adjusted with inflation.[295] A person

---

[293] Food and Drug Administration, Consumer Health Information, *FDA Beyond Our Borders*, 2 (2008), www.fda.gov/downloads/ForConsumers/ConsumerUpdates/ucm103044.pdf [hereinafter *FDA Beyond Our Borders*].

[294] H.R. 2749 §§ 101, 204, 205, 111th Cong. (as engrossed by House of Representatives, July 30, 2009).

[295] When the bill was introduced in the House, the fee amount was $1,000. At the mark-up session, an amendment in the nature of a substitute was agreed to by a voice vote that, among other things, lowered the registration fee from $1,000 to $500. H.R. Rep. No. 111-234, at 58 (2009); compare H.R. 2749 § 101 111th Cong. (as reported by the House Committee on Energy and Commerce) with H.R. 2749 § 101 111th Cong. (as introduced in House of Representatives, June 8, 2009).

who owns or operates multiple facilities will not have to pay more than $175,000 in registration fees in a single year.

The section defined a "facility" as, whether domestic or foreign, "any factory, warehouse, or establishment (including a factory, warehouse, or establishment of an importer) that manufactures, processes, packs, or holds food."[296] Each facility that would have been required to register would have had to submit electronically a registration by December 31 of every year.

The section required registrants to provide in the registration the name, address, emergency contact information, all trade names under which the facility conducted food-related business, and the primary purpose and business activity of the facility, including the facility's dates of operation if the facility is open seasonally. The registrant would have been required to provide the general food category being manufactured, processed, packed, or held at the facility and the name, address, and twenty-four-hour contact information of the US distribution agent who has access to the records the bill requires. If the facility were located outside the United States, the name, address, and emergency contact of a US agent for the facility would additionally have been provided. The registration must also have included the unique facility identifier that would have been required by Section 206, and any other information that may have been required by regulation. If there were any changes to the required information, the facility would have been required to notify the FDA no later than thirty days after the change.

Farms, private residences, restaurants, retail food establishments, and non-profit food establishments such as soup kitchens were not considered facilities, and would not have been required to register or pay a fee. A "farm" would have been defined as "an operation in one general physical location devoted to the growing and harvesting of crops, the raising of animals (including seafood), or both."[297] The exclusion for a "farm" covered the following types of farms:

1. An operation where food is packed or held, so long as all the food packed or held on the farm is grown, raised, or consumed on that farm or another farm under the same ownership

---

[296] H.R. 2749 § 101, 111th Cong. (as engrossed by House of Representatives, July 30, 2009).
[297] *Id.*

2. An operation that manufactures or processes food, so long as all the food manufactured or processed is consumed on the farm or another farm under the same ownership

3. An operation with annual sales to consumers that exceed sales to all other buyers

4. An operation that grows, harvests, and manufactures grain or other feedstuff on that farm or on another farm of the same ownership and distributes the grain or other feedstuff to one or more other farms for consumption by humans or animals on those farms

5. A fishery, a term that includes "a wild fishery, an aquaculture operation or bed, a fresh water fishery, and a saltwater fishery"[298]

All of these types of operations would have fallen under the definition of "farm" and were not considered facilities, and thus would not have to register or pay a yearly fee.

Retailers would have been excluded also. A retail food establishment would have included grocery stores, convenience stores, stores that sell animal feed directly to consumers, or vending machine locations if these entities primarily sell food products directly to consumers, meaning that the establishment's sales directly to consumers exceed its sales to other buyers. A retail food establishment would have been considered a facility, and would not have to register or pay the fee.[299]

---

[298] *Id.*

[299] The definitions added by this section in regard to facilities were not in the draft of the bill as reported by the House Committee on Energy and Commerce. According to the Committee report: "The Committee does not intent to alter the FDA's current regulatory definition of 'facility' governing which entities must register. For example, the Committee believes that any storage facility located on a farm does not need to be registered with the FDA if the commodities stored in such facility originate on that farm or another farm under the same ownership." H.R. Rep. No. 111-234, at 45 (2009). The definitions were added by the "amendment in the nature of a substitute to be considered as adopted" and represent a refinement to the current law, which does not exclude private residences from being a facility and does not define the term "farm" or "retail food establishment." Both terms are instead currently defined by regulations. According to the House Report, the "amendment in the nature of a substitute to be considered as adopted:" clarifie[d] who exactly does—and does not—have to register with FDA and pay the annual registration fee. For instance, the substitute amendment provides that farms, including those that process food and feed that they sell to other farms or primarily directly to consumers, do not have to register or pay. In addition, retail food establishments that sell products directly to consumers also do not have to register or pay. H.R. Rep. No. 111-235, at 2-3 (2009); compare H.R. 2749 § 101, 111th Cong. (as engrossed by House of Representatives, July 30, 2009) with H.R. 2749 § 101, 111th Cong. (as reported by the House Committee on Energy and Commerce, June 17, 2009).

Failure to Register a Site

The FDA could have *canceled* a facility registration, after providing at least ten days notice, if the facility did not update the registration in accordance with the Act, or if the registration included false, incomplete, or inaccurate information, or when a facility had not paid the registration fee within thirty days after the due date. If the facility updated or corrected the registration no later than seven days after notice is provided, the FDA could not have canceled the registration.

The FDA may have *suspended* the registration of a facility for a violation of the FDCA "that could result in serious adverse health consequences or death to humans and animals."[300]

Any food "manufactured, processed, packed, or held" in a facility that did not comply with this provision would have been deemed misbranded under 21 U.S.C. § 343.[301]

Fighting a Suspension

The FDA would have been required to give notice before suspension and offer the opportunity to an informal hearing. The FDA could vacate a suspension, based on an inspection or other information or at the request of the owner, operator, or agent of the facility, once the violation was corrected.

The authority to suspend or cancel a registration could not be delegated by the FDA "to any officer or employee other than the Commissioner of Food and Drugs, the Principal Deputy Commissioner, the Associate Commissioner for Regulatory Affairs, or the Director for the Center for Food Safety and Applied Nutrition, of the Food and Drug Administration."[302] In this provision, headquarters approval of the action by one of four people would have been required, making the decision

---

[300] H.R. 2749 § 101, 111th Cong. (as engrossed by House of Representatives, July 30, 2009).
[301] Id.
[302] Id. This provision was not included in the bill as introduced in the House, but was added by the bill reported out by the House Committee. Compare H.R. 2749 § 101, 111th Cong. (as reported by the House Committee on Energy and Commerce, June 17, 2009) with H.R. 2749 § 101, 111th Cong. (as introduced in House of Representatives, June 8, 2009).

unlike other sanctions under other laws, which FDA district directors can impose. In part, this was justified by a desire for tighter centralized control of decisions to shut down a facility. In part, it reflects the industry's ability to lobby and influence Washington executives even when a local FDA official is hostile to the particular site's behaviors.

Facility Registration Numbers

By guidance (a regulation would not have been required) and in consultation with Customs, the FDA would have been required to establish a unique numerical system and to establish the form, manner, and timing of the submission of that unique identifier.[303] The legislation required that the FDA take into account established "unique" identifier systems and consider compatibility with existing systems utilized by Customs.[304]

Upon registration, each facility, importer, and custom broker would have been required to submit a unique facility identifier specific to the facility, or for importers and custom brokers, specific to the principal place of business for which the person is registering. Whenever an importer or custom broker would have imported or offered food for import into the United States, they would have been required to provide the unique facility identifier for the article of food, or the article would have been refused admission.

---

[303] The bill as reported out by the House Committee did not include a provision requiring the FDA to consult with Customs. Requiring the FDA to work with Customs was added by the amendment in the nature of a substitute to be considered as adopted. H.R. Rep. 111-235, at 2-3 (2009); compare H.R. 2749 § 206, 111th Cong. (as engrossed by House of Representatives, July 30, 2009) with H.R. 2749 § 206 111th Cong. (as reported by the House Committee on Energy and Commerce, passed by House of Representatives, June 17, 2009). When the bill was introduced in the House, the provision required that in the absence of the FDA establishing a unique identifier system by guidance, a Dunn & Bradstreet Universal Numbering System was to be used for the unique identifier system. Compare H.R. 2749 § 206, 111th Cong. (as reported by the House Committee on Energy and Commerce) with H.R. 2749 § 206, 111th Cong. (as introduced in House of Representatives, June 8, 2009).

[304] Prior to the bill as engrossed by the House, this section did not include a provision requiring the FDA to take into account other established unique identifier systems. Compare H.R. 2749 § 206, 111th Cong. (as engrossed by House of Representatives, July 30, 2009) with H.R. 2749 § 206 111th Cong. (as reported by the House Committee on Energy and Commerce, passed by House of Representatives, June 17, 2009).

SEC. 102. REGISTRATION OF FOOD FACILITIES.

(a) Updating of Food Category Regulations; Biennial Registration Renewal.--Section 415(a) (21 U.S.C. 350d(a)) is amended--

> *(1) in paragraph (2), by--*

>> *(A) striking "conducts business and" and inserting "conducts business, the e-mail address for the contact person of the facility or, in the case of a foreign facility, the United States agent for the facility, and"; and*

>> *(B) inserting ," or any other food categories as determined appropriate by the Secretary, including by guidance" after "Code of Federal Regulations";*

> *(2) by redesignating paragraphs (3) and (4) as paragraphs (4) and (5), respectively; and*

> *(3) by inserting after paragraph (2) the following:*

>> *"(3) BIENNIAL REGISTRATION RENEWAL.--During the period beginning on October 1 and ending on December 31 of each even-numbered year, a registrant that has submitted a registration under paragraph (1) shall submit to the Secretary a renewal registration containing the information described in paragraph (2). The Secretary shall provide for an abbreviated registration renewal process for any registrant that has not had any changes to such information since the registrant submitted the preceding registration or registration renewal for the facility involved.".*

(b) Suspension of Registration.--

> *(1) IN GENERAL.--Section 415 (21 U.S.C. 350d) is amended--*

(A) in subsection (a)(2), by inserting after the first sentence the following: "The registration shall contain an assurance that the Secretary will be permitted to inspect such facility at the times and in the manner permitted by this Act.";

(B) by redesignating subsections (b) and (c) as subsections (c) and (d), respectively; and

(C) by inserting after subsection (a) the following:

"(b) Suspension of Registration.--

"(1) IN GENERAL.--If the Secretary determines that food manufactured, processed, packed, received, or held by a facility registered under this section has a reasonable probability of causing serious adverse health consequences or death to humans or animals, the Secretary may by order suspend the registration of a facility--

"(A) that created, caused, or was otherwise responsible for such reasonable probability; or

"(B)(i) that knew of, or had reason to know of, such reasonable probability; and

"(ii) packed, received, or held such food.

"(2) HEARING ON SUSPENSION.--The Secretary shall provide the registrant subject to an order under paragraph (1) with an opportunity for an informal hearing, to be held as soon as possible but not later than 2 business days after the issuance of the order or such other time period, as agreed upon by the Secretary and the

registrant, on the actions required for reinstatement of registration and why the registration that is subject to suspension should be reinstated. The Secretary shall reinstate a registration if the Secretary determines, based on evidence presented, that adequate grounds do not exist to continue the suspension of the registration.

"(3) POST-HEARING CORRECTIVE ACTION PLAN; VACATING OF ORDER.--

"(A) CORRECTIVE ACTION PLAN.--If, after providing opportunity for an informal hearing under paragraph (2), the Secretary determines that the suspension of registration remains necessary, the Secretary shall require the registrant to submit a corrective action plan to demonstrate how the registrant plans to correct the conditions found by the Secretary. The Secretary shall review such plan not later than 14 days after the submission of the corrective action plan or such other time period as determined by the Secretary.

"(B) VACATING OF ORDER.-- Upon a determination by the Secretary that adequate grounds do not exist to continue the suspension actions required by the order, or that such actions should be modified, the Secretary shall promptly vacate the order and reinstate the registration of the facility subject to

the order or modify the order, as appropriate.

"(4) EFFECT OF SUSPENSION.--If the registration of a facility is suspended under this subsection, no person shall import or export food into the United States from such facility, offer to import or export food into the United States from such facility, or otherwise introduce food from such facility into interstate or intrastate commerce in the United States.

"(5) REGULATIONS.--

"(A) IN GENERAL.--The Secretary shall promulgate regulations to implement this subsection. The Secretary may promulgate such regulations on an interim final basis.

"(B) REGISTRATION REQUIREMENT.--The Secretary may require that registration under this section be submitted in an electronic format. Such requirement may not take effect before the date that is 5 years after the date of enactment of the FDA Food Safety Modernization Act.

"(6) APPLICATION DATE.--Facilities shall be subject to the requirements of this subsection beginning on the earlier of--

"(A) the date on which the Secretary issues regulations under paragraph (5); or

"(B) 180 days after the date of enactment of the FDA Food Safety Modernization Act.

"(7) NO DELEGATION.--The authority conferred by this subsection to issue an order to suspend a registration or vacate an order of suspension shall not be delegated to any officer or employee other than the Commissioner.".

(2) SMALL ENTITY COMPLIANCE POLICY GUIDE.--Not later than 180 days after the issuance of the regulations promulgated under section 415(b)(5) of the Federal Food, Drug, and Cosmetic Act (as added by this section), the Secretary shall issue a small entity compliance policy guide setting forth in plain language the requirements of such regulations to assist small entities in complying with registration requirements and other activities required under such section.

(3) IMPORTED FOOD.--Section 801(l) (21 U.S.C. 381(l)) is amended by inserting "(or for which a registration has been suspended under such section)" after "section 415".

(c) Clarification of Intent.--

(1) RETAIL FOOD ESTABLISHMENT.--The Secretary shall amend the definition of the term "retail food establishment" in section in 1.227(b)(11) of title 21, Code of Federal Regulations to clarify that, in determining the primary function of an establishment or a retail food establishment under such section, the sale of food products directly to consumers by such establishment and the sale of food directly to consumers by such retail food establishment include--

(A) the sale of such food products or food directly to consumers by such establishment at a roadside stand or farmers' market where such stand or market is located other than where the food was manufactured or processed;

(B) the sale and distribution of such food through a community supported agriculture program; and

(C) the sale and distribution of such food at any other such direct sales platform as determined by the Secretary.

(2) DEFINITIONS.--For purposes of paragraph (1)--

(A) the term "community supported agriculture program" has the same meaning given the term "community supported agriculture (CSA) program" in section 249.2 of title 7, Code of Federal Regulations (or any successor regulation); and

(B) the term "consumer" does not include a business.

(d) Conforming Amendments.--

(1) Section 301(d) (21 U.S.C. 331(d)) is amended by inserting "415," after "404,".

(2) Section 415(d), as redesignated by subsection (b), is amended by adding at the end before the period "for a facility to be registered, except with respect to the reinstatement of a registration that is suspended under subsection (b)".

8

Requirements for Tracing and Recordkeeping of Food Shipments

What Do Managers Need To Know?

No express requirement for food tracing, from source to factory to retailer, was included in the final text of the 2010 Act.

Tracing of the original source of a food product is used when illness breaks out and the root cause of the contamination or infection is being examined. Without tracing data, the current food regulatory system plays "catch-up" each time the wave of illness is associated with food from an unknown source, and the task of tracing the cause takes days or weeks.

Instead, the final Act says the possibility for a future tracing rule will be studied and examined, but it may be years before actual rules are in force. Proponents had called for better FDA food tracing capabilities, so that faster response to food contaminant incidents could be achieved.

But the FDA got more power to require records to be kept. The FDA was given new power to designate "high-risk" foods, by December 2011, and will be required to propose a rule for recordkeeping for the movement of these high-risk foods by December 2012. In turn, aspects of that rule will be vigorously fought by some segments of the food industry, and the final rule may be imposed at some future time.

In the Senate process, the industry opponents of the Act won a partial victory in their ability to block a tracing rule, and in placing thirteen sets of conditions on any future FDA recordkeeping rules, enough to encumber the process for years. Consumer organizations and the FDA had won in the House version, but ultimately got far less than they had expected from the Act's tracing and recordkeeping provisions.

What Will the Tracing Study Requirement Produce?

The 2010 legislation mandates that the FDA conduct two studies with three foods. The FDA must study both processed food and raw agricultural commodities. In the study, the FDA must work in consultation with the USDA and representatives from state departments of health and agriculture to improve the capacity to effectively and rapidly track and trace food, in the event of an outbreak. This mandate for a mere study of a possible future tracing system in the final Act is weaker than and different from the mandate under the House bill. It also depends on funding for the study from the new 112th Congress. The Act, as it progressed through the Senate, became less explicit and more conditional as to the final system the FDA must develop.

The early versions of the bill made a grant of power to the FDA to trace movements of foods, under the House bill's prescriptive system, and this had caused alarm to industry trade associations such as the Food Marketing Institute, the Grocery Manufacturers Association, and the United Fresh Produce Association. The Grocery Manufacturers Association reminded Congress that foods and facilities are widely varied across the industry, and urged that extensive research be completed before the FDA implements specific tracing systems.[305] The Food Marketing Institute urged that the FDA "be allowed to design systems based on the information gathered and not be mandated to develop a specific type of system prior to those efforts."[306] The United Fresh Produce Association was opposed to including in the bill specific parameters for a tracing system, but advocated

---

[305] Hearing on Food Safety Enhancement Act of 2009, Before the Subcommittee on Health of the H. Committee on Energy and Commerce, 111th Cong. 2 (2009) [hereinafter Hearing on Food Safety Enhancement Act of 2009] (Prepared Statement of Pamela Bailey, President of Grocery Manufacturers Association).

[306] Hearing on Food Safety Enhancement Act of 2009, Before the Subcommittee on Health of the H. Committee on Energy and Commerce, 111th Cong. 5 (2009) [hereinafter Hearing on Food Safety Enhancement Act of 2009] (Prepared Statement of Mike Ambrosio, Food Marketing Institute, in Preliminary Transcript).

extensive research by the FDA: "As you weigh various traceability provisions, we urge that Congress set the goal for food traceability, not mandate the process."[307] Critics of the industry view noted that the slow pace of tracing leads to additional cases of the foodborne illness.

In response to this industry effort, the final Act is far less prescriptive in nature. Although it requires the FDA to study the potential for tracing, it does not specify a certain deadline for the identification of the source of a foodborne illness outbreak, nor does it specify the information that must be maintained within a tracing system.

What Is the Timing of FDA Tracing Rules?

Sometime in 2014, there will be a recordkeeping requirement for high-risk foods, and there may be a tracing requirement then or after, but the Act does not fix a date by which final tracing rules must be in place. Both the House bill and the Senate bill spoke of rules on tracing, but neither would specify a date by when the FDA must implement any tracing system. The conditions and complexities placed on the rulemaking obligation will make this a very lengthy rulemaking process, as the opponents intended by their efforts to win Senate exclusions, exemptions, and amendments.

The Act placed timelines by when the FDA must engage in pilot projects and report to Congress. By the end of May 2012, the FDA will report to Congress with recommendations and the results of the pilot studies.[308] The Act requires that the FDA, in coordination with the produce industry, must establish a pilot project with at least three foods, for a tracing system for raw agricultural commodities, and a pilot program for three processed foods.[309] The inclusion of a total of six foods in the pilot projects, as opposed to the single pilot project on fruit and vegetables that would have been required by the House bill, is in response to industry's arguments. Trade associations called for extensive research prior to standards being set for any tracing systems.

---

[307] Hearing on Food Safety Enhancement Act of 2009, Before the Subcommittee on Health of the H. Committee on Energy and Commerce, 111th Cong. 3-4 (2009) [hereinafter Hearing on Food Safety Enhancement Act of 2009] (Prepared Statement of Tom Stenzel, President of United Fresh Produce Association).
[308] Pub.L. 111-353 §204(c)(3).
[309] *Id.* at §204(c)(2).

The goal of the eventual food tracing system should be to allow the FDA, in the event of a foodborne illness outbreak, to quickly identify the source of the outbreak and the recipients of the contaminated food; that goal is likely to be achieved around 2015.[310] The pilot projects must be established within nine months of enactment of the Act, and are to include at least three different types of foods involved in foodborne illness outbreaks within the five-year period preceding the enactment of the Act.[311] Industry trade groups such as the United Fresh Association and the Food Marketing Institute urged Congress to consider efforts that had been voluntarily made through the industry Produce Traceability Initiative.[312]

The FDA is to report to Congress on the findings of the pilot projects and recommendations for a tracing system by the end of May 2012.[313]

Why Must Processed Foods Be Subjected To a Tracing Pilot Project?

In addition to requiring the FDA to investigate the establishment of a tracing system for raw agricultural commodities, the Act requires the FDA to establish a pilot project to explore and develop a tracing system for processed food.[314] Many in the produce industry were opposed to the idea that only produce would be subject to a tracing system, and were likely behind efforts to include this section.[315] The specific processed foods are

---

[310] The bill as reported by the Senate Committee altered the traceback provision by requiring that the FDA conduct at least three pilot programs before making suggestions to Congress on a traceback system. The bill as introduced in the Senate only required one pilot program. Additionally, language was added emphasizing the importance for a speedy identification of a source of an outbreak. Instead of only mandating that the traceback program allow the FDA to "quickly identify" the source of an outbreak, a clause was added stating that the traceback program should enable the FDA to "quickly identify, as soon as practicable," the source of an outbreak. Compare S. 510 § 204, 111th Cong. (as reported by the Senate HELP Committee, Nov. 18, 2009) with S. 510 § 204, 111th Cong. (as introduced in Senate, Mar. 3, 2009).

[311] Pub.L. 111-353 §204(a)(2).

[312] Priority Issues, Food Marketing Institute, www.fmi.org/gr/issues/gr_issues_display.cfm?id=26; Hearing on Food Safety Enhancement Act of 2009, Before the Subcommittee on Health of the H. Committee on Energy and Commerce, 111th Cong. 3-4 (2009) [hereinafter Hearing on Food Safety Enhancement Act of 2009] (Prepared Statement of Tom Stenzel, President of United Fresh Produce Association).

[313] Pub.L. 111-353 §204(a)(3).

[314] "Processed food" is defined by 21 U.S.C. 321(gg).

[315] Tom Karst, *Industry Largely Positive about House Food Safety Bill*, THE PACKER, http://thepacker.com/Industry-largely-positive-about-House-food-safety-bill/Article.aspx?articleid=367499&authorid=117&feedid=215&src=recent.

selected for the purpose of developing and demonstrating methods that are applicable and appropriate for small businesses; and technologies, including existing technologies, that enhance trace-back and trace-forward. The FDA is to report to Congress with the findings of the pilot project and with recommendations on establishing a tracing program for processed foods.[316]

What Are the Increased Recordkeeping Requirements Placed on High-Risk Foods?

Section 204 of the Act empowers the FDA to adopt rules for recordkeeping on high-risk foods. The FDA will make a determination as to whether a food is "high-risk" based on known safety risks, including a food's history of foodborne illness outbreaks and the likelihood of future outbreaks. The FDA may remove foods from the high-risk designation when appropriate.

The rules for high-risk foods will not go into effect immediately. The FDA has up to two years after enactment to provide notice of proposed rules for facilities "that manufacture, process, pack, or hold" high-risk foods, and the effective date for the rules must take into consideration the time required to comply with such requirements. The FDA must hold at least three public meetings in diverse areas to provide an opportunity to gain input from diverse persons prior to proposing rules.

But the rules are subject to a number of mandated requirements.[317] The rules must be science-based. Public health benefits achieved by the imposition of recordkeeping requirement rules must outweigh the costs. The records required will relate only to information reasonably available and appropriate. The rules will not require records to maintain the full pedigree of the food, the recipients of the food beyond the subsequent recipient, or "product tracking to the case level."[318] Further, rules are to be scale-appropriate and are not to prescribe specific technologies, but instead are to allow facilities to use current business systems to the extent appropriate.

---

[316] Pub.L. 111-353 §204(a)(3); *see* S. 510 § 205, 111th Cong. (as reported by the Senate HELP Committee, Nov. 18, 2009).
[317] Pub.L. 111-353 204(d)(1).
[318] Pub.L. 111-353, 204(d)(1)(L).

For facilities that handle more than one food, efforts will be made to minimize the number of different recordkeeping requirements. Waivers may be allowed for facilities that would face economic hardship in complying with the rules. Exceptions will be made for imported foods to take into account international trade obligations.

Protections must be built into the rules to prevent the disclosure of trade secrets or confidential information. The FDA may not require that any records be retained for any longer than two years. Instead, the length of time records are required to be maintained will take into consideration spoilage of food, loss of value, or loss of palatability of the food.

When the system is in place, the availability of food distribution records will assist in the investigation of outbreaks of illness. The bill specifies that nothing in the bill should be construed as allowing the FDA to "prescribe specific technologies for the maintenance of records."[319]

What Limits on FDA Requirements Appear in the New Act?

Although the tracing of a food depends on records about that food, the Act separates recordkeeping from tracing for purposes of the final statutory provisions. New rules will be adopted to require records to be kept.

Certain foods will be exempt from the increased recordkeeping requirements placed on high-risk foods. The FDA may modify the requirements as applied to farms participating in farm-to-school or farm-to-institution programs. Further, any foods produced on farms that have packaging that "maintains the integrity of the product and prevents subsequent contamination or alteration" and labeling that includes the contact information of the farm of origin will also not be subject to the recordkeeping requirements. Despite the fact that farms do not face recordkeeping requirements, the amendments require that farms, upon written notice, comply in a "prompt and reasonable manner" with food safety investigations.[320]

---

[319] *Id.* at 204(d)(1)(C).
[320] *Id.* at 204(f).

Further, no records are required to be kept on foods produced through the use of fishing vessels until the point the food is sold by the operator of the fishing vessel.[321] Comingled raw agricultural commodities,[322] meaning commodities that are combined or mixed after harvesting, but before processing,[323] will be subject to limited recordkeeping requirements. The FDA may exempt other foods where product tracing is not necessary to protect public health. These three categories—food produced on fishing vessels, comingled raw agricultural commodities, and other food exempted by the FDA—however, are subject to minimum recordkeeping requirements. If the person or food is subject to registration under 21 U.S.C. 350d, there must be a record of the previous source of such food and the immediate subsequent recipient of such food.

Grocery stores will not be required to maintain records other than the records documenting the farm that was the source of the food, and will not need to retain these records for longer than 180 days.[324] No records are required to be maintained on food sold by a farm directly to a consumer.[325]

Readers must note that these recordkeeping requirements only apply to high-risk foods. All other foods will be subject to any of the non-high-risk food recordkeeping requirements of 21 U.S.C. 350c.

What Is the Enforcement Mechanism for the Tracing and Recordkeeping Section?

There is no enforcement mechanism for the proposed tracing system or the recordkeeping requirements. FDA Commissioner Hamburg had testified at the Senate HELP Committee hearing on October 22, 2009, that:

> Section 204 (Enhanced Traceback and Recordkeeping) does not include any type of enforcement mechanism. To

---

[321] *Id.* at 204(d)(6)(C).

[322] *Id.* at 204(d)(6)(D)(ii). This does not include fruit and vegetables subject to produce safety standards under new section 419.

[323] *Id.* at 204(d)(2)(D)(ii)(III). "Processing" means the operations that alter the "general state of the commodity, such as canning, cooking, freezing, dehydration, milling, grinding, pasteurization, or homogenization."

[324] *Id.* at 204(d)(6)(G).

[325] *Id.* at 204(d)(6)(H).

encourage compliance and to have consequences for lack of compliance with these important requirements, it is necessary to include an effective enforcement mechanism.[326]

What Had the Pre-2010 Law Been?

This 2010 provision calls for a dramatic increase in tracing responsibility compared to the current system. Since the 2002 bioterrorism legislation, the FDA has required food firms to document the "immediate previous source and…subsequent recipients of food."[327] Because federal surveys of food facilities have demonstrated that many facilities are unaware of the current recordkeeping requirements, and that even more facilities are not in compliance with the requirements, [328] it will probably take some time after adoption of new tracing commands before the food facilities comply with even more exacting traceability requirements.

What Would the Earlier Proposals for a Tracing Rule Have Required, if Adopted?

At the time of the 2010 amendments, it could take the FDA, the Centers for Disease Control, and local officials several weeks to find the source of a serious health problem. The proponents of tracing in Congress wanted to change this problem into an opportunity for tracing higher-risk foods.

The original proposed legislation would have required the FDA to establish by regulation a tracing system for food located within the United States, or for import into the United States, that will enable the identification of "each person who grows, produces, manufactures, processes, packs, transports, holds, or sells such food in as short a timeframe as practicable, but no longer than two business days."[329] Traceability was supposed to be a key

---

[326] Hearing on Keeping America's Families Safe: Reforming the Food Safety System, S. Committee on Health, Education, Labor, and Pensions, 111th Cong. 9, Oct. 22, 2009 (Testimony of FDA Commissioner Hamburg).

[327] 21 U.S.C. 350c(b), Pub.L. 107-188 (2002).

[328] HHS, *Traceability in the Food Supply Chain* 12-17 (2009) [hereinafter *Traceability in the Food Supply Chain*].

[329] H.R. 2749 § 107, 111th Cong. (as engrossed by House of Representatives, July 30, 2009).

improvement in the food safety system that made the 2010 legislation necessary, but lobbying against the tracing powers won out.

The House bill chose not to specify the exact details of the tracing system, but instead entrusted the FDA with designing the program within a framework established by the statute. Before implementing such a system, the FDA would have been required to evaluate the costs, benefits, and feasibility of technologies and methodologies that enable identification of such an extensive background on the handling of each food item. In addition, before proposing regulations to implement this section, the FDA would have been required to hold pilot programs with one or more sectors of the food industry, and to hold public meetings to obtain input and information from different interest groups. The FDA would have been required to coordinate with the USDA in conducting the pilot program; the USDA's food programs include meat and poultry products.

The House bill provisions on establishing a tracing system appear to have resulted from various concerns cited in testimony and by trade associations. Industry asked that the section be less prescriptive with the details of the tracing system. Language was added instructing the FDA to take into account all information learned in public meetings and in the pilot programs required by the bill.

The bill that was passed by the House but not enacted would have provided the FDA the authority, but does not mandate it, to establish systems to maintain certain identifying information—something the bill as introduced in the House had done.[330] This change in language would have allowed the FDA to gather information on establishing successful tracing systems without being tied to specific parameters mandated by the legislation.

The effect of the agricultural lobbying organizations on the Act's exemptions is evident in three special provisions.[331] The FDA would have been required to consider the impact of regulations on farms and to

---

[330] Compare H.R. 2749 § 107, 111th Cong. (as engrossed by House of Representatives, July 30, 2009) with H.R. 2749 § 107, 111th Cong. (as reported by the House Committee on Energy and Commerce, June 17, 2009).

[331] Rory Harrington, *Food Safety Bill Defeated—or Just Delayed*, FOOD QUALITY NEWS, July 30, 2009, www.foodqualitynews.com/Publications/Food-Beverage-Nutrition/FoodProductionDaily.com/Quality-Safety/US-food-safety-bill-defeated-or-just-delayed.

coordinate with the USDA in issuing regulations that apply to farms. Certain types of farms would have been exempt from a tracing system requirement. Food that was produced on a farm and sold directly to a consumer, or to a restaurant or grocery store, would have been exempt from the tracing system requirement.

Another lobbying effort saved fisheries.[332] Food sold by fishing vessels would have been exempt from a tracing system, at least until the point it is sold by the operator of the fishing vessel.[333] The bill as introduced in the House did not exempt any seafood-related industries. Prior to the House bill being reported out by the House Committee, Representative Shadegg introduced and withdrew an amendment to exclude any "fishery (including an oyster bed, a wild fishery, an aquaculture facility, a fresh water fishery, and a salt water fishery)" from the tracing requirement, with the understanding that the House Committee would work on changes to the provision prior to floor vote.[334] Shadegg briefly got his request in the bill as reported by the House Committee, which added a provision exempting fisheries, including oyster beds, wild fisheries, aquaculture facilities, fresh water facilities, and saltwater fisheries. However, the language changed by the time the bill passed the House, and the bill exempted a narrower group of seafood industry players, specifically only fishing vessels, a term that means "any vessel, boat, ship, or other craft which is used for, equipped to be used for, or of a type which is normally used for fishing or aiding or

---

[332] Pub. L. 111-353, §204(d)(6)(C).

[333] The bill as reported by the House Committee exempted a broader group of those involved in the seafood industry. It exempted fisheries, including oyster beds, wild fisheries, aquaculture facilities, fresh water facilities, and saltwater fisheries. The bill as engrossed by the House exempts only fishing vessels, meaning "any vessel, boat, ship, or other craft which is used for, equipped to be used for, or of a type which is normally used for fishing or aiding or assisting one or more vessels at sea in the performance of any activity relating to fishing, including, but not limited to, preparation, supply, storage, refrigeration, transportation, or processing." Compare H.R. 2749 § 107, 111th Cong. (as engrossed by House of Representatives, July 30, 2009) with H.R. 2749 § 107, 111th Cong. (as reported by the House Committee on Energy and Commerce, passed by House of Representatives, June 17, 2009). The bill as introduced in the House did not exempt any seafood-related industries. Additionally the bill as introduced in the House did not limit the recordkeeping requirements of farms, restaurants, or grocery stores. Compare H.R. 2749 § 103, 111th Cong. (as reported by the House Committee on Energy and Commerce, June 17, 2009) with H.R. 2749 § 103, 111th Cong. (as introduced in House of Representatives, June 8, 2009).

[334] Terry Kivian, *Democrats Agree to Scale Back FDA User Fees in Food Safety Bill,* NATIONAL JOURNAL, June 10, 2009.

assisting one or more vessels at sea in the performance of any activity relating to fishing, including, but not limited to, preparation, supply, storage, refrigeration, transportation, or processing."[335]

In addition, the FDA could have exempted other foods or facilities from these requirements, by notice in the Federal Register, if the FDA determines a tracing system for that food "is not necessary to protect the public health."[336] A minimum set of requirements would have applied. A person who "produces, receives, manufactures, processes, packs, transports, distributes, or holds" a food the FDA exempts from this section still would have had to show to inspectors the previous source and the subsequent recipient of the food, as is presently required.[337]

What Did Congressional Sponsors Originally Intend?

According to the sponsor of the House Bill, Representative John Dingell, under this section the "FDA will establish a food trace-back system so that the public health officials can easily determine the source of foodborne disease outbreaks and protect farmers and producers against unwise and inadequate judgments because of lack of personnel and money."[338] The Senate did not wish to fight during the 2010 election year against the food industry, so it instead chose a future study of possible tracing, in the final text of the Act.

What Had the FDA Sought That It Did Not Receive?

Eventually, after tracing powers are confirmed in future legislation, the FDA will use the new powers for penalties, court actions, and import restrictions. According to FDA Commissioner Hamburg at the House Subcommittee on Health hearing on June 3, 2009:

> The requirement in section 107 to implement a product tracing system for food will also provide FDA with

---

[335] Compare H.R. 2749 § 107, 111th Cong. (as engrossed by House of Representatives, July 30, 2009) with H.R. 2749 § 107, 111th Cong. (as reported by the House Committee on Energy and Commerce, June 17, 2009).

[336] H.R. 2749 § 107, 111th Cong. (as engrossed by House of Representatives, July 30, 2009).

[337] H.R. 2749 § 206, 111th Cong. (as engrossed by House of Representatives, July 30, 2009).

[338] 155 Cong. Rec. H9157 (daily ed. July 30, 2009) (Statement of Rep. Dingell).

enhanced information that will help the Agency trace foods more quickly during an outbreak. The current requirement to keep records for the immediate previous source and immediate subsequent recipient (one up, [and] *one* back) requires the Agency to go to each point in the distribution chain during an outbreak to trace the source and distribution of the contaminated product, which is not a sufficiently expedient process when trying to prevent more people from becoming ill. The ability to trace the path of any food, including tomatoes, other fresh produce, and peanut butter, back through every point in the supply chain or forward through the supply chain, is crucial for limiting foodborne illness in an outbreak, for preventing future outbreaks, and for reducing the impact on the segments of the industry whose products were not associated with the illnesses.[339]

Commissioner Hamburg also indicated that the FDA does believe it is important that restaurant owners and small business owners maintain some level of records to facilitate transfer of information on the background of a food item. According to the Commissioner:

I think clearly we want to work with restaurant owners and small businesses in order to make sure that the systems are not too cumbersome, but it is very important that they keep records because if there is a tainted food that is in their facility, the implications for the health of their business as well as for the health of their consumers is very significant indeed. And I think that they would want to be able to assist in sharing their information about where the foods came from so that the traceback can occur and we can identify the source of an outbreak and control it.[340]

---

[339] Hearing on Food Safety Enhancement Act of 2009, Before the Subcommittee on Health of the H. Committee on Energy and Commerce, 111th Cong. 7 (2009) [hereinafter Hearing on Food Safety Enhancement Act of 2009] (Prepared Statement by Margaret A. Hamburg, Commissioner of FDA, HHS, Rockville, MD).

[340] Hearing on Food Safety Enhancement Act of 2009, Before the Subcommittee on Health of the H. Committee on Energy and Commerce, 111th Cong. 138 (2009) [hereinafter Hearing on Food Safety Enhancement Act of 2009] (Statement of FDA Commissioner Hamburg in Preliminary Transcript).

What Have Proponents and Opponents of Food Tracing Said?

The International Foodservice Distributors Association was supportive of retaining the pre-2010 law requirements for companies to retain records of their one supplier and one subsequent recipient, but it testified that the additional tracing requirements proposed by the House bill would put undue stress on its members.[341]

An executive of the American Wholesale Marketers Association told Congress of its concern that the House bill's "expanded FDA trace-back system calls for an expedition of records that is far too draconian, as it would call for an expedition of records allowing the FDA to identify every person in the chain of food distribution within two business days." These expanded recordkeeping and reporting requirements "would significantly impact our members, the majority of whom have nothing to do with food packaging or manufacturing."[342] The Grocery Manufacturers Association urged the FDA to engage in thorough pilot programs to determine that tracing systems are appropriately developed. The association testified that:

> Different products have multiple ingredients such as spices and herbs and we want to make sure enough research is conducted to determine the best way to ensure whether or not our companies will be able to trace all the ingredients within their products. There can be no one-size-fits-all approach to each product and each facility. All our facilities are very much different from each other, as is each product, so there needs to be some variability in the standards that are put in place. The pilot projects will help educate FDA about how varied and different those standards would have to be in order to create traceability systems for the range of products and processes. We want to make sure the language about the studies and pilots remains in the final law that is passed out of Congress.[343]

---

[341] See April Terreri, *Will New FDA Penalties Break your Bank?* FOOD LOGISTICS, Sept. 2009, at 26.

[342] *Id.*

[343] Hearing on Food Safety Enhancement Act of 2009, Before the Subcommittee on Health of the H. Committee on Energy and Commerce, 111th Cong. 9 (2009) [hereinafter Hearing on Food Safety Enhancement Act of 2009] (Prepared Statement by Pamela G. Bailey, President of the Grocery Manufacturers Association).

A representative of the Food Marketing Institute, a trade association that represents food retailers and wholesalers, testified at the House Energy and Commerce Committee's Subcommittee on Health hearing on food safety on June 3, 2009, stating:

> We recognize that collaboration with FDA is necessary to ensure that industry initiatives will better assist in the event of a foodborne illness outbreak. We support the draft's provisions requiring the Secretary to gather information to identify technologies for tracing and to assess the costs and benefits associated with the adoption of such systems, hold public meetings for input and conduct pilot projects when writing regulations. However, we would recommend that the Secretary be allowed to design systems based on the information gathered and not be mandated to develop a specific type of system prior to those efforts.
>
> Current traceability systems do not uniformly meet the needs of industry, the consumer, or government. Enhancing systems that will help minimize the time required to identify, isolate and remove product that may cause injury, illness or adverse health consequences is the most important goal of a traceability system. Development of a stronger food traceability system is not a static process. Technology improvements are being made everyday that improve both information transfer and food processing. Improving traceability is a long term commitment. A number of strong pilot projects addressing the unique needs of a particular product or industry are ongoing and are already resulting in improvements in best practices. One challenge that has been identified that we are working to alleviate is the need to develop consistent industry standards for messaging of data related to product that ensures interoperability among data capture and transfer systems, so that all elements of the supply chain can receive information about the product or commodity in a consistent, timely manner.

We also recommend including retailers in the section allowing direct sales by farms to be exempt from the requirements of the section. Wakefern and many other retailers support local farms in their communities by featuring locally grown produce in their stores in the same manner a local restaurant would make it available to its customers. We would like to be able to continue supporting our local economies and small farmers while also giving the consumer the opportunity to purchase fresh produce grown locally.[344]

Pamela Bailey, president of the Grocery Manufacturers Association, the world's largest trade association, representing more than 300 food, beverage, and consumer product companies, testified at the House Energy and Commerce Committee's Subcommittee on Health hearing on food safety on June 3, 2009:

We recognize that Section 107 of the discussion draft instructs FDA to assess the costs, benefits and feasibility of traceability technologies and gives FDA the power to exempt foods when FDA determines that a tracing system for such food is not necessary to protect public health. Furthermore, we recognize that the discussion draft instructs FDA to conduct pilot projects and public meetings. We believe these studies, public meetings, and pilot projects should be completed *before* FDA decides whether and how to assign the food industry the responsibility for tracking a food product and which coding and identification systems may be best suited for this task. Because many raw ingredients are commingled and blended to smooth out natural farm-to-farm variability, traceability will not always add value as we trace the origin of raw ingredients back to the farm, as the discussion draft implies. As you anticipate in Section

[344] Hearing on Food Safety Enhancement Act of 2009, Before the Subcommittee on Health of the H. Committee on Energy and Commerce, 111th Cong. 5 (2009) [hereinafter Hearing on Food Safety Enhancement Act of 2009] (Prepared Statement of Mike Ambrosio, Food Marketing Institute, in Preliminary Transcript).

107(c)(4)(B), the cost and feasibility of requiring every manufacturer to maintain the full pedigree of every ingredient in every food may outweigh the benefits.

To address concerns raised during the peanut product recall, we propose two important improvements while FDA and the food industry work together to identify additional improvements to our traceability systems. To ensure that food manufacturers know their ingredient suppliers, we suggest that the Committee explore whether to propose that intermediate distributors and brokers include in the labeling of their bulk ingredients the identity of the ingredient supplier. Distributors and brokers can create "blind spots" in the value chain when they fail to pass the identity of an ingredient supplier to their customers. A simple change in labeling rules for bulk ingredients could eliminate these "blind spots" by identifying ingredient suppliers on the label or sending identifying information in a form that accompanies the product, whichever is most practical. In addition, enforcement of the current "one step forward, one step back" systems created by the Bioterrorism Act can be improved in two ways: one, by working with FDA to better communicate industry responsibilities under the Act; and two, by making traceability records available during a routine inspection.[345]

After her testimony, Bailey was asked by Representative DeGette to elaborate on achieving a successful tracing system. Bailey stated:

[T]here is a difference between a single product like a strawberry that is ready to eat versus ingredients that may be co-mingled and...put into additional products... And we saw in the peanut paste problem that when there are

---

[345] Hearing on Food Safety Enhancement Act of 2009, Before the Subcommittee on Health of the H. Committee on Energy and Commerce, 111th Cong. 2 (2009) [hereinafter Hearing on Food Safety Enhancement Act of 2009] (Prepared Statement of Pamela Bailey, President of Grocery Manufacturers Association).

brokers involved, PCA would sell the paste to a broker who would then sell it to an end manufacturer. And that is why we included the recommendation that the distributor label it.

Now, going forward, what we have learned working with our member companies and other areas of the food industry, it can be enormously expensive when you start to deal with co-mingled ingredient commodity products, and that is where we caution. And we think the legislation has it absolutely right. Let us ask FDA to first identify cost/benefit because in the end resources are finite.[346]

In a letter on June 11, 2009, to the House Committee on Energy and Commerce, the American Spice Trade Association took issue with the proposed traceability requirements in the House bill. According to the group, spices that are commingled are impossible to trace. "For example, red peppers and chilies are grown in small batches by thousands of individual farmers, who bring their products to a local market where they are further processed by exporters. And rosemary and oregano are wild herbs grown on mountainsides and collected by local residents, ASTA executive director Cheryl Deem wrote, before being sold to processors and exporters."[347]

In a statement on the Food Marketing Institute website, the group indicated its position on traceability:

The Bio-Terrorism Act requires warehouses and retailers to trace produce one step forward and one step back. However, the 2008 salmonella outbreak and subsequent trace back of tomatoes and jalapeno peppers exposed the difficulty FDA had with going through different forms of records that individual companies used to comply with the

---

[346] Hearing on Food Safety Enhancement Act of 2009, Before the Subcommittee on Health of the H. Committee on Energy and Commerce, 111th Cong. 194 (2009) [hereinafter Hearing on Food Safety Enhancement Act of 2009] (Statement of Pamela Bailey, President of Grocery Manufacturers Association, in Preliminary Transcript).

[347] Peter Cohn, *Panel, Agencies Express Concerns About Food Safety Bill*, NATIONAL JOURNAL'S CONGRESS DAILY, June 23, 2009.

Bio-Terrorism Act. FMI supports language requiring systems that will improve the capability of commodity groups to trace back foods to their source and we believe that the government should require such systems. Each commodity group should be required to create an automated trace back system that is cost-effective and complements current business operations. The FMI Board of Directors has endorsed the industry developed Produce Traceability Initiative that has established industry standards to better trace produce through the supply chain.[348]

Tom Stenzel, president of the United Fresh Produce Association, a trade association representing growers, packers, shippers, fresh-cut processors, distributors, and marketers of fresh fruits and vegetables, testified at the House Energy and Commerce Committee's Subcommittee on Health hearing on food safety on June 3, 2009:

The fresh produce industry is committed to farm-to-fork traceability of our products. As I presented in my detailed testimony before the House Committee on Appropriations Agricultural Subcommittee on March 26 of this year, our industry has underway a massive commitment to a Produce Traceability Initiative (PTI) www.producetraceability.org to provide labeling and electronic traceability for the 6 billion cases of produce that move annually within the United States. This is a massive and extremely expensive long-term undertaking, but it is a commitment made by our industry to drive standardization and efficiency of traceability systems.

However, we are greatly concerned that the prescriptive nature of Section 107 could easily derail these important efforts to bring the most efficient and cost-effective technology to bear on this challenge. As you weigh various traceability provisions, we urge that Congress set the goal

---

[348] Priority Issues, Food Marketing Institute, www.fmi.org/gr/issues/gr_issues_display.cfm?id=26.

for food traceability, not mandate the process. The overly prescriptive mandates in this bill from the top down are not as likely to be as effective as bottom up efficiencies and real-world systems designed for unique challenges.

We also believe this legislation should set a goal for total supply chain traceability across the food industry, not single out individual food categories or processes for traceability. With that overall goal, we believe Congress should then mandate an intensive evaluation of technologies, systems and pilot tests that will truly lead to the end result we all desire—traceability across the entire food supply to determine the source of contamination in any food product. Let's not have Congress start inventing how the mousetrap should work, but instead set the path forward with clear direction that allows industry innovation to flourish.[349]

The United Fresh Produce Association was pleased with the traceability provision as passed by the House, especially that it required the FDA to engage in at least one pilot program. "We feel good about that, because that means they can come sit with us on (the Produce Traceability Initiative) and as long as it accomplishes what we all believe it will, we have a pretty good system already underway," Stenzel said in an article in *The Packer*, an industry newspaper for the produce industry. Additionally, Stenzel noted that committee members favored mandatory traceability: "What this legislation tells us is that there is going to be mandatory traceability—not just for produce but for all foods… Now that everybody realizes it will be mandatory across the industry, we're not going to have to worry that only 50 percent of the industry is going to do [Produce Traceability Initiative]."[350]

---

[349] Hearing on Food Safety Enhancement Act of 2009, Before the Subcommittee on Health of the H. Committee on Energy and Commerce, 111th Cong. 3-4 (2009) [hereinafter Hearing on Food Safety Enhancement Act of 2009] (Prepared Statement of Tom Stenzel, President of United Fresh Produce Association).

[350] Tom Karst, *Industry Largely Positive about House Food Safety Bill*, THE PACKER, http://thepacker.com/Industry-largely-positive-about-House-food-safetybill/Article.aspx? articleid=367499&authorid=117&feedid=215&src=recent.

A representative for the Food Marketing Institute testified at the Senate HELP Committee hearing on October 22, 2009:

> We support the legislation's establishment of pilot projects to test and evaluate new methods for rapidly and effectively tracking fruits and vegetables. Our industry recognizes that current traceability systems are not uniformly meeting the needs of industry, the consumer, and government. Enhancing systems that will help minimize the time required to identify, isolate and remove product that may cause injury, illness or adverse health consequences is the most important goal of a traceability system.
>
> Moving forward, this is not a static process as technology improvements that may revise procedures both on the information side and the food processing side are constantly being updated. Improving traceability is a long term commitment among all commodity groups. The food industry has proactively undertaken a number of strong pilot projects addressing the unique needs of a particular product or industry that are already resulting in improvements in best practices. We understand there will be technical challenges and significant costs associated with the implementation of traceability throughout the supply chain's infrastructure and that is why we see the pilot approach as being critical to developing best practices. Collaboration with FDA is necessary to ensure that industry initiatives will better assist in the event of a food safety outbreak.[351]

In a joint letter to the Senate HELP Committee with the National Organic Coalition, the National Farmers Union, the Organic Trade Association, and

---

[351] Hearing on Keeping America's Families Safe: Reforming the Food Safety System, S. Committee on Health, Education, Labor, and Pensions, 111th Cong. 5-6, Oct. 22, 2009 (Testimony of Michael Roberson, Director of Corporate Quality Assurance, Publix Super Markets Inc. on behalf of the Food Marketing Institute).

a number of other national, regional, and local food and agricultural groups just prior to mark-up, the groups urged that:

> In the case of a food borne illness it is imperative that the cause of the contamination be easily identified. Fruits and vegetables that are produced on a farm and sold directly to a consumer or restaurant or grocery stores are quickly and easily identified and, as in the House bill, should be exempt from new traceability requirements. The Senate bill should adopt that House language and also extend the same treatment to fruits and vegetables that are farm identity-preserved through to the final consumer. The Senate bill should also provide that one up, one down traceability that is already required by the National Organic Program fulfill traceback requirements for certified organic fruits and vegetables that are raw agricultural commodities. We also recommend that the same standard be applied to all other farms subject to traceability requirements.[352]

Text of the Law as Adopted

SEC. 204. ENHANCING TRACKING AND TRACING OF FOOD AND RECORDKEEPING.

(a) Pilot Projects.--

> *(1) IN GENERAL.--Not later than 270 days after the date of enactment of this Act, the Secretary of Health and Human Services (referred to in this section as the "Secretary"), taking into account recommendations from the Secretary of Agriculture and representatives of State departments of health and agriculture, shall establish pilot projects in coordination with the food industry to explore and evaluate methods to rapidly and effectively identify recipients of food to prevent or mitigate a foodborne illness outbreak and to address credible threats of serious adverse health consequences or death to humans or animals as a result of such food being adulterated under section 402 of the Federal Food,*

---

[352] Letter on Senate Food Safety Bill (S. 510) to members of Senate HELP Committee, National Sustainable Agriculture Coalition, Nov. 16, 2009, http://sustainableagriculture.net/wp-content/uploads/2008/08/Letter-to-HELP-on-S-510-11-16-092.pdf.

Drug, and Cosmetic Act (21 U.S.C. 342) or misbranded under section 403(w) of such Act (21 U.S.C. 343(w)).

(2) CONTENT.--The Secretary shall conduct 1 or more pilot projects under paragraph (1) in coordination with the processed food sector and 1 or more such pilot projects in coordination with processors or distributors of fruits and vegetables that are raw agricultural commodities. The Secretary shall ensure that the pilot projects under paragraph (1) reflect the diversity of the food supply and include at least 3 different types of foods that have been the subject of significant outbreaks during the 5-year period preceding the date of enactment of this Act, and are selected in order to--

(A) develop and demonstrate methods for rapid and effective tracking and tracing of foods in a manner that is practicable for facilities of varying sizes, including small businesses;

(B) develop and demonstrate appropriate technologies, including technologies existing on the date of enactment of this Act, that enhance the tracking and tracing of food; and

(C) inform the promulgation of regulations under subsection (d).

(3) REPORT.--Not later than 18 months after the date of enactment of this Act, the Secretary shall report to Congress on the findings of the pilot projects under this subsection together with recommendations for improving the tracking and tracing of food.

(b) Additional Data Gathering.--

(1) IN GENERAL.--The Secretary, in coordination with the Secretary of Agriculture and multiple representatives of State departments of health and agriculture, shall assess--

(A) the costs and benefits associated with the adoption and use of several product tracing technologies, including technologies used in the pilot projects under subsection (a);

(B) *the feasibility of such technologies for different sectors of the food industry, including small businesses; and*

(C) *whether such technologies are compatible with the requirements of this subsection.*

(2) *REQUIREMENTS.--To the extent practicable, in carrying out paragraph (1), the Secretary shall--*

(A) *evaluate domestic and international product tracing practices in commercial use;*

(B) *consider international efforts, including an assessment of whether product tracing requirements developed under this section are compatible with global tracing systems, as appropriate; and*

(C) *consult with a diverse and broad range of experts and stakeholders, including representatives of the food industry, agricultural producers, and nongovernmental organizations that represent the interests of consumers.*

(c) *Product Tracing System.--The Secretary, in consultation with the Secretary of Agriculture, shall, as appropriate, establish within the Food and Drug Administration a product tracing system to receive information that improves the capacity of the Secretary to effectively and rapidly track and trace food that is in the United States or offered for import into the United States. Prior to the establishment of such product tracing system, the Secretary shall examine the results of applicable pilot projects and shall ensure that the activities of such system are adequately supported by the results of such pilot projects.*

(d) *Additional Recordkeeping Requirements for High Risk Foods.--*

(1) *IN GENERAL.--In order to rapidly and effectively identify recipients of a food to prevent or mitigate a foodborne illness outbreak and to address credible threats of serious adverse health consequences or death to humans or animals as a result of such food being adulterated under section 402 of the Federal Food, Drug, and Cosmetic Act or misbranded under section 403(w) of such Act, not later than 2 years after the date of enactment of this Act, the Secretary shall publish a notice of proposed rulemaking to establish*

recordkeeping requirements, in addition to the requirements under section 414 of the Federal Food, Drug, and Cosmetic Act (21 U.S.C. 350c) and subpart J of part 1 of title 21, Code of Federal Regulations (or any successor regulations), for facilities that manufacture, process, pack, or hold foods that the Secretary designates under paragraph (2) as high-risk foods. The Secretary shall set an appropriate effective date of such additional requirements for foods designated as high risk that takes into account the length of time necessary to comply with such requirements. Such requirements shall--

(A) relate only to information that is reasonably available and appropriate;

(B) be science-based;

(C) not prescribe specific technologies for the maintenance of records;

(D) ensure that the public health benefits of imposing additional recordkeeping requirements outweigh the cost of compliance with such requirements;

(E) be scale-appropriate and practicable for facilities of varying sizes and capabilities with respect to costs and recordkeeping burdens, and not require the creation and maintenance of duplicate records where the information is contained in other company records kept in the normal course of business;

(F) minimize the number of different recordkeeping requirements for facilities that handle more than 1 type of food;

(G) to the extent practicable, not require a facility to change business systems to comply with such requirements;

(H) allow any person subject to this subsection to maintain records required under this subsection at a central or reasonably accessible location provided that such records can be made available to the Secretary not later than 24 hours after the Secretary requests such records;

(I) include a process by which the Secretary may issue a waiver of the requirements under this subsection if the Secretary determines that such requirements would result in an economic hardship for an individual facility or a type of facility;

(J) be commensurate with the known safety risks of the designated food;

(K) take into account international trade obligations;

(L) not require--

> *(i) a full pedigree, or a record of the complete previous distribution history of the food from the point of origin of such food;*

> *(ii) records of recipients of a food beyond the immediate subsequent recipient of such food; or*

> *(iii) product tracking to the case level by persons subject to such requirements; and*

(M) include a process by which the Secretary may remove a high-risk food designation developed under paragraph (2) for a food or type of food.

(2) DESIGNATION OF HIGH-RISK FOODS.--

> *(A) IN GENERAL.--Not later than 1 year after the date of enactment of this Act, and thereafter as the Secretary determines necessary, the Secretary shall designate high-risk foods for which the additional recordkeeping requirements described in paragraph (1) are appropriate and necessary to protect the public health. Each such designation shall be based on--*

>> *(i) the known safety risks of a particular food, including the history and severity of foodborne illness outbreaks attributed to such food, taking into consideration foodborne illness*

data collected by the Centers for Disease Control and Prevention;

(ii) the likelihood that a particular food has a high potential risk for microbiological or chemical contamination or would support the growth of pathogenic microorganisms due to the nature of the food or the processes used to produce such food;

(iii) the point in the manufacturing process of the food where contamination is most likely to occur;

(iv) the likelihood of contamination and steps taken during the manufacturing process to reduce the possibility of contamination;

(v) the likelihood that consuming a particular food will result in a foodborne illness due to contamination of the food; and

(vi) the likely or known severity, including health and economic impacts, of a foodborne illness attributed to a particular food.

(B) LIST OF HIGH-RISK FOODS.--At the time the Secretary promulgates the final rules under paragraph (1), the Secretary shall publish the list of the foods designated under subparagraph (A) as high-risk foods on the Internet website of the Food and Drug Administration. The Secretary may update the list to designate new high-risk foods and to remove foods that are no longer deemed to be high-risk foods, provided that each such update to the list is consistent with the requirements of this subsection and notice of such update is published in the Federal Register.

(3) PROTECTION OF SENSITIVE INFORMATION.--In promulgating regulations under this subsection, the Secretary shall take appropriate measures to ensure that there are effective procedures to prevent the unauthorized disclosure of any trade secret or confidential information that is

obtained by the Secretary pursuant to this section, including periodic risk assessment and planning to prevent unauthorized release and controls to--

(A) prevent unauthorized reproduction of trade secret or confidential information;

(B) prevent unauthorized access to trade secret or confidential information; and

(C) maintain records with respect to access by any person to trade secret or confidential information maintained by the agency.

(4) PUBLIC INPUT.--During the comment period in the notice of proposed rulemaking under paragraph (1), the Secretary shall conduct not less than 3 public meetings in diverse geographical areas of the United States to provide persons in different regions an opportunity to comment.

(5) RETENTION OF RECORDS.--Except as otherwise provided in this subsection, the Secretary may require that a facility retain records under this subsection for not more than 2 years, taking into consideration the risk of spoilage, loss of value, or loss of palatability of the applicable food when determining the appropriate timeframes.

(6) LIMITATIONS.--

(A) FARM TO SCHOOL PROGRAMS.--In establishing requirements under this subsection, the Secretary shall, in consultation with the Secretary of Agriculture, consider the impact of requirements on farm to school or farm to institution programs of the Department of Agriculture and other farm to school and farm to institution programs outside such agency, and shall modify the requirements under this subsection, as appropriate, with respect to such programs so that the requirements do not place undue burdens on farm to school or farm to institution programs.

(B) IDENTITY-PRESERVED LABELS WITH RESPECT TO FARM SALES OF FOOD THAT IS PRODUCED AND PACKAGED ON A FARM.--The

requirements under this subsection shall not apply to a food that is produced and packaged on a farm if--

> *(i) the packaging of the food maintains the integrity of the product and prevents subsequent contamination or alteration of the product; and*

> *(ii) the labeling of the food includes the name, complete address (street address, town, State, country, and zip or other postal code), and business phone number of the farm, unless the Secretary waives the requirement to include a business phone number of the farm, as appropriate, in order to accommodate a religious belief of the individual in charge of such farm.*

(C) FISHING VESSELS.--The requirements under this subsection with respect to a food that is produced through the use of a fishing vessel (as defined in section 3(18) of the Magnuson-Stevens Fishery Conservation and Management Act (16 U.S.C. 1802(18))) shall be limited to the requirements under subparagraph (F) until such time as the food is sold by the owner, operator, or agent in charge of such fishing vessel.

(D) COMMINGLED RAW AGRICULTURAL COMMODITIES.--

> *(i) LIMITATION ON EXTENT OF TRACING.--Recordkeeping requirements under this subsection with regard to any commingled raw agricultural commodity shall be limited to the requirements under subparagraph (F).*

> *(ii) DEFINITIONS.--For the purposes of this subparagraph--*

>> *(I) the term "commingled raw agricultural commodity" means any commodity that is combined or mixed after harvesting, but before processing;*

(II) the term "commingled raw agricultural commodity" shall not include types of fruits and vegetables that are raw agricultural commodities for which the Secretary has determined that standards promulgated under section 419 of the Federal Food, Drug, and Cosmetic Act (as added by section 105) would minimize the risk of serious adverse health consequences or death; and

(III) the term "processing" means operations that alter the general state of the commodity, such as canning, cooking, freezing, dehydration, milling, grinding, pasteurization, or homogenization.

(E) EXEMPTION OF OTHER FOODS.--The Secretary may, by notice in the Federal Register, modify the requirements under this subsection with respect to, or exempt a food or a type of facility from, the requirements of this subsection (other than the requirements under subparagraph (F), if applicable) if the Secretary determines that product tracing requirements for such food (such as bulk or commingled ingredients that are intended to be processed to destroy pathogens) or type of facility is not necessary to protect the public health.

(F) RECORDKEEPING REGARDING PREVIOUS SOURCES AND SUBSEQUENT RECIPIENTS.--In the case of a person or food to which a limitation or exemption under subparagraph (C), (D), or (E) applies, if such person, or a person who manufactures, processes, packs, or holds such food, is required to register with the Secretary under section 415 of the Federal Food, Drug, and Cosmetic Act (21 U.S.C. 350d) with respect to the manufacturing, processing, packing, or holding of the applicable food, the Secretary shall require such person to maintain records that identify the immediate previous source of such food and the immediate subsequent recipient of such food.

(G) GROCERY STORES.--With respect to a sale of a food described in subparagraph (H) to a grocery store, the Secretary shall

not require such grocery store to maintain records under this subsection other than records documenting the farm that was the source of such food. The Secretary shall not require that such records be kept for more than 180 days.

*(H) FARM SALES TO CONSUMERS.--*The Secretary shall not require a farm to maintain any distribution records under this subsection with respect to a sale of a food described in subparagraph (I) (including a sale of a food that is produced and packaged on such farm), if such sale is made by the farm directly to a consumer.

(I) SALE OF A FOOD.--A sale of a food described in this subparagraph is a sale of a food in which--

    (i) the food is produced on a farm; and

    (ii) the sale is made by the owner, operator, or agent in charge of such farm directly to a consumer or grocery store.

*(7) NO IMPACT ON NON-HIGH-RISK FOODS.--*The recordkeeping requirements established under paragraph (1) shall have no effect on foods that are not designated by the Secretary under paragraph (2) as high-risk foods. Foods described in the preceding sentence shall be subject solely to the recordkeeping requirements under section 414 of the Federal Food, Drug, and Cosmetic Act (21 U.S.C. 350c) and subpart J of part 1 of title 21, Code of Federal Regulations (or any successor regulations).

(e) Evaluation and Recommendations.--

*(1) REPORT.--*Not later than 1 year after the effective date of the final rule promulgated under subsection (d)(1), the Comptroller General of the United States shall submit to Congress a report, taking into consideration the costs of compliance and other regulatory burdens on small businesses and Federal, State, and local food safety practices and requirements, that evaluates the public health benefits and risks, if any, of limiting--

    (A) the product tracing requirements under subsection (d) to foods identified under paragraph (2) of such subsection, including whether

such requirements provide adequate assurance of traceability in the event of intentional adulteration, including by acts of terrorism; and

(B) the participation of restaurants in the recordkeeping requirements.

(2) DETERMINATION AND RECOMMENDATIONS.--In conducting the evaluation and report under paragraph (1), if the Comptroller General of the United States determines that the limitations described in such paragraph do not adequately protect the public health, the Comptroller General shall submit to Congress recommendations, if appropriate, regarding recordkeeping requirements for restaurants and additional foods, in order to protect the public health.

(f) Farms.--

(1) REQUEST FOR INFORMATION.--Notwithstanding subsection (d), during an active investigation of a foodborne illness outbreak, or if the Secretary determines it is necessary to protect the public health and prevent or mitigate a foodborne illness outbreak, the Secretary, in consultation and coordination with State and local agencies responsible for food safety, as appropriate, may request that the owner, operator, or agent of a farm identify potential immediate recipients, other than consumers, of an article of the food that is the subject of such investigation if the Secretary reasonably believes such article of food--

(A) is adulterated under section 402 of the Federal Food, Drug, and Cosmetic Act;

(B) presents a threat of serious adverse health consequences or death to humans or animals; and

(C) was adulterated as described in subparagraph (A) on a particular farm (as defined in section 1.227 of chapter 21, Code of Federal Regulations (or any successor regulation)).

(2) MANNER OF REQUEST.--In making a request under paragraph (1), the Secretary, in consultation and coordination with State and local agencies responsible for food safety, as appropriate, shall issue a written notice to

the owner, operator, or agent of the farm to which the article of food has been traced. The individual providing such notice shall present to such owner, operator, or agent appropriate credentials and shall deliver such notice at reasonable times and within reasonable limits and in a reasonable manner.

(3) DELIVERY OF INFORMATION REQUESTED.--The owner, operator, or agent of a farm shall deliver the information requested under paragraph (1) in a prompt and reasonable manner. Such information may consist of records kept in the normal course of business, and may be in electronic or non-electronic format.

(4) LIMITATION.--A request made under paragraph (1) shall not include a request for information relating to the finances, pricing of commodities produced, personnel, research, sales (other than information relating to shipping), or other disclosures that may reveal trade secrets or confidential information from the farm to which the article of food has been traced, other than information necessary to identify potential immediate recipients of such food. Section 301(j) of the Federal Food, Drug, and Cosmetic Act and the Freedom of Information Act shall apply with respect to any confidential commercial information that is disclosed to the Food and Drug Administration in the course of responding to a request under paragraph (1).

(5) RECORDS.--Except with respect to identifying potential immediate recipients in response to a request under this subsection, nothing in this subsection shall require the establishment or maintenance by farms of new records.

(g) No Limitation on Commingling of Food.--Nothing in this section shall be construed to authorize the Secretary to impose any limitation on the commingling of food.

(h) Small Entity Compliance Guide.--Not later than 180 days after promulgation of a final rule under subsection (d), the Secretary shall issue a small entity compliance guide setting forth in plain language the requirements of the regulations under such subsection in order to assist small entities, including farms and small businesses, in complying with the recordkeeping requirements under such subsection.

(i) Flexibility for Small Businesses.--Notwithstanding any other provision of law, the regulations promulgated under subsection (d) shall apply--

(1) to small businesses (as defined by the Secretary in section 103, not later than 90 days after the date of enactment of this Act) beginning on the date that is 1 year after the effective date of the final regulations promulgated under subsection (d); and

(2) to very small businesses (as defined by the Secretary in section 103, not later than 90 days after the date of enactment of this Act) beginning on the date that is 2 years after the effective date of the final regulations promulgated under subsection (d).

(j) Enforcement.--

(1) PROHIBITED ACTS.--Section 301(e) (21 U.S.C. 331(e)) is amended by inserting "; or the violation of any recordkeeping requirement under section 204 of the FDA Food Safety Modernization Act (except when such violation is committed by a farm)" before the period at the end.

(2) IMPORTS.--Section 801(a) (21 U.S.C. 381(a)) is amended by inserting "or (4) the recordkeeping requirements under section 204 of the FDA Food Safety Modernization Act (other than the requirements under subsection (f) of such section) have not been complied with regarding such article," in the third sentence before "then such article shall be refused admission".

9

FDA Inspections of Facilities and Records at Food Facilities in the United States and Foreign Nations

What Do Managers Need To Know?

More inspections, of more facilities, in more nations will occur under the 2010 congressional directions to the FDA about its domestic and foreign food program. With many new employees and new powers, the pace and intensity of food inspections is very likely to expand. If your category of food has had safety problems, you will be inspected much more intensely and more frequently than ever before.

Companies can expect that the new inspectors will find more violations and more safety risks. The companies then will pay the FDA for its costs for reinspection. In the worst cases, the inspection problems will be categorized in the FDA's system as "official action indicated," and the company may be forced into a food recall or penalized with civil penalties or court actions. More immediately, the FDA could put the food under temporary "detention" or suspend the registration of the plant, shutting it down.

Supply chains from non-US food sources are especially vulnerable. Many more FDA inspections will be done in non-US jurisdictions. If the foreign food facility refuses inspection by the FDA or its authorized foreign representative, after receiving twenty-four hours' notice or immediately at the door of the facility, the company should stop shipments to the United States, because an electronic notice to the FDA would lead to an import alert, and no food from that facility can enter the United States. When the facility later agrees to inspection, the FDA can charge the costs of the foreign reinspection to the US importer, whether or not the importer had any role in the denial of inspection. If the national government where the food facility is located prevents or prohibits FDA inspection, the food is barred from entry into the United States, and the importer must pay for any subsequent FDA travel and other costs of reinspection. Prudent managers at non-US plants will work with national authorities to make sure they are prepared to participate in the FDA's new wave of vigorous inspections.

What Will Inspections by the FDA Include, After the 2010 Legislation?

Records, especially about contamination hazards and testing results, will be the main focus of the new FDA inspection regime. This chapter and Chapter 2 should be read together, because a review of the food facility's safety plans and hazard analysis required by the new Act will be an important question at the beginning of virtually every inspection. The inspection is not limited to one lot of food that had contamination or infection problems. "Any other article of food that [FDA] reasonably believes is likely to be affected in a similar manner" can be checked if those records are "needed" to help the FDA decide "whether there is a reasonable probability that the use or exposure to the food will cause serious adverse health consequences or death to humans or animals."[353]

Farms and restaurants inside the United States will not be required to accept FDA inspections under the new Act, though they could voluntarily do so. (They must accept local health department and state health or agriculture inspectors, operating under state law.) But all other food handlers are subjected to FDA records inspections related to food safety issues. The FDA can visit the food facility either for a random inspection or for a targeted inspection of records that may be related to a serious adverse effect or death.

The words of the 2010 Act focus on records, allowing the FDA "at reasonable times and within reasonable limits and in a reasonable manner,

---

[353] 21 U.S.C. 350c(a)(2).

to have access to and copy all records."[354] These can be electronic, digital, paper, or other "records." It would be very rare that a food firm would refuse access to records under the highly charged event of an outbreak and contamination issue. If the firm chose to refuse records access, it would face a virtual barrage: suspension of registration for its facility, prevention of further US import shipments, civil penalties, possible court actions, and a bill from the FDA for all reinspections of the facility over the following year. If the FDA field inspector believed the withholding was the result of possible fraud, the FDA's Office of Criminal Investigations would be called in to interrogate the facility managers, possibly leading to a criminal charge against them and the importer.

The importer of food from other nations must allow FDA inspectors, "at all reasonable times" (which has been interpreted to include day or night times when the plant is operating), to inspect the food, including the inspector's option to copy and verify any documents.[355] The prior law[356] gave the FDA broad powers for records inspection, but had reserved a small set of categories, like pricing data, that were not subject to inspection.

How Will the Risk-Based Inspections Operate?

The 2010 legislation calls for the FDA to increase the inspection frequency of all facilities. Domestic high-risk facilities must be inspected at least once within the first five years after the enactment of this Act, and in the succeeding years at least once every third year. All other US food facilities must be inspected at first at seven-year intervals and then at least once every five years.

The FDA will use a risk profile of each facility to determine whether it is a high-risk or non-high-risk facility. Calculating a risk profile will require the FDA to consult the following factors for each facility:[357]

> (A) The known safety risk of the food manufactured, processed, packed, or held at the facility.

---

[354] *Id.*
[355] 21 U.S.C. 374, 21 U.S.C. 350c.
[356] 21 U.S.C. 374, 21 U.S.C. 350c.
[357] Pub.L. 111-353 §201, adding new 421(a)(1)

(B) The facility's compliance history, including with regard to food recalls, outbreaks, and violations of food safety standards.

(C) The rigor and effectiveness of the facility's hazard analysis and risk-based preventive controls.

(D) Whether the food manufactured, processed, packed, handled, prepared, treated, distributed, or stored at the facility meets the criteria for priority under section 801(h)(1) [possible intentional adulteration].

(E) Whether the facility has received a certificate as described in section 809(b). [see Chapter 5 of this text]

(F) Any other criteria deemed necessary and appropriate by the Secretary for purposes of allocating inspection resources.

In the bill as introduced in the Senate, among the list of factors the FDA was to consult in determining risk profiles of facilities was the "facility's history of food recalls, outbreak, and violations of food safety standards." In the bill as reported by the Senate Committee, this language was changed to the facility's "compliance history, including with regard to food recalls, outbreaks, and violations of food safety standards." An additional factor was modified in the bill reported out by the Senate Committee. Instead of only consulting the "rigor of the facility's hazard analysis and risk-based preventive controls," language was added to require consulting the "rigor and *effectiveness*" of the facility's hazard analysis and risk-based preventive controls.

Domestic facilities will be inspected by the FDA, or by state or local officials recognized by the FDA. The Secretary may recognize "Federal, State, and local officials and agencies and representatives of foreign countries" to inspect foreign facilities. Before recognizing federal, state, or local officials, or agencies and representatives of foreign countries, the FDA must determine that the federal, state, or local officials are able to meet standards established by the FDA for conducting inspections, according to the frequency determined by the risk-based schedule. Prior to 2010, about 80 percent of food inspections were performed by local or state health officials, some under contracts with the FDA.

What Are the Details of the Foreign Inspection System?

The 2010 Act will establish clear legal authority for inspections of foreign facilities. The earlier statutory provisions were not clear on that issue.[358] The Act recognizes the creation of a parallel domestic and foreign inspection system. This is a system whereby third-party organizations or counterpart agencies within a country will be certified by the FDA to inspect food intended for sale in the United States, to ensure that it conforms with FDCA requirements.[359] The FDA was empowered to delegate this role for inspection of medical devices in earlier legislation.[360]

The 2010 legislation allows the FDA to "enter into arrangements and agreements with foreign governments to facilitate the inspection of foreign facilities registered under section 415."[361] The FDA must direct resources toward the inspection of "foreign facilities, suppliers, and food types, especially such facilities, suppliers, and food types that present a high risk (as identified by the Secretary), to help ensure the safety and security of the food supply of the United States."[362]

Within the first year after the enactment of the Act, the FDA must inspect no fewer than 600 foreign facilities. In subsequent years, the FDA must inspect twice the number of foreign facilities inspected in the previous year.

Any food that comes from a facility where the owner, operator, or agent, or the government of the country in which the facility is located, "refuses to permit entry of United States inspectors, upon request, to inspect such facility," will be refused admission into the United States.[363] If a request to inspect a facility is refused for longer than twenty-four hours after the

---

[358] Hearing to Review Current Issues in Food Safety: Hearing Before the H. Committee on Agriculture, 111th Cong. 125 (2009) [hereinafter Hearing to Review Current Issues in Food Safety] (Prepared Statement of Michael R. Taylor, J.D. Senior Advisor to the Commissioner, FDA, HHS, Rockville, MD).

[359] FDA, Consumer Health Information, *FDA Beyond Our Borders*, 2 (2008), www.fda.gov/downloads/ForConsumers/ConsumerUpdates/ucm103044.pdf [hereinafter *FDA Beyond Our Borders*].

[360] 21 U.S.C. 374(g). Since 1997, the FDA has allowed accredited private entities to perform some of the FDA investigation functions.

[361] 21 U.S.C. 387(a)(1).

[362] 21 U.S.C. 387(a)(2), added by Pub.L. 111-353 §306 (2010).

[363] 21 U.S.C. 387(b), added by Pub.L. 111-353 §306(2010).

request is made, it will be considered a refusal.[364] It will be necessary for the coordinator of supply chain relations to immediately train the non-US facility operators about the new responsibilities for accepting the FDA or its agents as they implement the expanded systems of inspections.

What Access Must Food Facilities Allow the FDA?

Owners, operators, or agents must allow FDA employees, who have provided written notice, to enter "at reasonable times, any factory, warehouse, or establishment…in which food…are manufactured, processed, packed, or held," for the purpose of consumption of the food in the United States. FDA employees are allowed to inspect, within reasonable times, limits, and manner, the entered premises and "all pertinent equipment, finished and unfinished materials, materials, containers and labeling" within the premises. Existing Sections 704 (physical inspection) and 414 (records inspection) were affected by the changes. This was the baseline for upgrading the inspection powers in the 2010 Act. This language is very broad and allows the FDA to enter and inspect any establishment other than a farm or restaurant where food has been held for consumption in the United States. The 2010 Act will establish clear legal authority for inspections of foreign facilities. The earlier statutory provisions were not clear on that issue.

Under the 2010 Act, every food facility that registers must sign "an assurance that the [FDA] will be permitted to inspect such facility at the times and in the manner permitted by this Act."[365] The registration would be suspended for refusal and the imports would be blocked for "inability to inspect" the foreign site,[366] so very few sophisticated food companies would refuse FDA inspection.

The House bill had proposed that a food will be considered adulterated if a food has been "produced, manufactured, processed, packed, or held in a farm, factory, warehouse, or establishment and the owner, operator, or agent of such farm, factory, warehouse, or establishment…delays or limits

---

[364] 21 U.S.C. 387(b); see S. 510 § 307, 111th Cong. (as reported by the Senate HELP Committee, Nov. 18, 2009).
[365] 21 U.S.C. 350d(a)(2).
[366] 21 U.S.C. 387(b).

an inspection, or refuses to permit entry or inspection, under section 414 or 704 [of the FDCA]."[367] This did not survive into the final Act, but the FDA has other tools available to challenge the uncooperative firm.

What Was the Status of FDA Cooperation with Other Nations on Food Safety Prior to 2010 Law?

FDA Commissioner Margaret Hamburg's October 2009 speech on enforcement announced that the FDA would be "leaning forward" to enforce US food laws in the nations from which the food is exported to American consumers. In an effort to ensure broader compliance by foreign firms of US standards, the FDA increasingly partners with foreign governments to provide guidance on understanding FDA standards, laws, and regulations.[368] In addition, the FDA has over 100 formal agreements with counterpart agencies in twenty-nine other countries, including eighteen with European Union member countries.[369]

These agreements were entered into for the purpose of sharing resources and scientific expertise, and to promote responsible international standards and regulations. The FDA has made another thirty agreements with counterpart agencies in other countries for the purpose of obtaining information that can help the agency in determining the acceptability of imported articles of food and in prioritizing foreign inspection activities.[370]

Historically, the FDA had not been involved in ensuring that foreign facilities comply with US standards, but instead relied on inspections at ports of entry. Under the FDA's "Beyond Our Borders" initiative, the FDA is setting up offices overseas for the purpose of ensuring that facilities in exporting countries produce food that meets US health and safety standards

---

[367] H.R. 2749 § 207, 111th Cong. (as engrossed by House of Representatives, July 30, 2009).

[368] *See* FDA, Consumer Health Information, *FDA Beyond Our Borders*, 2 (2008), www.fda.gov/downloads/ForConsumers/ConsumerUpdates/ucm103044.pdf [hereinafter *FDA Beyond Our Borders*]; David P. Kelly and Lawrence L. Bachorik, *Promoting Public Health and Protecting Consumer in a Global Economy: An Overview of HHS/FDA's International Activities*, 60 FOOD DRUG L.J. 339 (2005).

[369] FDA, Consumer Health Information, *FDA Beyond Our Borders*, 2 (2008), www.fda.gov/downloads/ForConsumers/ConsumerUpdates/ucm103044.pdf [hereinafter *FDA Beyond Our Borders*].

[370] FDA, Consumer Health Information, *FDA Beyond Our Borders*, 2 (2008), www.fda.gov/downloads/ForConsumers/ConsumerUpdates/ucm103044.pdf [hereinafter *FDA Beyond Our Borders*].

by providing technical assistance and conducting inspections. In November 2008, the FDA opened its first overseas office in China. Offices in India and Mexico followed. The FDA plans to use its new statutory authority to open offices in other areas of the world.[371]

The FDA expects that information gained at the international offices, through working with its counterpart regulatory agencies, and through US expatriates' knowledge about local industries, will be passed on to FDA inspectors at US ports of entry and used to determine what shipments should be inspected.[372]

What Is the Dedicated Foreign Inspectorate?

The FDA was given authority "to provide assistance to the appropriate governmental entities of such countries with respect to measures to provide for the safety of articles of food and other products regulated by the Food and Drug Administration exported by such country to the United States, including by directly conducting risk-based inspections of such articles and supporting such inspections by such governmental entity."[373]

How Do FDA Inspections Interact with Third-Party Inspections?

The 2010 legislation recognizes the creation of a parallel domestic and foreign inspection system. This is a system whereby third-party organizations or counterpart agencies within a country will be certified by the FDA to inspect food intended for sale in the United States, to ensure that it conforms to FDCA requirements. The FDA was empowered to delegate this role for inspection of medical devices in earlier legislation.

Must the Company Show Records to the FDA?

The new Act increases the FDA's access to records.[374] Few will dispute the records access, and for those, the FDA can usually claim that a record has

---

[371] S. 510 § 309.
[372] GAO, *Food Safety: Agencies Need to Address Gaps in Enforcement and Collaboration to Enhance Safety of Imported Food* 31 (2009) [hereinafter *Agencies Need to Address Gaps in Enforcement and Collaboration to Enhance Safety of Imported Food*].
[373] S. 510 § 309.
[374] 21 U.S.C. §§350c, 374.

some bearing on a potential violation of the Act.[375] This command of records access includes records access to any hazard analysis or food safety plans required by the legislation.[376] Some disputes may arise. Courts are likely to give the FDA wide latitude in records access, since such broad language has been used in the Act and in its legislative history.

Did the FDA Get the Right to Get Remote Record Requests?

No. The House bill had a provision not included in the final Act. If a record was not required to be immediately available under this provision, the FDA could by letter identify the records to be made available during inspection. This authority should not be construed as permitting a person to refuse to produce required records until the FDA provides notice. The use of these subpoena-like demands was not included in the final Act, but the FDA usually obtains cooperation by phone or letter or e-mail despite the absence of express authority for the requests.

What Is the New Records Access Authority of the FDA?

The FDA's access to records is enlarged by the 2010 legislation. The following provision reflects the 2010 legislation increase in the scope of FDA access to records. The language added by the amendment is in italics:

> If the [FDA] has a reasonable belief that an article of food, *and any other article of food that the[FDA] reasonably believes is likely to be affected in a similar manner, is* adulterated and presents a threat of serious adverse health consequences or death to humans or animals, each person (excluding farms and restaurants) who manufactures, processes, packs, distributes, receives, holds, or imports such article shall, at the request of an officer or employee duly designated by the [FDA], permit such officer or employee, upon presentation of appropriate credentials and a written notice to such person, at reasonable times and within reasonable limits and in a reasonable manner, to have access to and copy all records relating to such article *and to any other article*

---

[375] H.R. 2749 § 106, 111th Cong. (as engrossed by House of Representatives, July 30, 2009).
[376] See text in Chapters 2 and 3.

*of food that the [FDA] reasonably believes is likely to be affected in
a similar manner* that are needed to assist the Secretary in
determining whether the food is adulterated and presents a
threat of serious adverse health consequences or death to
humans or animals.

This preempts the future argument that "Only food in Lot 22 was bad. You
can't see what was in Lot 23." If the FDA "believes that there is a
reasonable probability that the use of or exposure to an article of food, and
any other article of food that the [FDA] reasonably believes is likely to be
affected in a similar manner, will cause serious adverse health consequences
or death to humans or animals, each person (excluding farms and
restaurants) who manufactures, processes, packs, distributes, receives,
holds, or imports" must, "at reasonable times and within reasonable limits
and in a reasonable manner," allow an FDA officer or employee to access
all documents related to the food at issue and any other food "that the
[FDA] reasonably believes is likely to be affected in a similar manner, that
are needed to assist the [FDA] in determining whether there is a reasonable
probability that the use of or exposure to the food will cause serious
adverse health consequences or death to humans or animals."[377] This is full
of discretion and quite favorable to the FDA in a potential court defense by
the company wishing to avoid inspection.

The 2010 amendments preserved a sweeping authority when it modified
existing Section 414(a). Under the prior law, the scope of records the FDA
may request access to had included "all records relating to the manufacture,
processing, packing, distribution, receipt, holding, or importation of such
article maintained by or on behalf of such person in any format (including
paper and electronic formats) and at any location."[378] So the headquarters,
factory, receiving area, storage warehouse, and other areas were all within
"any" location. This was expanded to now also cover the original
"adulterated" food and the 2010 new category of "food of concern" (a food
that may cause serious adverse health effects or death).[379]

---

[377] 21 U.S.C. 350c(a)(2).
[378] 21 U.S.C. 350c(a).
[379] 21 U.S.C. 350c(a)(3).

The House bill had a provision not included in the final Act. If a record was not required to be immediately available under this provision, the FDA could by letter identify the records to be made available during inspection.[380] The use of these subpoena-like demands was not included in the final Act, but the FDA usually obtains cooperation by phone or letter or e-mail despite the absence of express authority for the requests.

Can Improper Import Entry Filings Be Punished?

The FDA can require, by regulation or guidance, that companies submit documentation and information on articles of food imported or offered for import into the United States, as a condition for granting admission of the food into US commerce.[381] The 2010 Act builds upon existing requirements for advance notice of food shipments.[382] Fraud on the FDA regarding imported food triggers criminal investigations, because more false statements cases[383] will be prosecuted as more import submissions are required,[384] and the 2010 Act defines "smuggled" food as "any food that a person introduces into the United States through fraudulent means or with the intent to defraud or mislead."[385] So an importer can trigger a criminal prosecution by manipulating the paperwork in a way that misleads the FDA. Prudent food companies will have an active compliance oversight of the groups responsible for sourcing food in foreign nations. The 2008–2009 melamine poisoning fraud from China that inspired Congress toward adopting the 2010 Act should not recur in the future, at least not among sophisticated firms.

In addition to prosecution risks for false statements in food import documentation, it is also a criminal offense for a third-party auditor to falsely certify or for an accrediting body to falsely accredit an entity.[386] The FDA in some past cases has criminally prosecuted fraud in import paperwork.

---

[380] The bill as introduced in the House did not include authority for the FDA to demand by letter records not immediately available on the commencement of an inspection. Compare H.R. 2749 § 105, 111th Cong. (as reported by the House Committee on Energy and Commerce, June 17, 2009) with H.R. 2749 § 105, 111th Cong. (as introduced in House of Representatives, June 8, 2009).

[381] 21 U.S.C. 381.

[382] 21 C.F.R. §1.279(a).

[383] 18 U.S.C. 1001.

[384] 21 U.S.C. 381(g).

[385] Pub.L. 111-353 §309(e).

[386] 21 U.S.C. 388(e) refers to 18 U.S.C. 1001, false official statements.

The House version that did not become law would have extended liability to customs brokers. But because of efforts against this aspect of the House bill by the brokers' lobbyists, a customs broker who commits such acts will not be subject to the civil penalty section.[387] (Existing Customs procedures and penalties were not altered.)

The implementing regulation, or FDA guidance document that is required by the 2010 law, may specify the mode of submission of any documents. When developing regulations or guidance, the FDA is required to consult with Customs if the collection of documentation will involve the records submitted to Customs.[388] This will probably be an expansion of the existing Customs-FDA sharing on incoming food shipments that occurs with the FDA's databases, OASIS, and the incoming PREDICT electronic data systems.

What Was the Background of These Provisions?

Under the unsuccessful House bill, all food facilities that are required to register would have been divided into three categories, based on their risk of foodborne illness. The House bill would have set a more rigorous timetable for inspections. A high-risk facility that manufactures or processes food would have been randomly inspected at least every six to twelve months.[389] A low-risk facility that manufactures or processes food, or a facility that packs or labels food, would have been randomly inspected at

---

[387] This section was not in the bill as reported out by the House Committee for floor action, but was added into the final House bill as engrossed. Compare H.R. 2749 § 205, 111th Cong. (as engrossed by House of Representatives, July 30, 2009) with H.R. 2749 § 205 111th Cong. (as reported by the House Committee on Energy and Commerce, passed by House of Representatives, June 17, 2009).

[388] The bill as reported out by the House Committee did not command the FDA to consult with Customs if the collection of documentation would involve Customs in developing regulations or guidance. Requiring the FDA to work with Customs was added by the amendment in the nature of a substitute to be considered as adopted. H.R. Rep. 111-235, at 2-3 (2009); compare H.R. 2749 § 105, 111th Cong. (as engrossed by House of Representatives, July 30, 2009) with H.R. 2749 § 105, 111th Cong. (as reported by the House Committee on Energy and Commerce, passed by House of Representatives, June 17, 2009).

[389] The bill as introduced in the House defined a Category 1 facility as "a high-risk facility that manufactures or process raw products of animal origin (including fish and fisheries products) or other food as designated by the [FDA]." These facilities were to be inspected every six to eighteen months. Compare H.R. 2749 § 105, 111th Cong. (as reported by the House Committee on Energy and Commerce, June 17, 2009) with H.R. 2749 § 105, 111th Cong. (as introduced in House of Representatives, June 8, 2009).

least every eighteen months to three years. A facility that merely "holds food" would be randomly inspected at least every five years.[390] The FDA could, by issuing a guidance document (which is easier than adopting a rule), alter the types of facilities within each category. Before modifying the categorization of food facilities, the FDA would have published a notice of the proposed categorization in the Federal Register, and provide sixty days for public comment.[391] (This blurs the distinctions between a "guidance" and a "rule," but was requested by industry to allow more time for input on the new requirements.) The House Committee report indicated that foreign government agency inspectors "will be heavily relied upon" to accomplish the inspections of foreign facilities. The FDA is expected "to recognize agencies and representatives of foreign countries to help fulfill the bill's requirements for inspection frequency."[392]

When the bill was reported by the Senate Committee, the language was changed to require consulting the *compliance* history of an importer, in regard to food recalls, outbreaks, and food safety standard violations, as opposed to the more broad "history of food recalls, outbreaks, and violations of food safety standards of the food importer." Additionally, instead of only consulting the "rigor of the foreign supplier verification program under section 805," the provision was modified to require the FDA to consult the "rigor *and effectiveness* of the foreign supplier verification program under section 805." One additional factor was changed by requiring the FDA to consult not only the "risk profile of the countries of origin and countries of transport of the food imported," as required when the bill was introduced,

---

[390] The bill as introduced in the House required Category 3 facilities to be inspected at least every three to four years. Compare H.R. 2749 § 105, 111th Cong. (as reported by the House Committee on Energy and Commerce, June 17, 2009) with H.R. 2749 § 105, 111th Cong. (as introduced in House of Representatives, June 8, 2009). On the House floor, one representative noted that subjecting grain-storage facilities to FDA inspections puts duplicative burdens on the facilities, since many of these facilities are already subject to USDA grain inspection authority. 155 Cong. Rec. H9133 (daily ed. July 30, 2009) (Statement of Rep. Moran).

[391] The bill as reported out by the House Committee did not include a provision requiring the FDA to publish a notice of the proposed categorization in the Federal Register and provide sixty days for public comment before modifying the categorization of food facilities. Compare H.R. 2749 § 105, 111th Cong. (as engrossed by House of Representatives, July 30, 2009) with H.R. 2749 § 105, 111th Cong. (as reported by the House Committee on Energy and Commerce, June 17, 2009).

[392] H.R. Rep. No. 111-234, at 40 (2009).

but by requiring the FDA to consult the "risk profile of the countries *or regions* of origin and countries of transport of the food imported."[393]

What New Powers Would the Unsuccessful House Bill Have Given?

In the House version that did not become law, once the FDA had a "reasonable belief" that an article of food "presents a serious adverse health consequence or risk of death to humans or animals," the FDA would have had additional authority to access records remotely without on-site inspection.[394] After receiving written notice, each person who "manufactures, processes, packs, transports, distributes, receives, holds, or imports" such food that the FDA determined may be affected, would have been required to submit "all records reasonably related to such article of food as soon as is reasonably practicable."[395] If the documents are available for electronic submission, the person would have been required to submit the records electronically.[396]

For those food facilities that are required to engage in hazard analysis and establish a food safety plan, the FDA may have required the "owner, operator, or agent of such facility to submit to the [FDA], as soon as reasonably practicable after receiving written notice of such requirement, the food safety plan, supporting information relied on by the facility to select the preventive controls to include in its food safety plan, and documentation of corrective actions, if any [were taken] within the preceding two years."[397] If the documents are available for electronic submission, the person would have been required to submit the records electronically.

---

[393] Compare S. 510 § 201, 111th Cong. (as reported by the Senate HELP Committee, Nov. 18, 2009) with S. 510 § 201, 111th Cong. (as introduced in Senate, Mar. 3, 2009) (emphasis added).

[394] This provision was not in the bill as introduced in the House but was adopted by a voice vote after the Chairmen offered a manager's amendment during the mark-up by the House Committee. According to the Committee report, the manager's amendment "clarifies the circumstances under which the [FDA] may access food records remotely." H.R. Rep. No. 111-234, at 58 (2009); Compare H.R. 2749 § 105, 111th Cong. (as reported by the House Committee on Energy and Commerce, June 17, 2009) with H.R. 2749 § 105, 111th Cong. (as introduced in House of Representatives, June 8, 2009).

[395] H.R. 2749 § 106, 111th Cong. (as engrossed by House of Representatives, July 30, 2009).

[396] H.R. 2749 § 106, 111th Cong. (as engrossed by House of Representatives, July 30, 2009).

[397] The bill as introduced in the House did not include authority to demand remote access to food safety plans, a provision later added by the Committee in the bill it reported. Compare H.R. 2749 § 105, 111th Cong. (as reported by the House Committee on Energy and Commerce, June 17, 2009) with H.R. 2749 § 105, 111th Cong. (as introduced in House of Representatives, June 8, 2009).

This section was heavily influenced by the agricultural lobbying groups. It limited FDA records inspection authority relating to farms by mandating access to records on farms in relation to only the following foods:

- A raw agricultural commodity, such as "fruit, vegetable, nut or fungus, subject to a standard"[398]
- A food that "is the subject of an active investigation by the [FDA] of a food borne illness outbreak and is not a grain or similarly handled commodity"[399]

The FDA would have been directed by the House bill to be selective, and to study patterns of past illness outbreaks that had been traced to raw agricultural commodities, then to consult with the USDA, and then to identify by guidance, following notice and public comment, which of the raw agricultural commodities will be subject to this record access provision. Presumably this was intended by the lobbying teams for industry to prevent the FDA from making a rule establishing a total right of access for all vegetables and fruits. The FDA also was to have specified the scope of the records to which it will have access. The Senate version was less prescriptive but also was influenced by the industry efforts.[400]

---

[398] A standard issued under the new authority in Section 419A.

[399] The bill as reported out by the House Committee did not include any provision limiting the record access on farms. In fact, the bill as reported out by the House Committee included authority for FDA employees to enter and inspect farms in which food is "produced, manufactured, processed, packed, or held," for introduction into interstate commerce. The section would have required any person subject to such an inspection to provide access to all required documents as established by the FDA. The section as reported out by the House Committee also included clear language indicating that individuals who produce food (i.e., farmers) would have been required to provide general access to records. Specifically, the general provision on record access would have required every person who "produces, manufactures, processes, packs, transports, distributes, receives, or holds an article of food in the United States or for import into the United States" to permit, "at reasonable times and within reasonable limits and in a reasonable manner," designated officers access and copies of all records bearing on a potential violation of the FDCA. The bill as engrossed by the House removed the word "produces" from the provision, indicating that farmers do not have to provide general record access. At no point during drafting did the provision providing the FDA emergency access to records in the event the FDA has a "reasonable belief" that an article of food "presents a serious adverse health consequence or risk of death to humans or animals" include language that a person who *produces* food would have to comply with the provision. Compare H.R. 2749 § 106, 111th Cong. (as engrossed by House of Representatives, July 30, 2009) with H.R. 2749 § 106, 111th Cong. (as reported by the House Committee on Energy and Commerce, passed by House of Representatives, June 17, 2009).

[400] 21 U.S.C. 350c.

The legislation giving new powers does not limit access to records under other existing statutory authority.

The House version of the legislation required the FDA to establish recordkeeping regulations that cover both establishment and (for no longer than three years) maintenance of records by persons who manufacture, process, pack, transport, distribute, receive, or hold food in the United States or for import into the United States.[401] When the FDA adopted its rules, it was to have taken into account the size of the business in establishing recordkeeping regulations. In addition, the FDA would have been required "to consult with the [USDA] in promulgating regulations with respect to farms...and shall take into account the nature and impact on farms in promulgating such regulations."[402] Provisions on records by restaurants were dropped in the Senate.[403]

Section 105 would have provided the FDA relatively broad power to modify the inspection schedule and the type of food facilities within each category, and did not require the FDA to promulgate regulations to implement the section. The language in the bill allowing the FDA, by

---

[401] In the bill as reported out by the House Committee, the FDA was not required to establish recordkeeping requirements, but was given the authority to, should the FDA decide to. In addition, the FDA was allowed to establish recordkeeping requirements for those who *produce* food (i.e., farmers), in addition to those who "manufacture, process, pack, transport, distribute, receive, or hold food in the United States or for import into the United States." The bill as engrossed by the House does not include in the list of those that will be subject to recordkeeping requirements persons who *produce* food. Although this may indicate that the FDA does not have the authority to promulgate recordkeeping requirements on those that *produce* food, another provision included in the bill as engrossed by the House indicates that Congress does in fact envision the FDA promulgating regulation with respect to farms. Specifically, the bill as engrossed by the House requires the FDA to "consult with the [FDA] of Agriculture in promulgating regulations with respect to farms under this subsection [on recordkeeping requirements] and shall take into account the nature and impact on farms in promulgating such regulations." Compare H.R. 2749 § 105, 111th Cong. (as engrossed by House of Representatives, July 30, 2009) with H.R. 2749 § 105, 111th Cong. (as reported by the House Committee on Energy and Commerce, passed by House of Representatives, June 17, 2009). The bill as introduced in the House allowed the FDA, in drafting regulations for recordkeeping requirements, to require all records to be maintained in a standardized electronic format. This provision was eliminated and not included in the draft as reported out by the House Committee. Compare H.R. 2749 § 105, 111th Cong. (as reported by the House Committee on Energy and Commerce, June 17, 2009) with H.R. 2749 § 105, 111th Cong. (as introduced in House of Representatives, June 8, 2009).

[402] H.R. 2749 § 106, 111th Cong. (as engrossed by House of Representatives, July 30, 2009).

[403] 21 U.S.C. §350c(a)(2).

guidance, to modify the type of food facilities within each category of inspected facilities remained the same through each stage of the drafting of the legislation. The only restriction on this FDA power was added in the bill as passed by the House, which required the FDA to publish a notice of the proposed categorization in the Federal Register and provide sixty days for public comment before modifying the categorization of food facilities.

Minor adjustments were made to the section in the bill as passed by the House qualifying the FDA's power to set the inspection frequency. A provision was added preventing the FDA from modifying the schedule for inspection of Category 1, high-risk facilities and requiring the FDA to wait to alter the inspection frequency of Category 2 and 3 facilities until the FDA had submitted the three-year report and allowed time for public comment. Some House Republicans had expressed concerns about the effect of the inspection schedule on small producers, but were assuaged by these changes adopted as part of the manager's amendment at the mark-up session. Additionally, language was added in the bill as passed by the House instructing the FDA, when making recommendations on altering the inspection schedule, to consider certain science-based factors, including:

- The nature of the food products being processed, stored, or transported
- The manner in which food products are processed, stored, or transported
- The inherent likelihood that the products will contribute to the risk of foodborne illness
- The best available evidence concerning reported illnesses associated with the foods processed, stored, held, or transported in the category of facilities
- The overall record of compliance with food safety law among facilities in the category, including compliance with applicable performance standards and the frequency of recalls

What Had Congress Debated About These Inspections?

Representative Deal pointed out at the House Energy and Commerce Committee's Subcommittee on Health hearing on food safety on June 3, 2009 that the inspection schedule as of that date reflected the consideration of risk profiles, but "fails to address the cost/benefit factor of conducting such frequent inspections and could possibly result in insufficient oversight of certain higher-risk facilities due to time and manpower limitations of our inspectors."[404] Changes to the inspection schedule in the bill as passed by the House appear to address this concern and are a compromise between food safety advocates' pleas for more frequent inspections and Commissioner Hamburg's reminder of limited FDA resources and the need for flexibility. While the inspection schedule for Category 3 facilities did become more relaxed—only every three to five years as opposed to every three to four years as required by the bill as introduced in the House—the inspection schedule for Category 1 facilities was altered to require inspection every six to twelve months, as opposed to six to eighteen months, as the bill as introduced required.[405] Coupled with the FDA's relatively broad power to alter the inspection frequency and modify the type of food facilities within each category, the language as passed encourages increased inspections of high-risk facilities, as advocates desired, while still allowing the FDA the flexibility to make changes as needed.

The House Committee noted in its report on the 2010 legislation that the provision for remote access to records is intended to assist the FDA in ascertaining a facility's food safety program and prioritizing on-site inspections, and it is not intended as a substitute for on-site inspections. The House Committee also acknowledged that large document productions may not be the most efficient method for the FDA to obtain information on a facility, and suggested that the FDA tailor the process to fit its needs.

For example, the House Committee suggested that if the FDA finds that sending a series of questions to a facility is useful prior to requesting access to records, it may do so. The House Committee expects the FDA to identify the records it seeks, when notifying a company of the need for "remote access" to records, to ensure that the "records collection process is properly tailored to assist FDA in its investigation and that the agency will

---

[404] Hearing on Food Safety Enhancement Act of 2009, Before the Subcommittee on Health of the H. Committee on Energy and Commerce, 111th Cong. 9 (2009) [hereinafter Hearing on Food Safety Enhancement Act of 2009] (Opening Statement of Representative Deal in Preliminary Transcript).
[405] Compare H.R. 2749 § 105, 111th Cong. (as reported by the House Committee on Energy and Commerce, June 17, 2009) with H.R. 2749 § 105, 111th Cong. (as introduced in House of Representatives, June 8, 2009).

not waste time sorting through a broader array of records that are not pertinent to its investigation."[406]

The House Committee also noted that it expects companies to comply with an FDA food safety records request "as soon as reasonably practicable." In stating the purpose of the section, the House Committee report noted:

> The Committee's goal is to facilitate good communication between FDA and the company to help FDA determine whether appropriate preventive controls are in place, whether there is a need for additional preventive controls, guidance, or regulations, and what circumstances caused food contamination. This provision should be applied by FDA with that goal in mind.

Some Representatives had remarked on the House floor that this provision will give the FDA too much access to records. The lobbyists worked to protect the grain industry. According to Representative John Dingell, this claim of excessive scope of power is not true: "FDA is already limited in the types of records they can access under the law, and they cannot access financial data, pricing data, personnel data, research data, or sales data other than shipment data regarding sales."[407]

According to Representative Peterson:

> We did have some concerns in the Agriculture Committee that we engaged in some discussions and negotiations with Mr. Dingell and others on the staff of the Energy and Commerce Committee on, and we think we have further improved the bill in terms of how it relates to agriculture. We were able to clarify things in terms of livestock and grain farmers that there was some concern about the language, so that we cleared up some things in terms of performance standards and record keeping.[408]

---

[406] H.R. Rep. No. 111-234, at 49.
[407] 155 Cong. Rec. H9157 (daily ed. July 30, 2009) (statement of Rep. Dingell).
[408] 155 Cong. Rec. H9160 (daily ed. July 30, 2009) (statement of Rep. Peterson).

Prior to the House bill being reported out by the House Committee, Representative Deal introduced and withdrew an amendment calling for the elimination of the standardized electronic format requirements.[409] In the amended bill, as passed by voice vote at the mark-up session, the requirement that records be maintained in an electronic format was eliminated. However, a provision was added stating that if the records requested by the FDA are available in electronic format, they must be submitted electronically.

Some representatives disapproved of the bill's provision on records access as it was reported out of the House Committee, stating that it allowed the "FDA the power to inspect the records of grain farmers and livestock operations. [Representative] Peterson said Dingell had said, 'Don't put FDA on the farm.'"[410] In a letter to the House Energy and Commerce Health Subcommittee in mid-June 2009, the American Farm Bureau Federation and other agribusiness groups expressed opposition to the records access provision included in the bill because, according to them, it allows the FDA to go on a "fishing expedition" of farms' records and release confidential business information.[411]

The bill as reported out by the House Committee did not include any provision limiting the records access on farms. In fact, the bill as reported out by the House Committee included authority for FDA employees to enter and inspect farms in which food is "produced, manufactured, processed, packed, or held" for introduction into interstate commerce. The section would have required any person subject to such an inspection to provide access to all documents required by the FDA.

The section as reported by the House Committee also included clear language indicating that individuals who produce food (i.e., farmers) would have been required to provide general access to records. Specifically, the general provision on record access would have required every person who "produces, manufactures, processes, packs, transports, distributes, receives,

---

[409] Terry Kivian, *Democrats Agree to Scale Back FDA User Fees in Food Safety Bill*, NATIONAL JOURNAL, June 10, 2009.

[410] *Food Safety Bill Expected on House Floor by Friday*, NATIONAL JOURNAL'S CONGRESS DAILY, July 22, 2009.

[411] *Group Blast Waxman Food Safety Bill*, NATIONAL JOURNAL'S HILL BRIEFS, June 15, 2009.

or holds an article of food in the United States or for import into the United States" to permit, "at reasonable times and within reasonable limits and in a reasonable manner," designated officers access to and copies of all records bearing on a potential violation of the FDCA.

These provisions were changed in response to opposition voiced by agribusiness. The bill as engrossed by the House would have limited record inspection authority in regard to farms, as defined by Section 415 of the FDCA, by mandating access to records on farms in relation to only the following foods: a raw agricultural commodity, such as "fruit, vegetable, nut or fungus, subject to a standard issued under section 419A [of the FDCA]," or a food that "is the subject of an active investigation by the Secretary of a food borne illness outbreak and is not a grain or similarly handled commodity." The bill as engrossed by the House removed the word *produces* from the provision listing who must provide general record access to the FDA, indicating that farmers do not have to provide general record access. The Senate and final bills were more restrictive.

Additionally, a provision was added requiring the FDA to "consult with the Secretary of Agriculture in promulgating regulations with respect to farms under this subsection [on recordkeeping requirements] and shall take into account the nature and impact on farms in promulgating such regulations."[412]

Representative Dingell discussed the bill just prior to the House vote:

> Some have expressed concern that FDA will have access to confidential farm records and make them available for distribution. This is not so. FDA is already limited in the types of records they can access under the law, and they cannot access financial data, pricing data, personnel data, research data, or sales data other than shipment data regarding sales.[413]

---

[412] Compare H.R. 2749 § 106, 111th Cong. (as engrossed by House of Representatives, July 30, 2009) with H.R. 2749 § 106, 111th Cong. (as reported by the House Committee on Energy and Commerce, June 17, 2009).
[413] 155 Cong. Rec. H9157 (daily ed. July 30, 2009).

What Was the FDA's View on the Inspection Changes?

At the House Energy and Commerce Committee's Subcommittee on Health hearing on food safety on June 3, 2009, FDA Commissioner Hamburg noted that the inspection schedule included in the bill as of that date would be difficult for the FDA to achieve, and suggested it be modified.

> I think we just have to recognize that this would be an enormous scale-up of activity and that we need the timeframe to enable us to do it right, to recruit the people and train the people to work with industry to develop the systems that work. So we like flexibility in that way, and we would like more general flexibility so that we can learn as we go in terms of the inspection schedule and some of the requirements in that regard.
>
> ...
>
> I would love to be able to sit here and say that FDA could take it on and fully achieve it, but there is a reality of limited resources, both dollar and human. And I think that is where we need some flexibility to really look at the numbers and really also begin to move swiftly in the direction outlined in this bill but also try to learn as we go so that we can find ways to do our inspections in a more efficient targeted way and really focus on the highest risk and really try to leverage other resources to achieve the goals as well through partnership with state and locals, partnership with foreign governments and potentially with third parties that are certified and overseen by the FDA to help us particularly with respect to the burgeoning number of foreign sites for inspection.[414]

---

[414] Hearing on Food Safety Enhancement Act of 2009, Before the Subcommittee on Health of the H. Committee on Energy and Commerce, 111th Cong. 139-40 (2009) [hereinafter Hearing on Food Safety Enhancement Act of 2009] (Statement of FDA Commissioner Hamburg in Preliminary Transcript).

...

Section 105 proposes a rigorous inspection schedule for food facilities, ranging from at least every six to 18 months for high-risk processing facilities, every 18 months to three years for lowrisk processing facilities and food labelers and packers, to every three to four years for warehouses. These requirements start 18 months after enactment. To meet these requirements, section 105 allows the Agency to use inspections conducted by inspectors from recognized State, local, other Federal, and foreign government officials.

FDA would like to raise three issues about section 105.

First, the amount of resources required to achieve these inspection goals would far exceed even the historic increases in the President's FY 2010 budget. It would be difficult, if not impossible, for FDA to hire and train thousands of additional staff so quickly—even while relying on inspections by state, local, and other federal and foreign government officials. As a result, FDA would support modification of these provisions to take into account the operational challenges involved, such as by changing these inspection frequencies.

Second, as we develop a new food safety system, FDA will have better information to guide the Agency's approach to inspection and oversight. We will understand where we must inspect more frequently because of the high risk of certain foods, facilities, and processes. We will also understand where we can protect public health without conducting inspections as frequently. As a result, FDA would support flexibility to modify the inspection requirements based on the best available data on risk.

Third, section 105 could do more to provide flexibility to FDA in meeting the inspection challenge. The draft legislation allows the Agency to rely on inspections by other Federal agencies as well as by state, local, and foreign governments. An additional promising mechanism for international inspections is certification by accredited third parties. FDA would like the flexibility to explore the use of such an accreditation system and audit the performance of accredited third parties. With strong standards and robust oversight by FDA, this approach could help address the oversight challenge posed by the more than 200,000 registered foreign facilities exporting to the United States.[415]

It does not appear that the House took Commissioner Hamburg's remarks into consideration in drafting Section 105. During drafting, the inspection schedule for Category 3 facilities did become more relaxed. Instead of every three to four years as required by the bill as introduced in the House, the bill as reported by the House Committee changed the schedule to once every three to five years. However, the bill does not allow the schedule for inspection of Category 1, high-risk facilities to be modified. In addition, the bill as introduced in the House required inspections of Category 1 facilities every six to eighteen months. The bill as reported by the House Committee requires inspections on a shorter timeframe: once every six to twelve months.[416]

The House bill[417] did not have a provision like the Senate section allowing for inspection by accredited third parties. It should be noted though that a provision was added to the certification program for imports allowing the Secretary to use an "accredited body" to recognize qualified certifying entities. These qualified certifying entities are the entities that will be required to certify that a food complies with the FDCA, if the Secretary requires certification as a condition of import. Thus, in some way, the FDA does have the authority to use accredited parties to help with some oversight of

---

[415] Hearing on Food Safety Enhancement Act of 2009, Before the Subcommittee on Health of the H. Committee on Energy and Commerce, 111th Cong. 8-9 (2009) [hereinafter Hearing on Food Safety Enhancement Act of 2009] (Prepared Statement by Margaret A. Hamburg, Commissioner of FDA, HHS, Rockville, MD).

[416] Compare H.R. 2749 § 105, 111th Cong. (as reported by the House Committee on Energy and Commerce, June 17, 2009) with H.R. 2749 § 105, 111th Cong. (as introduced in House of Representatives, June 8, 2009).

[417] H.R. 2749 (2009).

imported foods, but it does not have that authority specifically in regard to foreign inspections.

On July 16, after the H.R. 2749 had been reported by the House Committee, Michael Taylor, senior adviser to the FDA Commissioner, testified at a Hearing to Review Current Issues in Food Safety at the House Agriculture Committee. According to Taylor:

> Now, for FDA, one of the most important elements of the legislation that is before the Congress that has come out of Energy and Commerce is that it provides a mandate for FDA to achieve specified frequencies of inspection. The legislation also provides a funding source to help FDA fulfill its new responsibilities. A greater investment in inspection is critical to ensuring high rates of compliance with preventive control standards and other food safety performance standards that will help drive improvement in food safety and drive reduced rates of foodborne illness. FDA thus supports the bill's inspection frequencies for domestic facilities.

> However, food imports present a significant resource challenge. FDA plans to increase inspection of foreign food facilities, but we are concerned that the bill's foreign inspection mandate may not result in the best use of FDA's resources in light of the approximately 200,000 registered foreign facilities, and the high cost of overseas inspections.

> We believe we can achieve cost-effective oversight of imports by working with foreign governments, increasing targeted risk-based foreign inspections by FDA, strengthening importer accountability for the safety of the food they import, and supporting strong third party inspections. We think it will take a mix of these initiatives to provide the oversight of imports that we need.[418]

---

[418] Hearing to Review Current Issues in Food Safety: Hearing Before the H. Committee on Agriculture, 111th Cong. 117-18 (2009) [hereinafter Hearing to Review Current Issues in Food Safety] (Prepared Statement of Michael R. Taylor, J.D. Senior Advisor to the Commissioner, FDA, HHS, Rockville, MD).

. . .

Section 105 proposes a rigorous inspection schedule for food facilities, ranging from at least every 6 to 12 months for high-risk processing facilities, every 18 months to 3 years for low-risk processing facilities and food labelers and packers, to at least every 5 years for warehouses. These requirements start 18 months after enactment. To meet these requirements, section 105 allows the agency to use inspections conducted by inspectors from recognized state, local, and other Federal agencies, and foreign government officials.

FDA supports the bill's inspection goals for domestic food facilities. We also welcome the challenge and opportunity provided by the bill to develop and apply the most modern approaches to inspection, including wider use of microbial testing, to verify that companies are meeting their prevention responsibilities and to achieve our public health goals.

We also appreciate the flexibility the bill provides to adjust inspection frequencies based on solid information about where we can achieve the greatest public health benefit through wise use of our finite resources. This flexibility would allow for more frequent inspection of foods, facilities, and processes that we find to be high risk and possibly less frequent inspection of facilities that we can have confidence, based on evidence, pose low risk.

Food imports present a significant resource challenge. It is important that food imports meet the same requirements as domestic products, and we are pleased that the bill provides FDA with new tools to help achieve this, including the requirement that importers observe good importer practices and authorization to require certification of compliance for imported food under certain circumstances. FDA plans to increase inspection of foreign food facilities, but we are concerned that the bill's foreign inspection mandate may not result in the best use of FDA's resources, in light of the approximately 200,000 registered foreign facilities and the high cost of overseas inspections. We think we can achieve cost-effective oversight of imports by working with foreign governments, using the bill's new tools for import oversight, supporting strong third-party inspections, and increasing targeted, risk-based foreign inspections.[419]

The following is an exchange between Taylor and a representative about increasing the safety of imported food:

> *Mr. Moran:* Mr. Chairman, thank you very much. The on-farm performance standards that are being considered in this legislation, a couple of questions. What is the conclusion or the basis that FDA would be the better regulator than USDA in regard to those performance standards? And are those performance standards going to be compatible with what we can expect from foreign producers of agriculture products who import into the United States?
>
> Under current law, meat and poultry, we have some assurance that those meat and poultry products that are coming in are produced under similar standards. It seems to me that we are once again creating a significant competitive disadvantage, increasing costs for production of agriculture in the United States in a sector of our economy that continues to compete with foreign producers.
>
> *Mr. Taylor:* Let me address that second question first. Any standards we set domestically for domestic producers

---

[419] Hearing to Review Current Issues in Food Safety: Hearing Before the H. Committee on Agriculture, 111th Cong. 123 (2009) [hereinafter Hearing to Review Current Issues in Food Safety] (Prepared Statement of Michael R. Taylor, J.D. Senior Advisor to the Commissioner, FDA, HHS, Rockville, MD).

would have to be met by foreign producers. That is an absolute basic principle. We can't have a separate standard for domestic producers.

Mr. Moran: And our ability to ensure that those standards are being met would be what?

Mr. Taylor: Well, if this law were passed, it would be this combination of new authorities and tools that we would have to oversee and ensure compliance with those standards. So it would include working with foreign governments to step up what they do. It would include for the first time FDA clearly having legal authority to inspect foreign facilities and to prevent food coming in if companies overseas have prevented us from inspecting.

We need to look at strengthening, very fundamentally, the importer's duty to manage that supply chain. That is another important part of the puzzle. And third-party certifications done in a rigorous accredited sort of way are all elements of doing this. When you have 200,000 overseas facilities, it is very clear that there is not one sort of simple way to provide the level of assurance that we need. And I agree with you completely. We need that result.

Mr. Moran: Would the US be able to enforce those performance standards in foreign countries?

Mr. Taylor: We would do the enforceability at the point of entry. I mean, one of the elements of this bill is to require the importer to maintain good importer practices, which includes documentation of the controls that are in place overseas and the fact that those products have met our standards, so we have direct authority over the importer.

Plus, the bill would give FDA extraterritorial jurisdiction over violations of the Act so that again we can begin to address those problems upstream. I think that one of the strengths of the bill is that it addresses FDA's need for strengthened legal tools to oversee imports.

Mr. Moran: Are there scientific standards that are accepted globally in regard to food safety?

Mr. Taylor: For some commodities and some hazards, yes, and for some, no. I think in the case of produce this issue of how you set specific, quantitative standards to try to give benchmarks for controlling pathogens, that is a work in progress. We have more work to do with the scientific community, with USDA, with the agricultural community.

We have Good Agricultural Practices, sort of broad guidances and standards; and the industry itself has started to develop specific quantitative metrics for what would be the microbial quality of the water used in irrigation. And we need to move in that direction to use these science-based criteria so we can have objective benchmarks for safety. But that is a work in progress that this bill would really compel FDA to pursue; and, hopefully, we would invest in the science that makes that possible.

Mr. Moran: We have been trying for a long time to utilize scientific-based standards in regard to, for example, meat export, our battles with Japan and Korea and others to accept meat products from the United States. It seems to me it has been very difficult to reach a conclusion, and particularly when there is a competitive advantage or disadvantage based upon that scientific standard.

Mr. Taylor: Right. These are difficult issues, and there are always going to be disputes, and there is a long way to go to harmonize standards internationally. But that is a worthy goal.[420]

---

[420] Hearing to Review Current Issues in Food Safety: Hearing Before the H. Committee on Agriculture, 111th Cong. 125-26 (2009) [hereinafter Hearing to Review Current Issues in Food Safety] (Prepared Statement of Michael R. Taylor, J.D. Senior Advisor to the Commissioner, FDA, HHS, Rockville, MD).

FDA Commissioner Hamburg testified at the Senate HELP Committee hearing on October 22, 2009, that:

> FDA supports the intent of section 201 to require a minimum inspection frequency based on risk. However, we are concerned that the bill does not provide a guaranteed consistent funding source to help FDA fulfill its new responsibilities. The Administration supports inclusion of a registration fee, as provided in the President's Budget for FY 2010, which could be used, in part, to fund this inspection mandate. We also suggest the inclusion of language that provides FDA flexibility to adjust the inspection frequencies. Further, we suggest adding language to authorize FDA to use accredited third parties, such as foreign regulatory agencies, to meet the inspection frequency for foreign facilities.
>
> FDA supports the bill's inspection goals for domestic food facilities. However, food imports present a significant resource challenge. It is important that food imports meet the same requirements as domestic products, and we are pleased that the bill provides FDA with new tools to help ensure they do, including the requirement that importers verify that their foreign suppliers are in compliance and the authorization to require certification of compliance for imported food under certain circumstances.
>
> FDA plans to increase inspection of foreign food facilities, but we are concerned that the bill's foreign inspection mandate may not result in the best use of FDA's resources, in light of the approximately 230,000 registered foreign facilities (as of the beginning of this month) and the high cost of overseas inspections. We think we can achieve cost-effective oversight of imports by working with foreign governments, using the bill's new tools for import oversight, supporting a strong accredited third-party inspection program, and increasing targeted, risk-

based foreign inspections, consistent with the United States' international trade obligations.[421]

What Was the FDA's View on Record Access?

According to FDA Commissioner Hamburg at the Subcommittee on Health hearing on June 3, 2009:

> Section 106 provides FDA with explicit authority to access food records during routine inspections, thereby addressing one of the most significant gaps in FDA's existing authority. The authority provided in this provision is essential to enable FDA to identify problems and require corrections before people become ill. It also enables the Agency to verify during routine inspections that firms are maintaining proper records. Although FDA has routine records access for certain other FDA-regulated products, and USDA has similar authority for the food products it regulates, FDA does not have explicit authority for the vast majority of foods under its jurisdiction. This provision provides FDA with access to critical information to identify problems before an emergency occurs. Under current limited authority, FDA generally only has access to required records during an emergency situation involving serious threats to health or life. Records access and recordkeeping by all persons in the distribution chain are the key mechanisms of providing regulators with information on plant operations, product safety, and product distribution. Such information is necessary to verify compliance and to identify problems.[422]

---

[421] Hearing on Keeping America's Families Safe: Reforming the Food Safety System, S. Committee on Health, Education, Labor, and Pensions, 111th Cong. 9-10, Oct. 22, 2009 (Testimony of FDA Commissioner Hamburg).

[422] Hearing on Food Safety Enhancement Act of 2009, Before the Subcommittee on Health of the H. Committee on Energy and Commerce, 111th Cong. 6. (Prepared Statement by Margaret A. Hamburg, Commissioner of U.S. Food and Drug Administration, Department of Health and Human Services, Rockville, MD).

FDA Commissioner Hamburg has indicated that records access is an important aspect of establishing a safe US food supply. At the House Energy and Commerce Committee's Subcommittee on Health hearing on food safety on June 3, 2009, Hamburg stated:

> I would like to stress that I think access to routine records is extremely important to assuring a safe food supply. It is very important that when inspectors go into a facility, they can examine certain aspects of what have been the procedure during a preceding period of time and not just inspect what is happening at that moment.
>
> ...
>
> We need companies to keep appropriate records, and we need to be able to have it to be able to inform our routine inspectional activities, to be able to work with the companies to make sure that they have adequate preventive controls in place. And we need it certainly in the event of a serious outbreak of public health concern to enable us to swiftly get the information we need for action.

When questioned about whether the records access provisions in the House bill would be sufficient, Commissioner Hamburg responded, "You know I think we would want this to be a dynamic process as we learn more, putting in place the programs and policies and then learning from experience. But I think the bill lays out a very sensible and doable approach."[423]

Changes made to the section by the manager's amendment adopted by voice vote at the mark-up session appear to have been in response to Commissioner Hamburg's emphasis placed on the importance of FDA access to both routine and emergency facility records. A provision was added allowing the FDA to demand remote access to records related to food safety plans and to records when there is a "reasonable belief" that an

---

[423] Hearing on Food Safety Enhancement Act of 2009, Before the Subcommittee on Health of the H. Committee on Energy and Commerce, 111th Cong. 96, 119-20 (2009) [hereinafter Hearing on Food Safety Enhancement Act of 2009] (Statement of FDA Commissioner Hamburg in Preliminary Transcript).

article of food "presents a serious adverse health consequence or risk of death to humans or animals."

Also, FDA Commissioner Hamburg testified at the Senate HELP Committee hearing on October 22, 2009, that S. 510 does not provide the FDA with explicit authority to access food records during routine inspections, one of the key authorities identified by the working group. Routine records access is a critical component of a food safety regulatory framework, and it is one of the most significant gaps in the FDA's existing authority. Although the FDA has routine records access for certain other FDA-regulated products, and the USDA has routine records access for USDA-regulated products, the FDA does not have explicit authority for routine access to records for the vast majority of foods under its jurisdiction. This authority is essential to enable the FDA to identify problems and require corrections before people become ill. Under current limited authority, the FDA generally only has access to required records during an emergency situation involving serious threats to health or life. Routine records access also enables the agency to verify during routine inspections that firms are maintaining the required records. An investigation this year by the HHS Office of Inspector General found significant lapses in compliance with recordkeeping requirements.[424]

What Was the Response from Trade Associations?

The Food Marketing Institute, an association composed of more than 1,500 member companies, both food retailers and wholesalers, that operate in the United States and around the world, endorsed H.R. 2749, but the association was critical of the recordkeeping requirements set by the bill. According to John Billings, director of government relations for the association, "We support the Bioterrorism Act's one-up, one-back process. Since retailers are at the end of the food logistics supply chain, we would be concerned if it was our responsibility to be a data collector for the entire chain."

---

[424] Hearing on Keeping America's Families Safe: Reforming the Food Safety System, S. Committee on Health, Education, Labor, and Pensions, 111th Cong. 6-7, Oct. 22, 2009 (Testimony of FDA Commissioner Hamburg).

According to Jon Eisen, senior vice president of government relations for the International Foodservice Distributors Association:

> While we are supportive of the approach taken, especially in the Senate legislation, I am concerned regarding the additional paperwork and recordkeeping requirements. Most members already have HACCP plans in place and the harsh civil monetary penalties involved for not complying with additional recordkeeping requirements could put undue stress on companies.[425]

A representative of the Food Marketing Institute testified at the House Energy and Commerce Committee's Subcommittee on Health hearing on food safety on June 3, 2009, stating that the institute is:

> pleased to see that Section 105 directs FDA to target its inspection resources based on the risks associated with different types of facilities. For prevention to have the greatest chance of success, particularly with limited resources, resources should be deployed using a risk-based model. In terms of factors to consider for assessing the risk presented by the facility, we are pleased to see that the FDA will be considering whether a facility importing food has been certified in accordance with Section 801 (p). Certification by a qualified certification body can also be used as a factor to assess the risk of domestic food producers and would further assist FDA in targeting its resources based on risk.[426]

Tom Stenzel, president of the United Fresh Produce Association, a trade association representing growers, packers, shippers, fresh-cut processors, distributors, and marketers of fresh fruits and vegetables, testified at the

---

[425] *See* April Terreri, *Will New FDA Penalties Break Your Bank?* FOOD LOGISTICS, Sept. 2009, at 26.

[426] Hearing on Food Safety Enhancement Act of 2009, Before the Subcommittee on Health of the H. Committee on Energy and Commerce, 111th Cong. 4 (2009) [hereinafter Hearing on Food Safety Enhancement Act of 2009] (Prepared Statement of Mike Ambrosio, Food Marketing Insitute, in Preliminary Transcript).

House Energy and Commerce Committee's Subcommittee on Health hearing on food safety on June 3, 2009:

> We support the concept of risk-based inspections, including increased frequency of inspections for certain facilities. However, we believe FDA should be required to complete rulemaking to establish a science-based transparent system for determining classifications for what facilities shall be included in different categories, rather than be left to the Secretary's discretion. In addition, we recommend that the terms "high-risk" and "low-risk" not be used to define category 1 or category 2. Any individual facility can be either a high or low-risk facility based on how it's operated, and there should be no general pejorative terms applied to whole classes of facilities. The statute can require a science-based process for determining appropriate inspection frequency for individual facilities, which may at times vary in risk profile and inspection need.[427]

A representative for the Food Marketing Institute testified at the Senate HELP Committee hearing on October 22, 2009:

> We support directing FDA to allocate limited inspection resources depending on the "risk profile of the facility." The risk of food-borne illness and contamination varies greatly depending on the type of product that the facility produces. For example, at Publix one manufacturing facility may produce bottled water while a different facility produces spinach and artichoke dip. Understandably, the spinach and artichoke dip is comprised of many additional ingredients, requires refrigeration control, and would be considered a food with greater risks than bottled water. We would also encourage that FDA be allowed to develop a

---

[427] Hearing on Food Safety Enhancement Act of 2009, Before the Subcommittee on Health of the H. Committee on Energy and Commerce, 111th Cong. 4 (2009) [hereinafter Hearing on Food Safety Enhancement Act of 2009] (Prepared Statement of Tom Stenzel, President of United Fresh Produce Association).

separate classification for warehouse facilities that only hold foods that are not exposed to the environment as is allowed in Section 103.

In addition, we would encourage FDA be directed to consider the inspections performed by state and local officials. Our retail stores are inspected by state departments of agriculture and local health departments. Our manufacturing facilities and distribution centers are inspected by the USDA, FDA, and state departments of agriculture. With proper training and coordination, we believe that state and local inspections should assist FDA with its responsibilities in a cost-effective and efficient manner.[428]

In a joint letter to the Senate HELP Committee from the National Organic Coalition, the National Farmers Union, the Organic Trade Association, and a number of other national, regional, and local food and agricultural groups just prior to mark-up, the groups urged that:

Farmers are understandably concerned about the prospect of multiple inspectors on their farms. USDA's National Organic Program has developed an accredited inspection system in which organic inspectors, acting as agents of the USDA, annually inspect certified organic farms. We believe these accredited inspectors should be provided the opportunity on a voluntary basis to become accredited food safety inspectors and to combine organic and food safety inspection in a single annual field visit. We urge you to direct FDA and USDA to develop such a mutually advantageous and cost-effective dual inspection system.[429]

---

[428] Hearing on Keeping America's Families Safe: Reforming the Food Safety System, S. Committee on Health, Education, Labor, and Pensions, 111th Cong. 5, Oct. 22, 2009 (Testimony of Michael Roberson, Director of Corporate Quality Assurance, Publix Super Markets Inc. on behalf of the Food Marketing Institute).

[429] Letter on Senate Food Safety Bill (S. 510) to members of Senate HELP Committee, National Sustainable Agriculture Coalition, Nov. 16, 2009, http://sustainableagriculture.net/wp-content/uploads/2008/08/Letter-to-HELP-on-S-510-11-16-092.pdf.

What Was the Response from Consumer Groups?

After H.R. 2749 was reported out of the House Committee on Energy and Commerce, Donna Rosenbaum, executive director of Safe Tables Our, Priority, stated that the public health group was pleased with changes made, to the bill, but that the group would continue to lobby for the language in the bill to be clarified, including asking for a definition of high-risk facilities.[430] The bill as introduced in the House defined a Category 1 facility as "a high-risk facility that manufactures or processes raw products of animal origin (including fish and fisheries products) or other food as designated by the Secretary." These facilities were to be inspected every six to eighteen months.[431] This language was changed in the bill reported out by the House Committee, and a high-risk facility, known as a Category 1 facility, is a facility "that manufactures or processes food" and must be randomly inspected at least every six to twelve months.[432] This language was not further refined by the bill as passed by the House, and it is left to the FDA to determine a more precise definition.

Caroline Smith DeWaal, director of food safety at the Center for Science in the Public Interest, testified at the House Energy and Commerce Committee's Subcommittee on Health hearing on food safety on June 3, 2009:

> While [the bill provision on inspections] is a vast improvement over FDA's existing program, we continue to believe that more frequent inspections than called for in this bill are needed—particularly of high-risk facilities. We understand that, though not perfect, the bill attempts to strike a reasonable balance between the realistic budget and workforce constraints at FDA, and an ideal inspection system.
>
> However, we think it is important for the Committee to understand the need to look at the concept of risk-based

---

[430] Jane Zhang, *Bill Boosting FDA Oversight of Food Wins Panel Approval*, WALL STREET JOURNAL, June 18, 2009, http://online.wsj.com/article/SB124526262358724091.html.
[431] Compare H.R. 2749 § 105, 111th Cong. (as reported by the House Committee on Energy and Commerce, June 17, 2009) with H.R. 2749 § 105, 111th Cong. (as introduced in House of Representatives, June 8, 2009).
[432] H.R. 2749 § 105, 111th Cong. (as engrossed by House of Representatives, July 30, 2009).

inspection across the entire spectrum of food products, not just those regulated by FDA. Thus, any definition of high risk must start with the understanding that slaughter and processing raw meat and poultry are exceptionally high-risk activities. Most meat and poultry slaughter fall under USDA's responsibility and that Department is required to inspect these functions on a continuous basis. The Food Safety and Inspection Service (FSIS) is present in every plant every day. That is appropriate for meat and even seafood processing because of the risk of zoonotic disease and pathogens. FDA's responsibility with regard to meat or poultry is limited to slaughter and processing of animals and birds not specifically itemized in the FMIA and PPIA. Oversight of processing game birds and animals is FDA's primary activity in this area.

The USDA system of continuous inspection of these high risk products provides important protection that is not in the discussion draft, and we urge the committee to address it. First the bill should explicitly recognize the need for continuous inspection of very high risk raw animal products, and second it should authorize FDA to contract with USDA to have the Agriculture Department's inspectors provide continuous inspection for the very limited number of such plants currently under FDA's jurisdiction. Such authority could be used if FDA determines that it does not have a sufficient number of inspectors to allow for continuous inspection of the small number of plants that slaughter so-called "non-amenable species" of animals, or that process raw meat from such animals for sale to the public (such as plants grinding fresh venison).[433]

---

[433] Hearing on Food Safety Enhancement Act of 2009, Before the Subcommittee on Health of the H. Committee on Energy and Commerce, 111th Cong. 5 (2009) [hereinafter Hearing on Food Safety Enhancement Act of 2009] (Prepared Statement of Caroline Smith DeWaal, Director of Food Safety at the Center for Science in the Public Interest).

Caroline Smith DeWaal, director of food safety at the Center for Science in the Public Interest, testified at the Senate HELP Committee hearing on October 22, 2009:

> We believe it is critical to establish categories of risk to ensure that FDA will establish meaningful schedules of inspection. To be adequate, the statutory provisions on federal inspection should do three things:
>
> - Establish a minimum of three risk categories;
> - Set inspection frequencies based on these categories, with the minimum frequency of once every 6 to 12 months for high-risk facilities; and
> - Prohibit FDA from using certification by a private entity as a factor in setting the frequency of federal inspection for a domestic facility.[434]

The Make Our Food Safe Coalition called for S. 510 to be amended to:

> establish a minimum inspection frequency consistent with H.R. 2749 of once every 6–12 months for high-risk products, and at least once every 18 months–3 years for lower-risk foods. Food warehouses can be inspected once every four to five years.[435]

---

[434] Hearing on Keeping America's Families Safe: Reforming the Food Safety System, S. Committee on Health, Education, Labor, and Pensions, 111th Cong. 7-8 Oct. 22, 2009 (Testimony of Caroline Smith DeWaal, Director of the Center for Science in the Public Interest, testimony supported by Center for Foodborne Illness Research and Prevention, Consumer Federation of America, Consumers Union, Food and Water Watch, National Consumers League, Safe Tables Our Priority, and Trust for America's Health).

[435] *The Senate Must Pass Strong FDA Food Safety Legislation This Year*, Make Our Food Safe Coalition, Dec. 1, 2009, www.makeourfoodsafe.org/tools/assets/files/PDF-Senate-Fall-Fact-Sheet.pdf.

Text of the Law as Adopted

SEC. 101. INSPECTIONS OF RECORDS.

(a) In General.--Section 414(a) (21 U.S.C. 350c(a)) is amended--

> *(1) by striking the heading and all that follows through "of food is" and inserting the following: "Records Inspection.--*
>
>> *"(1) ADULTERATED FOOD.--If the Secretary has a reasonable belief that an article of food, and any other article of food that the Secretary reasonably believes is likely to be affected in a similar manner, is";*
>
> *(2) by inserting ," and to any other article of food that the Secretary reasonably believes is likely to be affected in a similar manner," after "relating to such article";*
>
> *(3) by striking the last sentence; and*
>
> *(4) by inserting at the end the following:*
>
>> *"(2) USE OF OR EXPOSURE TO FOOD OF CONCERN.--If the Secretary believes that there is a reasonable probability that the use of or exposure to an article of food, and any other article of food that the Secretary reasonably believes is likely to be affected in a similar manner, will cause serious adverse health consequences or death to humans or animals, each person (excluding farms and restaurants) who manufactures, processes, packs, distributes, receives, holds, or imports such article shall, at the request of an officer or employee duly designated by the Secretary, permit such officer or employee, upon presentation of appropriate credentials and a written notice to such person, at reasonable times and within reasonable limits and in a reasonable manner, to have access to and copy all records relating to such article and to any other article of food that the Secretary reasonably believes is likely to be affected in a similar manner, that are needed to assist the Secretary in determining whether there is a reasonable probability that the use of or exposure to*

the food will cause serious adverse health consequences or death to humans or animals.

"*(3) APPLICATION.--The requirement under paragraphs (1) and (2) applies to all records relating to the manufacture, processing, packing, distribution, receipt, holding, or importation of such article maintained by or on behalf of such person in any format (including paper and electronic formats) and at any location.*".

(b) Conforming Amendment.--Section 704(a)(1)(B) (21 U.S.C. 374(a)(1)(B)) is amended by striking "section 414 when" and all that follows through "subject to" and inserting "section 414, when the standard for records inspection under paragraph (1) or (2) of section 414(a) applies, subject to".

<<*see bracketed insert below*>>

Sec. 374. Inspection

(a) Right of agents to enter; scope of inspection; notice; promptness; exclusions

(1) For purposes of enforcement of this chapter, officers or employees duly designated by the Secretary, upon presenting appropriate credentials and a written notice to the owner, operator, or agent in charge, are authorized (A) to enter, at reasonable times, any factory, warehouse, or establishment in which food, drugs, devices, or cosmetics are manufactured, processed, packed, or held, for introduction into interstate commerce or after such introduction, or to enter any vehicle being used to transport or hold such food, drugs, devices, or cosmetics in interstate commerce; and (B) to inspect, at reasonable times and within reasonable limits and in a reasonable manner, such factory, warehouse, establishment, or vehicle and all pertinent equipment, finished and unfinished materials, containers, and labeling therein. In the case of any person (excluding farms and restaurants) who manufactures, processes, packs, transports, distributes, holds, or imports foods, the inspection shall extend to all records and other information described in [[section 414, when the standard for records inspection under paragraph (1) or (2) of section 414(a) applies, subject to]] the limitations established in section 350c(d) of this title.

SEC. 201. TARGETING OF INSPECTION RESOURCES FOR DOMESTIC FACILITIES, FOREIGN FACILITIES, AND PORTS OF ENTRY; ANNUAL REPORT.

(a) Targeting of Inspection Resources for Domestic Facilities, Foreign Facilities, and Ports of Entry.--Chapter IV (21 U.S.C. 341 et seq.), as amended by section 106, is amended by adding at the end the following:

421. TARGETING OF INSPECTION RESOURCES FOR DOMESTIC FACILITIES, FOREIGN FACILITIES, AND PORTS OF ENTRY; ANNUAL REPORT.

"*(a) Identification and Inspection of Facilities.--*

"*(1) IDENTIFICATION.--The Secretary shall identify high-risk facilities and shall allocate resources to inspect facilities according to the known safety risks of the facilities, which shall be based on the following factors:*

"*(A) The known safety risks of the food manufactured, processed, packed, or held at the facility.*

"*(B) The compliance history of a facility, including with regard to food recalls, outbreaks of foodborne illness, and violations of food safety standards.*

"*(C) The rigor and effectiveness of the facility's hazard analysis and risk-based preventive controls.*

"*(D) Whether the food manufactured, processed, packed, or held at the facility meets the criteria for priority under section 801(h)(1).*

"*(E) Whether the food or the facility that manufactured, processed, packed, or held such food has received a certification as described in section 801(q) or 806, as appropriate.*

"(F) *Any other criteria deemed necessary and appropriate by the Secretary for purposes of allocating inspection resources.*

"(2) *INSPECTIONS.--*

"(A) IN GENERAL.--*Beginning on the date of enactment of the FDA Food Safety Modernization Act, the Secretary shall increase the frequency of inspection of all facilities.*

"(B) DOMESTIC HIGH-RISK FACILITIES.--*The Secretary shall increase the frequency of inspection of domestic facilities identified under paragraph (1) as high-risk facilities such that each such facility is inspected--*

"(i) *not less often than once in the 5-year period following the date of enactment of the FDA Food Safety Modernization Act; and*

"(ii) *not less often than once every 3 years thereafter.*

"(C) DOMESTIC NON-HIGH-RISK FACILITIES.--*The Secretary shall ensure that each domestic facility that is not identified under paragraph (1) as a high-risk facility is inspected--*

"(i) *not less often than once in the 7-year period following the date of enactment of the FDA Food Safety Modernization Act; and*

"(ii) *not less often than once every 5 years thereafter.*

"*(D) FOREIGN FACILITIES.--*

"*(i) YEAR 1.--In the 1-year period following the date of enactment of the FDA Food Safety Modernization Act, the Secretary shall inspect not fewer than 600 foreign facilities.*

"*(ii) SUBSEQUENT YEARS.--In each of the 5 years following the 1-year period described in clause (i), the Secretary shall inspect not fewer than twice the number of foreign facilities inspected by the Secretary during the previous year.*

"*(E) RELIANCE ON FEDERAL, STATE, OR LOCAL INSPECTIONS.--In meeting the inspection requirements under this subsection for domestic facilities, the Secretary may rely on inspections conducted by other Federal, State, or local agencies under interagency agreement, contract, memoranda of understanding, or other obligation.*

"*(b) Identification and Inspection at Ports of Entry.--The Secretary, in consultation with the Secretary of Homeland Security, shall allocate resources to inspect any article of food imported into the United States according to the known safety risks of the article of food, which shall be based on the following factors:*

"*(1) The known safety risks of the food imported.*

"*(2) The known safety risks of the countries or regions of origin and countries through which such article of food is transported.*

"*(3) The compliance history of the importer, including with regard to food recalls, outbreaks of foodborne illness, and violations of food safety standards.*

"(4) The rigor and effectiveness of the activities conducted by the importer of such article of food to satisfy the requirements of the foreign supplier verification program under section 805.

"(5) Whether the food importer participates in the voluntary qualified importer program under section 806.

"(6) Whether the food meets the criteria for priority under section 801(h)(1).

"(7) Whether the food or the facility that manufactured, processed, packed, or held such food received a certification as described in section 801(q) or 806.

"(8) Any other criteria deemed necessary and appropriate by the Secretary for purposes of allocating inspection resources.

"(c) Interagency Agreements With Respect to Seafood.--

"(1) IN GENERAL.--The Secretary of Health and Human Services, the Secretary of Commerce, the Secretary of Homeland Security, the Chairman of the Federal Trade Commission, and the heads of other appropriate agencies may enter into such agreements as may be necessary or appropriate to improve seafood safety.

"(2) SCOPE OF AGREEMENTS.--The agreements under paragraph (1) may include--

"(A) cooperative arrangements for examining and testing seafood imports that leverage the resources, capabilities, and authorities of each party to the agreement;

"(B) coordination of inspections of foreign facilities to increase the percentage of imported seafood and seafood facilities inspected;

"(C) standardization of data on seafood names, inspection records, and laboratory testing to improve interagency coordination;

"(D) coordination to detect and investigate violations under applicable Federal law;

"(E) a process, including the use or modification of existing processes, by which officers and employees of the National Oceanic and Atmospheric Administration may be duly designated by the Secretary to carry out seafood examinations and investigations under section 801 of this Act or section 203 of the Food Allergen Labeling and Consumer Protection Act of 2004;

"(F) the sharing of information concerning observed non-compliance with United States food requirements domestically and in foreign nations and new regulatory decisions and policies that may affect the safety of food imported into the United States;

"(G) conducting joint training on subjects that affect and strengthen seafood inspection effectiveness by Federal authorities; and

"(H) outreach on Federal efforts to enhance seafood safety and compliance with Federal food safety requirements.

"(d) Coordination.--The Secretary shall improve coordination and cooperation with the Secretary of Agriculture and the Secretary of Homeland Security to target food inspection resources.

"(e) Facility.--For purposes of this section, the term 'facility' means a domestic facility or a foreign facility that is required to register under section 415.".

(b) Annual Report.--Section 1003 (21 U.S.C. 393) is amended by adding at the end the following:

"(h) *Annual Report Regarding Food.*--Not later than February 1 of each year, the Secretary shall submit to Congress a report, including efforts to coordinate and cooperate with other Federal agencies with responsibilities for food inspections, regarding--

"(1) information about food facilities including--

"(A) the appropriations used to inspect facilities registered pursuant to section 415 in the previous fiscal year;

"(B) the average cost of both a non-high-risk food facility inspection and a high-risk food facility inspection, if such a difference exists, in the previous fiscal year;

"(C) the number of domestic facilities and the number of foreign facilities registered pursuant to section 415 that the Secretary inspected in the previous fiscal year;

"(D) the number of domestic facilities and the number of foreign facilities registered pursuant to section 415 that were scheduled for inspection in the previous fiscal year and which the Secretary did not inspect in such year;

"(E) the number of high-risk facilities identified pursuant to section 421 that the Secretary inspected in the previous fiscal year; and

"(F) the number of high-risk facilities identified pursuant to section 421 that were scheduled for inspection in the previous fiscal year and which the Secretary did not inspect in such year.

"(2) information about food imports including--

"(A) the number of lines of food imported into the United States that the Secretary physically inspected or sampled in the previous fiscal year;

"(B) the number of lines of food imported into the United States that the Secretary did not physically inspect or sample in the previous fiscal year; and

"(C) the average cost of physically inspecting or sampling a line of food subject to this Act that is imported or offered for import into the United States; and

"(3) information on the foreign offices of the Food and Drug Administration including--

"(A) the number of foreign offices established; and

"(B) the number of personnel permanently stationed in each foreign office.

"(i) Public Availability of Annual Food Reports.--The Secretary shall make the reports required under subsection (h) available to the public on the Internet Web site of the Food and Drug Administration.".

(c) Advisory Committee Consultation.--In allocating inspection resources as described in section 421 of the Federal Food, Drug, and Cosmetic Act (as added by subsection (a)), the Secretary may, as appropriate, consult with any relevant advisory committee within the Department of Health and Human Services.

SEC. 306. INSPECTION OF FOREIGN FOOD FACILITIES.

(a) In General.--Chapter VIII (21 U.S.C. 381 et seq.), as amended by section 302, is amended by inserting at the end the following:

"SEC. 807. INSPECTION OF FOREIGN FOOD FACILITIES.

"(a) Inspection.--The Secretary--

"(1) may enter into arrangements and agreements with foreign governments to facilitate the inspection of foreign facilities registered under section 415; and

"(2) shall direct resources to inspections of foreign facilities, suppliers, and food types, especially such facilities, suppliers, and food types that present a high risk (as identified by the Secretary), to help ensure the safety and security of the food supply of the United States.

"(b) Effect of Inability To Inspect.--Notwithstanding any other provision of law, food shall be refused admission into the United States if it is from a foreign factory, warehouse, or other establishment of which the owner, operator, or agent in charge, or the government of the foreign country, refuses to permit entry of United States inspectors or other individuals duly designated by the Secretary, upon request, to inspect such factory, warehouse, or other establishment. For purposes of this subsection, such an owner, operator, or agent in charge shall be considered to have refused an inspection if such owner, operator, or agent in charge does not permit an inspection of a factory, warehouse, or other establishment during the 24-hour period after such request is submitted, or after such other time period, as agreed upon by the Secretary and the foreign factory, warehouse, or other establishment.".

(b) Inspection by the Secretary of Commerce.--

(1) IN GENERAL.--The Secretary of Commerce, in coordination with the Secretary of Health and Human Services, may send 1 or more inspectors to a country or facility of an exporter from which seafood imported into the United States originates. The inspectors shall assess practices and processes used in connection with the farming, cultivation, harvesting, preparation for market, or transportation of such seafood and may provide technical assistance related to such activities.

(2) INSPECTION REPORT.--

(A) IN GENERAL.--The Secretary of Health and Human Services, in coordination with the Secretary of Commerce, shall--

(i) prepare an inspection report for each inspection conducted under paragraph (1);

(ii) provide the report to the country or exporter that is the subject of the report; and

(iii) provide a 30-day period during which the country or exporter may provide a rebuttal or other comments on the findings of the report to the Secretary of Health and Human Services.

(B) DISTRIBUTION AND USE OF REPORT.--The Secretary of Health and Human Services shall consider the inspection reports described in subparagraph (A) in distributing inspection resources under section 421 of the Federal Food, Drug, and Cosmetic Act, as added by section 201.

10

Enforcement Tools:
Recalls, Detention, and Penalties

What Do Managers Need to Know?

A new standard of action is applied that puts teeth into the recall process. Previously, food recalls were voluntary and were usually performed by the maker, with or without an FDA request, when the food was adulterated or misbranded. If the company then refused to make a recall, the FDA would need to go to court and seek multiple court orders and seizures of food shipments, perhaps also asking a court to issue an injunction against further shipments.

After the 2010 legislation, if the food is within one of the many categories of "adulterated," or if it fails to disclose an allergen that could be harmful, the FDA can order a recall if certain preconditions are met. The FDA can use "detention" to stop the movement of suspect foods. An expanded duty to notify consumers and downstream customers accompanies the expanded duty to perform recalls. The company that resists a recall has an uphill battle to show to the Commissioner of the FDA that "adequate grounds" exist for vacating or modifying the recall order, a standard that is very discretionary in favor of the FDA's initial decision.

The new recall orders come with civil penalties, and potential for refusals or violations. The FDA also gets an easier power of food "detention," stopping shipments. Added authority for web and press release of details of the recall order make it much less likely that companies will resist an FDA recall order, because resistance to recalls carries with it high risks of bad publicity and higher risks of significant punishments.

What Is a Food Recall?

A food "recall" is the rapid, publicly announced return to a food seller of some of the food that seller has distributed, in response to a potential risk that food poses for consumers.[436] Recalls of marketed food products are never happy events, before, during, or after the implementation of the recall. Careers are sometimes ended by the failure to manage a recall or by the recognition of accountability for what had gone wrong that caused the need for a recall. There are no heroes or prizes awarded in managing a recall, but there can be serious negative consequences for companies and managers.

The 2010 legislation increases the legal requirements and consequences of food recall situations, in Section 206, and thereby increases the pressure upon companies to carefully execute a necessary recall with close attention to the FDA's expectations. In short, power shifts toward the FDA, and a long history of negotiations about voluntary recall is replaced with powerful directives that pack a strong punitive consequence.

Of all the sections of the 2010 law, this newly expanded one is the least explored in formal legislative history documentation, and was probably the provision that was most eagerly sought by FDA field office enforcement managers who deal with the practicalities of food problems. Unlike the 2010 law's more complex sections that evolved over years of effort, these recall provisions largely developed in the Senate as part of the summer 2010 manager's amendments.

What Changes Are Made by the 2010 Law?

Before the 2010 amendments, the FDA had to informally negotiate to convince a food company to voluntarily cooperate and remove its food from sale. The company could lawfully refuse the request to recall.[437] The

---

[436] 21 C.F.R. 7.; 2 James O'Reilly, *Food & Drug Administration* chap. 22 (3d Ed. 2010 Supp.).
[437] But most companies cooperated. *Id.*

FDA then would have to ask the Justice Department to obtain a court order seizing identified lots of the food, where those lots were located (and assuming that the food containers were still there when the court papers were delivered and the seizure was executed). Alternatively, the FDA could ask a state health agency director to issue an embargo under state law that forbade movement of the food within that state. If the FDA opted not to act in the face of the refusal, and a food consumer died, the FDA would be criticized sharply in the news media, and the recalcitrant food company was likely to face serious product liability claims, bankruptcy, and perhaps an FDA prosecution. Once the firm cooperated with the request for voluntary recall, the FDA would publicly announce the recall, inspect the facility, sample the recalled packages, and use scientific measurements to determine the extent of the contamination. The FDA would be in the driver's seat, and the firm would "fully cooperate" even if did not wish to do so, yet under the rubric of voluntary action.

What Are the Elements of the Recall?

The 2010 amendments established new powers of mandatory recall in new Section 423. This was added almost at the very end of the Senate process, at the FDA's strong urging, as national news media focused on massive recalls of Iowa eggs that were contaminated with salmonella.

If the FDA determines that an article of food other than infant formula

1. Has a "reasonable probability" of adulteration or a misbranding relating to allergen warnings,
2. And consumer use or exposure to this food "will cause" serious adverse health consequences or death,

the FDA must provide to the company or person responsible an opportunity to stop distribution and recall the food, and if the responsible person refuses or does not stop distributing the food, then (only) the FDA Commissioner can require that the movement of the food must stop and required notices must be given (see below).

To parse this more clearly, a food company with a bad product already has a "reasonable probability" that the FDA would find the product to be adulterated. The FDA then looks at human health risk. Will (not just might) the bad food cause "serious" illness? Then the FDA encourages a voluntary recall. If the company refuses, then (and only then) can the Commissioner (not a lower-level official) make the determination that it must stop shipment, be brought back, and consumers must be notified.

Additionally, the FDA may allow for the assistance of other individuals in providing notice to the persons affected by the recall, including health professionals and state and local officials. This Senate provision includes a non-delegation provision[438] added at the request of industry lobbyists that allows only the Commissioner of the FDA to issue an order for emergency mandatory recall.[439]

What Notifications Are Required?

Recalls are high-speed campaigns to stop the consumer from getting sick. Time is of the essence.[440] For the plaintiff who was harmed weeks after the defect in the food was known, an inadequate and slow recall caused that avoidable harm, and a slow, tepid response is worse than none at all in the context of a later liability lawsuit.[441]

The FDA will use press releases, email, social media alerts, and postings on its web pages to get the word out. Each notice will:

- Describe the product
- Describe the risk
- Post a web photo of the product
- Consider publicizing the main recipients (e.g., retail chains)

---

[438] Pub. L. 111-353, Title II sec. 423(g).

[439] The bill as introduced in the House did not include a non-delegation provision stipulating who is allowed to order an emergency mandatory recall. Compare H.R. 2749 § 111, 111th Cong. (as reported by the House Committee on Energy and Commerce, June 17, 2009) with H.R. 2749 § 111, 111th Cong. (as introduced in House of Representatives, June 8, 2009).

[440] See James O'Reilly, Food Crisis Management Manual 2d Ed. 2008 (fdli.org).

[441] In tort law, a bungled effort to protect a person gives rise to liability greater than ignoring the person; see Restatement of Product Liability 3d and James O'Reilly, Product Recalls and the Third Restatement: Consumers Lose Twice from Defects in Products and in the Restatement Itself (2004).

- Describe (apparently at food industry association insistence) other forms of the same type of food that are not "affected by" the recall[442]

Additionally, the FDA is required to add a search engine to the FDA website that would allow consumers to easily look up information on recalled items.[443]

What Are the Procedural Safeguards?

Speed matters. Faced with risks of illness and death, the FDA does not want to be held back by formalities and delaying mechanisms. In drafting this provision during the 2010 egg recalls, congressional negotiators gave much more weight to the public interest, and cut back on opportunities that industry sought to enhance companies' ability to fight over the recall.

Most recalls will continue to be voluntary. For those that are mandatory, the affected firm has a right to request an informal hearing under Section 423(b)(1)—probably a conference phone call or hastily arranged visit to the FDA's district office—within forty-eight hours of the FDA order to recall. Very few of these very informal "hearings" will succeed—but the firm that opposes the recall must begin here with this required step to begin its appeal. A federal court probably will refuse to hear a company's plea if it has not "exhausted its remedy" at the FDA.

Who Has the Power to Act?

Only the FDA Commissioner herself or himself may act. Usually this means a rapid rubber-stamp approval via electronic mail using FDA standard internal emergency communication channels.

A cynical view might be that industry defenders defeated themselves during the summer 2010 drafting. They insisted that only the Commissioner could decide to order the recall, and so congressional negotiators included that

---

[442] New 423(g).
[443] Compare S. 510 § 207, 111th Cong. (as reported by the Senate HELP Committee, Nov. 18, 2009) with S. 510 § 207, 111th Cong. (as introduced in Senate, Mar. 3, 2009).

constraint at the end of the recall powers.[444] They wrote this into the bill that already had an appeal step, after the Commissioner's determination, consisting of a rapid informal meeting with local managers of the FDA to protest the determination.[445] Reading this wording closely, industry lobbyists seem to have defeated their clients' needs. How rare will it be for the lower-level supervisor in the field office of an 11,500-member agency, at a quick informal hearing, to overrule the decision of the single most powerful official at the head of that agency? The anonymous client whose lobbyist "won" the addition of a Commissioner-only power, in clause 423(h), should demand its money back.

Because the appeal of a determination must be taken to the FDA within two days of the order,[446] the presence of this statutory process will likely prevent a federal court from issuing a temporary restraining order against the FDA until after the "exhaustion of remedies" is completed by the company. This well-known feature of administrative procedure binds federal courts. Because of the presence of a statutory requirement for administrative appeal, the issue is not ripe for federal courts until after the statutory process has first been utilized.[447] One can imagine that a less sophisticated food company's local lawyer would rush to federal court to sue against their recall order. But the FDA has many precedents on its side of a motion to dismiss for lack of exhaustion of the available administrative remedies.[448]

What Enforcement Tools Are Available?

Refusal to recall food after an FDA order has been issued, or failure to recall after an FDA order has been issued, is now considered in the 2010 law to be a "prohibited act,"[449] and it can be criminally prosecuted[450] or

---

[444] New 423(h) was added in the summer 2010 Manager's Amendment, where many of the negotiated concessions were made toward industry by the sponsors.

[445] New 423(c) was in place before the addition of the 423(h) requirement that only the Commissioner could make the "determination."

[446] New 423(c).

[447] For background on exhaustion of remedies as a barrier to lawsuits, see 1 James O'Reilly, *Food & Drug Administration* (3d Ed. 2010 Supp.).

[448] More of the exhaustion case law is found in James O'Reilly, *Administrative Rulemaking* (2010 Ed.).

[449] New 21 U.S.C. 331(xx).

subjected to a large administrative civil penalty,[451] the equivalent of a large fine. If there is a refusal to recall and a refusal to notify downstream recipients of the food, the FDA will probably get court orders to seize the shipments that can be located, and use its new 2010 powers to "detain" what is still in the factory, and may turn the case over to the FDA Office of Criminal Investigations to work up a prosecution recommendation. So as a practical matter, the company's best option is to immediately meet with the FDA and present its best science data to rebut the assertions of adulteration.

What Happens To Logistics Companies Not Associated with Food Production?

Truck, rail, and warehousing companies were concerned about the impact of the recall provisions on their business. Special mention of their situation was made, but they remained subject to the same recall orders as food companies are. Section 423(b)(2) forces the food company to provide to logistics firms and carriers specific details of where the shipments went and how they can be identified.

Are the 2010 FDA Recall Powers Unusual?

No. The FDA mandatory recall powers are much more recent than those of the enhanced recall powers added in recent years to auto safety, consumer product safety, and other systems. The National Highway Traffic Safety Administration has had this power since 1966, expanded by the TREAD Act in 2000,[452] and the Consumer Product Safety Commission received greatly expanded authority for mandatory recalls in 2008,[453] expanding its original 1972 authorities. The FDA is moving up toward the norm, driven by public alarm about the massive egg recalls of 2010.

Civil damage cases have often considered the effects of the product recall on liability to injured users. The Third Restatement of Torts in 1997 made

---

[450] Note that the responsible corporate officers can be fined or jailed under strict liability norms for failure to comply. 21 U.S.C. 333.

[451] New 21 U.S.C. 333(f)(2)(A).

[452] 49 U.S.C. 30101 et seq.

[453] 15 U.S.C. 2064.

special provision for inadequate recalls. In those states that follow that document's controversial suggestions, failure to adequately conduct a recall where one is required will be a basis for tort liability to injured consumers, whose harm would have been avoided by the proper conduct of retrieving the food or consumer product.

Does the Law Compensate an Innocent Farmer?

No, or at least not yet. Erroneous calls for recall do not trigger any payment obligation by the FDA to the companies impacted by the error. The 2010 amendments responded to a related farm state lobbying complaint. Federal Torts Claims Act authority for compensation does not currently include "discretionary" matters such as decisions by the FDA to order a recall.[454] Under the 2010 law, the Government Accountability Office must prepare a study on how much compensation could be awarded to farmers in the event that an error in the recall process results in loss to the farmers.[455] Spinach, grapes, peanuts, and other crops have been badly impacted by safety-related recalls in past years, but the 2010 Congress did not have the votes needed to expand Federal Torts Claims Act remedies to the losses that might be incurred by "innocent farmers" when their crop commodities lose sales as a result of contamination cases. The study of farmer restitution may be a complex research project. In the event that a particular future error causes such great displacement, Congress might then pass a special legislative appropriation and claims mechanism for farmers whose income dropped as a result of inaccurate claims of health problems.

What Has Shifted Costs of a Recall?

The FDA can use its new 2010 authority to order a recall to be conducted, and the FDA will be repaid by the company for its costs of managing the recall. The FDA can require "the responsible party for a domestic facility (as defined in section 415(b)) and an importer who does not comply with a recall order under section 423 or under section 412(f) [infant formulas] in such fiscal year, to cover food recall activities associated with such order performed by the Secretary, including technical assistance, follow-up effectiveness checks, and public notifications, for such year."

---

[454] 28 US.C. 2680(h).
[455] Act 206(c).

How Will Administrative Detention Work?

The 2010 legislation gives an FDA inspector the power to detain an article of food inspected, examined, or investigated under a section of the FDCA, if the inspector has "reason to believe" the article is adulterated or misbranded. The "reason to believe" that the article is "adulterated or misbranded" is not a difficult standard, since "adulteration" covers many aspects of food safety. This will enhance an FDA employee's power to detain food. Under pre-2010 law, the inspector who wished to impose a detention order must show that he or she has "credible evidence or information indicating" that the food presents "a threat of serious adverse health consequences to death to humans or animals." Lowering the bar suggests more detentions will occur.

In addition, the period of time for which an article of food can be detained is extended by this section from the prior time limit of thirty days to sixty days. The deadline for when the FDA must offer the opportunity for an informal hearing at which the detention can be challenged is increased from five days to fifteen days.[456]

When Can the FDA Begin To Use Detentions?

Administrative detention authority will take effect 180 days after enactment of the Act. The Senate bill requires the FDA to implement the changes through regulations—an interim final rule issued no later than 120 days after enactment.

According to FDA Commissioner Hamburg at the House Subcommittee on Health hearing on June 3, 2009, "Section 132 makes the Agency's administrative detention authority more useful by expanding the circumstances under which the Agency can detain a food, thereby preventing its movement or distribution while the Agency takes appropriate regulatory action."[457] The House bill provision regarding administrative detention was quite similar to the provision passed into law.

---

[456] H.R. 2749 § 132, 111th Cong. (as engrossed by House of Representatives, July 30, 2009).
[457] Hearing on Food Safety Enhancement Act of 2009, Before the Subcommittee on Health of the H. Committee on Energy and Commerce, 111th Cong. 4-5 (2009) [hereinafter Hearing on Food Safety Enhancement Act of 2009] (Prepared Statement by Margaret A. Hamburg, Commissioner of FDA, HHS, Rockville, MD).

FDA Commissioner Hamburg testified at the Senate HELP Committee hearing on October 22, 2009, that:

> Section 207 provides important revisions to the existing standard for the administrative detention of foods. The current standard of "credible evidence or information" of "a threat of serious adverse health consequences or death to humans or animals" is too high given that a key purpose of the provision is to provide time to gather information regarding the product's potential to cause significant harm. As a result, the existing authority is often not useful in situations where it otherwise could help us prevent or minimize the harmful effects of an adulterated or misbranded food.[458]

What Is Most Significant About the 2010 Changes?

The major expansion of food safety enforcement and penalties under the 2010 legislation is one of the most impactful aspects of the amendments. Regulators get power when Congress gets alarmed. Enforcement power delegations tend to flow from public crises. Egg recalls, melamine, and other safety issues led to public pressure for new federal powers to deal with these problems.

Beyond the FDA's impacts, there will be extensive media attention on enforcement cases. There will be a high risk of adverse publicity to companies if errors occur by the company or by the FDA and the enforcement cases are mishandled. For publicly traded shareholder-owned companies, news of the FDA use of the new enforcement powers against a company whose shares are listed on an exchange may generate a negative overreaction, for the interruption of sales may be a major disruption to corporate productivity and sales.

---

[458] Hearing on Keeping America's Families Safe: Reforming the Food Safety System, S. Committee on Health, Education, Labor, and Pensions, 111th Cong. 6-7, Oct. 22, 2009 (Testimony of FDA Commissioner Hamburg).

What Effects Will Be Felt Outside the United States?

From the FDA's viewpoint, the 2010 legislation will have significant offshore impacts, and a substantial educational effort for "sister agencies" around the world will be needed. Inter-governmental liaison roles will be extremely important, through the FDA's Office of International Affairs, as the FDA seeks to get the word out concerning international shipment requirements, communicated through embassies and US missions abroad. International agreements will be used to shift inspection roles to governmental, and in some cases to third-party private-sector, certification and inspectional entities.[459]

The food industry may be snowed under paperwork revisions in the first months of the new law, to deal with recall obligations. Lawyers and regulatory professionals, consultants, and logistics managers will be required to change all of the conventional assumptions about the buyer and seller responsibilities for imported food. There will be a need for revision of virtually all contractual indemnification and compliance guarantees. A company signing a certification risks severe punishment if the food is contaminated at the port of entry or in the vehicle carrying the food into the US port.

Must the Food Company Report Its Violative Food to the FDA?

Since the 2007 amendments, the Reportable Food Registry has required that any FDA-registered food facilities that manufacture, process, pack, or hold food for human or animal consumption in the United States under Section 415(a) (21 U.S.C. 350d) is required to report to the FDA when there is a reasonable probability that the use of, or exposure to, an article of food will cause serious adverse health consequences or death to humans or animals. A labeling error can result in a reportable event. If the food has an allergen that is not disclosed, it is "misbranded" under Section 403(w) where "serious adverse health consequences" could result. Other forms of misbranding by inadequate label statements are not expressly discussed in the 2010 law. Prudent food companies that have found a mislabeling they believe could have serious adverse health consequences should voluntarily report.

---

[459] S. 510 § 309 (2009).

The electronic portal www.safetyreporting.hhs.gov also will receive reports from federal agencies like the Centers for Disease Control, state health or agriculture departments, and local government officials. These entities may voluntarily use the Reportable Food Registry portal to report information that may come to them about reportable foods. No change to the content of this standard is made by the 2010 amendments. But the separate standard for what the FDA can do with the incoming information (from whatever source the information comes) is now clarified: the test for recalls, like for required reports to the FDA, is now whether "there is a reasonable probability that an article of food (other than infant formula) is adulterated under section 402 or misbranded under section 403(w) and the use of or exposure to such article will cause serious adverse health consequences or death to humans or animals."

What About Potential Risks Found with Meat, Eggs, and Poultry?

Safety problems should be reported to the US Department of Agriculture hotline at mphotline.fsis@usda.gov or 1-888-mphotline.

How Will Recalls and Imports Intersect?

While the FDA mandatory recall is underway, the food company should be hesitant to risk shipping any more of the same food into the United States. If the FDA believes, from the examination of a sample of food, that the food is subject to an order to cease distribution or recall the article, the food will be denied entry into the United States, and may be destroyed at the port.

What Did Members of Congress Intend?

Representative Shimkus took issue at the House Energy and Commerce Committee's Subcommittee on Health hearing on food safety on June 3, 2009 with the standard applied to recalls. He stated that he believed the standard, which included the language "reason to believe the use of, or consumption of, or exposure to, an article of food may cause serious adverse health consequences or death to humans or animals" was too vague, and commented that "I hope we can work to clean up that language."[460] Shimkus additionally urged that certain increased powers of the FDA should be entrusted only to the Commissioner, such as the authority to order a mandatory recall, suspend a facility, and issue subpoenas. Commissioner Hamburg responded:

> Well, these are important and powerful authorities that shouldn't be used lightly. However, I think that experience shows that senior level officials can be entrusted with these authorities along with the Commissioner, but it is certainly something that we would want to work with Congress on in order to put in place the system that people have the most confidence in.[461]

What Did the FDA Tell Congress About Recall Authority?

FDA Commissioner Hamburg was questioned at the House Energy and Commerce Committee's Subcommittee on Health hearing on food safety on June 3, 2009, about the recall standard included in the bill. Representative Whitfield remarked, "The FDA would have the authority for recall if an article of food may cause adverse health consequences. That would be the legal standard, may cause. But in the Senate bill, it says that there must be a reasonable probability of serious adverse health consequences or death." He then asked Commissioner Hamburg if the less precise standard included in the House bill bothered her. Commissioner Hamburg replied:

> Well, I certainly understand the concern that you are raising, and I think there may be some opportunities for some wordsmithing. Certainly we would never seek to recall a product without, you know, some reasonable expectation that there was serious adverse consequences and harm related to that product. A recall is no small issue both in terms of resources and efforts on the part of the FDA and

---

[460] Hearing on Food Safety Enhancement Act of 2009, Before the Subcommittee on Health of the H. Committee on Energy and Commerce, 111th Cong. 185-86 (2009) [hereinafter Hearing on Food Safety Enhancement Act of 2009] (Statement of Representative Shimkus in Preliminary Transcript).

[461] Hearing on Food Safety Enhancement Act of 2009, Before the Subcommittee on Health of the H. Committee on Energy and Commerce, 111th Cong. 126 (2009) [hereinafter Hearing on Food Safety Enhancement Act of 2009] (Statement of FDA Commissioner Hamburg in Preliminary Transcript).

also its implications on industry and consumers who want access to those products.

So I think it is an area that we would like to work with you on for language. We wouldn't want it to be too overwhelmingly prescriptive because you want to have the flexibility in that kind of potentially emergency situation to move forward.[462]

At the House Energy and Commerce Committee's Subcommittee on Health hearing on food safety on June 3, 2009, Commissioner Hamburg indicated that the increased FDA authority for mandatory recalls will be utilized if necessary:

> I think the history is that voluntary recall is often effective in getting those potentially harmful products off the shelves and protecting consumers but that you do need that emergency mandatory recall function as a backup. There certainly have been cases where the mandatory recall of a dangerous product has been delayed because of a reluctance on the part of the company to pull that product, and there has been a back-and-forth and lawyers involved and delays of weeks, putting consumers at risk.
>
> So I think that to have the mandatory recall as a emergency measure is very, very important. And sadly in a world where we might also need to address intentional contamination of food, that emergency mandatory recall becomes a very, very important tool. You know I think the reality is that having that as an enforcement tool probably makes it easier to also work with companies on the voluntary recall.[463]

---

[462] Hearing on Food Safety Enhancement Act of 2009, Before the Subcommittee on Health of the H. Committee on Energy and Commerce, 111th Cong. 9 (2009) [hereinafter Hearing on Food Safety Enhancement Act of 2009] (Opening Statement of Representative Deal in Preliminary Transcript).

[463] Hearing on Food Safety Enhancement Act of 2009, Before the Subcommittee on Health of the H. Committee on Energy and Commerce, 111th Cong. 124-26 (2009) [hereinafter Hearing on Food Safety Enhancement Act of 2009] (Statement of FDA Commissioner Hamburg in Preliminary Transcript).

What Did Trade Associations Say?

A number of groups, including the American Wholesale Marketers Association, the International Foodservice Distributors Association, and the International Warehouse Logistics Association, have voiced concerns that Congress is too unfamiliar with food industry logistics to draft comprehensive food safety reform whereby the burdens are placed on the right players.[464] The food distribution chain is a long one. As food moves from production to the point of sale, it may change hands a number of times. First, it is produced, grown, or manufactured. This first step alone might involve multiple ingredients from many different suppliers. If the food is made in a foreign country, perhaps the original producer or a separate importer will decide to ship the food into the United States. A broker will then prepare the import documents and oversee moving the shipment through Customs. At some point along the way, the food may be temporarily placed in a warehouse. From there, distributors and wholesalers may purchase and transport the food to a retailer, at which point it will finally be sold to consumers.[465] Warehouse owners believe it will be physically impossible for them to comply with recall requirements, and that large per-unit and per-day fines for violations have the potential of hurting their businesses. According to Joel Anderson, president of the International Warehouse Logistics Association, the legislation:

> presupposes that [warehouses] have chain of ownership as well as knowledge of product characteristics that [warehouses] simply do not have… They view the supply chain as if there are only two players—the shipper and the receiver. They don't understand there are many others involved in the movement of food products, including truckers, warehouses, brokers and retailers.[466]

The American Wholesale Marketers Association, the International Foodservice Distributors Association, and the International Warehouse

---

[464] *See* April Terreri, *Will New FDA Penalties Break Your Bank?* FOOD LOGISTICS, Sept. 2009, at 26.

[465] *See Food Supply Chain Handbook*, Grocery Manufacturer Association 4-6 (2008), www.gmabrands.com/publications/GMA_SupplyChain2.pdf.

[466] *See* April Terreri, *Will New FDA Penalties Break Your Bank?* FOOD LOGISTICS, Sept. 2009, at 26.

Logistics Association worked throughout the drafting of the legislation to have liabilities be placed on the companies that are responsible for contamination. According to Joel Anderson, president of the International Warehouse Logistics Association, "Anytime you see contamination along the food logistics supply chain it has not occurred on the warehousing or trucking side—it has occurred at the origin of production."[467]

A representative of the Food Marketing Institute, a trade association that represents food retailers and wholesalers, testified at the House Energy and Commerce Committee's Subcommittee on Health hearing on food safety on June 3, 2009, stating that the institute:

> believe[s] that FDA should be given the authority to mandate a recall in only those cases where a company responsible for adulterated food does not act promptly to recall a food that presents a reasonable probability of causing serious health problems or death. This authority would allow FDA to act when a firm refuses to recall product or when a company is no longer in business and is not able to conduct the recall. Penalties and other punitive measures should also be limited to those responsible for the adulteration.

> We are however concerned with the proposal to give FDA the authority to issue a "cease distribution" order as a result of its impact on retail operations. Stores have very little room to hold foods for an extended period of time, particularly frozen or perishable foods. If FDA issues a "cease distribution" order for a product, retailers will treat that order as if the product had been recalled. Stores would immediately remove the product from the shelf and implement other measures to ensure the consumer could not purchase the specific item. We need to be able to transport these items out of the store both

---

[467] *See* April Terreri, *Will New FDA Penalties Break Your Bank?* FOOD LOGISTICS, Sept. 2009, at 26.

for space reasons and because we would not want to hold food subject to a "cease distribution" order near food that will be sold to the consumer.[468]

Pamela Bailey, president of the Grocery Manufacturers Association, the world's largest trade association, representing more than 300 food, beverage, and consumer product companies, testified at the House Energy and Commerce Committee's Subcommittee on Health hearing on food safety on June 3, 2009, noting her concerns about the recall provision:

> We believe that certain enforcement provisions of the discussion draft, such as mandatory recall and suspension of registration, should only be exercised by senior agency officials, should only be exercised when there is a risk of serious adverse health consequences, and that companies should be afforded certain due process protections, such as an administrative hearing.

> As we saw during the recent recalls of tomatoes, jalapeno peppers, spinach, and other food products, recalls can have devastating financial impacts. FDA, CDC and others must be given new tools and resources to understand the source of contamination before taking action, and we applaud the Committee for expanding our existing surveillance systems and research to better determine the sources of contamination. We believe that new powers created in the discussion draft can be improved to ensure that enforcement actions, such as mandatory recalls and suspension of registration, reflect the best science and agency judgment.[469]

---

[468] Hearing on Food Safety Enhancement Act of 2009, Before the Subcommittee on Health of the H. Committee on Energy and Commerce, 111th Cong. 6 (2009) [hereinafter Hearing on Food Safety Enhancement Act of 2009] (Prepared Statement of Mike Ambrosio in Preliminary Transcript).

[469] Hearing on Food Safety Enhancement Act of 2009, Before the Subcommittee on Health of the H. Committee on Energy and Commerce, 111th Cong. 4 (2009) [hereinafter Hearing on Food Safety Enhancement Act of 2009] (Prepared Statement of Pamela Bailey, President of Grocery Manufacturers Association).

In a statement on the Food Marketing Institute website, the institute indicated its position on recall authority:

> FDA should be given the authority to mandate a recall in those cases where a company found to be responsible for adulterating food does not act promptly to recall a food that presents a reasonable probability of causing serious health problems or death. The FMI Board of Directors approved a policy statement that supports providing federal regulatory agencies with the authority to require a recall under these circumstances.[470]

A representative for the Food Marketing Institute testified at the Senate HELP Committee hearing on October 22, 2009:

> In 2007, FMI's Board of Directors adopted a policy urging Congress to grant the Food and Drug Administration the authority to require a recall of seriously adulterated food when the entity responsible for its adulteration refuses to or delays in recalling the food. The provision in S. 510 requires FDA to give a responsible party the opportunity to cease distribution of an adulterated or misbranded food product while authorizing the Agency to issue a cease distribution order and a mandatory recall order if necessary.

> We support the mandatory recall provision and the procedural limits in the bill, including the direction to FDA to work with state and local public health officials, who are often valuable resources, and the limitation that the authority may only be exercised by the Commissioner. Mandatory recall is a significant action and should only be directed by the highest knowledgeable authority within the Agency and the Agency should be accountable for executing that authority.[471]

---

[470] Priority Issues, Food Marketing Institute, www.fmi.org/gr/issues/gr_issues_display.cfm?id=26.

[471] Hearing on Keeping America's Families Safe: Reforming the Food Safety System, S. Committee on Health, Education, Labor, and Pensions, 111th Cong. 6, Oct. 22, 2009 (Testimony of Michael Roberson, Director of Corporate Quality Assurance, Publix Super Markets Inc. on behalf of the Food Marketing Institute).

Matters Debated But Not Adopted

These form part of the history but not the final content of the 2010 legislation.

What Criminal Penalties Were Proposed But Removed from the 2010 Final Legislation?

Prior law made it possible for the FDA to criminally charge companies and their executives for violations of the FDCA. The persons who had responsible relationships to operate the business within compliance with the law, such as senior company executives, could be criminally punished without proof of their knowledge of the offense.[472] The House version of the 2010 legislation was not adopted. It would have increased criminal penalties for persons who "knowingly" commit certain prohibited acts "with respect to any food that is misbranded or adulterated." The penalty is increased to ten years in prison and a large fine. The selected prohibited acts that carry the longer prison term would have included virtually all of the food violations in the code:

1. Introducing or delivering to introduce any adulterated or misbranded food into interstate commerce
2. Adulterating or misbranding any food that is in interstate commerce
3. Receiving in interstate commerce or delivering, or offering to deliver, any adulterated or misbranded food
4. Altering the label of any food after shipment in interstate commerce that results in the article being deemed adulterated or misbranded
5. Introducing or delivering for introduction into interstate commerce an unsafe dietary supplement[473]

The House Committee report showed the intention to increase criminal penalties for all "knowing" prohibited acts related to food.[474] This section

---

[472] This responsible relationship test is explored in depth in 1 James O'Reilly, *Food & Drug Administration* ch 8 (3d Ed. 2009 Supp.), westgroup.com.
[473] H.R. 2749 § 134, 111th Cong. (as engrossed by House of Representatives, July 30, 2009).
[474] H.R. Rep. No. 111-234, at 42 (2009).

would have been self-executing and did not require rulemaking, and does not include an "effective date."

The bill did not change other criminal penalties already in force for non-knowing offenses, and did not alter the strict liability for executives. The criminal penalty for committing a prohibited act under 21 U.S.C. § 331 had been one year maximum imprisonment and/or a maximum $1,000 fine, or three years and/or a maximum $10,000 fine, if the violation was committed with the intent to defraud or mislead.[475] Since this is relatively small punishment, prosecutors usually added fraud or other violations along with the FDCA criminal charges.

Although this section would have implemented a fine for violations, revenues from criminal penalties would have been deposited in the Crime Victims Fund, and the Congressional Budget Office did not expect there to be significant revenues from criminal penalties.[476]

What Civil Penalties Were Proposed But Removed from the Final 2010 Legislation?

The House bill would have established new power to assess civil penalties for committing a prohibited act relating to food under 21 U.S.C. § 331. In the case of an individual, the penalty would have been not more than $20,000, not to exceed $50,000 in a single proceeding. For others, the penalty would have been not more than $250,000, not to exceed $1 million in a single proceeding.

The FDA would not have needed to show proof "beyond a reasonable doubt," since the penalty would not have been a criminal fine. A person who "knowingly" commits a prohibited act relating to food could have been assessed a civil penalty not more than $50,000, and not to exceed $100,000 in a single proceeding. For entities that commit knowing violations, like a corporation whose managers fraudulently dilute infant formula, the civil penalty would have been not more than $500,000, not to

---

[475] 21 U.S.C. § 333 (2009).
[476] H.R. Rep. No. 111-234, at 54 (2009).

exceed $7.5 million in a single proceeding.[477] This section also specified that each violation and each day during which the violation continued would have been a separate offense.

How Would the Proposed FDA Local Quarantine Power Have Worked?

The FDA would have received new authority to prohibit or restrict the movement of food, under Section 133 of the House bill, that was not adopted. This section would have been rarely utilized, but it would have empowered the FDA to quarantine food to an area or region within a state. For example, tomatoes with a particular plant infection might have been quarantined in Ohio and barred from shipment to other states. The bill specifically stated:

> After consultation with the Governor or other appropriate
> official of an affected State, if the [FDA] determines that
> there is credible evidence that an article of food presents
> an imminent threat of serious adverse health consequences
> or death to humans or animals, the [FDA] may prohibit or
> restrict the movement of an article of food within a State
> or portion of a State for which the [FDA] has credible
> evidence that such food is located within, or originated
> from, such State or portion thereof.[478]

The FDA would not have been limited to a quarantine of the specific food that is considered a danger. The FDA additionally "may prohibit or restrict the movement within a State or portion of a State of any article of food or

---

[477] When the bill was introduced in the House, it called for only one class of civil penalties and did not include penalties for "knowing" violations. The penalty for committing a prohibited act relating to food under 21 U.S.C. § 331 was to have been not more than $100,000 in the case of an individual, and $500,00 in the case of any other person. Compare H.R. 2749 § 135, 111th Cong. (as reported by the House Committee on Energy and Commerce) with H.R. 2749 § 135, 111th Cong. (as introduced in House of Representatives, June 8, 2009).

[478] H.R. 2749 § 133, 111th Cong. (as engrossed by House of Representatives, July 30, 2009). The bill as introduced in the House did not require the threat to be "imminent" for the FDA to impose a quarantine. Compare H.R. 2749 § 133, 111th Cong. (as reported by the House Committee on Energy and Commerce, June 17, 2009) with H.R. 2749 § 133, 111th Cong. (as introduced in House of Representatives, June 8, 2009).

means of conveyance of such article of food, if the FDA determines that the prohibition or restriction is a necessary protection from an imminent threat of serious adverse health consequences or death to humans or animals."[479] Congress responded to the industry lobby with another restriction of the delegation level at which quarantine orders can be decided. The FDA Commissioner or the Principal Deputy Commissioner could have ordered a quarantine, but not the district director at the local FDA office, without special approval from those two executives at FDA headquarters.[480]

The FDA was told in the House proposed legislation that it would need to adopt rules. These rules were required to have been "consistent with national security interests and as appropriate for known hazards, establish by regulation standards for conducting [quarantines] including, as appropriate, sanitation standards and procedures to restore any affected equipment or means of conveyance to its status prior to [a quarantine]."[481] Thus, if violative corn was put into tanks and rail cars, the FDA could have ordered the corn to be scrapped and could have ordered the tanks and rail cars to be cleaned by (or at the expense of) the food company.

The FDA would have been required to "notify the Governor or other appropriate office of the State affected by the proposed action" and "issue a public announcement of the proposed action" when issuing a quarantine. Furthermore, the FDA would have been required to publish the findings that

---

[479] The bill as reported out by the House Committee allowed the FDA to restrict the movement of food and transport but did not restrict that authority by requiring the FDA to first determine that it was a "a necessary protection from an imminent threat of serious adverse health consequences or death to humans or animals." Compare H.R. 2749 § 133, 111th Cong. (as engrossed by House of Representatives, July 30, 2009) with H.R. 2749 § 133, 111th Cong. (as reported by the House Committee on Energy and Commerce, June 17, 2009).

[480] The bill as introduced in the House did not include a provision limiting who could order a quarantine. Compare H.R. 2749 § 133, 111th Cong. (as reported by the House Committee on Energy and Commerce, June 17, 2009) with H.R. 2749 § 133, 111th Cong. (as introduced in House of Representatives, June 8, 2009). The bill as reported out by the House Committee only allowed the FDA Commissioner, the Principal Deputy Commissioner, and the Associate Commissioner for Regulatory Affairs of the FDA to order a quarantine. Compare H.R. 2749 § 133, 111th Cong. (as engrossed by House of Representatives, July 30, 2009) with H.R. 2749 § 133, 111th Cong. (as reported by the House Committee on Energy and Commerce, June 17, 2009).

[481] This provision was not in the bill as reported out by the House Committee. Compare H.R. 2749 § 133, 111th Cong. (as engrossed by House of Representatives, July 30, 2009) with H.R. 2749 § 133, 111th Cong. (as reported by the House Committee on Energy and Commerce, June 17, 2009).

support the proposed action in the Federal Register, along with "a statement of the reasons for the proposed action" and "a description of the proposed action."[482] Before the quarantine order could have been issued, the FDA findings must be (1) that such a quarantine would be "adequate to prevent the imminent threat of serious adverse health consequences or death to humans or animals," and (2) that no less drastic action is feasible.[483]

Quarantines exist under many state laws; they are intended to be short-term temporary halts to food movement. In the House bill that was not adopted, if after fourteen days of establishing a quarantine "the [FDA] determines it is necessary to continue the action," the FDA must "notify the Governor or other appropriate office of the State affected of the continuation of the action; issue a public announcement of the continuation of the action; and publish in the Federal Register the findings of the [FDA] that support the continuation of the action, including an estimate of the anticipated duration of the action," and must repeat these actions at fourteen-day intervals until the FDA discontinues the quarantine.[484] This power was not adopted, but in reality, the FDA field officials could ask their state counterparts to use state powers to do so.

Under the House bill, before the FDA could impose the quarantine, the FDA would have been required to determine that there was no less drastic action that is feasible, and that a quarantine would be "adequate to prevent the imminent threat of serious adverse health consequences or death to humans or animals."[485]

---

[482] The bill as reported out by the House Committee did not require the FDA to publish the announcement in the Federal Register but allowed the FDA to make a public announcement of the quarantine through "newspaper, radio, television, the Internet, or any reasonable means to make such announcement." Compare H.R. 2749 § 133, 111th Cong. (as engrossed by House of Representatives, July 30, 2009) with H.R. 2749 § 133, 111th Cong. (as reported by the House Committee on Energy and Commerce, June 17, 2009).

[483] H.R. 2749 sec. 133.

[484] This provision was not in the bill as reported out by the House Committee. Compare H.R. 2749 § 133, 111th Cong. (as engrossed by House of Representatives, July 30, 2009) with H.R. 2749 § 133, 111th Cong. (as reported by the House Committee on Energy and Commerce, June 17, 2009).

[485] The bill as introduced in the House did not include this provision. In the bill as reported out by the House Committee, a provision was added to caution the FDA that "any quarantine under this paragraph shall be no greater than is appropriate, as determined by the [FDA], to protect the public health." Compare H.R. 2749 § 133, 111th Cong. (as reported by the House Committee on Energy and Commerce, June 17, 2009) with H.R. 2749 § 133, 111th Cong. (as introduced in House of Representatives, June 8, 2009).

Violation of a quarantine would have been a prohibited act under 21 U.S.C. § 331. Criminal or civil remedies can be used when the defendant violated any provision under Section 331.

What Did the FDA Say About Quarantine Powers?

On July 16, 2009, after H.R. 2749 had been reported by the House Committee, Michael Taylor, the senior advisor to the FDA Commissioner, testified at a hearing to review current issues in food safety at the House Agriculture Committee. In response to a remark by a representative characterizing the use of a quarantine as a "punishment to a geographic area," Taylor said:

> As I read the quarantine provision, though, that is a provision that is aimed at a very unusual situation where there is an imminent risk of very significant harm to the public health… Quarantine simply addresses what you do if you do traceback to a situation where the only way that you can protect the ag sector and the public is to contain the food that you believe is at most risk… One of the values of traceback would be to target where the problem is. Quarantine is going to be a very unusual remedy. I mean, in the ordinary case if you traceback and you know the scope of the problem and you can take care of the problem there is no need for quarantine. That would be a very unusual remedy where there was no other alternative way to contain a problem.[486]

What Did Trade Associations Successfully Argue Against Quarantines?

Tom Stenzel, president of the United Fresh Produce Association, a trade association representing growers, packers, shippers, fresh-cut processors, distributors, and marketers of fresh fruits and vegetables, testified at the

---

[486] Hearing to Review Current Issues in Food Safety, Before the H. Committee on Agriculture, 111th Cong. 124-25 (2009) [hereinafter Hearing to Review Current Issues in Food Safety] (Prepared Statement of Michael R. Taylor, J.D. Senior Advisor to the Commissioner, FDA, HHS, Rockville, MD).

House Energy and Commerce Committee's Subcommittee on Health hearing on food safety on June 3, 2009:

> We oppose this section giving HHS authority to quarantine foods from vast geographic areas within the United States, based only on the modest standard that "FDA reasonably believes" such food may have originated from a particular region. First, food safety is not determined by geographical or political boundaries such as state or county lines, but by the preventive controls and practices applied by any individual producer or manufacturer. With the intensive new regulatory requirements of this bill, such a broad-based swipe against entire regions of food production is certainly regulatory overkill, and fraught with potential unintended consequences.
>
> Consider our industry's experience last summer, in which the combined efforts of the CDC and FDA advised consumers against consuming tomatoes from vast regions of the country for suspected Salmonella contamination, only to find months later that the real source of the problem was contaminated jalapeno peppers from a farm 500 miles south of the U.S.-Mexican border. Or, consider the spinach outbreak in 2006, when our entire industry immediately pulled all spinach from shelves nationwide, and the nation's primary spinach growing regions were under an FDA public relations cloud for weeks and weeks. In fact, we now know that the only contaminated product came from one 50-acre farm, packaged in one processing plant, and only on one production shift.
>
> Should FDA have had the simple ability to quarantine vast geographical regions, I fear the stampede to action that could have occurred in either of these cases. We see no wisdom in providing statutory authority to magnify the damage of this type of decision-making. We support mandatory product recall, but not mandatory

"geographical recall" based on local, county, state or
country boundaries.[487]

Changes were made to the section in response to concerns that the FDA's
authority under the section as introduced was too broad. The standard was
changed as to what particular food the FDA can quarantine. There must
not just be a threat of serious adverse health consequences or death to
humans or animals before the FDA may quarantine a particular food, as
was required by the bill as introduced in the House, but there must be an
imminent threat of serious adverse health consequences or death to humans
or animals. Additionally, instead of needing a "reasonable belief," the FDA
must have "credible evidence" that a food is located in or originated from a
particular region before quarantining a type of food in a geographic area.
The FDA's authority to carry out a quarantine of a specific food through
prohibiting or restricting the means of conveyance of any article of food
was tempered by an amendment that allows the FDA the authority only
when the FDA "determines that the prohibition or restriction is a necessary
protection from an imminent threat of serious adverse health consequences
or death to humans or animals."

The bill as introduced in the House did not include a provision limiting
who could order a quarantine, but the bill amended to allow only the
secretary or, when specifically designated by the secretary, the FDA
Commissioner or the Principal Deputy Commissioner, to order a
quarantine.[488]

Why Was the FDA Denied Subpoena Authority in the Final Bill?

The House bill would have given the FDA authority to issue subpoenas for
"requiring the attendance and testimony of witnesses and the production of
records and other things" at hearings, proceedings, and investigations in

---

[487] Hearing on Food Safety Enhancement Act of 2009, Before the Subcommittee on
Health of the H. Committee on Energy and Commerce, 111th Cong. 4 (2009) [hereinafter
Hearing on Food Safety Enhancement Act of 2009] (Prepared Statement of Tom Stenzel,
President of United Fresh Produce Association).
[488] Compare H.R. 2749 § 133, 111th Cong. (as engrossed by House of Representatives,
July 30, 2009) with H.R. 2749 § 133, 111th Cong. (as reported by the House Committee
on Energy and Commerce, June 17, 2009).

regard to a violation of the FDCA, the Public Health Service Act, or the Federal Anti-Tampering Act.

At the House Energy and Commerce Committee's Subcommittee on Health hearing on food safety on June 3, 2009, FDA Commissioner Hamburg noted that the FDA supported the House bill's addition of subpoenas to FDA enforcement authority. When asked if the subpoena authority granted by the bill was too broad a grant of power, Commissioner Hamburg responded:

> Well, I think that we have enough work to do without going on fishing expeditions. We would be seeking information that would be of vital importance to addressing the tasks at hand. It would be of great value to have the ability to access critical information, to inform the inspection process as well as to inform outbreak investigations. And I think that if we are going to be able to really move forward to ensure the safety of the food supply, this is one of a number of tools that will enable us to really do what needs to be done.[489]

Representative Shimkus took issue at the House Energy and Commerce Committee's Subcommittee on Health hearing on food safety on June 3, 2009 with the standard included in the bill for the FDA to issue a subpoena. He stated that it provided too vague a power to the FDA to allow the FDA to issue subpoenas in "any other matter relative to the Commissioner's jurisdiction under [the FDCA], the Public Health Service Act, and the Federal Anti-Tampering Act," and suggested that the language should be clarified.[490]

---

[489] Hearing on Food Safety Enhancement Act of 2009, Before the Subcommittee on Health of the H. Committee on Energy and Commerce, 111th Cong. 132 (2009) [hereinafter Hearing on Food Safety Enhancement Act of 2009] (Statement of FDA Commissioner Hamburg in Preliminary Transcript).

[490] Hearing on Food Safety Enhancement Act of 2009, Before the Subcommittee on Health of the H. Committee on Energy and Commerce, 111th Cong. 186-87 (2009) [hereinafter Hearing on Food Safety Enhancement Act of 2009] (Statement of Representative Shimkus in Preliminary Transcript).

The language was changed by the manager's amendment passed by voice vote at the mark-up session, eliminating the exercise of a subpoena for the purpose of "any other matter relative to the Commissioner's jurisdiction over food under this Act, the Public Health Service Act, or the Federal Anti-Tampering Act." The final provision allows the exercise of subpoenas for the purpose of:

> (1) any hearing, investigation, or other proceeding respecting a violation of a provision of this Act, the Public Health Service Act, or the Federal Anti-Tampering Act, relating to food; or

> (2) any hearing, investigation, or other proceeding to determine if a person is in violation of a specific provision of this Act, the Public Health Service Act, or the Federal Anti-Tampering Act, relating to food.

Additionally, a non-delegation provision was added allowing only the secretary or an official designated by the secretary to issue a subpoena.[491]

How Would the House "Extraterritorial Jurisdiction" Provision Have Operated?

The House-passed legislation's Section 213 was deleted in the final bill. It would have made it a prohibited act to "produce, manufacture, process, prepare, pack, hold, or distribute an adulterated or misbranded food with the knowledge or intent such an article will be imported into the United States."[492] This section would have established extraterritorial jurisdiction over any violation of the FDCA relating to food "intended for import into the United States or if any act in furtherance of the violation was committed in the United States."[493] This would have filled a gap that courts consider when a non-US person protests lack of jurisdiction for an enforcement case. Here, Congress expressly claims the authority to impose

---

[491] Compare H.R. 2749 § 135, 111th Cong. (as reported by the House Committee on Energy and Commerce) with H.R. 2749 § 135, 111th Cong. (as introduced in House of Representatives, June 8, 2009).
[492] H.R. 2749 § 213, 111th Cong. (as engrossed by House of Representatives, July 30, 2009).
[493] Id.

penalties for actions outside the United States that had been intended to affect the food entering the United States.

During congressional deliberations, FDA Food Safety Chief Michael Taylor told Congress, "The bill would give FDA extraterritorial jurisdiction over violations of the Act so that again we can begin to address those problems upstream. I think that one of the strengths of the bill is that it addresses FDA's need for strengthened legal tools to oversee imports."[494] But the provision did not survive lobbying by opponents in the Senate proceedings.

According to a statement by Representative John Dingell on the House floor, the bill's provisions on imported food not only would have given the FDA the authority needed to keep the US food supply safe, but also the:

> Legislation does something else of importance to our people, and that is, it sees to it that where misbehavior occurs abroad, those same penalties that would be assessed against Americans are assessed against foreigners. This is an important matter of competition to American producers and manufacturers. It sees to it that they are fairly treated, and that there is *no more unfair competition by people who could market unsafe commodities* to the detriment of American consumers and American growers, producers and processors... Food and Drug has the authority to *terminate the ability of foreigners to sell in this country* for the first time in a way which is consistent with American trade laws and the obligations of American people with regard to the safety of food.[495] (emphasis added)

The 2010 law's addition of extraterritorial power would have been significant. Although currently an importing firm may have its food shipment denied entry into the United States, its losses are limited to the value of the cargo destroyed. The FDA has been unable to impose penalties for violations of the FDCA that happen outside of the United States.

---

[494] Testimony before House Agriculture Committee, July 16, 2009.
[495] 155 Cong. Rec. H9161 (daily ed. July 30, 2009) (statement of Rep. Dingell).

According to the FDA, civil penalties are integral to discouraging violations of the FDCA.[496]

Arguments will still be made. Importers may attempt to argue that criminal and civil penalties cannot be enforced against actions that occur in a foreign country. It is a longstanding principle of American jurisprudence that Congress has the power to enforce laws that operate outside the territorial boundaries of the United States.[497] This practice is not unique to the United States, but is customary international law.[498] Congress's power to adopt laws with extraterritorial application arises from the same authority that empowers it to legislate domestically—its enumerated powers laid out in Article I of the Constitution.[499]

Extraterritorial application of US law is circumscribed by a general presumption that US law is to apply only domestically, if Congress had not "clearly expressed" the intent for extraterritorial application.[500] This canon of statutory construction has not been uniformly applied throughout history. Traditionally the application of extraterritorial jurisdiction required explicit congressional authorization.[501] However, as cross-border interactions became commonplace, courts more frequently faced the question of whether a specific area of law had exterritorial application, and a different rule developed. The bright-line application transformed into a more nuanced, searching inquiry, one that has allowed for extraterritorial jurisdiction in some areas of law and not others, despite similar levels of ambiguous guidance from Congress.[502]

---

[496] See GAO, *Food Safety: Agencies Need to Address Gaps in Enforcement and Collaboration to Enhance Safety of Imported Food* 6 (2009) [hereinafter *Agencies Need to Address Gaps in Enforcement and Collaboration to Enhance Safety of Imported Food*].

[497] See *Equal Employment Opportunity Comm'n v. Arabian Am. Oil Co.*, 499 U.S. 244, 248 (1991).

[498] Restatement (Third) of the Foreign Relations Law of the U.S. § 402 (2009).

[499] U.S. Const. Art. I.

[500] See *Benz v. Compania*, 353 U.S. 138, 147 (1957).

[501] See *American Banana Co. v. United Fruit Co.*, 213 U.S. 347, 356 (1909).

[502] See *Equal Employment Opportunity Comm'n v. Arabian Am. Oil Co.*, 499 U.S. 244 (1991) (labor); *United States v. Aluminum Co. of Am.*, 148 F.2d 416 (2d Cir. 1945). (antitrust); *Schoenbaum v. Firstbrook*, 405 F.2d 200 (2d Cir. 1968) (securities). Some commentators hypothesize that courts have been more likely to find extraterritorial jurisdiction when doing so will protect US market interests. This has led to exterritorial application of antitrust and securities law, but not labor and environmental law. See Jonathan Turley, *Legal Theory: "When in Rome:" Multinational Misconduct and the Presumption Against Extraterritoriality*, 84 Nw. U.L. Rev. 598, 634 (1990).

Did Congress Intend for the FDA to Be Enforcing Its Laws Globally?

Yes. The 2010 law expressly empowers international involvement for the FDA in food enforcement efforts. According to the FDA's mission statement, the FDA is, among other things, to "participate through appropriate processes with representatives of other countries to reduce the burden of regulation, harmonize regulatory requirements, and achieve appropriate reciprocal arrangements."[503] The FDA has developed international programs within its current framework, such as those mentioned above through the FDA's Beyond Our Borders Initiative, and so it has requested and received international enforcement authority.[504] Section 308 of the new law expressly establishes this foreign inspection power.

The House version of the 2010 law responded to global food sourcing concerns by not only mandating extensive programs to be applied on a global level, but by establishing extraterritorial jurisdiction over "any violation of [the FDCA] relating to any article of food if such article was intended for import into the United States or if any act in furtherance of the violation was committed in the United States."[505] Congress could have found its power to legislate extraterritorial jurisdiction for H.R. 2749 in the "Necessary and Proper Clause" of the Constitution.[506] The law's specific inclusion of extraterritorial jurisdiction would have enabled the criminal and civil penalties to be applied to actions affecting US food that occur outside of the United States. The FDA argued that this authority would be "pivotal in discouraging the importation of substandard foods and will be a dramatic improvement to the FDA's ability to ensure that the US food supply is safe."[507] But it did not survive into the final text of the law.

---

[503] 21 U.S.C. § 393 (2009).

[504] FDA, Consumer Health Information, *FDA Beyond Our Borders*, 2 (2008), www.fda.gov/downloads/ForConsumers/ConsumerUpdates/ucm103044.pdf [hereinafter *FDA Beyond Our Borders*]; See HHS, FDA, *Food Protection Plan: An Integrated Strategy for Protecting the Nation's Food Supply* (2007).

[505] H.R. 2749 §213, 111th Cong. (as passed by House of Representatives July 29, 2009).

[506] H.R. Rep. No. 111-234, at 37. Article I, Section 8, Clause 18 of the Constitution grants Congress the power "to make all Laws which shall be necessary and proper for carrying into Execution the foregoing Powers, and all other Powers vested by this Constitution in the Government of the United States, or in any Department or Officer thereof." U.S. Const. art. I, § 8, cl. 18.

[507] *See* GAO, *Food Safety: Agencies Need to Address Gaps in Enforcement and Collaboration to Enhance Safety of Imported Food* 6 (2009) [hereinafter *Agencies Need to Address Gaps in Enforcement and Collaboration to Enhance Safety of Imported Food*].

What Is the Difference in Enforcement Actions That Rely on the Use of "Prohibited Acts" Instead of "Misbranding" and "Adulteration"?

Caroline Smith DeWaal, director of food safety at the Center for Science in the Public Interest, testified at the House Energy and Commerce Committee's Subcommittee on Health hearing on food safety on June 3, 2009:

> We agree with basing enforcement actions on the adulteration and misbranding provisions in sections 402 and 403 of the Food, Drug, and Cosmetic Act. Many of the food safety bills currently being discussed rely on the prohibited acts section, which would limit the use of enforcement tools discussed above such as detention, seizure, and mandatory recall. Importantly, using the prohibited acts section—rather than adulteration or misbranding—would provide FDA with little ability to respond to unsafe imports. We urge the committee to resist changes that would weaken enforcement of sections 101, 102, 103, 104, and 109.[508]

Text of the Law as Adopted

SEC. 206. MANDATORY RECALL AUTHORITY.

(a) In General.--Chapter IV (21 U.S.C. 341 et seq.), as amended by section 202, is amended by adding at the end the following:

"SEC. 423. MANDATORY RECALL AUTHORITY.

"(a) Voluntary Procedures.--If the Secretary determines, based on information gathered through the reportable food registry under section 417 or through any other means, that there is a reasonable probability that an article of food (other than infant formula) is adulterated under section 402 or misbranded under section 403(w) and the use of or exposure to such article will cause serious

---

[508] Hearing on Food Safety Enhancement Act of 2009, Before the Subcommittee on Health of the H. Committee on Energy and Commerce, 111th Cong. 8 (2009) [hereinafter Hearing on Food Safety Enhancement Act of 2009] (Prepared Statement of Caroline Smith DeWaal, Director of Food Safety at the Center for Science in the Public Interest).

adverse health consequences or death to humans or animals, the Secretary shall provide the responsible party (as defined in section 417) with an opportunity to cease distribution and recall such article.

"(b) Prehearing Order To Cease Distribution and Give Notice.--

"(1) IN GENERAL.--If the responsible party refuses to or does not voluntarily cease distribution or recall such article within the time and in the manner prescribed by the Secretary (if so prescribed), the Secretary may, by order require, as the Secretary deems necessary, such person to--

"(A) immediately cease distribution of such article; and

"(B) as applicable, immediately notify all persons--

"(i) manufacturing, processing, packing, transporting, distributing, receiving, holding, or importing and selling such article; and

"(ii) to which such article has been distributed, transported, or sold, to immediately cease distribution of such article.

"(2) REQUIRED ADDITIONAL INFORMATION.--

"(A) IN GENERAL.--If an article of food covered by a recall order issued under paragraph (1)(B) has been distributed to a warehouse-based third party logistics provider without providing such provider sufficient information to know or reasonably determine the precise identity of the article of food covered by a recall order that is in its possession, the notice provided by the responsible party subject to the order issued under paragraph (1)(B) shall include such information as is necessary for the warehouse-based third party logistics provider to identify the food.

"(B) RULES OF CONSTRUCTION.--*Nothing in this paragraph shall be construed--*

"(i) to exempt a warehouse-based third party logistics provider from the requirements of this Act, including the requirements in this section and section 414; or

"(ii) to exempt a warehouse-based third party logistics provider from being the subject of a mandatory recall order.

"(3) DETERMINATION TO LIMIT AREAS AFFECTED.--*If the Secretary requires a responsible party to cease distribution under paragraph (1)(A) of an article of food identified in subsection (a), the Secretary may limit the size of the geographic area and the markets affected by such cessation if such limitation would not compromise the public health.*

"(c) Hearing on Order.--*The Secretary shall provide the responsible party subject to an order under subsection (b) with an opportunity for an informal hearing, to be held as soon as possible, but not later than 2 days after the issuance of the order, on the actions required by the order and on why the article that is the subject of the order should not be recalled.*

"(d) Post-hearing Recall Order and Modification of Order.--

"(1) AMENDMENT OF ORDER.--*If, after providing opportunity for an informal hearing under subsection (c), the Secretary determines that removal of the article from commerce is necessary, the Secretary shall, as appropriate--*

"(A) amend the order to require recall of such article or other appropriate action;

"(B) specify a timetable in which the recall shall occur;

"(C) require periodic reports to the Secretary describing the progress of the recall; and

"(D) provide notice to consumers to whom such article was, or may have been, distributed.

"(2) VACATING OF ORDER.--If, after such hearing, the Secretary determines that adequate grounds do not exist to continue the actions required by the order, or that such actions should be modified, the Secretary shall vacate the order or modify the order.

"(e) Rule Regarding Alcoholic Beverages.--The Secretary shall not initiate a mandatory recall or take any other action under this section with respect to any alcohol beverage until the Secretary has provided the Alcohol and Tobacco Tax and Trade Bureau with a reasonable opportunity to cease distribution and recall such article under the Alcohol and Tobacco Tax and Trade Bureau authority.

"(f) Cooperation and Consultation.--The Secretary shall work with State and local public health officials in carrying out this section, as appropriate.

"(g) Public Notification.--In conducting a recall under this section, the Secretary shall--

"(1) ensure that a press release is published regarding the recall, as well as alerts and public notices, as appropriate, in order to provide notification--

"(A) of the recall to consumers and retailers to whom such article was, or may have been, distributed; and

"(B) that includes, at a minimum--

"(i) the name of the article of food subject to the recall;

"(ii) a description of the risk associated with such article; and *"(iii) to the extent practicable, information for consumers about similar articles of food that are not affected by the recall;*

"(2) consult the policies of the Department of Agriculture regarding providing to the public a list of retail consignees receiving products involved in a Class I recall and shall consider providing such a list to the public, as determined appropriate by the Secretary; and

"(3) if available, publish on the Internet Web site of the Food and Drug Administration an image of the article that is the subject of the press release described in (1).

"(h) No Delegation.--The authority conferred by this section to order a recall or vacate a recall order shall not be delegated to any officer or employee other than the Commissioner.

"(i) Effect.--Nothing in this section shall affect the authority of the Secretary to request or participate in a voluntary recall, or to issue an order to cease distribution or to recall under any other provision of this Act or under the Public Health Service Act.

"(j) Coordinated Communication.--

"(1) IN GENERAL.--To assist in carrying out the requirements of this subsection, the Secretary shall establish an incident command operation or a similar operation within the Department of Health and Human Services that will operate not later than 24 hours after the initiation of a mandatory recall or the recall of an article of food for which the use of, or exposure to, such article will cause serious adverse health consequences or death to humans or animals.

"(2) REQUIREMENTS.--To reduce the potential for miscommunication during recalls or regarding investigations of a food borne illness outbreak associated with a food that is subject to a recall, each incident command operation or similar operation under paragraph (1) shall use regular staff and resources of the Department of Health and Human Services to--

"*(A) ensure timely and coordinated communication within the Department, including enhanced communication and coordination between different agencies and organizations within the Department;*

"*(B) ensure timely and coordinated communication from the Department, including public statements, throughout the duration of the investigation and related foodborne illness outbreak;*

"*(C) identify a single point of contact within the Department for public inquiries regarding any actions by the Secretary related to a recall;*

"*(D) coordinate with Federal, State, local, and tribal authorities, as appropriate, that have responsibilities related to the recall of a food or a foodborne illness outbreak associated with a food that is subject to the recall, including notification of the Secretary of Agriculture and the Secretary of Education in the event such recalled food is a commodity intended for use in a child nutrition program (as identified in section 25(b) of the Richard B. Russell National School Lunch Act (42 U.S.C. 1769f(b)); and*

"*(E) conclude operations at such time as the Secretary determines appropriate.*

"*(3) MULTIPLE RECALLS.--The Secretary may establish multiple or concurrent incident command operations or similar operations in the event of multiple recalls or foodborne illness outbreaks necessitating such action by the Department of Health and Human Services.*".

(b) Search Engine.--Not later than 90 days after the date of enactment of this Act, the Secretary shall modify the Internet Web site of the Food and Drug Administration to include a search engine that--

(1) is consumer-friendly, as determined by the Secretary; and

(2) provides a means by which an individual may locate relevant information regarding each article of food subject to a recall under section 423 of the Federal Food, Drug, and Cosmetic Act and the status of such recall (such as whether a recall is ongoing or has been completed).

(c) Civil Penalty.--Section 303(f)(2)(A) (21 U.S.C. 333(f)(2)(A)) is amended by inserting "or any person who does not comply with a recall order under section 423" after "section 402(a)(2)(B)".

(d) Prohibited Acts.--Section 301 (21 U.S.C. 331 et seq.), as amended by section 106, is amended by adding at the end the following:

> *"(xx) The refusal or failure to follow an order under section 423.".*

(e) GAO Review.--

> *(1) IN GENERAL.--Not later than 90 days after the date of enactment of this Act, the Comptroller General of the United States shall submit to Congress a report that--*

>> *(A) identifies State and local agencies with the authority to require the mandatory recall of food, and evaluates use of such authority with regard to frequency, effectiveness, and appropriateness, including consideration of any new or existing mechanisms available to compensate persons for general and specific recall-related costs when a recall is subsequently determined by the relevant authority to have been an error;*

>> *(B) identifies Federal agencies, other than the Department of Health and Human Services, with mandatory recall authority and examines use of that authority with regard to frequency, effectiveness, and appropriateness, including any new or existing mechanisms available to compensate persons for general and specific recall-related costs when a recall is subsequently determined by the relevant agency to have been an error;*

(C) considers models for farmer restitution implemented in other nations in cases of erroneous recalls; and

(D) makes recommendations to the Secretary regarding use of the authority under section 423 of the Federal Food, Drug, and Cosmetic Act (as added by this section) to protect the public health while seeking to minimize unnecessary economic costs.

(2) EFFECT OF REVIEW.--If the Comptroller General of the United States finds, after the review conducted under paragraph (1), that the mechanisms described in such paragraph do not exist or are inadequate, then, not later than 90 days after the conclusion of such review, the Secretary of Agriculture shall conduct a study of the feasibility of implementing a farmer indemnification program to provide restitution to agricultural producers for losses sustained as a result of a mandatory recall of an agricultural commodity by a Federal or State regulatory agency that is subsequently determined to be in error. The Secretary of Agriculture shall submit to the Committee on Agriculture of the House of Representatives and the Committee on Agriculture, Nutrition, and Forestry of the Senate a report that describes the results of the study, including any recommendations.

(f) Annual Report to Congress.--

(1) IN GENERAL.--Not later than 2 years after the date of enactment of this Act and annually thereafter, the Secretary of Health and Human Services (referred to in this subsection as the "Secretary") shall submit a report to the Committee on Health, Education, Labor, and Pensions of the Senate and the Committee on Energy and Commerce of the House of Representatives on the use of recall authority under section 423 of the Federal Food, Drug, and Cosmetic Act (as added by subsection (a)) and any public health advisories issued by the Secretary that advise against the consumption of an article of food on the ground that the article of food is adulterated and poses an imminent danger to health.

(2) CONTENT.--The report under paragraph (1) shall include, with respect to the report year--

(A) the identity of each article of food that was the subject of a public health advisory described in paragraph (1), an opportunity to cease

distribution and recall under subsection (a) of section 423 of the Federal Food, Drug, and Cosmetic Act, or a mandatory recall order under subsection (b) of such section;

(B) the number of responsible parties, as defined in section 417 of the Federal Food, Drug, and Cosmetic Act, formally given the opportunity to cease distribution of an article of food and recall such article, as described in section 423(a) of such Act;

(C) the number of responsible parties described in subparagraph (B) who did not cease distribution of or recall an article of food after given the opportunity to cease distribution or recall under section 423(a) of the Federal Food, Drug, and Cosmetic Act;

(D) the number of recall orders issued under section 423(b) of the Federal Food, Drug, and Cosmetic Act; and

(E) a description of any instances in which there was no testing that confirmed adulteration of an article of food that was the subject of a recall under section 423(b) of the Federal Food, Drug, and Cosmetic Act or a public health advisory described in paragraph (1).

SEC. 207. ADMINISTRATIVE DETENTION OF FOOD.

(a) In General.--Section 304(h)(1)(A) (21 U.S.C. 334(h)(1)(A)) is amended by--

(1) striking "credible evidence or information indicating" and inserting "reason to believe"; and

(2) striking "presents a threat of serious adverse health consequences or death to humans or animals" and inserting "is adulterated or misbranded".

(b) Regulations.--Not later than 120 days after the date of enactment of this Act, the Secretary shall issue an interim final rule amending subpart K of part 1 of title 21, Code of Federal Regulations, to implement the amendment made by this section.

(c) Effective Date.--The amendment made by this section shall take effect 180 days after the date of enactment of this Act.

11

Costs and Fees

What Do Managers Need To Know?

The only mandated payment to be collected under the 2010 Act is from a person or entity that fails an inspection, or fails to properly execute a recall, and then only for the FDA's costs for one year after the event. The FDA can also collect a fee from voluntary participants in the Qualified Importer Program[509] to cover the costs of this fast-track alternative. This Senate-negotiated outcome was a major defeat for the FDA's intent to assure a stronger food safety budget.

The FDA now has the authority to charge domestic and foreign facilities for the costs of returning for a second or subsequent inspection, if the company facility does not satisfy FDA standards in the first inspection.

The FDA also has been given express authority to bill the company whose food is ordered to be recalled, for the FDA's total costs for overseeing the recall. This could amount to a very considerable charge, delayed by government accounting until months after the recall is undertaken. The fee amount will be set by the Secretary based on the costs of covering food recall activities including "technical assistance, follow-up effectiveness checks, and public notifications."

The FDA allows the option for a company that brings food into the United States to register as a "qualified importer" under Section 806 of the new Act. The costs of setting up the program in its first year, plus the overhead

---

[509] Pub.L. 111-353 §806 (2010).

cost of operating the program in each year, can be collected from these volunteer companies.[510]

What Was the Intent Underlying the Final (Senate) Version of the Act?

Unlike the House bill, the Senate bill as introduced included no registration fee for facilities or importers. The Senate bill did include fees related to reinspection, recall, and importation activities.

The "responsible party for each domestic facility" and the "United States agent for each foreign facility" must pay a fee that covers 100 percent of the FDA's costs associated with a reinspection. A clause was added to this provision in the bill as reported by the Senate Committee levying such fees on the US agent of each foreign facility subject to reinspection.[511] In the bill as introduced, reinspection fees were only levied on domestic facilities.

The "responsible party for each domestic facility" and "an importer who does not comply with a recall order under section 423 or under section 412(f)" must pay for all costs associated with a food recall, including "technical assistance, follow-up effectiveness checks, and public notifications, for such year." The language in this provision was changed to levy the fee only in the instance of non-compliance with a recall order, whereas the bill as introduced in the Senate levied the fee on any facility or importer subject to a food recall.

Each importer participating in the voluntary Qualified Importer Program must pay yearly to cover the administrative costs of the program, as well as a portion of the startup costs for that program.[512]

Any importer subject to reinspection must bear the costs associated with the reinspection. The language was changed in this provision as reported out by the Senate Committee to capture all instances of importers subject to reinspection, not only when an importer is subject to reinspection at a port of entry, as was the case in the bill introduced in the Senate.

---

[510] Pub.L. 111-353 §107 (2010).

[511] *Id.*, new 743(a)(1)(C, D).

[512] *Id.*, new 743(b)(2)(B)(i).

A provision was added in the bill reported by the Senate Committee requiring the FDA to publish "a proposed set of guidelines in consideration of the burden of fee amounts on small business. Such consideration may include reduced fee amounts for small businesses. The Secretary shall provide for a period of public comment on such guidelines. The Secretary shall adjust the fee schedule for small businesses subject to such fees only through notice and comment rulemaking."

A provision on compliance with World Trade Organization agreements that was in the bill when introduced in the Senate was removed from the bill in the version reported by the Senate Committee. The provision had stated: "Nothing in this section shall be construed to authorize the assessment of any fee inconsistent with the agreement establishing the World Trade Organization or any other treaty or international agreement to which the United States is a party."[513] However, a section providing that no term of the entire bill should be construed inconsistently with World Trade Organization obligations was added to the bill when reported by the Senate Committee.[514]

What Would the Unsuccessful House Bill Have Provided?

The House gave the FDA extensive fee-gathering authority to pay for the programs created under the 2010 amendments.[515] The $500 per-food facility registration fees adopted by the House, but resisted by the food industry in the Senate, would have gone toward defraying the costs of food safety activities, which are:

> activities related to compliance by facilities registered under section 415 with the requirements of this Act relating to food (including research related to and the development of standards (such as performance standards and preventive controls), risk assessments, hazard analyses,

---

[513] Compare S. 510 § 107, 111th Cong. (as reported by the Senate HELP Committee, Nov. 18, 2009) with S. 510 § 107, 111th Cong. (as introduced in Senate, Mar. 3, 2009).
[514] S. 510 § 404, 111th Cong. (as reported by the Senate HELP Committee, Nov. 18, 2009) www.wisconsinagconnection.com/story-national.php?Id=2424&yr=2009; *Fears Over Trade Linger After Senate Committee Reports Food Safety Bill*, INSIDE HEALTH POLICY, Nov. 25, 2009.
[515] These fee proposals failed in the Senate.

inspection   planning   and   inspections,   third-party
inspections, compliance review and enforcement, import
review, information technology support, test development,
product sampling, risk communication, and administrative
detention).[516]

A person who owns or operates multiple facilities would not have had to
pay more than $175,000 in registration fees in a single year. A sunset
provision stated that no fee would be collected after 2014. History suggests
that such a sunset clause simply improves the negotiating room that pro-
industry members can use to oppose costs and burdens of the new law.

The House Committee noted in its report that the money appropriated
through the fees would have been directed toward food safety activities, but
additionally detailed which activities should be given priority in allocating
the funds, perhaps indicating the committee's value of each activity:

Because an effective food safety program must be a
combined effort of the scientific and regulatory food safety
activities of the Center for Food Safety and Applied
Nutrition (CFSAN) and support for the food safety
inspection-related activities of the Office of Regulatory
Affairs (ORA), the Committee expresses its intent that the
agency give highest priority for use of these funds to
activities that directly support implementation of this bill,
including: (1) regulations and guidance, particularly with
respect to hazard analyses, preventive controls, and food
safety plans, both with respect to packaged food and to
fresh produce; (2) risk assessment activities underlying
development of performance standards; (3) information

---

[516] H.R, 2749 § 101, 111th Cong. (as engrossed by House of Representatives, July 30,
2009). On the House floor, Representative Lucas made a motion to insert a provision in
the bill that would allow the FDA to devote a portion of the registration fees appropriated
through Section 415 to preemptive purchases of food products from producers as a matter
of food safety activities. He claimed this provision would address the issue of
indemnification for the wrongful attribution of a food outbreak to a food item and would
strengthen FDA accountability. Although Representative Dingell argued that the
amendment could not be considered under the closed rule, the Speaker *pro tempore*
allowed the amendment to be considered. It was defeated by a vote of 861 yeas to 240
nays. 155 Cong. Rec. H9162-64 (daily ed. July 30, 2009).

gathering steps prior to developing regulations on traceability and reporting results of finished product testing, including required pilot projects, technology assessments, and feasibility studies; (4) maintenance of an enhanced registration system; (5) maintenance of an up-to-date reportable food registry; (6) information technology systems to support domestic and import inspectional activities; (7) scientific equipment to conduct needed research and perform product sampling; (8) training of agency and state officials in the proper conduct of inspectional activities; (9) development of an expedited safe and secure importation program; (10) surveillance, public education, and research activities in support of improving food safety; (11) review of infant formula and GRAS submissions; and (12) creation and implementation of a risk-based inspection schedule.

How Did the FDA Respond?

According to FDA Commissioner Hamburg at the Subcommittee on Health hearing on June 3, 2009:

> The draft legislation makes an important investment in the resources needed for major progress. After all, FDA must have the resources necessary to meet its responsibilities. Otherwise, the public will not benefit from the promise of a modern food safety system, and the Agency will fail to meet the expectations of the President, Congress, and the public.

> The bill authorizes three fees that are also requested in the President's FY 2010 budget. For example, section 101 provides for a registration fee. This fee is of critical importance to enable the Agency to increase its inspection coverage of the approximately 378,000 registered facilities and to enhance its other food safety activities. Section 108 provides for a reinspection fee for a food facility that commits a violation that requires additional inspections by

FDA. This will help cover the costs of reinspecting FDA-regulated facilities that fail to meet current Good Manufacturing Practices (cGMPs) or other FDA requirements. Section 144 authorizes the Secretary to charge and collect a fee for the issuance of export certificates for food and animal feed which would facilitate trade. This fee will help cover the cost of this program, which is necessary for firms to do business with countries that require such certificates.[517]

What Was the Intent of the House Version, Which Was Not Adopted?

The House bill anticipated that the costs of these new food safety activities would have, in part, been funded by the collection of new fees required by the 2010 legislation. The 2010 legislation establishes only one of the two proposed programs, a facility reinspection and recall fee program, but not also an importer registration fee program. According to the House report, the 2010 legislation would have required "food facilities, importers, custom brokers, and filers" to annually register with the Secretary and "provide certain information related to the entity" in order "to enable the Secretary to better account for entities involved in the manufacture, processing, packing, holding, and import of food."[518]

In summarizing the bill, the House Committee report noted:

> H.R. 2947 would require [FDA] to strengthen federal efforts related to ensuring the safety of commercially distributed food. H.R. 2947 would also broaden the [FDA's] authority to regulate food products, and would require the agency to assess fees on food facilities, as well as importers and exporters of food products to cover the costs of registering and inspecting facilities authorized in the bill.[519]

---

[517] Hearing on Food Safety Enhancement Act of 2009, Before the Subcommittee on Health of the H. Committee on Energy and Commerce, 111th Cong. 3-8 (2009) [hereinafter Hearing on Food Safety Enhancement Act of 2009] (Prepared Statement by Margaret A. Hamburg, Commissioner of FDA, HHS, Rockville, MD).

[517] H.R. Rep. No. 111-234, at 46 (2009).

[518] H.R. Rep. No. 111-234, at 35-36 (2009).

[519] H.R. Rep. No. 111-234, at 38 (2009).

The amendment retained the provisions of the bill as reported by the House Committee, but clarified a few provisions.[520] Specifically:

> It clarifie[d] who exactly does—and does not—have to register with FDA and pay the annual registration fee. For instance, the substitute amendment provides that farms, including those that process food and feed that they sell to other farms or primarily directly to consumers, do not have to register or pay. In addition, retail food establishments that sell products directly to consumers also do not have to register or pay.[521]

How Did Trade Associations Respond?

A representative of the Food Marketing Institute, a trade association that represents food retailers and wholesalers, testified at the House Energy and Commerce Committee's Subcommittee on Health hearing on food safety on June 3, 2009, stating that the institute is "willing to support a fair registration or user fee provided that it is utilized by the FDA in a transparent and accountable manner to improve the safety of our food supply through means such as conducting research and consumer education programs."[522]

Pamela Bailey, president of the Grocery Manufacturers Association, the world's largest trade association, representing more than 300 food, beverage, and consumer product companies, testified at the House Energy and Commerce Committee's Subcommittee on Health hearing on food safety on June 3, 2009. She noted the association's concern about the registration fees:

> If enacted, the fees proposed would provide roughly 40 percent of FDA food-related spending—an unprecedented increase in industry financing of a public health agency that

---

[520] H.R. Rep. No. 111-235 (2009).

[521] H.R. Rep. No. 111-234, at 2-3 (2009).

[522] Hearing on Food Safety Enhancement Act of 2009, Before the Subcommittee on Health of the H. Committee on Energy and Commerce, 111th Cong. 148 (2009) [hereinafter Hearing on Food Safety Enhancement Act of 2009] (Statement of Mike Ambrosio, Food Marketing Institute, in Preliminary Transcript).

has been financed through general revenue for more than a century. As FDA's science advisory board has noted, a combination of fees and inspection mandates could drain critically needed resources from science and standard-setting functions. In particular, we are concerned that a broadly applied fee to finance basic FDA functions, including inspections and enforcement, creates an inherent conflict of interest that will erode, rather than improve, consumer confidence in our food supplies. Our industry is ultimately responsible for the safety of its products, but securing the safety of the food supply is a government function which should be largely financed with government resources.[523]

Tom Stenzel, president of the United Fresh Produce Association, a trade association representing growers, packers, shippers, fresh-cut processors, distributors, and marketers of fresh fruits and vegetables, testified at the House Energy and Commerce Committee's Subcommittee on Health hearing on food safety on June 3, 2009:

We continue to advocate strongly that user fees are an inappropriate means of funding food safety inspections. Assuring a rigorous food safety inspection system is properly the responsibility of the nation at large, and thus appropriated funds, rather than a role for individual food companies. This is a long-held principle shared by many stakeholders in this debate, and one that should not be compromised for short-term budget expediency.

Should any type of fees be included in a final bill, we strongly urge that they must not be used for inspection programs; must be targeted to specific and justified needs not met through recent and potential increased appropriations; must be transparent and capped in

---

[523] Hearing on Food Safety Enhancement Act of 2009, Before the Subcommittee on Health of the H. Committee on Energy and Commerce, 111th Cong. 5 (2009) [hereinafter Hearing on Food Safety Enhancement Act of 2009] (Prepared Statement of Pamela Bailey, President of Grocery Manufacturers Association).

legislation (we oppose the open-ended fee concept of Section 201); must be fair and equitable to both imports and domestically produced foods; and must not create trade barriers that are likely to result in reciprocal financial barriers established by other countries to US exports.[524]

In a statement on the Food Marketing Institute website, the institute indicated its position on registration fees:

FMI acknowledges that FDA food safety programs are woefully under-funded, but increasing FDA funds will not in and of itself minimize food safety risks to consumers. A more effective food safety system needs to be designed before Congress can accurately assess the funds needed by FDA to accomplish its mission. We are concerned that additional broad-based fees will also raise the cost of food for consumers in a time of rising food prices and a difficult economy.[525]

In response to concerns voiced by trade associations and Republican House members, the manager's amendment to the House bill adopted by voice vote at the mark-up session lowered the annual facility registration fee from $1,000 to $500 and capped fees at $175,000 annually per company.[526] The National Sustainable Agriculture Coalition and the National Organic Council asserted throughout the passage of the legislation that the registration fee would be costly for small processors. The associations were displeased even with the reduced fee of $500 yearly for each facility included in the House bill.[527] In an article in *The Packer*, an industry newspaper for the produce industry, right after the Subcommittee on

---

[524] Hearing on Food Safety Enhancement Act of 2009, Before the Subcommittee on Health of the H. Committee on Energy and Commerce, 111th Cong. 5 (2009) [hereinafter Hearing on Food Safety Enhancement Act of 2009] (Prepared Statement of Tom Stenzel, President of United Fresh Produce Association).

[525] Priority Issues, Food Marketing Institute, www.fmi.org/gr/issues/gr_issues_display.cfm?id=26.

[526] Amy Tsui, *House Commerce Health Panel Passes Food Safety Bill, Including Import Provisions*, 26 INTL TRADE REPORTER 806 (2009); Kathryn Wolfe, *Panel Approves Measure to Improve Food Safety*, CQ WEEKLY ONLINE, June 15, 2009.

[527] Jerry Hagstrom, *Timing of Senate Food Safety Bill Uncertain*, CONGRESS DAILY, Aug. 19, 2009.

Health reported out the legislation, Erik Olson, director of food and consumer product safety for the Pew Health Group, was reported as having stated that Pew would have preferred the $1,000 registration fee to have remained, that "it's not an inconsequential change in terms of the money that could be raised."[528]

What Was Said About Funding the 2010 Legislation?

From the beginning, skeptics of the Senate bill questioned where funding would come from for the bill's expansive provisions. When the bill was introduced, there was no provision similar to the House bill provision mandating a registration fee. Senator Harkin was skeptical of including such a provision, saying that taxpayers should fund the costs of food safety activities, not food companies. Senator Mike Enzi, the ranking Republican on the committee, adamantly voiced his opposition: "Asking a regulated industry to cough up for their own basic regulation is a tax, plain and simple. Not to mention a potential conflict of interest, as the public-health watchdog becomes ever more dependent on the industry it is supposed to be watching."[529] However, Harkin did not rule out the inclusion of a registration fee, instead waiting to make a final determination until the Congressional Budget Office provided an estimate on the costs of the bill.[530] He acknowledged that he did not want a bill passed that did not provide the FDA with enough resources to fulfill bill mandates.[531] Commentators expected that the user fee provision would not be addressed in the passage of the Senate bill, but during conference committee.[532]

Advocates for food safety pointed out to Harkin that a "dedicated revenue stream" for the bill is pivotal, since Congress may be tempted to lower

---

[528] Tom Karst, *House Subcommittee Passes Food Safety Bill*, THE PACKER, June 15, 2009, http://thepacker.com/House-subcommittee-passes-food-safety-bill/Article.aspx?articleid=367395&authorid=117&feedid=215&src=recent.

[529] Jane Zhang, *Senate Panel OKs Giving FDA More Power to Police Food Safety*, THE WALL STREET JOURNAL, Nov. 18, 2009, http://online.wsj.com/article/SB125856363184153895.html.

[530] Rory Harrington, *US Food Safety Bill Enters Final Lap*, FOOD SAFETY NEWS, Nov. 19, 2009, www.foodqualitynews.com/Legislation/US-food-safety-bill-enters-final-lap.

[531] Jerry Hagstrom, *Senate Panel Takes up Food Safety, and Optimism Grows*, NATIONAL JOURNAL'S CONGRESS DAILY, Oct. 23, 2009.

[532] Sam Baker, *With Health Care on the Ropes, Opening Emerges for Food Safety Bill*, INSIDE HEALTH POLICY, Jan. 29, 2010.

appropriations if no contaminations occur for a period of time.[533] FDA Commissioner Hamburg stated that demands of food safety programs already outstrip resources, and that moving forward it will be essential to have "sustained, predictable funding."[534]

Many groups were opposed to the idea of a user fee. The Alliance for a Stronger FDA was particularly displeased with any proposal that would force the FDA to rely heavily on user fees to fulfill its mandate. While the alliance was firmly behind a significant FDA budget increase, noting that the FDA plays a pivotal role in ensuring safety of food and drugs and in maintaining consumer confidence in food safety, the alliance was troubled by an increase that would not be through taxes on the general public.[535] A number of groups opposed to the idea of a user fee proposed alternatives and conditions. A representative for the Grocery Manufacturers Association stated that the association was not outright opposed to paying fees, but that fees should be devoted to science, prevention, and detection, not inspections.[536] The National Sustainable Agriculture Coalition was adamantly opposed to a flat fee for each facility, and stated that the association would only endorse a user fee if it was applied on "a sliding scale progressive fee structure based on ability to pay."[537] Roger Johnson, president of the National Farmers Union, saw the Senate bill as an opportunity to correct the mistakes make in H.R. 2749, stating that if a user fee was added to the Senate bill, the amount should be scaled to production levels.[538]

---

[533] Rory Harrington, *US Food Safety Bill Enters Final Lap*, FOOD SAFETY NEWS, Nov. 19, 2009, www.foodqualitynews.com/Legislation/US-food-safety-bill-enters-final-lap.

[534] Hearing on Keeping America's Families Safe: Reforming the Food Safety System, S. Committee on Health, Education, Labor, and Pensions, 111th Cong., Oct. 22, 2009 (Oral Testimony of FDA Commissioner Hamburg).

[535] Andrew Zajac, *FDA Budget Draws Cries of Not Enough*, L.A. TIMES, Feb. 11, 2010, http://articles.latimes.com/2010/feb/11/nation/la-na-fda-budget11-2010feb11.

[536] Jerry Hagstrom, *Senate Panel Takes up Food Safety, and Optimism Grows*, NATIONAL JOURNAL'S CONGRESS DAILY, Oct. 23, 2009.

[537] NSAC Talking Points for Amendments to the S. 510 Food Safety Modernization Act, National Sustainable Agriculture Coalition, http://sustainableagriculture.net/wp-content/uploads/2008/08/NSAC-S-510-Talking-Points-11-10-09.pdf.

[538] Kevin Bogardus, *Ag Groups Lobby Senate on Food Safety Bill*, THE HILL, Aug. 09, 2009, http://thehill.com/homenews/house/53137-ag-groups-lobby-senate-on-food-safety-bill.

President Obama's proposal for a three-year spending freeze announced in mid-January 2010 immediately caused concern that it would slow or reverse a trend of financial increases for the FDA, an event that could jeopardize the FDA's ability to fulfill its responsibilities under new legislation.[539] While the Congressional Budget Office had not yet estimated the costs of S. 510, the office had estimated that H.R. 2749 would require appropriations of $2 billion over the course of the next five years, with user fees covering the additional $1.5 billion expected to be spent by the FDA on food safety activities.[540]

A week later, however, President Obama released his 2011 budget request, calling for a 6 percent increase in the FDA budget to $2.51 billion. User fees from the food, drug, and tobacco industry would make up the remainder of the agency's resources, contributing to a grand total of $4 billion. Employment at the agency would rise by 1,251 additional full-time employees to total 13,586. At the time of the request, it was expected that a large amount of the budget would be spent on food safety. Some observed that the budget was overly optimistic, considering that the Senate still had not passed its bill and the budget projection depends on $250 million in user fees envisioned by the House bill but not included in the Senate bill.[541] Despite this relatively large budget increase for the FDA in comparison to budget allocations for other agencies, food safety advocates decried that it was not enough.[542]

---

[539] Sam Baker, *Spending Freeze Raises Questions on Food Bill, May Stymie FDA Efforts*, INSIDE HEALTH POLICY, Jan. 29, 2010.

[540] Sam Baker, *With Health Care on the Ropes, Opening Emerges for Food Safety Bill*, INSIDE HEALTH POLICY, Jan. 29, 2010.

[541] Lyndsey Layton, *Obama 2011 Budget Request: Food and Drug Administration*, THE WASHINGTON POST, Feb. 1, 2010, www.washingtonpost.com/wp-dyn/content/article/2010/02/01/AR2010020102093.html.

[542] Andrew Zajac, *FDA Budget Draws Cries of Not Enough*, L.A. TIMES, Feb. 11, 2010, http://articles.latimes.com/2010/feb/11/nation/la-na-fda-budget11-2010feb11.

<u>Text of the Law as Adopted</u>

SEC. 107. AUTHORITY TO COLLECT FEES.

(a) Fees for Reinspection, Recall, and Importation Activities.--Subchapter C of chapter VII (21 U.S.C. 379f et seq.) is amended by adding at the end the following:

"PART 6--FEES RELATED TO FOOD

"SEC. 743. AUTHORITY TO COLLECT AND USE FEES.

"(a) In General.--

> *"(1) PURPOSE AND AUTHORITY.--For fiscal year 2010 and each subsequent fiscal year, the Secretary shall, in accordance with this section, assess and collect fees from--*

>> *"(A) the responsible party for each domestic facility (as defined in section 415(b)) and the United States agent for each foreign facility subject to a reinspection in such fiscal year, to cover reinspection-related costs for such year;*

>> *"(B) the responsible party for a domestic facility (as defined in section 415(b)) and an importer who does not comply with a recall order under section 423 or under section 412(f) in such fiscal year, to cover food recall activities associated with such order performed by the Secretary, including technical assistance, follow-up effectiveness checks, and public notifications, for such year;*

>> *"(C) each importer participating in the voluntary qualified importer program under section 806 in such year, to cover the administrative costs of such program for such year; and*

>> *"(D) each importer subject to a reinspection in such fiscal year, to cover reinspection-related costs for such year.*

"*(2) DEFINITIONS.--For purposes of this section--*

"*(A) the term 'reinspection' means--*

"*(i) with respect to domestic facilities (as defined in section 415(b)), 1 or more inspections conducted under section 704 subsequent to an inspection conducted under such provision which identified noncompliance materially related to a food safety requirement of this Act, specifically to determine whether compliance has been achieved to the Secretary's satisfaction; and*

"*(ii) with respect to importers, 1 or more examinations conducted under section 801 subsequent to an examination conducted under such provision which identified noncompliance materially related to a food safety requirement of this Act, specifically to determine whether compliance has been achieved to the Secretary's satisfaction;*

"*(B) the term 'reinspection-related costs' means all expenses, including administrative expenses, incurred in connection with--*

"*(i) arranging, conducting, and evaluating the results of reinspections; and*

"*(ii) assessing and collecting reinspection fees under this section; and*

"*(C) the term 'responsible party' has the meaning given such term in section 417(a)(1).*

"*(b) Establishment of Fees.--*

"*(1) IN GENERAL.--Subject to subsections (c) and (d), the Secretary shall establish the fees to be collected under this section for* each fiscal year specified in subsection (a)(1), based on the methodology described under paragraph (2), and shall publish such fees in a Federal Register notice not later than 60 days before the start of each such year.

"(2) FEE METHODOLOGY.--

"(A) FEES.--Fees amounts established for collection--

"(i) under subparagraph (A) of subsection (a)(1) for a fiscal year shall be based on the Secretary's estimate of 100 percent of the costs of the reinspection-related activities (including by type or level of reinspection activity, as the Secretary determines applicable) described in such subparagraph (A) for such year;

"(ii) under subparagraph (B) of subsection (a)(1) for a fiscal year shall be based on the Secretary's estimate of 100 percent of the costs of the activities described in such subparagraph (B) for such year;

"(iii) under subparagraph (C) of subsection (a)(1) for a fiscal year shall be based on the Secretary's estimate of 100 percent of the costs of the activities described in such subparagraph (C) for such year; and

"(iv) under subparagraph (D) of subsection (a)(1) for a fiscal year shall be based on the Secretary's estimate of 100 percent of the costs of the activities described in such subparagraph (D) for such year.

"(B) OTHER CONSIDERATIONS.--

"(i) VOLUNTARY QUALIFIED IMPORTER PROGRAM.--

"(I) PARTICIPATION.--In establishing the fee amounts under subparagraph (A)(iii) for a fiscal year, the Secretary shall provide for the number of importers who have submitted to the Secretary a notice under section 806(c) informing the Secretary of the intent of such importer to participate in the program under section 806 in such fiscal year.

"(II) RECOUPMENT.--In establishing the fee amounts under subparagraph (A)(iii) for the first 5 fiscal years after the date of enactment of this section, the Secretary shall include in such fee a reasonable surcharge that provides a recoupment of the costs expended by the Secretary to establish and implement the first year of the program under section 806.

"(ii) CREDITING OF FEES.--In establishing the fee amounts under subparagraph (A) for a fiscal year, the Secretary shall provide for the crediting of fees from the previous year to the next year if the Secretary overestimated the amount of fees needed to carry out such activities, and consider the need to account for any adjustment of fees and such other factors as the Secretary determines appropriate.

"(iii) PUBLISHED GUIDELINES.--Not later than 180 days after the date of enactment of the FDA Food Safety Modernization Act, the Secretary shall publish in the Federal Register a proposed set of guidelines in consideration of the burden of fee amounts on small business. Such consideration may include reduced fee amounts for small businesses. The Secretary shall provide for a period of public comment on such guidelines. The Secretary shall adjust the fee schedule for small businesses subject to such fees only through notice and comment rulemaking.

"(3) USE OF FEES.--The Secretary shall make all of the fees collected pursuant to clause (i), (ii), (iii), and (iv) of paragraph (2)(A) available solely to pay for the costs referred to in such clause (i), (ii), (iii), and (iv) of paragraph (2)(A), respectively.

"(c) Limitations.--

"(1) IN GENERAL.--Fees under subsection (a) shall be refunded for a fiscal year beginning after fiscal year 2010 unless the amount of the total appropriations for food safety activities at the Food and Drug Administration for such fiscal year (excluding the amount of fees appropriated for such fiscal year) is equal to or greater than the amount of appropriations for food safety activities at the Food and Drug Administration for fiscal year 2009 (excluding the amount of fees appropriated for such fiscal year), multiplied by the adjustment factor under paragraph (3).

"(2) AUTHORITY.--If--

"(A) the Secretary does not assess fees under subsection (a) for a portion of a fiscal year because paragraph (1) applies; and

"(B) at a later date in such fiscal year, such paragraph (1) ceases to apply,

the Secretary may assess and collect such fees under subsection (a), without any modification to the rate of such fees, notwithstanding the provisions of subsection (a) relating to the date fees are to be paid.

"*(3) ADJUSTMENT FACTOR.--*

"*(A) IN GENERAL.--The adjustment factor described in paragraph (1) shall be the total percentage change that occurred in the Consumer Price Index for all urban consumers (all items; United States city average) for the 12-month period ending June 30 preceding the fiscal year, but in no case shall such adjustment factor be negative.*

"*(B) COMPOUNDED BASIS.--The adjustment under subparagraph (A) made each fiscal year shall be added on a compounded basis to the sum of all adjustments made each fiscal year after fiscal year 2009.*

"*(4) LIMITATION ON AMOUNT OF CERTAIN FEES.--*

"*(A) IN GENERAL.--Notwithstanding any other provision of this section and subject to subparagraph (B), the Secretary may not collect fees in a fiscal year such that the amount collected--*

"*(i) under subparagraph (B) of subsection (a)(1) exceeds $20,000,000; and*

"*(ii) under subparagraphs (A) and (D) of subsection (a)(1) exceeds $25,000,000 combined.*

"*(B) EXCEPTION.--If a domestic facility (as defined in section 415(b)) or an importer becomes subject to a fee described in subparagraph (A), (B), or (D) of subsection (a)(1) after the maximum amount of fees has been collected by the Secretary under subparagraph (A), the Secretary may collect a fee from such facility or importer.*

"(d) Crediting and Availability of Fees.--Fees authorized under subsection (a) shall be collected and available for obligation only to the extent and in the amount provided in appropriations Acts. Such fees are authorized to remain available until expended. Such sums as may be necessary may be transferred from the Food and Drug Administration salaries and expenses account without fiscal year limitation to such appropriation account for salaries and expenses with such fiscal year limitation. The sums transferred shall be available solely for the purpose of paying the operating expenses of the Food and Drug Administration employees and contractors performing activities associated with these food safety fees.

"(e) Collection of Fees.--

> *"(1) IN GENERAL.--The Secretary shall specify in the Federal Register notice described in subsection (b)(1) the time and manner in which fees assessed under this section shall be collected.*

> *"(2) COLLECTION OF UNPAID FEES.--In any case where the Secretary does not receive payment of a fee assessed under this section within 30 days after it is due, such fee shall be treated as a claim of the United States Government subject to provisions of subchapter II of chapter 37 of title 31, United States Code.*

"(f) Annual Report to Congress.--Not later than 120 days after each fiscal year for which fees are assessed under this section, the Secretary shall submit a report to the Committee on Health, Education, Labor, and Pensions of the Senate and the Committee on Energy and Commerce of the House of Representatives, to include a description of fees assessed and collected for each such year and a summary description of the entities paying such fees and the types of business in which such entities engage.

"(g) Authorization of Appropriations.--For fiscal year 2010 and each fiscal year thereafter, there is authorized to be appropriated for fees under this section an amount equal to the total revenue amount determined under subsection (b)

for the fiscal year, as adjusted or otherwise affected under the other provisions of this section.".

(b) Export Certification Fees for Foods and Animal Feed.--

> *(1) AUTHORITY FOR EXPORT CERTIFICATIONS FOR FOOD, INCLUDING ANIMAL FEED.--Section 801(e)(4)(A) (21 U.S.C. 381(e)(4)(A)) is amended--*

>> *(A) in the matter preceding clause (i), by striking "a drug" and inserting "a food, drug";*

>> *(B) in clause (i) by striking "exported drug" and inserting "exported food, drug"; and*

>> *(C) in clause (ii) by striking "the drug" each place it appears and inserting "the food, drug".*

> *(2) CLARIFICATION OF CERTIFICATION.--Section 801(e)(4) (21 U.S.C. 381(e)(4)) is amended by inserting after subparagraph (B) the following new subparagraph:*

>> *"(C) For purposes of this paragraph, a certification by the Secretary shall be made on such basis, and in such form (including a publicly available listing) as the Secretary determines appropriate.".*

Also see new 21 U.S.C. 388(c)(8):

NEUTRALIZING COSTS.--The Secretary shall establish by regulation a reimbursement (user fee) program, similar to the method described in section 203(h) of the Agriculture Marketing Act of 1946, by which the Secretary assesses fees and requires accredited third-party auditors and audit agents to reimburse the Food and Drug Administration for the work performed to establish and administer the accreditation system under this section. The Secretary shall make operating this program revenue-neutral and shall not generate surplus revenue from such a reimbursement mechanism. Fees authorized under this paragraph shall be collected and available for obligation only to the extent and in the amount provided in advance in appropriation Acts. Such fees are authorized to remain available until expended.

12

International Trade Constraints on FDA Import Controls

What Do Managers Need To Know?

The FDA's ability to implement the new law on issues relating to foreign commerce, specifically new standards on imported food, will be subject to US treaties, including individual national bilateral trade agreements and the General Agreement on Tariffs and Trade, the multinational treaty administered by the World Trade Organization (WTO) in Geneva, Switzerland. The final Act included at its end a specific reservation that Congress did not intend that the new Act would violate WTO requirements.

How Will the 2010 Legislation Be Affected by International Trade Obligations?

Will international treaty obligations be utilized to invalidate some portions of the 2010 food safety legislation? Although the US Congress has the right and obligation to adopt laws to protect the health of US citizens, international trade principles encourage governments not to create barriers to trade. Measures adopted to protect consumers from unsafe imported food can act as non-tariff barriers, by increasing the transaction costs of importing food into a country, and by giving special privileges to domestic producers over foreign competitors.[543]

---

[543] *Understanding the WTO Agreement on Sanitary and Phytosanitary Measures, available at* www.wto.org/english/tratop_e/sps_e/spsund_e.htm.

With advice from other federal agencies, the FDA may be moderate and cautious in rolling out its expanded powers. The FDA has established offices abroad,[544] and with its hope for positive relationships with local governments, the FDA may freely grant variances for those foods that the local government can adequately inspect and approve for shipment.[545]

The 2010 legislation contains an express statement recognizing that international treaties[546] have primary authority. The early drafts contained some rather defensive references to compliance with international standards. Nonetheless, there are likely to be international conflicts over the new requirements. Congress's intent in drafting the new legislation is to increase food safety within the United States. Nevertheless, the provisions of the legislation might have the secondary effect of discouraging some firms from shipping food into the United States.

The WTO Agreement on the Application of Sanitary and Phytosanitary Measures (SPS Agreement) was negotiated to prevent WTO countries like the United States from enacting spurious or excessive "food safety" measures that act as barriers to trade. Specifically, the SPS Agreement recognizes that WTO member countries have the right to enact food safety measures to protect "human, animal or plant life or health," but it requires that the measures are based on scientific principles and are only applied to the "extent necessary to protect human, animal or plant life or health." These food safety measures—called "sanitary and phytosanitary measures" under the agreement—must not "arbitrarily or unjustifiably discriminate" against other member countries and must not operate as a "disguised restriction on trade."[547]

The SPS Agreement is applicable to the new FDA food imports law, so it should be considered by companies that operate in multiple nations.[548] This agreement specifically takes into account human health and the importing

---

[544] 21 U.S.C. 2243, adopted as Pub. L. 111-353, Title IV sec. 309.

[545] 21 U.S.C. 350h(c)(2).

[546] 21 U.S.C. 2252, adopted as Pub. L. 111-353, Title IV sec. 404.

[547] Agreement on the Application of Sanitary and Phytosanitary Measures art. 2, April 15, 1994, 1867 U.N.T.S. 493 art 2 [hereinafter SPS Agreement], *available at* www.wto.org/english/docs_e/legal_e/15-sps.pdf.

[548] www.wto.org/english/docs_e/legal_e/legal_e.htm.

countries' needs to protect their consumers by regulating imported products that may not be safe.[549] Its scope is broad:

> Sanitary or phytosanitary measures include all relevant laws, decrees, regulations, requirements and procedures including, *inter alia*, end product criteria; processes and production methods; testing, inspection, certification and approval procedures; quarantine treatments including relevant requirements associated with the transport of animals or plants, or with the materials necessary for their survival during transport; provisions on relevant statistical methods, sampling procedures and methods of risk assessment; and packaging and labelling requirements directly related to food safety.[550]

Several of these are elements of the new Food Safety Modernization Act, especially certification, inspection, and risk assessment.[551]

WTO member nations are required to accept as equivalent the sanitary and phytosanitary measures (SPS measures) of other members, "even if these measures differ from their own or from those used by other Members trading in the same product, if the exporting Member objectively demonstrates to the importing Member that its measures achieve the importing Member's appropriate level of sanitary or phytosanitary protection."[552] Step one is to identify the regulatory control, step two is to identify the differences with the other nation's standards, step three is to have the "receiving" nation defend its standards, and step four is to "objectively" assemble data to show that the sending nation's "measures" will achieve the same level of protection that the receiving nation wants. For example, Sweden might claim that its fish-cleaning processes make it unnecessary for the US FDA to have an import alert for contamination against jars of undercooked fish from Sweden. Member nations are allowed to determine their own appropriate level of

---

[549] Agreement on the Application of Sanitary and Phytosanitary Measures, www.wto.org/english/docs_e/legal_e/legal_e.htm.

[550] Agreement on the Application of Sanitary and Phytosanitary Measures, Annex A, Definitions 1 www.wto.org/english/docs_e/legal_e/legal_e.htm.

[551] Pub.L. 111-353 (2010), and see Chapters 5, 6, and 9 of this text.

[552] Agreement on the Application of Sanitary and Phytosanitary Measures art. 2, April 15, 1994, 1867 U.N.T.S. 493 art 4.1 [hereinafter SPS Agreement], available at www.wto.org/english/docs_e/legal_e/15-sps.pdf.

protection. However, members are to strive to harmonize SPS measures "on as wide a basis as possible" by utilizing "international standards."[553]

An SPS measure that conforms to international standards enjoys a presumption of validity.[554] If a member adopts an SPS measure that establishes a higher level of protection than the international standard, then in the event of challenge by a food-exporting nation, the food-importing member must demonstrate that the SPS measure is justified by scientific analysis and evidence,[555] and they are required to engage in a risk assessment to ensure that SPS measures "are not more trade-restrictive than required to achieve their appropriate level of sanitary and phytosanitary protection."[556] Control, inspection, and approval procedures cannot arbitrarily or unjustifiably prevent the importation of food.[557]

While private firms are not able to challenge the 2010 legislation under the SPS Agreement, if the firm operates within a country that is a member of the WTO, the firm can approach their government and ask their country to file a challenge under the SPS Agreement against the new statute or its implementing regulations.[558] When a WTO member believes another

---

[553] Agreement on the Application of Sanitary and Phytosanitary Measures Annex A5, art. 3.1., April 15, 1994, 1867 U.N.T.S. 493 art. 2 [hereinafter SPS Agreement], *available at* www.wto.org/english/docs_e/legal_e/15-sps.pdf.

[554] Agreement on the Application of Sanitary and Phytosanitary Measures Annex A5, art. 3.1., April 15, 1994, 1867 U.N.T.S. 493 arts. 2.4, 3.2 [hereinafter SPS Agreement], *available at* www.wto.org/english/docs_e/legal _e/15-sps.pdf.

[555] Agreement on the Application of Sanitary and Phytosanitary Measures Annex A5, art. 3.1., April 15, 1994, 1867 U.N.T.S. 493 art. 3.3 [hereinafter SPS Agreement], *available at* www.wto.org/english/docs_e/legal_e/15-sps.pdf.

[556] Agreement on the Application of Sanitary and Phytosanitary Measures Annex A5, art. 3.1., April 15, 1994, 1867 U.N.T.S. 493 art. 5.6 [hereinafter SPS Agreement], *available at* www.wto.org/english/docs_e/legal_e/15-sps.pdf.

[557] Agreement on the Application of Sanitary and Phytosanitary Measures Annex A5, art. 3.1., April 15, 1994, 1867 U.N.T.S. 493 art. 8, Annex C. [hereinafter SPS Agreement], *available at* www.wto.org/english/docs_e/legal_e/15-sps.pdf.

[558] Private parties have no formal recognized role in a WTO dispute. Only Member-states can file challenges with the WTO. Understanding on Rules and Procedures Governing the Settlement of Disputes art. 1, Apr. 15, 1994, 1869 U.N.T.S. 401, 33 I.L.M. 1125, available at www.wto.org/english/docs_e/legal_e/28-dsu.pdf [hereinafter Rules on WTO Disputes]. Private parties have, however, been involved in providing input for briefs and arguments, but this is purely within the discretion of the Member-state and its counsel. In addition, the WTO dispute settlement body has accepted amicus briefs in a few cases from non-governmental organizations, but their role has been limited. Kathleen W. Cannon, *15th Judicial Conference of the United States Court of International Trade Symposium: Trade Litigation before the WTO, NAFTA, and U.S. Courts: A Petitioner's Perspective*, 17 TUL. J. INT'L & COMP. L. 389, 392-93 (2009).

member has violated the SPS Agreement, the member may initiate informal dialogue to resolve the concern, or can resort to the SPS Agreement dispute procedures found in the WTO's "Understanding on Rules and Procedures Governing the Settlement of Disputes."[559] The vast majority of challenges brought before the dispute panel actually have been resolved through mutually agreed settlements.[560] Among the active disputes at the WTO are food-related objections to US regulations by China,[561] Canada,[562] and Mexico.[563] There will be more of these in the rollout of the 2010 Act.

However, if a dispute does not settle, the WTO will appoint a three-member neutral dispute panel that will make a ruling. There are some helpful precedents, but there is no rule of *stare decisis* in a WTO dispute requiring the panels to follow past precedent. The dispute panel can neither add to nor diminish the rights and obligations established in the agreement.[564] If the dispute panel finds a violation of the SPS Agreement, the country is expected to withdraw the offending measure.[565]

---

[559] Agreement on the Application of Sanitary and Phytosanitary Measures art. 11, (Apr. 15, 1994), 1867 U.N.T.S. 493 art 2 [hereinafter SPS Agreement], *available at* www.wto.org/english/docs_e/legal_e/15-sps.pdf.; Geoffrey S.Becker, CRS Report for Congress, *Sanitary snd Phytosanitary (Sps) Concerns in Agricultural Trade* 8 (2006) [hereinafter *Sanitary snd Phytosanitary*] (discussing the utility of informal dialogue); *Understanding on Rules and Procedures Governing the Settlement of Disputes* Annex 2, (Apr. 15, 1994), 1869 U.N.T.S. 401, 33 I.L.M. 1125, *available at* www.wto.org/english/docs_e/legal_e/28-dsu.pdf [hereinafter Rules on WTO Disputes].

[560] World Trade Organization, Committee on Sanitary and Phytosanitary Measures, Reference Documents, *WTO Disputes Invoking the SPS Agreement*, www.wto.org/english/tratop_e/sps_e/decisions06_e.htm.

[561] *United States—Certain Measures Affecting Imports of Poultry from China*, Report of the Panel, WT/DS392/R, 29 September 2010, p. 183. http://docsonline.wto.org/imrd/gen_searchResult.asp?RN=0&searchtype=browse&q1=%28+%40meta%5FSymbol+G%FCSPS%FCN%FCUSA%FC%2A%29&language=1.

[562] *United States—Certain Country of Origin Labeling Requirements*, Request for the Establishment of a Panel of a Panel by Canada, WT/DS384/8, 9 October 2009, http://docsonline.wto.org/imrd/gen_searchResult.asp?RN=0&searchtype=browse&q1=%28+%40meta%5FSymbol+G%FCSPS%FCN%FCUSA%FC%2A%29&language=1.

[563] *United States—Certain Country of Origin Labeling Requirements*, Request for the Establishment of a Panel of a Panel by Mexico, WT/DS386/7, 13 October 2009, http://docsonline.wto.org/imrd/gen_searchResult.asp?RN=0&searchtype=browse&q1=%28+%40meta%5FSymbol+G%FCSPS%FCN%FCUSA%FC%2A%29&language=1.

[564] *Understanding on Rules and Procedures Governing the Settlement of* Disputes art. 3.2 (Apr. 15, 1994), 1869 U.N.T.S. 401, 33 I.L.M. 1125, *available at* www.wto.org/english/docs_ e/legal_e/28-dsu.pdf [hereinafter Rules on WTO Disputes].

[565] Understanding on Rules and Procedures Governing the Settlement of Disputes art. 3.7 (Apr. 15, 1994), 1869 U.N.T.S. 401, 33 I.L.M. 1125, *available at* www.wto.org/english/docs_e/legal_e/28-dsu.pdf [hereinafter Rules on WTO Disputes].

How Could a WTO Challenge Be Asserted?

A WTO member may bring a challenge against the United States claiming that particular provisions in the 2010 food legislation violate the SPS Agreement. Because of this potential, it is worth contemplating the framework for such a challenge.[566] At the outset, it must be determined whether the SPS Agreement applies. The SPS Agreement applies to "all sanitary and phytosanitary measures which may, directly or indirectly, affect international trade."

It must first be determined whether the 2010 food legislation is an SPS measure. According to the SPS Agreement, an SPS measure is "any measure" applied to "protect human or animal life or health within the territory of the Member from risks" arising from "additives, contaminants, toxins, or disease-causing organisms in foods, beverages, or feedstuffs" and from "diseases carried by animals, plants, or products thereof, or from the entry, establishment or spread of pests."[567] The SPS Agreement does not define the word "measure," and does not distinguish between measures that are established against a specific food, or measures established to regulate the process by which food enters a country since the object of both is protection of human health.[568] The 2010 legislation is designed to "protect human or animal life or health" in the United States by increasing food safety.[569] The legislation contains numerous references to protecting the health of US citizens and empowers the FDA, an agency dedicated to

---

[566] *See* Geoffrey S. Becker, CRS Report for Congress, *U.S. Food and Agricultural Imports: Safeguards and Selected Issues* 7 (2009) [hereinafter *Safeguards and Selected Issues*]; Brian Knowlton, *He Called for a Ban on Produce That Doesn't Meet U.S. Rules: Clinton Sounds Food Safety Alarm*, N.Y. TIMES, Oct. 3, 1997 (demonstrating that past government attempts at import food reform have been met with accusations of protectionism).

[567] Agreement on the Application of Sanitary and Phytosanitary Measures Annex 1A (Apr. 15, 1994), 1867 U.N.T.S. 493 [hereinafter SPS Agreement], available at www.wto.org/english/docs_e/legal_e/15-sps.pdf.

[568] According to the WTO, it does not matter whether the measure is a "technical requirement." What matters is the purpose of the measure, and the "SPS Agreement covers all measures whose purpose is to protect: human or animal health from food-borne risks; human health from animal- or plant-carried diseases; animals and plants from pests or diseases." World Trade Organization, *Sanitary and Phytosanitary Measures: Introduction, Understanding the WTO Agreement on Sanitary and Phytosanitary Measures*, www.wto.org/english/tratop_e/sps_e/spsund_e.htm.

[569] 155 Cong. Rec. H900 (daily ed. July 29, 2009) (Statement of Rep. Dingell).

health issues, to implement the legislation. Thus, it appears that the 2010 legislation is an SPS measure.

In addition to meeting the criteria of an SPS measure, the 2010 law will affect international trade. Among other things, the law will require each importer to comply with the Foreign Supplier Verification Program, and imported food must be accompanied by a certification or assurance that it complies with US food safety laws. These requirements will be burdensome and costly for foreign facilities and importers, and might cause some foreign firms to leave the industry.[570] It is too early to evaluate the extent of the impact on international trade, but it is clear that the provisions will affect international trade.

Thus, the 2010 legislation is an SPS measure that will affect international trade and, accordingly, complaints about its international impacts will be scrutinized under the SPS Agreement. At this early juncture, it is unclear whether all aspects of the 2010 law will be upheld under the SPS Agreement in a WTO dispute. The provisions of the statute will need to be compared to international standards.[571]

If a particular US regulatory provision does not conform to an international standard, either because an international standard does not exist or because the provision does not adhere to the standard, there will be no presumption of validity of the US rule. The United States will have to demonstrate that the 2010 legislation is "based" on a risk assessment that takes into account techniques established by relevant international organizations and available scientific evidence.[572] The risk assessment will have to show that domestically produced foods are subject to the same level of scrutiny under the 2010 legislation that imported foods face, where there are identical or similar conditions.[573] The SPS Agreement does allow the 2010 legislation to

---

[570] *Don't Eat That! Legal Issues in Food Safety*, supra note 9 (Remarks by Stuart Pape); Geoffrey S. Becker, CRS Report for Congress, *Sanitary and Phytosanitary (SPS) Concerns in Agricultural Trade* 4 (2006) [hereinafter *Sanitary and Phytosanitary*].

[571] Shannon May, *Importing a Change in Diet: The Proposed Food Safety Law of 2010 and the Possible Impact on Importers and International Trade*, 65 FOOD & DRUG L.J. 1 (2010).

[572] *See* Agreement on the Application of Sanitary and Phytosanitary Measures art. 5 (Apr. 15, 1994), 1867 U.N.T.S. 493 art. 5 [hereinafter SPS Agreement], *available at* www.wto.org/english/docs_e/legal_e/15-sps.pdf.

[573] Agreement on the Application of Sanitary and Phytosanitary Measures art. 2.3 (Apr. 15, 1994), 1867 U.N.T.S. 493 [hereinafter SPS Agreement], *available at* www.wto.org/english/docs_e/legal_e/15-sps.pdf.

take into account real differences in conditions between domestically produced and imported foods, but the provisions of the 2010 legislation may not constitute a "disguised restriction on international trade."[574]

A claim can be asserted that the United States has not engaged in the thorough risk-assessment protocol required by the SPS Agreement. There has been no government review released on the topic of the 2010 legislation's potential for violating the SPS Agreement. According to the senior advisor to the Commissioner of the FDA, Michael Taylor, the Office of the US Trade Representative, the executive agency responsible for developing and coordinating US international trade policy, has considered at least the House bill that initially formed the legislation. Taylor stated that the US Trade Representative had engaged in an "internal administration process to look at all aspects of the bill" that may implicate WTO obligations, and has "come to good conclusions."[575] This statement is indicative of the muted, but pivotal role WTO obligations have played throughout the drafting of import safety legislation.

Did the Senate Consider WTO Issues?

Yes. The Senate appears to have put more outright emphasis on WTO obligations in drafting S. 510 than did the House in its more aggressive regulatory controls. The Act's Section 404 is a "savings clause" to preserve WTO and other international treaty obligations.[576] The bill contains no importer-specific fee provisions. It was suggested at a Senate hearing that imposing fees only on imported food and not domestic food will violate WTO agreements.[577]

Although much of the trade-related language was not amended at the mark-up, some changes were made. A provision was added stating that nothing in the bill should be construed in a manner that is inconsistent with any

---

[574] Agreement on the Application of Sanitary and Phytosanitary Measures art. 2.3 (Apr. 15, 1994), 1867 U.N.T.S. 493 [hereinafter SPS Agreement], *available at* www.wto.org/english/docs_e/legal_e/15-sps.pdf.

[575] *See Expert Q&A on Import Food Safety*, FOOD SAFETY NEWS, Oct. 18, 2009, www.foodsafetynews.com/2009/10/gover.

[576] Pub.L. 111-353 §404 (2010).

[577] *See Amy Tsui, Standards: Durbin, Gregg Introduce Food Safety Bill, Avoiding User Fees That Could Violate WTO*, 26 INT'L TRADE REPORTER 317 (2009).

obligations under any trade agreements to which the United States is a party.[578] This language is similar to language included in other legislation that may implicate trade agreement concerns and is not language included in H.R. 2749.[579] Language was added to S. 510 requiring that "internationally-recognized standards" be considered in drafting specific regulations.[580] Section 204(d) limits FDA control on records at foreign high-risk food plants so as to "take into account international trade obligations." Working with the private sector to develop recovery plans to rapidly resume "international trade" was added to the list of recovery goals after a food emergency.[581]

Indicating further the Senate's intention that S. 510 not violate any WTO obligations, the US Trade Representative was added to a list of individuals who should be consulted when developing plans for strengthening the safety of importing countries' food systems. The section had already included that the FDA consult the secretaries of Agriculture, State, Treasury, and Commerce, as well as "representatives of the food industry, appropriate foreign government officials, nongovernmental organizations that represent the interests of consumers, and other stakeholders."[582] The provision, however, mentions that the plans should include recommendations on "*whether* and *how* to harmonize requirements under the Codex Alimentarius," the most widely agreed upon set of international food standards and specifically mentioned in the SPS Agreement.[583] This

---

[578] Compare S. 510 § 404, 111th Cong. (as reported by the Senate HELP Committee, Nov. 18, 2009) with S. 510 § 404, 111th Cong. (as introduced in Senate, Mar. 3, 2009); *Food Safety Bill Approved by Senate HELP Committee*, USAGNET, Nov. 23, 2009, www.wisconsinagconnection.com/story-national.php?Id=2424&yr=2009; *Fears Over Trade Linger After Senate Committee Reports Food Safety Bill*, INSIDE HEALTH POLICY, Nov. 25, 2009.

[579] *Fears Over Trade Linger After Senate Committee Reports Food Safety Bill*, INSIDE HEALTH POLICY, Nov. 25, 2009. H.R. 2749, includes references to international obligations in some specific sections, but does not include a provision applying to the entire bill.

[580] S. 510 §§ 103, 204, 111th Cong. (as reported by the Senate HELP Committee, Nov. 18, 2009); *Fears Over Trade Linger After Senate Committee Reports Food Safety Bill*, INSIDE HEALTH POLICY, Nov. 25, 2009.

[581] Compare S. 510 § 108, 111th Cong. (as reported by the Senate HELP Committee, Nov. 18, 2009) with S. 510 § 108, 111th Cong. (as introduced in Senate, Mar. 3, 2009).

[582] *See* S. 510, 111th Cong. § 306 (as introduced in the Senate on March 3, 2009).

[582] Compare S. 510 § 306, 111th Cong. (as reported by the Senate HELP Committee, Nov. 18, 2009) with S. 510 § 306, 111th Cong. (as introduced in Senate, Mar. 3, 2009).

[583] *See* S. 510, 111th Cong. § 306 (as introduced in the Senate on March 3, 2009).

language is different from its former incarnation, which required the plans to include "recommendations to harmonize requirements under the Codex Alimentarius," suggesting that the decision to harmonize under Codex Alimentarius was rethought prior to the committee mark-up.[584] Working with the private sector to develop recovery plans to rapidly resume "international trade" was added to the list of recovery goals after a food emergency. In the bill introduced in the Senate, the recovery goal in working with the private sector was only to resume "agriculture, and food production," not "international trade."

Was the FDA Aware of the International Treaty Issues?

The consideration of trade obligations in implementing food safety laws does not appear to be a sentiment coming only from within Congress. The FDA has already expressed its intention of collaborating with other countries through international trade channels to increase the safety of US food supply.

Addressing the Codex Committee on Food Hygiene in November 2009, FDA Commissioner Hamburg urged that "public health protection is a global endeavor" that requires engaging in information sharing, utilizing advanced scientific techniques across borders and "on increasing harmonization of food safety standards." She noted that "international bodies like the World Health Organization, the Food and Agriculture Organization and, of course, Codex are so critically important." Underlying Commissioner Hamburg's speech was an acceptance of international trade as a reality of the global marketplace that exists today. According to Commissioner Hamburg, free trade and safe food are not inapposite, but instead should "drive each other." Emphasizing their equal importance, she said, "All people in the world deserve food that is safe, and all nations deserve the opportunity to participate, and prosper, in the global economy." Shedding light on some of the more open-ended provisions included in H.R. 2749, Commissioner Hamburg mentioned that the food safety plans

---

[583] Compare S. 510 § 306, 111th Cong. (as reported by the Senate HELP Committee, Nov. 18, 2009) with S. 510 § 306, 111th Cong. (as introduced in Senate, Mar. 3, 2009) (emphasis added).

[584] *See* S. 510, 111th Cong. § 306 (as introduced in the Senate on March 3, 2009).

[584] Compare S. 510 § 306, 111th Cong. (as reported by the Senate HELP Committee, Nov. 18, 2009) with S. 510 § 306, 111th Cong. (as introduced in Senate, Mar. 3, 2009).

that would be required of all food facilities "would be grounded in the basic principles of food hygiene adopted by "the Codex Committee."[585]

Could Parts of the 2010 Legislation Be Challenged Successfully Before the WTO?

While EU sources stated that as of the Senate bill mark-up session, a number of the programs envisioned by the bill are similar to ones enforced in the European Union, there were still concerns about specific Senate bill provisions. A section that called for a review of the regulatory authority of foreign countries initially in the bill as introduced was flagged as possibly triggering trade agreement problems and was eliminated. In the bill as introduced in the Senate, the section required that the FDA find a "country can provide reasonable assurances that the food supply of the country is equivalent in safety to food manufactured, processed, packed, or held in the United States." The bill as reported by the Senate Committee changed the language to require that the FDA find that a "country can provide reasonable assurances that the food supply of the country *meets or exceeds* the safety of food manufactured, processed, packed, or held in the United States."[586] By the time the bill was passed, the section was entirely eliminated.

As to other provisions focusing on import safety, such as the Voluntary Qualified Importer Program, whereby the importer can receive expedited entry of food imports if they are able to meet certain requirements, or the certification program for certain imported foods, whereby the FDA can require that certain foods meet a certification process before entry into the United States, the EU sources stated that the programs are similar to what is done in the European Union.[587]

---

[585] Margaret A. Hamburg, Commissioner of U.S. Food and Drug Administration, Department of Health and Human Services, Rockville, MD, Speech Before the Codex Committee on Food Hygiene, San Diego, CA, Nov. 16, 2009, www.fda.gov/NewsEvents/Speeches/ucm191342.htm.

[586] Compare S. 510 § 305, 111th Cong. (as reported by the Senate HELP Committee, Nov. 18, 2009) with S. 510 § 305, 111th Cong. (as introduced in Senate, Mar. 3, 2009); *Fears Over Trade Linger After Senate Committee Reports Food Safety Bill*, INSIDE HEALTH POLICY, Nov. 25, 2009.

[587] *Fears Over Trade Linger After Senate Committee Reports Food Safety Bill*, INSIDE HEALTH POLICY, Nov. 25, 2009

Respected commentators on food law have mixed feelings on the potential for a substantive WTO challenge under the 2010 legislation. The paperwork and documentation requirements may be challenged, but much will depend on the panel as to whether a challenge will be successful. Stuart Pape of Patton Boggs in Washington, D.C., a specialist in food and drug law, sees less of a potential for a WTO challenge by the European Union since, according to Pape, the 2010 legislation will in some ways bring US law up to what the European Union put in place a few years ago. Pape believes a developing country will be the most likely to raise a challenge, since the SPS Agreement makes more exceptions for developing countries that the 2010 legislation does not specifically take into account. Neal Fortin, director of the Institute for Food Laws and Regulation at Michigan State University, however, believes any challenge a WTO member might have will not go to the dispute panel but will instead go to negotiations.[588] These projections represent educated projections as to whether the 2010 legislation will trigger a WTO challenge. However, at this stage in the passage of the legislation— with the final terms of the legislation yet undecided—it is impossible to determine whether the new food safety legislation will violate the SPS Agreement.

What If the WTO Rejects Provisions of the 2010 Law?

Under the Constitution, treaties signed by the United States with other nations are binding and have the effect of law. A WTO decision could result in penalty tariffs or other sanctions. As a practical matter, the US Trade Representative has so many other issues to deal with in international trade, that a food import rejection by a WTO panel would probably cause the administrative agencies such as the FDA to suspend operation of the rule, or there may be congressional action to modify the 2010 legislation to avoid the problem that led to the dispute panel's decision. In either case, all affected firms, not just the first to instigate the international complaint system, would be affected by the forced change in policies.

---

[588] *Don't Eat That! Legal Issues in Food Safety*, Roundtable Discussion with Neal Fortin, James O'Reilly, and Stuart Pape, ABA Center for Continuing Legal Education (Sept. 16, 2009) [hereinafter *Don't Eat That! Legal Issues in Food Safety*].

What Had the Unadopted House Version Proposed?

For example, an earlier congressional proposal to impose user fees to screen food imports was unsuccessful after receiving negative criticism for the bill's potential for violating WTO commitments.[589] The House version of the 2010 legislation did impose various fees on imported food, but additionally they imposed comparable sets of fees on domestically produced foods.

The House had a limited focus on international trade concerns. A few provisions referencing international standards were added to the bill. The section on certification was amended to include a provision requiring the FDA to implement the section in a manner consistent with US obligations under international agreements and a provision allowing the FDA to rely on or incorporate international standards in issuing regulations to ensure qualified certified entities and auditors are free from conflict of interests.[590] A provision was added to the section on food safety plans and hazard analysis requiring the FDA to take international standards on hazard analysis and preventive controls into consideration when issuing guidance or regulations.[591]

What Criticisms Did the Legislation Draw?

Conservative activists opposed the global accommodation because it would "undermine DSHEA and move the US one step closer to harmonizing its standards under the Codex Alimentarius with those of restrictive regimes like the European Union. (DSHEA, or the Dietary Supplement Health and Education Act of 1994, says that supplements are food and are safe for consumption unless proven otherwise—ensuring that millions of Americans are able to enjoy access to safe, effective and affordable dietary supplements)."[592] The National Health Federation said its "concerns, and the concerns of others in the health-freedom community, were heard, as the

---

[589] *See* Rossella Brevetti, *Standards: Proposed User Fee to Screen Food Imports Violates WTO, Industry Tells Finance Panel,* 24 INT'L TRADE REPORTER 1492 (2007).
[590] H.R. 2749 § 109, 111th Cong. (as engrossed by House of Representatives, July 30, 2009).
[591] *Id.*
[592] *See* www.democracyinaction.org website, "S. 510, Food Safety Bill: A Threat to Health Food Stores, Farms and Consumers" (last visited Dec. 30, 2009).

statutory language on Codex harmonization was changed to direct the Food and Drug Administration to report to Congress on 'whether and how to harmonize requirements under the Codex Alimentarius' on the issue of foreign conventional food processing standards. This is an important but partial victory... We are all grateful to those Senators active in eliminating the harmonization wording."[593] The same group criticized the bill during House debate, saying the "legislation...would bury American farmers, food producers, and other food and cosmetic businesses in yet more red tape and regulations."[594]

According to the *National Journal*, in an article prior to the House bill's passage, the US Trade Representative voiced some opposition to the House bill, presumably because of the fear that other countries might react to the more stringent legislation by mirroring restrictions against US exports. The US Trade Representative noted that the House bill would have implemented policies that do not adhere to international standards and that other countries could retaliate.[595] These concerns were not unfounded. In a report issued by the European Union in 2009, worries were voiced about the impact of the 2010 food safety legislation, specifically that EU exporters may be negatively impacted by the requirements in the legislation, such as "import inspection fees, country-of-origin labeling and mandatory certification of 'high-risk foods.'"[596]

What Did Trade Associations Say About International Trade Obligations?

Pamela Bailey, president of the Grocery Manufacturers Association, the world's largest trade association, representing more than 300 food, beverage, and consumer product companies, testified at the House Energy and Commerce Committee's Subcommittee on Health hearing on food safety on June 3, 2009, and indicated the assocation's desire to work with

---

[593] National Health Federation press statement, www.thenhf.org (Nov. 20, 2009).
[594] National Health Federation press statement, "The Goon Squad Advances Its 'Food Safety' Bill" (July 18, 2009), www.thenhf.org.
[595] Peter Cohn, *Panel, Agencies Express Concerns About Food Safety Bill*, NATIONAL JOURNAL'S CONGRESS DAILY, June 23, 2009.
[596] Peter Cohn, *EU Report Warns of New Barriers, Duties*, NATIONAL JOURNAL'S CONGRESS DAILY, July 27, 2009.

the Committee in aligning the proposed legislation with "internationally recognized standards."[597]

Tom Stenzel, president of the United Fresh Produce Association, a trade association representing growers, packers, shippers, fresh-cut processors, distributors, and marketers of fresh fruits and vegetables, testified at the House Energy and Commerce Committee's Subcommittee on Health hearing on food safety on June 3, 2009:

> We strongly recommend that the committee examine all imported food provisions to ensure that they comply with all legal trade responsibilities and assure equal treatment and standards for both imported and domestically produced foods. This should be a principle maintained throughout all provisions.[598]

Text of the Law as Adopted

SEC. 404. COMPLIANCE WITH INTERNATIONAL AGREEMENTS.

Nothing in this Act (or an amendment made by this Act) shall be construed in a manner inconsistent with the agreement establishing the World Trade Organization or any other treaty or international agreement to which the United States is a party.

---

[597] Hearing on Food Safety Enhancement Act of 2009, Before the Subcommittee on Health of the H. Committee on Energy and Commerce, 111th Cong. 2 (2009) [hereinafter Hearing on Food Safety Enhancement Act of 2009] (Prepared Statement of Pamela Bailey, President of Grocery Manufacturers Association).

[598] Hearing on Food Safety Enhancement Act of 2009, Before the Subcommittee on Health of the H. Committee on Energy and Commerce, 111th Cong. 4 (2009) [hereinafter Hearing on Food Safety Enhancement Act of 2009] (Prepared Statement of Tom Stenzel, President of United Fresh Produce Association).

SEC. 107. AUTHORITY TO COLLECT FEES

"SEC. 743. AUTHORITY TO COLLECT AND USE FEES.

"(a) In General.--

"(1) PURPOSE AND AUTHORITY.--For fiscal year 2010 and each subsequent fiscal year, the Secretary shall, in accordance with this section, assess and collect fees from--

"(A) the responsible party for each domestic facility (as defined in section 415(b)) and the United States agent for each foreign facility subject to a reinspection in such fiscal year, to cover reinspection-related costs for such year;

"(B) the responsible party for a domestic facility (as defined in section 415(b)) and an importer who does not comply with a recall order under section 423 or under section 412(f) in such fiscal year, to cover food recall activities associated with such order performed by the Secretary, including technical assistance, follow-up effectiveness checks, and public notifications, for such year;

"(C) each importer participating in the voluntary qualified importer program under section 806 in such year, to cover the administrative costs of such program for such year; and

"(D) each importer subject to a reinspection in such fiscal year, to cover reinspection-related costs for such year.

[See also sections 301-306 of the Act, Pub.L. 111-353, discussed in other chapters]

13

Impacts on Existing
Food Registry and Controls

What Do Managers Need To Know?

Congress tightened the existing food "early warning" system, established in 2007, with the 2010 amendments. The Reportable Food Registry dealt with mandating reports of food problems to the FDA when it was adopted by Congress in 2007.[599] The Reportable Food Registry went into full effect in 2009.[600] Under new rules, a food seller who knowingly and willfully fails to give consumers notice of a reportable food can be prosecuted.[601]

The 2010 Act deals with the outflow of warning information from the FDA to the consumer, as the FDA seeks to act consistently upon the incoming reports. Retailers have new legal obligations for food they sell. Food companies must alter their grocery outlet notification systems[602] or create new and effective mechanisms for downstream warnings about serious health concerns with a food that has been distributed. Rules must be in place in 2012.[603]

Why this 2010 legislation? A massive recall of egg products in 2010 after a huge recall of peanut-containing products in 2009 built pressure for a more

---

[599] 21 U.S.C. 350f.
[600] FDA Notice, 75 Fed.Reg. 44973 (July 30, 2010).
[601] New 21 U.S.C. 331(yy).
[602] 21 U.S.C. 350f(h)(1).
[603] 21 U.S.C. 350f(h)(2).

uniform and much more consistent disclosure system that could actually reach the food consumers.

Faster disclosure of the critical food recall information, compelled by the new law, will reach from the food company to the FDA and from the FDA on a standard warning format to the grocery outlet where the food was distributed.[604] The significance of the change is the explicit use of grocery store recall notifications in a consumer-visible "prominent" location.[605] This is hoped to expand the responsiveness of the average food consumer, who might "tune out" routine news accounts of a current set of recalls. Because the front line of the recall now will run through the retail store, lobbyists for the food marketers were extensively involved in fine-tuning these details.

What Is the Reportable Food Registry?

This is a federal food safety program, enacted by Congress in 2007 and officially launched in September 2009, whose title is a euphemism for the "food problems list." If there is a "reasonable probability" that a food problem could cause "serious adverse health consequences or death," a report by the food company must be made to the FDA under the electronic reporting system.[606] Congress basically took the FDA's definition of a Class I (most serious) recall and mandated that a report be made within twenty-four hours of a food company's notice of a food problem. In the Reportable Food Registry's first year, 228 primary reports were filed, and when amended and supplementary reports are counted, 2,600 submissions were made.[607]

In the 2010 Act, Congress is correcting some weaknesses of the 2007 statutory system providing warnings about food problems and recalls, spreading the news of new risk information from the FDA Reportable Food Registry out to consumers. Hundreds of reports had been filed with the FDA, and a smaller number were actively pursued as product recalls

---

[604] 21 U.S.C. 350f(h).
[605] 21 U.S.C. 350f(h)(2).
[606] 21 U.S.C. 350f.
[607] Jennifer Thomas, FDA CFSAN Office of Compliance, Presentation to Regulatory Affairs Prof. Society Annual Meeting (October 2010).

(numerous duplicative reports were screened out, but padded the reported numbers).

The focus of this amendment is on uniformity of food recall warning notices that consumers can readily understand, with requirements that the warnings be put in stores and other sites where the food buyer will notice them. The Reportable Food Registry information flow is intended to be much faster. Note that the 2010 legislation reflects the lobbying efforts of the fruit and vegetable growers to be excluded when final rules are issued in 2012.

Although much of the 2010 Act had been compromised in order to win support from retail chains, this requirement is a significant step forward in outreach. It is likely to improve the responses consumers give to the warning or recall notice. Readers should note that the law gives flexibility for the FDA in writing the rules, and allows for punishment of retail food stores that refuse to post their notifications as required.

Text of the Law as Adopted

Section 417 (21 U.S.C. 350f) is amended--

(1) by redesignating subsections (f) through (k) as subsections (i) through (n), respectively; and

(2) by inserting after subsection (e) the following:

> *"(f) Critical Information.--Except with respect to fruits and vegetables that are raw agricultural commodities, not more than 18 months after the date of enactment of the FDA Food Safety Modernization Act, the Secretary may require a responsible party to submit to the Secretary consumer-oriented information regarding a reportable food, which shall include--*

>> *"(1) a description of the article of food as provided in subsection (e)(3);*

"(2) as provided in subsection (e)(7), affected product identification codes, such as UPC, SKU, or lot or batch numbers sufficient for the consumer to identify the article of food;

"(3) contact information for the responsible party as provided in subsection (e)(8); and

"(4) any other information the Secretary determines is necessary to enable a consumer to accurately identify whether such consumer is in possession of the reportable food.

"(g) Grocery Store Notification.--

"(1) ACTION BY SECRETARY.--The Secretary shall--

"(A) prepare the critical information described under subsection (f) for a reportable food as a standardized one-page summary;

"(B) publish such one-page summary on the Internet website of the Food and Drug Administration in a format that can be easily printed by a grocery store for purposes of consumer notification.

"(2) ACTION BY GROCERY STORE.--A notification described under paragraph (1)(B) shall include the date and time such summary was posted on the Internet website of the Food and Drug Administration.

"(h) Consumer Notification.--

"(1) IN GENERAL.--If a grocery store sold a reportable food that is the subject of the posting and such establishment is part of chain of establishments with 15 or more physical locations, then such establishment shall, not later than 24 hours after a one page summary described in subsection (g) is published, prominently display such summary or the information from such summary via at least one

of the methods identified under paragraph (2) and maintain the display for 14 days.

"(2) LIST OF CONSPICUOUS LOCATIONS.--Not more than 1 year after the date of enactment of the FDA Food Safety Modernization Act, the Secretary shall develop and publish a list of acceptable conspicuous locations and manners, from which grocery stores shall select at least one, for providing the notification required in paragraph (1). Such list shall include--

"(A) posting the notification at or near the register;

"(B) providing the location of the reportable food;

"(C) providing targeted recall information given to customers upon purchase of a food; and

"(D) other such prominent and conspicuous locations and manners utilized by grocery stores as of the date of the enactment of the FDA Food Safety Modernization Act to provide notice of such recalls to consumers as considered appropriate by the Secretary.".

(b) Prohibited Act.--Section 301 (21 U.S.C. 331), as amended by section 206, is amended by adding at the end the following:

"(yy) The knowing and willful failure to comply with the notification requirement under section 417(h).".

(c) Conforming Amendment.--Section 301(e) (21 U.S.C. 331(e)) is amended by striking "417(g)" and inserting "417(j)".

What Does the 2010 Act Do in Response to Smuggled Food?

Some foods are kept off the US market because their ingestion could harm the consumer's health. An example would be a fish with toxic effects, which cannot be allowed in the food supply because of its toxicity. This section adopted in 2010 deals squarely with that situation of severe health risk.

Action by the FDA to ban a food is rare. But even after the FDA uses its import alerts, seizures, and detentions against the food shipments that come in through legitimate import channels, there are still some people who may want to eat this particular food despite its risks (e.g., for a cultural or religious celebration for which the food plays some role).

This section targets and punishes smugglers of food that cannot legitimately be imported (or that was rejected at the border). The FDA and Customs are directed to cooperate. Fraudulent or counterfeit baby formula is an example of a food that some unscrupulous importers will smuggle into the channels of commerce because of the high profit margins that can be earned from the counterfeits.

Smuggling for purely economic tariff avoidance reasons would be barred by Customs laws and rules. Presumably, the 2010 Act provisions will not be used for conventional food importers who disobey a Customs paperwork rule, for there are ample remedies there, but the new section is targeted for the malicious violators.

If the FDA learns of a smuggled food and believes the food would cause serious adverse health consequences or death, the FDA must notify Homeland Security. The FDA may publish a public notification if there is reason to believe the food has entered domestic commerce.

Text of the Law as Adopted

SEC. 309. SMUGGLED FOOD.

(a) In General.--Not later than 180 days after the enactment of this Act, the Secretary shall, in coordination with the Secretary of Homeland Security, develop and implement a strategy to better identify smuggled food and prevent entry of such food into the United States.

(b) Notification to Homeland Security.--Not later than 10 days after the Secretary identifies a smuggled food that the Secretary believes would cause serious adverse health consequences or death to humans or animals, the Secretary shall provide to the Secretary of Homeland Security a notification under section 417(n) of the Federal Food, Drug, and Cosmetic Act (21 U.S.C. 350f(k)) describing the smuggled food

and, if available, the names of the individuals or entities that attempted to import such food into the United States.

(c) Public Notification.--If the Secretary-

> *(1) identifies a smuggled food;*

> *(2) reasonably believes exposure to the food would cause serious adverse health consequences or death to humans or animals; and*

> *(3) reasonably believes that the food has entered domestic commerce and is likely to be consumed,*

the Secretary shall promptly issue a press release describing that food and shall use other emergency communication or recall networks, as appropriate, to warn consumers and vendors about the potential threat.

(d) Effect of Section.--Nothing in this section shall affect the authority of the Secretary to issue public notifications under other circumstances.

(e) Definition.--In this subsection, the term "smuggled food" means any food that a person introduces into the United States through fraudulent means or with the intent to defraud or mislead.

14

Employee Concerns and Whistleblower Risks

What Do Managers Need To Know?

Dissatisfied employees at food plants have a new weapon against management. Food industry workers who believe there is a food safety problem will now be shielded from employer discipline by the 2010 Act,[608] or at least the more sophisticated employers will be more cautious about the downsides of firing the disgruntled employees. If a food safety problem exists at a plant, pay close attention to the possible existence of an angry worker who may "blow the whistle." Because of expansive wording of the 2010 law, the proof needed by the worker in a later case claiming wrongful retaliation is much lighter and more dubious than would be the case in conventional workplace controversies.

What Is a Whistleblower?

This term describes a worker or manager who complains that food is unsafe because of some factor relating to the company, its facility, or its operations. Blowing the figurative "whistle" is intended to call to the public's attention an unsafe condition of the food. Most of these situations are those in which the plant's filthy conditions, reported by a worker to a government hotline, lead to a recall or other cleanup measures.

---

[608] Pub.L. 111-353 §1012, added by S. 510 §402 (2010).

What Are the Elements of the Claim by the Employee?

The food industry employee can assert either:

> I was discharged or otherwise discriminated against by a food company, because I gave information relating to a violation (or was about to give that information) to the company or to the FDA or to the state attorney general, and the information was about a violation of a regulation or provision of the FD&C Act, and I gave the information or testified or assisted in a government proceeding; or,

> I refused to participate in or I objected to an activity that I reasonably believed was a violation of an FDA order, rule, standard, or other provision of the FD&C Act.[609]

These are very broad options when read in conjunction with the subjective measure of "about to" disclose the violation.

What Is Different about the Act's New Term "About To"?

Compared to twenty other federal laws also shielding worker safety complaints,[610] this section is one of the very few that uses an odd retrospective look-back: the protection prevents or mitigates any food industry discipline against a worker who was "about to" report to the government about the food safety concern.[611]

Under most such laws, the worker makes a complaint about bad conditions (e.g., to a federal inspector). Then the worker is disciplined for making the complaint, files a whistleblower action, and then shows in an administrative proceeding that the discipline flowed from the making of that complaint. The government then can order back pay and reinstatement. Documents

---

[609] *Id.*

[610] *See* list at www.whistleblowers.gov/index.html.

[611] Compare similar language in the 2008 Consumer Product Safety Improvements Act, Pub.L. 110-314 §219 (2008); see James O'Reilly, *Consumer Product Safety Regulation* (PLI, 2008).

and a paper trail or recorded phone call support the worker's complaint of retaliatory punishment.

Here the worker, after discipline occurs, tells the government that even though no complaint about food safety was made, he or she was about to make such a complaint about safety of food. The credibility of the witness can be attacked in the Labor Department hearing, but there need not be any tangible showing of a transmitted message making a complaint about food safety. There is an inherent, built-in temptation to retrospection—yes, before my job was cut, I knew the plant was insanitary and I was about to report its poor safety conditions.

Bringing testimony on the claim of "about to" reporting, into a disputed adjudication hearing, months after the firing, is a great gift for the worker and his or her union. No documentation exists of an actual complaint. Subjective intention of the person, examined in hindsight, governs whether he or she was about to complain. Employers are far more likely to settle such cases, as there is no way to disprove a worker's post-hoc statement of intention.

Where Does the Claim Go?

Within six months of the company's action against him or her, the worker must notify the local office of the US Department of Labor. The company then gets a letter describing the charge and the Labor Department process. Within sixty days, the Labor Department investigator will come to the company and investigate, and will notify the company and the complainant of the determination as to whether there was "reasonable cause that the complaint has merit." This same notice to the company will be accompanied by a preliminary order of protection or reinstatement. Within thirty days, the company or the employee can object and request a hearing. If the company fails to act, the preliminary order becomes final. If the company requests a hearing, an administrative law judge will hold a hearing "expeditiously," usually in a local courthouse hearing room. The employee wins if his or her report to government or refusal to act illegally was "a contributing factor" to the company's "unfavorable personnel action." The company wins if it shows by "clear and convincing evidence" that even without the employee objection or refusal related to a food regulatory issue, the employer "would have taken the same unfavorable personnel action in the absence of that behavior."[612]

What Should My Company Do if Confronted with a Whistleblower Claim?

First, inform managers to use careful wording in their messages about the situation, while the company retains the specialized lawyer assistance that is needed for these peculiarly difficult cases. Do not allow e-mail or written speculation and outrage to be expressed by managers who feel personally offended. The company's ability to sustain a decision about the errant employee may be lost if the paper trail shows wrong decisions or, more likely, wrong expressions.

Second, retain an additional lawyer (an undesired cost for most managers) who has the special expertise to handle Labor Department whistleblower cases. These are not classic discrimination claims. These are not labor union claims, but they have a kind of specific process that is best managed by experienced labor counsel who has mastered the whistleblower process.

Third, work with legal counsel to find patterns of deficient performance evaluations, punitive warnings, and other "clear and convincing evidence that the employer would have taken the same unfavorable personnel action in the absence of that behavior."

Fourth, if the employee claim was indeed "frivolous" or "in bad faith," then after its dismissal, ask the imposition of the agency' legal expenses upon the challenger.

Finally, route all the correspondence from managers through legal counsel to set up a future argument for privilege from disclosure.

---

[612] Pub.L. 111-353 §1012(b)(2)(C).

Text of the Law as Adopted

SEC. 402. EMPLOYEE PROTECTIONS.

Chapter X of the Federal Food, Drug, and Cosmetic Act (21 U.S.C. 391 et seq.), as amended by section 209, is further amended by adding at the end the following:

"SEC. 1012. EMPLOYEE PROTECTIONS.

"(a) In General.--No entity engaged in the manufacture, processing, packing, transporting, distribution, reception, holding, or importation of food may discharge an employee or otherwise discriminate against an employee with respect to compensation, terms, conditions, or privileges of employment because the employee, whether at the employee's initiative or in the ordinary course of the employee's duties (or any person acting pursuant to a request of the employee)--

"(1) provided, caused to be provided, or is about to provide or cause to be provided to the employer, the Federal Government, or the attorney general of a State information relating to any violation of, or any act or omission the employee reasonably believes to be a violation of any provision of this Act or any order, rule, regulation, standard, or ban under this Act, or any order, rule, regulation, standard, or ban under this Act;

"(2) testified or is about to testify in a proceeding concerning such violation;

"(3) assisted or participated or is about to assist or participate in such a proceeding; or

"(4) objected to, or refused to participate in, any activity, policy, practice, or assigned task that the employee (or other such person) reasonably believed to be in violation of any provision of this Act, or any order, rule, regulation, standard, or ban under this Act.

"(b) Process.--

"(1) IN GENERAL.--A person who believes that he or she has been discharged or otherwise discriminated against by any person in

violation of subsection (a) may, not later than 180 days after the date on which such violation occurs, file (or have any person file on his or her behalf) a complaint with the Secretary of Labor (referred to in this section as the 'Secretary') alleging such discharge or discrimination and identifying the person responsible for such act. Upon receipt of such a complaint, the Secretary shall notify, in writing, the person named in the complaint of the filing of the complaint, of the allegations contained in the complaint, of the substance of evidence supporting the complaint, and of the opportunities that will be afforded to such person under paragraph (2).

"(2) INVESTIGATION.--

"(A) IN GENERAL.--Not later than 60 days after the date of receipt of a complaint filed under paragraph (1) and after affording the complainant and the person named in the complaint an opportunity to submit to the Secretary a written response to the complaint and an opportunity to meet with a representative of the Secretary to present statements from witnesses, the Secretary shall initiate an investigation and determine whether there is reasonable cause to believe that the complaint has merit and notify, in writing, the complainant and the person alleged to have committed a violation of subsection (a) of the Secretary's findings.

"(B) REASONABLE CAUSE FOUND; PRELIMINARY ORDER.--If the Secretary concludes that there is reasonable cause to believe that a violation of subsection (a) has occurred, the Secretary shall accompany the Secretary's findings with a preliminary order providing the relief prescribed by paragraph (3)(B). Not later than 30 days after the date of notification of findings under this paragraph, the person alleged to have committed the violation or the complainant may file objections to the findings or preliminary order, or both, and request a hearing on the record. The filing of such objections shall not operate to stay any reinstatement remedy contained in the

preliminary order. Any such hearing shall be conducted expeditiously. If a hearing is not requested in such 30-day period, the preliminary order shall be deemed a final order that is not subject to judicial review.

"(C) DISMISSAL OF COMPLAINT.--

"(i) STANDARD FOR COMPLAINANT.--*The Secretary shall dismiss a complaint filed under this subsection and shall not conduct an investigation otherwise required under subparagraph (A) unless the complainant makes a prima facie showing that any behavior described in paragraphs (1) through (4) of subsection (a) was a contributing factor in the unfavorable personnel action alleged in the complaint.*

"(ii) STANDARD FOR EMPLOYER.-- *Notwithstanding a finding by the Secretary that the complainant has made the showing required under clause (i), no investigation otherwise required under subparagraph (A) shall be conducted if the employer demonstrates, by clear and convincing evidence, that the employer would have taken the same unfavorable personnel action in the absence of that behavior.*

"(iii) VIOLATION STANDARD.--*The Secretary may determine that a violation of subsection (a) has occurred only if the complainant demonstrates that any behavior described in paragraphs (1) through (4) of subsection (a) was a contributing factor in the unfavorable personnel action alleged in the complaint.*

"(iv) RELIEF STANDARD.--Relief may not be ordered under subparagraph (A) if the employer demonstrates by clear and convincing evidence that the employer would have taken the same unfavorable personnel action in the absence of that behavior.

"(3) FINAL ORDER.--

"(A) IN GENERAL.--Not later than 120 days after the date of conclusion of any hearing under paragraph (2), the Secretary shall issue a final order providing the relief prescribed by this paragraph or denying the complaint. At any time before issuance of a final order, a proceeding under this subsection may be terminated on the basis of a settlement agreement entered into by the Secretary, the complainant, and the person alleged to have committed the violation.

"(B) CONTENT OF ORDER.--If, in response to a complaint filed under paragraph (1), the Secretary determines that a violation of subsection (a) has occurred, the Secretary shall order the person who committed such violation--

"(i) to take affirmative action to abate the violation;

"(ii) to reinstate the complainant to his or her former position together with compensation (including back pay) and restore the terms, conditions, and privileges associated with his or her employment; and

"(iii) to provide compensatory damages to the complainant.

"(C) PENALTY.--If such an order is issued under this paragraph, the Secretary, at the request of the complainant, shall assess against the person against whom the order is issued a sum equal to the aggregate amount of all costs and expenses (including attorneys' and expert witness fees) reasonably incurred, as determined by the Secretary, by the complainant for, or in connection with, the bringing of the complaint upon which the order was issued.

"(D) BAD FAITH CLAIM.--If the Secretary finds that a complaint under paragraph (1) is frivolous or has been brought in bad faith, the Secretary may award to the prevailing employer a reasonable attorneys' fee, not exceeding $1,000, to be paid by the complainant.

"(4) ACTION IN COURT.--

"(A) IN GENERAL.--If the Secretary has not issued a final decision within 210 days after the filing of the complaint, or within 90 days after receiving a written determination, the complainant may bring an action at law or equity for de novo review in the appropriate district court of the United States with jurisdiction, which shall have jurisdiction over such an action without regard to the amount in controversy, and which action shall, at the request of either party to such action, be tried by the court with a jury. The proceedings shall be governed by the same legal burdens of proof specified in paragraph (2)(C).

"(B) RELIEF.--The court shall have jurisdiction to grant all relief necessary to make the employee whole, including injunctive relief and compensatory damages, including--

"(i) reinstatement with the same seniority status that the employee would have had, but for the discharge or discrimination;

"(ii) the amount of back pay, with interest; and

"(iii) compensation for any special damages sustained as a result of the discharge or discrimination, including litigation costs, expert witness fees, and reasonable attorney's fees.

"(5) REVIEW.--

"(A) IN GENERAL.--Unless the complainant brings an action under paragraph (4), any person adversely affected or aggrieved by a final order issued under paragraph (3) may obtain review of the order in the United States Court of Appeals for the circuit in which the violation, with respect to which the order was issued, allegedly occurred or the circuit in which the complainant resided on the date of such violation. The petition for review must be filed not later than 60 days after the date of the issuance of the final order of the Secretary. Review shall conform to chapter 7 of title 5, United States Code. The commencement of proceedings under this subparagraph shall not, unless ordered by the court, operate as a stay of the order.

"(B) NO JUDICIAL REVIEW.--An order of the Secretary with respect to which review could have been obtained under subparagraph (A) shall not be subject to judicial review in any criminal or other civil proceeding.

"(6) FAILURE TO COMPLY WITH ORDER.--Whenever any person has failed to comply with an order issued under paragraph (3), the Secretary may file a civil action in the United States district court for the district in which the violation was found to occur, or in the United States district court for the District of Columbia, to enforce such order. In actions brought under this paragraph, the district courts shall have jurisdiction to grant all appropriate relief including, but not limited to, injunctive relief and compensatory damages.

"(7) CIVIL ACTION TO REQUIRE COMPLIANCE.--

"(A) IN GENERAL.--A person on whose behalf an order was issued under paragraph (3) may commence a civil action against the person to whom such order was issued to require compliance with such order. The appropriate United States district court shall have jurisdiction, without regard to the amount in controversy or the citizenship of the parties, to enforce such order.

"(B) AWARD.--The court, in issuing any final order under this paragraph, may award costs of litigation (including reasonable attorneys' and expert witness fees) to any party whenever the court determines such award is appropriate.

"(c) Effect of Section.--

"(1) OTHER LAWS.--Nothing in this section preempts or diminishes any other safeguards against discrimination, demotion, discharge, suspension, threats, harassment, reprimand, retaliation, or any other manner of discrimination provided by Federal or State law.

"(2) RIGHTS OF EMPLOYEES.--Nothing in this section shall be construed to diminish the rights, privileges, or remedies of any employee under any Federal or State law or under any collective bargaining agreement. The rights and remedies in this section may not be waived by any agreement, policy, form, or condition of employment.

"(d) Enforcement.--Any nondiscretionary duty imposed by this section shall be enforceable in a mandamus proceeding brought under section 1361 of title 28, United States Code.

"(e) Limitation.--Subsection (a) shall not apply with respect to an employee of an entity engaged in the manufacture, processing, packing, transporting, distribution, reception, holding, or importation of food who, acting without direction from such entity (or such entity's agent), deliberately causes a violation of any requirement relating to any violation or alleged violation of any order, rule, regulation, standard, or ban under this Act.".

15

Dietary Supplements
and Other Provisions

What Is the Impact of the New Act on Dietary Supplements?

This Act does not directly affect the claims made for dietary supplement products, but two aspects tighten the regulatory regime for these products while leaving most supplement products unaffected.

One new section seeks to track down and report to the Drug Enforcement Administration, the federal overseers of illicit drugs, those companies that promote as "dietary supplements" the steroid-like materials that are addictive or promote dependency. While the FDA and the Drug Enforcement Administration have informally cooperated, this gives new authority and direction to root out the steroid equivalents being sold as diet products. The current marketing wave of body builder ads for power and strength from diet supplement products are likely to attract heavier regulatory attention when the Drug Enforcement Administration moves in on their marketers.

The new and complex Section 418 hazard analysis requirements expressly exclude dietary supplement facilities under new 418(g).

How Are New Dietary Ingredients Covered?

In addition, the specific words of Section 413 of the new Act give the FDA expanded powers in control of the general scope of dietary supplements, not just steroids. The Act addresses an area of confused definitions. "New dietary ingredient" notification to the FDA has been confusing as to coverage, with multiple questions left open by earlier legislation. The 2010 Act's Section 113 forces the FDA to define (though in an easily changed guideline, not a firm rule) two "when" answers, a "what" answer, and a "how" answer.

The new guidelines the FDA is required to issue must describe four things:

1. When a dietary supplement ingredient is a "new" dietary ingredient
2. When the manufacturer or distributor of a dietary ingredient or dietary supplement should provide the FDA with "published articles" and other scientific data supporting safe use experience with the ingredient
3. The evidence needed to document the safety of new dietary ingredients
4. Appropriate methods for establishing the identity of a new dietary ingredient

Note that these are not set up as binding rules, because the diet supplement industry used its political strength to limit the changes. There is significance to the choice of "guidance." Congress did not clarify its view of this field in definitive terms, allowing more room for the FDA to maneuver. The Act did not require the FDA to lock in its definitions in a final, binding rule. Other FDA rules in the diet supplement field have been fought hard by the industry's advocates for "commercial free speech" rights. Courts are likely to uphold the FDA guidelines because of this new statute's express congressional delegation. It helps the outcome of such a challenge for the FDA to point to Congress as the decision-maker, as compared to defending a totally FDA-initiated decision to make this important definitional area clearer.

Text of the Law as Adopted

SEC. 113. NEW DIETARY INGREDIENTS.

(a) In General.--Section 413 of the Federal Food, Drug, and Cosmetic Act (21 U.S.C. 350b) is amended--

> *(1) by redesignating subsection (c) as subsection (d); and*

> *(2) by inserting after subsection (b) the following:*

>> *"(c) Notification.--*

>>> *"(1) IN GENERAL.--If the Secretary determines that the information in a new dietary ingredient notification submitted under this section for an article purported to be a new dietary ingredient is inadequate to establish that a dietary supplement containing such article will reasonably be expected to be safe because the article may be, or may contain, an anabolic steroid or an analogue of an anabolic steroid, the Secretary shall notify the Drug Enforcement Administration of such determination. Such notification by the Secretary shall include,at a minimum, the name of the dietary supplement or article, the name of the person or persons who marketed the product or made the submission of information regarding the article to the Secretary under this section, and any contact information for such person or persons that the Secretary has.*

>>> *"(2) DEFINITIONS.--For purposes of this subsection--*

>>>> *"(A) the term 'anabolic steroid' has the meaning given such term in section 102(41) of the Controlled Substances Act; and*

>>>> *"(B) the term 'analogue of an anabolic steroid' means a substance whose chemical structure is*

substantially similar to the chemical structure of an anabolic steroid.".

(b) Guidance.--Not later than 180 days after the date of enactment of this Act, the Secretary shall publish guidance that clarifies when a dietary supplement ingredient is a new dietary ingredient, when the manufacturer or distributor of a dietary ingredient or dietary supplement should provide the Secretary with information as described in section 413(a)(2) of the Federal Food, Drug, and Cosmetic Act, the evidence needed to document the safety of new dietary ingredients, and appropriate methods for establishing the identify of a new dietary ingredient.

What Does the Act Do Regarding the Transportation of Food?

In the face of its recent diminished resources and complex constituent desires, the FDA dragged its feet on the implementation of 2007 legislation on food transportation safety. This provision in the new Act forces the FDA to issue its long-delayed rules.

Text of the Law as Adopted

SEC. 111. SANITARY TRANSPORTATION OF FOOD.

(a) In General.--Not later than 18 months after the date of enactment of this Act, the Secretary shall promulgate regulations described in section 416(b) of the Federal Food, Drug, and Cosmetic Act (21 U.S.C. 350e(b)).

(b) Food Transportation Study.--The Secretary, acting through the Commissioner of Food and Drugs, shall conduct a study of the transportation of food for consumption in the United States, including transportation by air, that includes an examination of the unique needs of rural and frontier areas with regard to the delivery of safe food.

What Does the Act Do for Allergy Issues in Childrens' Educational Settings?

Special advocacy efforts for children's causes have led to attachment of this section belatedly into the food safety law. Unlike the command and control models used in the remainder of the legislation, this is a social education policy program to encourage K–8 schools to screen more kids for food allergies.

Its dubious connection to imported food safety makes it the least congruent aspect of the statute. Most food companies are already doing their part, so this is more likely to affect educational entities.

Text of the Law as Adopted

SEC. 112. FOOD ALLERGY AND ANAPHYLAXIS MANAGEMENT.

(a) Definitions.--In this section:

> *(1) EARLY CHILDHOOD EDUCATION PROGRAM.--The term "early childhood education program" means--*
>
> > *(A) a Head Start program or an Early Head Start program carried out under the Head Start Act (42 U.S.C. 9831 et seq.);*
> >
> > *(B) a State licensed or regulated child care program or school; or*
> >
> > *(C) a State prekindergarten program that serves children from birth through kindergarten.*
>
> *(2) ESEA DEFINITIONS.--The terms "local educational agency", "secondary school", "elementary school", and "parent" have the meanings given the terms in section 9101 of the Elementary and Secondary Education Act of 1965 (20 U.S.C. 7801).*
>
> *(3) SCHOOL.--The term "school" includes public--*
>
> > *(A) kindergartens;*
> >
> > *(B) elementary schools; and*
> >
> > *(C) secondary schools.*

(4) SECRETARY.--The term "Secretary" means the Secretary of Health and Human Services.

(b) Establishment of Voluntary Food Allergy and Anaphylaxis Management Guidelines.--

(1) ESTABLISHMENT.--

(A) IN GENERAL.--Not later than 1 year after the date of enactment of this Act, the Secretary, in consultation with the Secretary of Education, shall--

(i) develop guidelines to be used on a voluntary basis to develop plans for individuals to manage the risk of food allergy and anaphylaxis in schools and early childhood education programs; and

(ii) make such guidelines available to local educational agencies, schools, early childhood education programs, and other interested entities and individuals to be implemented on a voluntary basis only.

(B) APPLICABILITY OF FERPA.--Each plan described in subparagraph (A) that is developed for an individual shall be considered an education record for the purpose of section 444 of the General Education Provisions Act (commonly referred to as the "Family Educational Rights and Privacy Act of 1974") (20 U.S.C. 1232g).

(2) CONTENTS.--The voluntary guidelines developed by the Secretary under paragraph (1) shall address each of the following and may be updated as the Secretary determines necessary:

(A) Parental obligation to provide the school or early childhood education program, prior to the start of every school year, with--

(i) documentation from their child's physician or nurse--

(I) *supporting a diagnosis of food allergy, and any risk of anaphylaxis, if applicable;*

(II) *identifying any food to which the child is allergic;*

(III) *describing, if appropriate, any prior history of anaphylaxis;*

(IV) *listing any medication prescribed for the child for the treatment of anaphylaxis;*

(V) *detailing emergency treatment procedures in the event of a reaction;*

(VI) *listing the signs and symptoms of a reaction; and*

(VII) *assessing the child's readiness for self-administration of prescription medication; and*

(ii) *a list of substitute meals that may be offered to the child by school or early childhood education program food service personnel.*

(B) *The creation and maintenance of an individual plan for food allergy management, in consultation with the parent, tailored to the needs of each child with a documented risk for anaphylaxis, including any procedures for the self-administration of medication by such children in instances where--*

(i) *the children are capable of self-administering medication; and*

(ii) *such administration is not prohibited by State law.*

(C) *Communication strategies between individual schools or early childhood education programs and providers of emergency medical services, including appropriate instructions for emergency medical response.*

(D) Strategies to reduce the risk of exposure to anaphylactic causative agents in classrooms and common school or early childhood education program areas such as cafeterias.

(E) The dissemination of general information on life-threatening food allergies to school or early childhood education program staff, parents, and children.

(F) Food allergy management training of school or early childhood education program personnel who regularly come into contact with children with life-threatening food allergies.

(G) The authorization and training of school or early childhood education program personnel to administer epinephrine when the nurse is not immediately available.

(H) The timely accessibility of epinephrine by school or early childhood education program personnel when the nurse is not immediately available.

(I) The creation of a plan contained in each individual plan for food allergy management that addresses the appropriate response to an incident of anaphylaxis of a child while such child is engaged in extracurricular programs of a school or early childhood education program, such as non-academic outings and field trips, before- and after-school programs or before- and after-early child education program programs, and school-sponsored or early childhood education program-sponsored programs held on weekends.

(J) Maintenance of information for each administration of epinephrine to a child at risk for anaphylaxis and prompt notification to parents.

(K) Other elements the Secretary determines necessary for the management of food allergies and anaphylaxis in schools and early childhood education programs.

(3) RELATION TO STATE LAW.--Nothing in this section or the guidelines developed by the Secretary under paragraph (1) shall be construed to preempt State law, including any State law regarding whether students at risk for anaphylaxis may self-administer medication.

(c) School-based Food Allergy Management Grants.--

(1) IN GENERAL.--The Secretary may award grants to local educational agencies to assist such agencies with implementing voluntary food allergy and anaphylaxis management guidelines described in subsection (b).

(2) APPLICATION.--

(A) IN GENERAL.--To be eligible to receive a grant under this subsection, a local educational agency shall submit an application to the Secretary at such time, in such manner, and including such information as the Secretary may reasonably require.

(B) CONTENTS.--Each application submitted under subparagraph (A) shall include--

(i) an assurance that the local educational agency has developed plans in accordance with the food allergy and anaphylaxis management guidelines described in subsection (b);

(ii) a description of the activities to be funded by the grant in carrying out the food allergy and anaphylaxis management guidelines, including--

(I) how the guidelines will be carried out at individual schools served by the local educational agency;

(II) how the local educational agency will inform parents and students of the guidelines in place;

(III) how school nurses, teachers, administrators, and other school-based staff will be made aware of, and given training on, when applicable, the guidelines in place; and

(IV) any other activities that the Secretary determines appropriate;

(iii) an itemization of how grant funds received under this subsection will be expended;

(iv) a description of how adoption of the guidelines and implementation of grant activities will be monitored; and

(v) an agreement by the local educational agency to report information required by the Secretary to conduct evaluations under this subsection.

(3) USE OF FUNDS.--Each local educational agency that receives a grant under this subsection may use the grant funds for the following:

(A) Purchase of materials and supplies, including limited medical supplies such as epinephrine and disposable wet wipes, to support carrying out the food allergy and anaphylaxis management guidelines described in subsection (b).

(B) In partnership with local health departments, school nurse, teacher, and personnel training for food allergy management.

(C) Programs that educate students as to the presence of, and policies and procedures in place related to, food allergies and anaphylactic shock.

(D) Outreach to parents.

(E) Any other activities consistent with the guidelines described in subsection (b).

(4) DURATION OF AWARDS.--*The Secretary may award grants under this subsection for a period of not more than 2 years. In the event the Secretary conducts a program evaluation under this subsection, funding in the second year of the grant, where applicable, shall be contingent on a successful program evaluation by the Secretary after the first year.*

(5) LIMITATION ON GRANT FUNDING.--*The Secretary may not provide grant funding to a local educational agency under this subsection after such local educational agency has received 2 years of grant funding under this subsection.*

(6) MAXIMUM AMOUNT OF ANNUAL AWARDS.--*A grant awarded under this subsection may not be made in an amount that is more than $50,000 annually.*

(7) PRIORITY.--*In awarding grants under this subsection, the Secretary shall give priority to local educational agencies with the highest percentages of children who are counted under section 1124(c) of the Elementary and Secondary Education Act of 1965 (20 U.S.C. 6333(c)).*

(8) MATCHING FUNDS.--

(A) IN GENERAL.--*The Secretary may not award a grant under this subsection unless the local educational agency agrees that, with respect to the costs to be incurred by such local educational agency in carrying out the grant activities, the local educational agency shall make available (directly or through donations from public or private entities) non-Federal funds toward such costs in an amount equal to not less than 25 percent of the amount of the grant.*

(B) DETERMINATION OF AMOUNT OF NON-FEDERAL CONTRIBUTION.--*Non-Federal funds required under subparagraph (A) may be cash or in kind, including plant, equipment, or services. Amounts provided by the Federal Government, and any portion of any service subsidized by the Federal Government, may not be included in determining the amount of such non-Federal funds.*

(9) ADMINISTRATIVE FUNDS.--A local educational agency that receives a grant under this subsection may use not more than 2 percent of the grant amount for administrative costs related to carrying out this subsection.

(10) PROGRESS AND EVALUATIONS.--At the completion of the grant period referred to in paragraph (4), a local educational agency shall provide the Secretary with information on how grant funds were spent and the status of implementation of the food allergy and anaphylaxis management guidelines described in subsection (b).

(11) SUPPLEMENT, NOT SUPPLANT.--Grant funds received under this subsection shall be used to supplement, and not supplant, non-Federal funds and any other Federal funds available to carry out the activities described in this subsection.

(12) AUTHORIZATION OF APPROPRIATIONS.--There is authorized to be appropriated to carry out this subsection $30,000,000 for fiscal year 2011 and such sums as may be necessary for each of the 4 succeeding fiscal years.

(d) Voluntary Nature of Guidelines.--

(1) IN GENERAL.--The food allergy and anaphylaxis management guidelines developed by the Secretary under subsection (b) are voluntary. Nothing in this section or the guidelines developed by the Secretary under subsection (b) shall be construed to require a local educational agency to implement such guidelines.

(2) EXCEPTION.--Notwithstanding paragraph (1), the Secretary may enforce an agreement by a local educational agency to implement food allergy and anaphylaxis management guidelines as a condition of the receipt of a grant under subsection (c).

Organizing a Food Business for Compliance

What Do Managers Need To Know?

The first duty a public company owes is to its shareholders. A close second is its general obligation to the customer, the public, and the community to deliver its products safely in a manner that will conform to the expectations of the public. A food company that fails to keep the public's trust will soon lose the profitability that retains shareholder loyalty. Prudent food company managers understand these duties. These duties underlie the compliance changes that prudent managers will make as a result of the 2010 food law changes. Institutional vulnerability is higher now. Supply chains are more strictly overseen by government, and individual liability of managers for misdemeanor crimes of prohibited acts will be substantially more impactful. Laws can't change attitudes, but the prudent food manager will use this book to teach the team what must be done. And, along the way, attitudes toward compliance will improve for those who want to keep their companies and their personal careers on track.

What Is To Be Done First?

Step one inside the company will be to convene meetings among the leaders of the company's purchasing department, supply chain managers, food manufacturing managers, quality control, receiving department, and regulatory managers. The initial meeting should be informational, and the company's attorney should participate actively in responding to the early concerns. The impact of the new law should be explained, both as to what is known and what is not known.

The "trainers" about the new law should listen as well as train. Obstacles not apparent at the corporate level will be addressed only if staff listens to the line managers' daily experiences. Subsequent meetings will track how the new FDA regulations are being formulated, and managers should listen for operational level comments on what the company should be expressing to trade associations and to the FDA in the public comment phases of the FDA rule-writing process. Is there a need to change Customs warehouse procedures, accounting recordkeeping, contingency plans, etc.?

The meetings should emphasize reasonable changes to get along with the new law. Whatever rules the FDA adopts to implement the 2010 Act will be in place for years or decades, like the FDA's good manufacturing practice rules of the 1970s. Don't believe tough talk from lawyers who are paid by the hour; paying them to litigate in search of a court reversal is a "very long shot" for those who dislike the Act and hate the FDA's final regulations. Living with a flexible set of requirements that can be adapted to the company's compliance efforts is optimal; facing a rigid rule that clashes directly with the company's operations is a serious management challenge. The aphorism that the world is divided into those who make things happen, those who watch things happen, and those who wonder what happened, applies in FDA food rule-making. Which will you be?

What Role Should Trade Groups Play?

Step two should be a trade association participation plan for the company. The FDA is writing rules affecting the segment of the food industry in which your company operates. The rules will have a big impact. Early acceptance by the FDA of the need for tailored exceptions and waivers may be very important to the company. So the trade association is the optimal vehicle for expressing collective concerns to the FDA. In the member companies, managers will identify which parts of the FDA rules implementing would hurt the company most. What can the company do to maximize the impact of the company's objections upon awareness of the rule-writing team inside the FDA? Numbers matter greatly. Accounting for the costs of compliance, likely delays and disruptions of the supply chain, etc. will be done before the trade association finalizes its comments. The FDA pays attention to costs and to lower-cost means of achieving the law's objectives. The company may also file its own comments and seek to have its local member of Congress support its views with a letter to the FDA. But remaining silent and unheard is a recipe for failure; "maybe they just won't notice us" is fallacious. The rule-writers want to know where the practical implementation problems would be. Inside the FDA, rule drafters generally do not interact much with the operational inspection and compliance teams who actually monitor ports and factories. Trade association comments to change the practical effect of the FDA's proposed rule will be most helpful if they contain numbers and speak to the actual difficulty presented by aspects of the rule that can be altered in final texts.

How Will Customs Brokers Respond?

Step three should be a meeting with the firm's import managers and customs brokers. They now have a more personal sense of involvement, since they will be confronting more FDA staff members with more discretion and more legal tools to compel strict compliance. Customs brokers would have been personally vulnerable under earlier versions of the bill, but the final Act deleted the FDA power over these agents. Compliance at the ports of entry is vital now that more powerful weapons are available to the FDA and more records and reports are required.

Will Companies That Depend on a Supply Chain of Foreign Vendors Use the WTO?

Step four should be an assessment of whether to use leverage against the FDA proposed rules. The United States is one of many nations that is bound by an international trade agreement; disputes under the agreement are resolved in Geneva by multi-nation dispute resolution panels of the WTO. If the proposed FDA rule affects food facilities in and food exports from a foreign nation, with which the company works closely on its imported food needs, the company can help that nation prepare its WTO complaint. WTO member nation challenges to FDA rules as "trade barriers" are going to be a pressure point on the FDA's implementing regulations. If done deftly, the final implementing rule will grant an exception that accommodates the needs of the food-exporting nation. An exception or modification to the FDA proposed rule would appease the nation that exports food, and may lead that nation to withdraw its complaint before a WTO dispute panel proceeding is convened. Within the administration, coordination among the FDA, the US Trade Representative, and the State Department will absolutely be needed to deal with these challenges.

This approach to a regulated firm's leverage against US programs involves some delicate interactions with lawyers who are experienced with international trade remedies. A very significant assessment will need to be made of the other nation's need for the US market for its export food items. Delicate negotiations on other issues may preclude that foreign government from irritating US diplomats with what their nation may perceive as a minor issue. Probable US government responses to the challenge will be sensitive. The food company should consider the foreign government's likely answer to its community of food exporters. The most skilled legal advisors will understand the probable responses from the WTO team at the Office of the US Trade Representative, if an aspect of implementing the new law were to be directly challenged in a WTO proceeding. The best outcome of a WTO case is withdrawal, without need for a panel decision, because the FDA has responded with an exception. The worst case would be a yearlong debate at the WTO leading to a decision, then US refusal, and a trade sanction brought against the recalcitrant US position. The globalization of the food supply chain is a reality, but few US food companies fully appreciate the leverage opportunity of the WTO mechanism.

Has the Company Modified Our Contingency Plans?

Step five will be a change to the company's existing contingency plan for supply outages. If the FDA put a particular nation's food export operations on the import alert list and has refused admission (e.g., to all Philippine pineapples), or if the FDA barred apples from Alberta or tomatoes from Mexico, the contingencies that are now plausible under the 2010 legislation there will need to be some planning of an alternative source.

Who Pays for All the Extra Overhead Cost?

Step six will be a pricing plan to recapture additional costs. All the competing firms with similar supply chains will incur more handling costs, as the import agents and customs brokers will need to charge more. The company sales director may argue for the firm to absorb the extra overhead, rather than raise prices during the current recession; but for some firms, the profit margins are too narrow and food prices will rise to reflect the new overhead costs. At this writing, no one can predict what cost amounts will be passed along, but most of the new regulatory costs will involve extra expenses consumers will pay as prices increase. (A cautionary note is that pricing decisions have such great antitrust sensitivity that discussions about costs should go through a well-operated trade association, not done bilaterally with competing food companies.)

Must We Train Foreign Managers of the Food Suppliers?

Step seven will be a quality compliance program with training at the foreign supply points. Getting the US regulatory requirements translated and explained out in the world from which food supplies come is a challenging assignment. Presumably the inter-governmental communications will be done by the FDA in embassy meetings. But the actual farm-level, factory-level, or food transit point meetings will be held in the local language with the local agents (hopefully following a script tailored to the specific crop and the experience of quality issues in the past).

What Should the Board of Directors Learn?

Step eight for public companies is a board briefing. "No surprises for the directors" is a prudent policy for company managers. In the wake of the Sarbanes-Oxley law, most publicly held company boards strengthened their audit committee to assure compliance. The 2010 food legislation will affect hundreds of significant publicly held companies and thousands of smaller entities. The board of directors audit committee should pay close attention to the potential risks the company faces if a regulatory crisis like an import alert, detention, or recall suddenly constricts the flow of foods to key customers. Regulatory professionals will need to be given the travel budget, training support, and personnel to comply with the new requirements, for the option of doing nothing is inconsistent with the audit committee's responsibility for anticipating vulnerabilities. A board that chooses to ignore the new requirements may be vulnerable to future suits by angered shareholders when the supply chain is shut down for noncompliance.

What Additional Compliance Staff or Consultancies Are Needed?

Step nine is the staffing decision. Veterans of the food safety field will regard this legislation as a "force multiplier" for the FDA, in numbers of additional regulators, new powers to demand records, and more volumes of regulatory effort. The food company cannot do it alone, without more help, and this can be facilitated via intermediary service providers or inhouse. Among intermediaries, experienced law firms will have a role, and international Customs trade firms will be quite busy. Perishable food sellers and importers are especially vulnerable if the pipeline is stopped and the weeks of remedial procedures are invoked, during which time the food rots (literally) in a bonded warehouse or on a pier somewhere in transit. Staffing choices to anticipate the likely vulnerability are a good investment for the future.

What Public Face Should Food Companies Put on the New Requirements?

Step ten is to be honest with consumers: the company is committed to safety and to fair compliance with all applicable laws. The company should explain what it takes to deliver the safe and wholesome food product to the consumer, and should explain that we all pay the price for a safe food supply. Retail chains and associations can carry the same message: enhanced food safety is not free of costs.

How Should This Book Be Used?

Don't leave one copy on the shelf in your lawyer's office. Share copies of this book with key customers, especially with food-exporting suppliers in other nations. Train import managers and plant managers. In publicly traded companies, make certain that the compliance officer has a copy so he or she can aid the board in meeting its responsibilities. Give the human resources officer a copy so that whistleblower cases can be properly handled, especially during layoff waves. Make the transportation and import teams aware of what will be changing around them as the new powers of the FDA are asserted in their zones of responsibility. We have included throughout the book segments of the previous versions that were not adopted, so managers can be thankful that the burdens they face are actually more tolerable than the adventures that could have confronted them before the final Act was completed.

Appendix: Final Text of the Statute

Congressional Record S8067-8093 (Nov. 30, 2010)

SA 4715. Mr. REID (for Mr. HARKIN) proposed an amendment to the bill S. 510, to amend the Federal Food, Drug, and Cosmetic Act with respect to the safety of the food supply; as follows:

Strike all after the enacting clause and insert the following:

SECTION 1. SHORT TITLE; REFERENCES; TABLE OF CONTENTS.

(a) Short Title.--This Act may be cited as the "FDA Food Safety Modernization Act".

(b) References.--Except as otherwise specified, whenever in this Act an amendment is expressed in terms of an amendment to a section or other provision, the reference shall be considered to be made to a section or other provision of the Federal Food, Drug, and Cosmetic Act (21 U.S.C. 301 et seq.).

(c) Table of Contents.--The table of contents for this Act is as follows:

Sec..1..Short title; references; table of contents.

TITLE I--IMPROVING CAPACITY TO PREVENT FOOD SAFETY PROBLEMS

Sec..101..Inspections of records.

Sec..102..Registration of food facilities.

Sec..103..Hazard analysis and risk-based preventive controls.

Sec..104..Performance standards.

Sec..105..Standards for produce safety.

Sec..106..Protection against intentional adulteration.

Sec..107..Authority to collect fees.

Sec..108..National agriculture and food defense strategy.

Sec..109..Food and Agriculture Coordinating Councils.

Sec..110..Building domestic capacity.

Sec..111..Sanitary transportation of food.

Sec..112..Food allergy and anaphylaxis management.

Sec..113..New dietary ingredients.

Sec..114..Requirement for guidance relating to post harvest processing of raw oysters.

Sec..115..Port shopping.

Sec..116..Alcohol-related facilities.

TITLE II--IMPROVING CAPACITY TO DETECT AND RESPOND TO FOOD SAFETY PROBLEMS

Sec..201..Targeting of inspection resources for domestic facilities, foreign facilities, and ports of entry; annual report.

Sec..202..Laboratory accreditation for analyses of foods.

Sec..203..Integrated consortium of laboratory networks.

Sec..204..Enhancing tracking and tracing of food and recordkeeping.

Sec..205..Surveillance.

Sec..206..Mandatory recall authority.

Sec..207..Administrative detention of food.

Sec..208..Decontamination and disposal standards and plans.

Sec..209..Improving the training of State, local, territorial, and tribal food safety officials.

Sec..210..Enhancing food safety.

Sec..211..Improving the reportable food registry.

TITLE III--IMPROVING THE SAFETY OF IMPORTED FOOD

Sec..301..Foreign supplier verification program.

Sec..302..Voluntary qualified importer program.

Sec..303..Authority to require import certifications for food.

Sec..304..Prior notice of imported food shipments.

Sec..305..Building capacity of foreign governments with respect to food safety.

Sec..306..Inspection of foreign food facilities.

Sec..307..Accreditation of third-party auditors.

Sec..308..Foreign offices of the Food and Drug Administration.

Sec..309..Smuggled food.

TITLE IV--MISCELLANEOUS PROVISIONS

Sec..401..Funding for food safety.

Sec..402..Employee protections.

Sec..403..Jurisdiction; authorities.

Sec..404..Compliance with international agreements.

Sec..405..Determination of budgetary effects.

TITLE I--IMPROVING CAPACITY TO PREVENT FOOD SAFETY PROBLEMS

SEC. 101. INSPECTIONS OF RECORDS.

(a) In General.--Section 414(a) (21 U.S.C. 350c(a)) is amended--

(1) by striking the heading and all that follows through "of food is" and inserting the following: "Records Inspection.--

"(1) ADULTERATED FOOD.--If the Secretary has a reasonable belief that an article of food, and any other article of food that the Secretary reasonably believes is likely to be affected in a similar manner, is";

(2) by inserting ," and to any other article of food that the Secretary reasonably believes is likely to be affected in a similar manner," after "relating to such article";

(3) by striking the last sentence; and

(4) by inserting at the end the following:

"(2) USE OF OR EXPOSURE TO FOOD OF CONCERN.--If the Secretary believes that there is a reasonable probability that the use of or exposure to an article of food, and any other article of food that the Secretary reasonably believes is likely to be affected in a similar manner, will cause serious adverse health consequences or death to humans or animals, each person (excluding farms and restaurants) who manufactures, processes, packs, distributes, receives, holds, or imports such article shall, at the request of an officer or employee duly designated by the Secretary, permit such officer or employee, upon presentation of appropriate credentials and a written notice to such person, at reasonable times and within reasonable limits and in a reasonable manner, to have access to and copy all records relating to such article and to any other article of food that the Secretary reasonably believes is likely to be affected in a similar manner, that are needed to assist the Secretary in determining whether there is a reasonable probability that the use of or exposure to the food will cause serious adverse health consequences or death to humans or animals.

"(3) APPLICATION.--The requirement under paragraphs (1) and (2) applies to all records relating to the manufacture, processing, packing, distribution, receipt, holding, or importation of such article maintained by or on behalf of such person in any format (including paper and electronic formats) and at any location.".

(b) Conforming Amendment.--Section 704(a)(1)(B) (21 U.S.C. 374(a)(1)(B)) is amended by striking "section 414 when" and all that follows through "subject to" and inserting "section 414, when the standard for records inspection under paragraph (1) or (2) of section 414(a) applies, subject to".

SEC. 102. REGISTRATION OF FOOD FACILITIES.

(a) Updating of Food Category Regulations; Biennial Registration Renewal.--Section 415(a) (21 U.S.C. 350d(a)) is amended--

(1) in paragraph (2), by--

(A) striking "conducts business and" and inserting "conducts business, the e-mail address for the contact person of the facility or, in the case of a foreign facility, the United States agent for the facility, and"; and

(B) inserting ," or any other food categories as determined appropriate by the Secretary, including by guidance" after "Code of Federal Regulations";

(2) by redesignating paragraphs (3) and (4) as paragraphs (4) and (5), respectively; and

(3) by inserting after paragraph (2) the following:

"(3) BIENNIAL REGISTRATION RENEWAL.--During the period beginning on October 1 and ending on December 31 of each even-numbered year, a registrant that has submitted a registration under paragraph (1) shall submit to the Secretary a renewal registration containing the information described in paragraph (2). The Secretary shall provide for an abbreviated registration renewal process for any registrant that has not had any changes to such information since the registrant submitted the preceding registration or registration renewal for the facility involved.".

(b) Suspension of Registration.--

(1) IN GENERAL.--Section 415 (21 U.S.C. 350d) is amended--

(A) in subsection (a)(2), by inserting after the first sentence the following: "The registration shall contain an assurance that the Secretary will be permitted to inspect such facility at the times and in the manner permitted by this Act.";

(B) by redesignating subsections (b) and (c) as subsections (c) and (d), respectively; and

(C) by inserting after subsection (a) the following:

"(b) Suspension of Registration.--

"(1) IN GENERAL.--If the Secretary determines that food manufactured, processed, packed, received, or held by a facility registered under this section has a reasonable probability of causing serious adverse health consequences or death to humans or animals, the Secretary may by order suspend the registration of a facility--

"(A) that created, caused, or was otherwise responsible for such reasonable probability; or

"(B)(i) that knew of, or had reason to know of, such reasonable probability; and

"(ii) packed, received, or held such food.

"(2) HEARING ON SUSPENSION.-- The Secretary shall provide the registrant subject to an order under paragraph (1) with an opportunity for an informal hearing, to be held as soon as possible but not later than 2 business days after the issuance of the order or such other time period, as agreed upon by the Secretary and the registrant, on the actions required for reinstatement of registration and why the registration that is subject to suspension should be reinstated. The Secretary shall reinstate a registration if the Secretary determines, based on evidence presented, that adequate grounds do not exist to continue the suspension of the registration.

"(3) POST-HEARING CORRECTIVE ACTION PLAN; VACATING OF ORDER.--

"(A) CORRECTIVE ACTION PLAN.--If, after providing opportunity for an informal hearing under paragraph (2), the Secretary determines that the suspension of registration remains necessary, the Secretary shall require the registrant to submit a corrective action plan to demonstrate how the registrant plans to correct the conditions found by the Secretary. The Secretary shall review such plan not later than 14 days after the submission of the corrective action plan or such other time period as determined by the Secretary.

"(B) VACATING OF ORDER.--Upon a determination by the Secretary that adequate grounds do not exist to continue the suspension actions required by the order, or that such actions should be modified, the Secretary shall promptly vacate the order and reinstate the registration of the facility subject to the order or modify the order, as appropriate.

"(4) EFFECT OF SUSPENSION.--If the registration of a facility is suspended under this subsection, no person shall import or export food into the United States from such facility, offer to import or export food into the United States from such facility, or otherwise introduce food from such facility into interstate or intrastate commerce in the United States.

"(5) REGULATIONS.--

"(A) IN GENERAL.--The Secretary shall promulgate regulations to implement this subsection. The Secretary may promulgate such regulations on an interim final basis.

"(B) REGISTRATION REQUIREMENT.--The Secretary may require that registration under this section be submitted in an electronic format. Such requirement may not take effect before the date that is 5 years after the date of enactment of the FDA Food Safety Modernization Act.

"(6) APPLICATION DATE.--Facilities shall be subject to the requirements of this subsection beginning on the earlier of--

"(A) the date on which the Secretary issues regulations under paragraph (5); or

"(B) 180 days after the date of enactment of the FDA Food Safety Modernization Act.

"(7) NO DELEGATION.--The authority conferred by this subsection to issue an order to suspend a registration or vacate an order of suspension shall not be delegated to any officer or employee other than the Commissioner.".

(2) SMALL ENTITY COMPLIANCE POLICY GUIDE.--Not later than 180 days after the issuance of the regulations promulgated under section 415(b)(5) of the Federal Food, Drug, and Cosmetic Act (as added by this section), the Secretary shall issue a small entity compliance policy guide setting forth in plain language the requirements of such regulations to assist small entities in complying with registration requirements and other activities required under such section.

(3) IMPORTED FOOD.--Section 801(l) (21 U.S.C. 381(l)) is amended by inserting "(or for which a registration has been suspended under such section)" after "section 415".

(c) Clarification of Intent.--

(1) RETAIL FOOD ESTABLISHMENT.--The Secretary shall amend the definition of the term "retail food establishment" in section in 1.227(b)(11) of title 21, Code of Federal Regulations to clarify that, in determining the primary function of an establishment or a retail food establishment under such section, the sale of food products directly to consumers by such establishment and the sale of food directly to consumers by such retail food establishment include--

(A) the sale of such food products or food directly to consumers by such establishment at a roadside stand or farmers' market where such stand or market is located other than where the food was manufactured or processed;

(B) the sale and distribution of such food through a community supported agriculture program; and

(C) the sale and distribution of such food at any other such direct sales platform as determined by the Secretary.

(2) DEFINITIONS.--For purposes of paragraph (1)--

(A) the term "community supported agriculture program" has the same meaning given the term "community supported agriculture (CSA) program" in section 249.2 of title 7, Code of Federal Regulations (or any successor regulation); and

(B) the term "consumer" does not include a business.

(d) Conforming Amendments.--

(1) Section 301(d) (21 U.S.C. 331(d)) is amended by inserting "415," after "404,".

(2) Section 415(d), as redesignated by subsection (b), is amended by adding at the end before the period "for a facility to be registered, except with respect to the reinstatement of a registration that is suspended under subsection (b)".

SEC. 103. HAZARD ANALYSIS AND RISK-BASED PREVENTIVE CONTROLS.

(a) In General.--Chapter IV (21 U.S.C. 341 et seq.) is amended by adding at the end the following:

"SEC. 418. HAZARD ANALYSIS AND RISK-BASED PREVENTIVE CONTROLS.

"(a) In General.--The owner, operator, or agent in charge of a facility shall, in accordance with this section, evaluate the hazards that could affect food manufactured, processed, packed, or held by such facility, identify and implement preventive controls to significantly minimize or prevent the occurrence of such hazards and provide assurances that such food is not adulterated under section 402 or misbranded under section 403(w), monitor the performance of those controls, and maintain records of this monitoring as a matter of routine practice.

"(b) Hazard Analysis.--The owner, operator, or agent in charge of a facility shall--

"(1) identify and evaluate known or reasonably foreseeable hazards that may be associated with the facility, including--

"(A) biological, chemical, physical, and radiological hazards, natural toxins, pesticides, drug residues, decomposition, parasites, allergens, and unapproved food and color additives; and

"(B) hazards that occur naturally, or may be unintentionally introduced; and

"(2) identify and evaluate hazards that may be intentionally introduced, including by acts of terrorism; and

"(3) develop a written analysis of the hazards.

"(c) Preventive Controls.--The owner, operator, or agent in charge of a facility shall identify and implement preventive controls, including at critical control points, if any, to provide assurances that--

"(1) hazards identified in the hazard analysis conducted under subsection (b)(1) will be significantly minimized or prevented;

"(2) any hazards identified in the hazard analysis conducted under subsection (b)(2) will be significantly minimized or prevented and addressed, consistent with section 420, as applicable; and

"(3) the food manufactured, processed, packed, or held by such facility will not be adulterated under section 402 or misbranded under section 403(w).

"(d) Monitoring of Effectiveness.--The owner, operator, or agent in charge of a facility shall monitor the effectiveness of the preventive controls implemented under subsection (c) to provide assurances that the outcomes described in subsection (c) shall be achieved.

"(e) Corrective Actions.--The owner, operator, or agent in charge of a facility shall establish procedures to ensure that, if the preventive controls implemented under subsection (c) are not properly implemented or are found to be ineffective--

"(1) appropriate action is taken to reduce the likelihood of recurrence of the implementation failure;

"(2) all affected food is evaluated for safety; and

"(3) all affected food is prevented from entering into commerce if the owner, operator or agent in charge of such facility cannot ensure that the affected food is not adulterated under section 402 or misbranded under section 403(w).

"(f) Verification.--The owner, operator, or agent in charge of a facility shall verify that--

"(1) the preventive controls implemented under subsection (c) are adequate to control the hazards identified under subsection (b);

"(2) the owner, operator, or agent is conducting monitoring in accordance with subsection (d);

"(3) the owner, operator, or agent is making appropriate decisions about corrective actions taken under subsection (e);

"(4) the preventive controls implemented under subsection (c) are effectively and significantly minimizing or preventing the occurrence of identified hazards, including through the use of environmental and product testing programs and other appropriate means; and

"(5) there is documented, periodic reanalysis of the plan under subsection (i) to ensure that the plan is still relevant to the raw materials, conditions and processes in the facility, and new and emerging threats.

"(g) Recordkeeping.--The owner, operator, or agent in charge of a facility shall maintain, for not less than 2 years, records documenting the monitoring of the preventive controls implemented under subsection (c), instances of nonconformance material to food safety, the results of testing and other appropriate means of verification under subsection (f)(4), instances when corrective actions were implemented, and the efficacy of preventive controls and corrective actions.

"(h) Written Plan and Documentation.--The owner, operator, or agent in charge of a facility shall prepare a written plan that documents and describes the procedures used by the facility to comply with the requirements of this section, including analyzing the hazards under subsection (b) and identifying the preventive controls adopted under subsection (c) to address those hazards. Such written plan, together with the documentation described in subsection (g), shall be made promptly available to a duly authorized representative of the Secretary upon oral or written request.

"(i) Requirement To Reanalyze.--The owner, operator, or agent in charge of a facility shall conduct a reanalysis under subsection (b) whenever a significant change is made in the activities conducted at a facility operated by such owner, operator, or agent if the change creates a reasonable potential for a new hazard or a significant increase in a previously identified hazard or not less frequently than once every 3 years, whichever is earlier. Such reanalysis shall be completed and additional preventive controls needed to address the hazard identified, if any, shall be implemented before the change in activities at the facility is operative. Such owner, operator, or agent shall revise the written plan required under subsection (h) if such a significant change is made or document the basis for the conclusion that no additional or revised preventive controls are needed. The Secretary may require a reanalysis under this section to respond to new hazards and developments in scientific understanding, including, as appropriate, results from the Department of Homeland Security biological, chemical, radiological, or other terrorism risk assessment.

"(j) Exemption for Seafood, Juice, and Low-acid Canned Food Facilities Subject to HACCP.--

"(1) IN GENERAL.--This section shall not apply to a facility if the owner, operator, or agent in charge of such facility is required to comply with, and is in compliance with, 1 of the following standards and regulations with respect to such facility:

"(A) The Seafood Hazard Analysis Critical Control Points Program of the Food and Drug Administration.

"(B) The Juice Hazard Analysis Critical Control Points Program of the Food and Drug Administration.

"(C) The Thermally Processed Low-Acid Foods Packaged in Hermetically Sealed Containers standards of the Food and Drug Administration (or any successor standards).

"(2) APPLICABILITY.--The exemption under paragraph (1)(C) shall apply only with respect to microbiological hazards that are regulated under the standards for Thermally Processed Low-Acid Foods Packaged in Hermetically Sealed Containers under part 113 of chapter 21, Code of Federal Regulations (or any successor regulations).

"(k) Exception for Activities of Facilities Subject to Section 419.-- This section shall not apply to activities of a facility that are subject to section 419.

"(l) Modified Requirements for Qualified Facilities.--

"(1) QUALIFIED FACILITIES.--

"(A) IN GENERAL.--A facility is a qualified facility for purposes of this subsection if the facility meets the conditions under subparagraph (B) or (C).

"(B) VERY SMALL BUSINESS.--A facility is a qualified facility under this subparagraph--

"(i) if the facility, including any subsidiary or affiliate of the facility, is, collectively, a very small business (as defined in the regulations promulgated under subsection (n)); and "(ii) in the case where the facility is a subsidiary or affiliate of an entity, if such subsidiaries or affiliates, are, collectively, a very small business (as so defined).

"(C) LIMITED ANNUAL MONETARY VALUE OF SALES.--

"(i) IN GENERAL.--A facility is a qualified facility under this subparagraph if clause (ii) applies--

"(I) to the facility, including any subsidiary or affiliate of the facility, collectively; and

"(II) to the subsidiaries or affiliates, collectively, of any entity of which the facility is a subsidiary or affiliate.

"(ii) AVERAGE ANNUAL MONETARY VALUE.--This clause applies if--

"(I) during the 3-year period preceding the applicable calendar year, the average annual monetary value of the food manufactured, processed, packed, or held at such facility (or the collective average annual monetary value of such food at any subsidiary or affiliate, as described in clause (i)) that is sold directly to qualified end-users during such period exceeded the average annual monetary value of the food manufactured, processed, packed, or held at such facility (or the collective average annual monetary value of such food at any subsidiary or affiliate, as so described) sold by such facility (or collectively by any such subsidiary or affiliate) to all other purchasers during such period; and

"(II) the average annual monetary value of all food sold by such facility (or the collective average annual monetary value of such food sold by any subsidiary or affiliate, as described in clause (i)) during such period was less than $500,000, adjusted for inflation.

"(2) EXEMPTION.--A qualified facility--

"(A) shall not be subject to the requirements under subsections (a) through (i) and subsection (n) in an applicable calendar year; and

"(B) shall submit to the Secretary--

"(i)(I) documentation that demonstrates that the owner, operator, or agent in charge of the facility has identified potential hazards associated with the food being produced, is implementing preventive controls to address the hazards, and is monitoring the preventive controls to ensure that such controls are effective; or

"(II) documentation (which may include licenses, inspection reports, certificates, permits, credentials, certification by an appropriate agency (such as a State department of agriculture), or other evidence of oversight), as specified by the Secretary, that the facility is in compliance with State, local, county, or other applicable non-Federal food safety law; and

"(ii) documentation, as specified by the Secretary in a guidance document issued not later than 1 year after the date of enactment of this section, that the facility is a qualified facility under paragraph (1)(B) or (1)(C).

"(3) WITHDRAWAL; RULE OF CONSTRUCTION.--

"(A) IN GENERAL.--In the event of an active investigation of a foodborne illness outbreak that is directly linked to a qualified facility subject to an exemption under this subsection, or if the Secretary determines that it is necessary to protect the public health and prevent or mitigate a foodborne illness outbreak based on conduct or conditions associated with a qualified facility that are material to the safety of the food manufactured, processed, packed, or held at such facility, the Secretary may withdraw the exemption provided to such facility under this subsection.

"(B) RULE OF CONSTRUCTION.--Nothing in this subsection shall be construed to expand or limit the inspection authority of the Secretary.

"(4) DEFINITIONS.--In this subsection:

"(A) AFFILIATE.--The term 'affiliate' means any facility that controls, is controlled by, or is under common control with another facility.

"(B) QUALIFIED END-USER.--The term 'qualified end-user', with respect to a food, means--

"(i) the consumer of the food; or

"(ii) a restaurant or retail food establishment (as those terms are defined by the Secretary for purposes of section 415) that--

"(I) is located--

"(aa) in the same State as the qualified facility that sold the food to such restaurant or establishment; or

"(bb) not more than 275 miles from such facility; and

"(II) is purchasing the food for sale directly to consumers at such restaurant or retail food establishment.

"(C) CONSUMER.--For purposes of subparagraph (B), the term 'consumer' does not include a business.

"(D) SUBSIDIARY.--The term 'subsidiary' means any company which is owned or controlled directly or indirectly by another company.

"(5) STUDY.--

"(A) IN GENERAL.--The Secretary, in consultation with the Secretary of Agriculture, shall conduct a study of the food processing sector regulated by the Secretary to determine--

"(i) the distribution of food production by type and size of operation, including monetary value of food sold;

"(ii) the proportion of food produced by each type and size of operation;

"(iii) the number and types of food facilities co-located on farms, including the number and proportion by commodity and by manufacturing or processing activity;

"(iv) the incidence of foodborne illness originating from each size and type of operation and the type of food facilities for which no reported or known hazard exists; and

"(v) the effect on foodborne illness risk associated with commingling, processing, transporting, and storing food and raw agricultural commodities, including differences in risk based on the scale and duration of such activities.

"(B) SIZE.--The results of the study conducted under subparagraph (A) shall include the information necessary to enable the Secretary to define the terms 'small business' and 'very small business', for purposes of promulgating the regulation under subsection (n). In defining such terms, the Secretary shall include consideration of harvestable acres, income, the number of employees, and the volume of food harvested.

"(C) SUBMISSION OF REPORT.--Not later than 18 months after the date of enactment the FDA Food Safety Modernization Act, the Secretary shall submit to Congress a report that describes the results of the study conducted under subparagraph (A).

"(6) NO PREEMPTION.--Nothing in this subsection preempts State, local, county, or other non-Federal law regarding the safe production of food. Compliance with this subsection shall not relieve any person from liability at common law or under State statutory law.

"(7) NOTIFICATION TO CONSUMERS.--

"(A) IN GENERAL.--A qualified facility that is exempt from the requirements under subsections (a) through (i) and subsection (n) and does not prepare documentation under paragraph (2)(B)(i)(I) shall--

"(i) with respect to a food for which a food packaging label is required by the Secretary under any other provision of this Act, include prominently and conspicuously on such label the name and business address of the facility where the food was manufactured or processed; or "(ii) with respect to a food for which a food packaging label is not required by the Secretary under any other provisions of this Act, prominently and conspicuously display, at the point of purchase, the name and business address of the facility where the food was manufactured or processed, on a label, poster, sign, placard, or documents delivered contemporaneously with the food in the normal course of business, or, in the case of Internet sales, in an electronic notice.

"(B) NO ADDITIONAL LABEL.--Subparagraph (A) does not provide authority to the Secretary to require a label that is in addition to any label required under any other provision of this Act.

"(m) Authority With Respect to Certain Facilities.--The Secretary may, by regulation, exempt or modify the requirements for compliance under this section with respect to facilities that are solely engaged in the production of food for animals other than man, the storage of raw agricultural commodities (other than fruits and vegetables) intended for further distribution or processing, or the storage of packaged foods that are not exposed to the environment.

"(n) Regulations.--

"(1) IN GENERAL.--Not later than 18 months after the date of enactment of the FDA Food Safety Modernization Act, the Secretary shall promulgate regulations--

"(A) to establish science-based minimum standards for conducting a hazard analysis, documenting hazards, implementing preventive controls, and documenting the implementation of the preventive controls under this section; and

"(B) to define, for purposes of this section, the terms 'small business' and 'very small business', taking into consideration the study described in subsection (l)(5).

"(2) COORDINATION.--In promulgating the regulations under paragraph (1)(A), with regard to hazards that may be intentionally introduced, including by acts of terrorism, the Secretary shall coordinate with the Secretary of Homeland Security, as appropriate.

"(3) CONTENT.--The regulations promulgated under paragraph (1)(A) shall--

"(A) provide sufficient flexibility to be practicable for all sizes and types of facilities, including small businesses such as a small food processing facility co-located on a farm;

"(B) comply with chapter 35 of title 44, United States Code (commonly known as the 'Paperwork Reduction Act'), with special attention to minimizing the burden (as defined in section 3502(2) of such Act) on the facility, and collection of information (as defined in section 3502(3) of such Act), associated with such regulations;

"(C) acknowledge differences in risk and minimize, as appropriate, the number of separate standards that apply to separate foods; and

"(D) not require a facility to hire a consultant or other third party to identify, implement, certify, or audit preventative controls, except in the case of negotiated enforcement resolutions that may require such a consultant or third party.

"(4) RULE OF CONSTRUCTION.--Nothing in this subsection shall be construed to provide the Secretary with the authority to prescribe specific technologies, practices, or critical controls for an individual facility.

"(5) REVIEW.--In promulgating the regulations under paragraph (1)(A), the Secretary shall review regulatory hazard analysis and preventive control programs in existence on the date of enactment of the FDA Food Safety Modernization Act, including the Grade 'A' Pasteurized Milk Ordinance to ensure that such regulations are consistent, to the extent practicable, with applicable domestic and internationally-recognized standards in existence on such date.

"(o) Definitions.--For purposes of this section:

"(1) CRITICAL CONTROL POINT.--The term 'critical control point' means a point, step, or procedure in a food process at which control can be applied and is essential to prevent or eliminate a food safety hazard or reduce such hazard to an acceptable level.

"(2) FACILITY.--The term 'facility' means a domestic facility or a foreign facility that is required to register under section 415.

"(3) PREVENTIVE CONTROLS.--The term 'preventive controls' means those risk-based, reasonably appropriate procedures, practices, and processes that a person knowledgeable about the safe manufacturing, processing, packing, or holding of food would employ to significantly minimize or prevent the hazards identified under the hazard analysis conducted under subsection (b) and that are consistent with the current scientific understanding of safe food manufacturing, processing, packing, or holding at the time of the analysis. Those procedures, practices, and processes may include the following:

> "(A) Sanitation procedures for food contact surfaces and utensils and food-contact surfaces of equipment.
>
> "(B) Supervisor, manager, and employee hygiene training.
>
> "(C) An environmental monitoring program to verify the effectiveness of pathogen controls in processes where a food is exposed to a potential contaminant in the environment.
>
> "(D) A food allergen control program.
>
> "(E) A recall plan.
>
> "(F) Current Good Manufacturing Practices (cGMPs) under part 110 of title 21, Code of Federal Regulations (or any successor regulations).
>
> "(G) Supplier verification activities that relate to the safety of food.".

(b) Guidance Document.--The Secretary shall issue a guidance document related to the regulations promulgated under subsection (b)(1) with respect to the hazard analysis and preventive controls under section 418 of the Federal Food, Drug, and Cosmetic Act (as added by subsection (a)).

(c) Rulemaking.--

> (1) PROPOSED RULEMAKING.--
>
> > (A) IN GENERAL.--Not later than 9 months after the date of enactment of this Act, the Secretary of Health and

Human Services (referred to in this subsection as the "Secretary") shall publish a notice of proposed rulemaking in the Federal Register to promulgate regulations with respect to--

> (i) activities that constitute on-farm packing or holding of food that is not grown, raised, or consumed on such farm or another farm under the same ownership for purposes of section 415 of the Federal Food, Drug, and Cosmetic Act (21 U.S.C. 350d), as amended by this Act; and

> (ii) activities that constitute on-farm manufacturing or processing of food that is not consumed on that farm or on another farm under common ownership for purposes of such section 415.

(B) CLARIFICATION.--The rulemaking described under subparagraph (A) shall enhance the implementation of such section 415 and clarify the activities that are included as part of the definition of the term "facility" under such section 415. Nothing in this Act authorizes the Secretary to modify the definition of the term "facility" under such section.

(C) SCIENCE-BASED RISK ANALYSIS.--In promulgating regulations under subparagraph (A), the Secretary shall conduct a science-based risk analysis of--

> (i) specific types of on-farm packing or holding of food that is not grown, raised, or consumed on such farm or another farm under the same ownership, as such packing and holding relates to specific foods; and

> (ii) specific on-farm manufacturing and processing activities as such activities relate to specific foods

that are not consumed on that farm or on another farm under common ownership.

(D) AUTHORITY WITH RESPECT TO CERTAIN FACILITIES.--

(i) IN GENERAL.--In promulgating the regulations under subparagraph (A), the Secretary shall consider the results of the science-based risk analysis conducted under subparagraph (C), and shall exempt certain facilities from the requirements in section 418 of the Federal Food, Drug, and Cosmetic Act (as added by this section), including hazard analysis and preventive controls, and the mandatory inspection frequency in section 421 of such Act (as added by section 201), or modify the requirements in such sections 418 or 421, as the Secretary determines appropriate, if such facilities are engaged only in specific types of on-farm manufacturing, processing, packing, or holding activities that the Secretary determines to be low risk involving specific foods the Secretary determines to be low risk.

(ii) LIMITATION.--The exemptions or modifications under clause (i) shall not include an exemption from the requirement to register under section 415 of the Federal Food, Drug, and Cosmetic Act (21 U.S.C. 350d), as amended by this Act, if applicable, and shall apply only to small businesses and very small businesses, as defined in the regulation promulgated under section 418(n) of the Federal Food, Drug, and Cosmetic Act (as added under subsection (a)).

(2) FINAL REGULATIONS.--Not later than 9 months after the close of the comment period for the proposed rulemaking under paragraph (1), the Secretary shall adopt final rules with respect to--

(A) activities that constitute on-farm packing or holding of food that is not grown, raised, or consumed on such farm or another farm under the same ownership for purposes of section 415 of the Federal Food, Drug, and Cosmetic Act (21 U.S.C. 350d), as amended by this Act;

(B) activities that constitute on-farm manufacturing or processing of food that is not consumed on that farm or on another farm under common ownership for purposes of such section 415; and

(C) the requirements under sections 418 and 421 of the Federal Food, Drug, and Cosmetic Act, as added by this Act, from which the Secretary may issue exemptions or modifications of the requirements for certain types of facilities.

(d) Small Entity Compliance Policy Guide.--Not later than 180 days after the issuance of the regulations promulgated under subsection (n) of section 418 of the Federal Food, Drug, and Cosmetic Act (as added by subsection (a)), the Secretary shall issue a small entity compliance policy guide setting forth in plain language the requirements of such section 418 and this section to assist small entities in complying with the hazard analysis and other activities required under such section 418 and this section.

(e) Prohibited Acts.--Section 301 (21 U.S.C. 331) is amended by adding at the end the following:

"(uu) The operation of a facility that manufactures, processes, packs, or holds food for sale in the United States if the owner, operator, or agent in charge of such facility is not in compliance with section 418.".

(f) No Effect on HACCP Authorities.--Nothing in the amendments made by this section limits the authority of the Secretary under the Federal Food, Drug, and Cosmetic Act (21 U.S.C. 301 et seq.) or the Public Health Service Act (42 U.S.C. 201 et seq.) to revise, issue, or enforce Hazard Analysis

Critical Control programs and the Thermally Processed Low-Acid Foods Packaged in Hermetically Sealed Containers standards.

(g) Dietary Supplements.--Nothing in the amendments made by this section shall apply to any facility with regard to the manufacturing, processing, packing, or holding oa dietary supplement that is in compliance with the requirements of sections 402(g)(2) and 761 of the Federal Food, Drug, and Cosmetic Act (21 U.S.C. 342(g)(2), 379aa-1).

(h) Updating Guidance Relating to Fish and Fisheries Products Hazards and Controls.--The Secretary shall, not later than 180 days after the date of enactment of this Act, update the Fish and Fisheries Products Hazards and Control Guidance to take into account advances in technology that have occurred since the previous publication of such Guidance by the Secretary.

(i) Effective Dates.--

(1) GENERAL RULE.--The amendments made by this section shall take effect 18 months after the date of enactment of this Act.

(2) FLEXIBILITY FOR SMALL BUSINESSES.-- Notwithstanding paragraph (1)--

(A) the amendments made by this section shall apply to a small business (as defined in the regulations promulgated under section 418(n) of the Federal Food, Drug, and Cosmetic Act (as added by this section)) beginning on the date that is 6 months after the effective date of such regulations; and

(B) the amendments made by this section shall apply to a very small business (as defined in such regulations) beginning on the date that is 18 months after the effective date of such regulations.

SEC. 104. PERFORMANCE STANDARDS.

(a) In General.--The Secretary shall, in coordination with the Secretary of Agriculture, not less frequently than every 2 years, review and evaluate relevant health data and other relevant information, including from toxicological and epidemiological studies and analyses, current Good Manufacturing Practices issued by the Secretary relating to food, and relevant recommendations of relevant advisory committees, including the Food Advisory Committee, to determine the most significant foodborne contaminants.

(b) Guidance Documents and Regulations.--Based on the review and evaluation conducted under subsection (a), and when appropriate to reduce the risk of serious illness or death to humans or animals or to prevent adulteration of the food under section 402 of the Federal Food, Drug, or Cosmetic Act (21 U.S.C. 342) or to prevent the spread by food of communicable disease under section 361 of the Public Health Service Act (42 U.S.C. 264), the Secretary shall issue contaminant-specific and science-based guidance documents, including guidance documents regarding action levels, or regulations. Such guidance, including guidance regarding action levels, or regulations--

(1) shall apply to products or product classes;

(2) shall, where appropriate, differentiate between food for human consumption and food intended for consumption by animals other than humans; and

(3) shall not be written to be facility-specific.

(c) No Duplication of Efforts.--The Secretary shall coordinate with the Secretary of Agriculture to avoid issuing duplicative guidance on the same contaminants.

(d) Review.--The Secretary shall periodically review and revise, as appropriate, the guidance documents, including guidance documents regarding action levels, or regulations promulgated under this section.

SEC. 105. STANDARDS FOR PRODUCE SAFETY.

(a) In General.--Chapter IV (21 U.S.C. 341 et seq.), as amended by section 103, is amended by adding at the end the following:

"SEC. 419. STANDARDS FOR PRODUCE SAFETY.

"(a) Proposed Rulemaking.--

"(1) IN GENERAL.--

"(A) RULEMAKING.--Not later than 1 year after the date of enactment of the FDA Food Safety Modernization Act, the Secretary, in coordination with the Secretary of Agriculture and representatives of State departments of agriculture (including with regard to the national organic program established under the Organic Foods Production Act of 1990), and in consultation with the Secretary of Homeland Security, shall publish a notice of proposed rulemaking to establish science-based minimum standards for the safe production and harvesting of those types of fruits and vegetables, including specific mixes or categories of fruits and vegetables, that are raw agricultural commodities for which the Secretary has determined that such standards minimize the risk of serious adverse health consequences or death.

"(B) DETERMINATION BY SECRETARY.--With respect to small businesses and very small businesses (as such terms are defined in the regulation promulgated under subparagraph (A)) that produce and harvest those types of fruits and vegetables that are raw agricultural commodities that the Secretary has determined are low risk and do not present a risk of serious adverse health consequences or death, the Secretary may determine not to include production and harvesting of such fruits and vegetables in such rulemaking, or may modify the applicable requirements of regulations promulgated pursuant to this section.

"(2) PUBLIC INPUT.--During the comment period on the notice of proposed rulemaking under paragraph (1), the Secretary shall conduct not less than 3 public meetings in diverse geographical areas of the United States to provide persons in different regions an opportunity to comment.

"(3) CONTENT.--The proposed rulemaking under paragraph (1) shall--

"(A) provide sufficient flexibility to be applicable to various types of entities engaged in the production and harvesting of fruits and vegetables that are raw agricultural commodities, including small businesses and entities that sell directly to consumers, and be appropriate to the scale and diversity of the production and harvesting of such commodities;

"(B) include, with respect to growing, harvesting, sorting, packing, and storage operations, science-based minimum standards related to soil amendments, hygiene, packaging, temperature controls, animals in the growing area, and water;

"(C) consider hazards that occur naturally, may be unintentionally introduced, or may be intentionally introduced, including by acts of terrorism;

"(D) take into consideration, consistent with ensuring enforceable public health protection, conservation and environmental practice standards and policies established by Federal natural resource conservation, wildlife conservation, and environmental agencies;

"(E) in the case of production that is certified organic, not include any requirements that conflict with or duplicate the requirements of the national organic program established under the Organic Foods Production Act of 1990, while providing the same level of public health protection as the requirements under guidance documents, including guidance documents regarding action levels, and regulations under the FDA Food Safety Modernization Act; and

"(F) define, for purposes of this section, the terms 'small business' and 'very small business'

"(4) PRIORITIZATION.--The Secretary shall prioritize the implementation of the regulations under this section for specific fruits and vegetables that are raw agricultural commodities based on known risks which may include a history and severity of foodborne illness outbreaks.

"(b) Final Regulation.--

"(1) IN GENERAL.--Not later than 1 year after the close of the comment period for the proposed rulemaking under subsection (a), the Secretary shall adopt a final regulation to provide for minimum science-based standards for those types of fruits and vegetables, including specific mixes or categories of fruits or vegetables, that are raw agricultural commodities, based on known safety risks, which may include a history of foodborne illness outbreaks.

"(2) FINAL REGULATION.--The final regulation shall--

"(A) provide for coordination of education and enforcement activities by State and local officials, as designated by the Governors of the respective States or the appropriate elected State official as recognized by State statute; and

"(B) include a description of the variance process under subsection (c) and the types of permissible variances the Secretary may grant.

"(3) FLEXIBILITY FOR SMALL BUSINESSES.-- Notwithstanding paragraph (1)--

"(A) the regulations promulgated under this section shall apply to a small business (as defined in the regulation promulgated under subsection (a)(1)) after the date that is 1 year after the effective date of the final regulation under paragraph (1); and

"(B) the regulations promulgated under this section shall apply to a very small business (as defined in the regulation promulgated under subsection (a)(1)) after the date that is 2 years after the effective date of the final regulation under paragraph (1).

"(c) Criteria.--

"(1) IN GENERAL.--The regulations adopted under subsection (b) shall--

"(A) set forth those procedures, processes, and practices that the Secretary determines to minimize the risk of serious adverse health consequences or death, including procedures, processes, and practices that the Secretary determines to be reasonably necessary to prevent the introduction of known or reasonably foreseeable biological, chemical, and physical hazards, including hazards that occur naturally, may be unintentionally introduced, or may be intentionally introduced, including by acts of terrorism, into fruits and vegetables, including specific mixes or categories of fruits and vegetables, that are raw agricultural commodities and to provide reasonable assurances that the produce is not adulterated under section 402;

"(B) provide sufficient flexibility to be practicable for all sizes and types of businesses, including small businesses such as a small food processing facility co-located on a farm;

"(C) comply with chapter 35 of title 44, United States Code (commonly known as the 'Paperwork Reduction Act'), with special attention to minimizing the burden (as defined in section 3502(2) of such Act) on the business, and collection of information (as defined in section 3502(3) of such Act), associated with such regulations;

"(D) acknowledge differences in risk and minimize, as appropriate, the number of separate standards that apply to separate foods; and

"(E) not require a business to hire a consultant or other third party to identify, implement, certify, compliance with these procedures, processes, and practices, except in the case of negotiated enforcement resolutions that may require such a consultant or third party; and

"(F) permit States and foreign countries from which food is imported into the United States to request from the Secretary variances from the requirements of the regulations, subject to paragraph (2), where the State or foreign country determines that the variance is necessary in light of local growing conditions and that the procedures, processes, and practices to be followed under the variance are reasonably likely to ensure that the produce is not adulterated under section 402 and to provide the same level of public health protection as the requirements of the regulations adopted under subsection (b).

"(2) VARIANCES.--

"(A) REQUESTS FOR VARIANCES.--A State or foreign country from which food is imported into the United States may in writing request a variance from the Secretary. Such request shall describe the variance requested and present information demonstrating that the variance does not increase the likelihood that the food for which the variance is requested will be adulterated under section 402, and that the variance provides the same level of public health protection as the requirements of the regulations adopted under subsection (b). The Secretary shall review such requests in a reasonable timeframe.

"(B) APPROVAL OF VARIANCES.--The Secretary may approve a variance in whole or in part, as appropriate, and may specify the scope of applicability of a variance to other similarly situated persons.

"(C) DENIAL OF VARIANCES.--The Secretary may deny a variance request if the Secretary determines that such variance is not reasonably likely to ensure that the food is not adulterated under section 402 and is not reasonably likely to provide the same level of public health protection as the requirements of the regulation adopted under subsection (b). The Secretary shall notify the person requesting such variance of the reasons for the denial.

"(D) MODIFICATION OR REVOCATION OF A VARIANCE.--The Secretary, after notice and an opportunity for a hearing, may modify or revoke a variance if the Secretary determines that such variance is not reasonably likely to ensure that the food is not adulterated under section 402 and is not reasonably likely to provide the same level of public health protection as the requirements of the regulations adopted under subsection (b).

"(d) Enforcement.--The Secretary may coordinate with the Secretary of Agriculture and, as appropriate, shall contract and coordinate with the agency or department designated by the Governor of each State to perform activities to ensure compliance with this section.

"(e) Guidance.--

"(1) IN GENERAL.--Not later than 1 year after the date of enactment of the FDA Food Safety Modernization Act, the Secretary shall publish, after consultation with the Secretary of Agriculture, representatives of State departments of agriculture, farmer representatives, and various types of entities engaged in the production and harvesting or importing of fruits and vegetables that are raw agricultural commodities, including small businesses, updated good agricultural practices and guidance for the safe production and harvesting of specific types of fresh produce under this section.

"(2) PUBLIC MEETINGS.--The Secretary shall conduct not fewer than 3 public meetings in diverse geographical areas of the United States as part of an effort to conduct education and outreach regarding the guidance described in paragraph (1) for persons in different regions who are involved in the production and harvesting of fruits and vegetables that are raw agricultural commodities, including persons that sell directly to consumers and farmer representatives, and for importers of fruits and vegetables that are raw agricultural commodities.

"(3) PAPERWORK REDUCTION.--The Secretary shall ensure that any updated guidance under this section will--

"(A) provide sufficient flexibility to be practicable for all sizes and types of facilities, including small businesses such as a small food processing facility co-located on a farm; and

"(B) acknowledge differences in risk and minimize, as appropriate, the number of separate standards that apply to separate foods.

"(f) Exemption for Direct Farm Marketing.--

"(1) IN GENERAL.--A farm shall be exempt from the requirements under this section in a calendar year if--

"(A) during the previous 3-year period, the average annual monetary value of the food sold by such farm directly to qualified end-users during such period exceeded the average annual monetary value of the food sold by such farm to all other buyers during such period; and

"(B) the average annual monetary value of all food sold during such period was less than $500,000, adjusted for inflation.

"(2) NOTIFICATION TO CONSUMERS.--

"(A) IN GENERAL.--A farm that is exempt from the requirements under this section shall--

"(i) with respect to a food for which a food packaging label is required by the Secretary under any other provision of this Act, include prominently and conspicuously on such label the name and business address of the farm where the produce was grown; or

"(ii) with respect to a food for which a food packaging label is not required by the Secretary under any other provision of this Act, prominently and conspicuously display, at the point of purchase, the name and business address of the farm where the produce was grown, on a label, poster, sign, placard, or documents delivered contemporaneously with the food in the normal course of business, or, in the case of Internet sales, in an electronic notice.

"(B) NO ADDITIONAL LABEL.--Subparagraph (A) does not provide authority to the Secretary to require a label that is in addition to any label required under any other provision of this Act.

"(3) WITHDRAWAL; RULE OF CONSTRUCTION.--

"(A) IN GENERAL.--In the event of an active investigation of a foodborne illness outbreak that is directly linked to a farm subject to an exemption under this subsection, or if the Secretary determines that it is necessary to protect the public health and prevent or mitigate a foodborne illness outbreak based on conduct or conditions associated with a farm that are material to the safety of the food produced or harvested at such farm, the Secretary may withdraw the exemption provided to such farm under this subsection.

"(B) RULE OF CONSTRUCTION.--Nothing in this subsection shall be construed to expand or limit the inspection authority of the Secretary.

"(4) DEFINITIONS.--

"(A) QUALIFIED END-USER.--In this subsection, the term 'qualified end-user', with respect to a food means--

"(i) the consumer of the food; or

"(ii) a restaurant or retail food establishment (as those terms are defined by the Secretary for purposes of section 415) that is located--

"(I) in the same State as the farm that produced the food; or

"(II) not more than 275 miles from such farm.

"(B) CONSUMER.--For purposes of subparagraph (A), the term 'consumer' does not include a business.

"(5) NO PREEMPTION.--Nothing in this subsection preempts State, local, county, or other non-Federal law regarding the safe production, harvesting, holding, transportation, and sale of fresh fruits and vegetables. Compliance with this subsection shall not relieve any person from liability at common law or under State statutory law.

"(6) LIMITATION OF EFFECT.--Nothing in this subsection shall prevent the Secretary from exercising any authority granted in the other sections of this Act.

"(g) Clarification.--This section shall not apply to produce that is produced by an individual for personal consumption.

"(h) Exception for Activities of Facilities Subject to Section 418.-- This section shall not apply to activities of a facility that are subject to section 418.".

(b) Small Entity Compliance Policy Guide.--Not later than 180 days after the issuance of regulations under section 419 of the Federal Food, Drug, and Cosmetic Act (as added by subsection (a)), the Secretary of Health and Human Services shall issue a small entity compliance policy guide setting forth in plain language the requirements of such section 419 and to assist small entities in complying with standards for safe production and harvesting and other activities required under such section.

(c) Prohibited Acts.--Section 301 (21 U.S.C. 331), as amended by section 103, is amended by adding at the end the following:

"(vv) The failure to comply with the requirements under section 419.".

(d) No Effect on HACCP Authorities.--Nothing in the amendments made by this section limits the authority of the Secretary under the Federal Food, Drug, and Cosmetic Act (21 U.S.C. 301 et seq.) or the Public Health Service Act (42 U.S.C. 201 et seq.) to revise, issue, or enforce product and category-specific regulations, such as the Seafood Hazard Analysis Critical Controls

Points Program, the Juice Hazard Analysis Critical Control Program, and the Thermally Processed Low-Acid Foods Packaged in Hermetically Sealed Containers standards.

SEC. 106. PROTECTION AGAINST INTENTIONAL ADULTERATION.

(a) In General.--Chapter IV (21 U.S.C. 341 et seq.), as amended by section 105, is amended by adding at the end the following:

"SEC. 420. PROTECTION AGAINST INTENTIONAL ADULTERATION.

"(a) Determinations.--

"(1) IN GENERAL.--The Secretary shall--

"(A) conduct a vulnerability assessment of the food system, including by consideration of the Department of Homeland Security biological, chemical, radiological, or other terrorism risk assessments;

"(B) consider the best available understanding of uncertainties, risks, costs, and benefits associated with guarding against intentional adulteration of food at vulnerable points; and

"(C) determine the types of science-based mitigation strategies or measures that are necessary to protect against the intentional adulteration of food.

"(2) LIMITED DISTRIBUTION.--In the interest of national security, the Secretary, in consultation with the Secretary of Homeland Security, may determine the time, manner, and form in which determinations made under paragraph (1) are made publicly available.

"(b) Regulations.--Not later than 18 months after the date of enactment of the FDA Food Safety Modernization Act, the Secretary, in coordination with the Secretary of Homeland Security and in consultation with the Secretary of Agriculture, shall promulgate regulations to protect against the intentional adulteration of food subject to this Act. Such regulations shall--

"(1) specify how a person shall assess whether the person is required to implement mitigation strategies or measures intended to protect against the intentional adulteration of food; and

"(2) specify appropriate science-based mitigation strategies or measures to prepare and protect the food supply chain at specific vulnerable points, as appropriate.

"(c) Applicability.--Regulations promulgated under subsection (b) shall apply only to food for which there is a high risk of intentional contamination, as determined by the Secretary, in consultation with the Secretary of Homeland Security, under subsection (a), that could cause serious adverse health consequences or death to humans or animals and shall include those foods--

"(1) for which the Secretary has identified clear vulnerabilities (including short shelf-life or susceptibility to intentional contamination at critical control points); and

"(2) in bulk or batch form, prior to being packaged for the final consumer.

"(d) Exception.--This section shall not apply to farms, except for those that produce milk.

"(e) Definition.--For purposes of this section, the term 'farm' has the meaning given that term in section 1.227 of title 21, Code of Federal Regulations (or any successor regulation).".

(b) Guidance Documents.--

(1) IN GENERAL.--Not later than 1 year after the date of enactment of this Act, the Secretary of Health and Human Services, in consultation with the Secretary of Homeland Security and the Secretary of Agriculture, shall issue guidance documents related to protection against the intentional adulteration of food, including mitigation strategies or measures to guard against such adulteration as required under section 420 of the Federal Food, Drug, and Cosmetic Act, as added by subsection (a).

(2) CONTENT.--The guidance documents issued under paragraph (1) shall--

(A) include a model assessment for a person to use under subsection (b)(1) of section 420 of the Federal Food, Drug, and Cosmetic Act, as added by subsection (a);

(B) include examples of mitigation strategies or measures described in subsection (b)(2) of such section; and

(C) specify situations in which the examples of mitigation strategies or measures described in subsection (b)(2) of such section are appropriate.

(3) LIMITED DISTRIBUTION.--In the interest of national security, the Secretary of Health and Human Services, in consultation with the Secretary of Homeland Security, may determine the time, manner, and form in which the guidance documents issued under paragraph (1) are made public, including by releasing such documents to targeted audiences.

(c) Periodic Review.--The Secretary of Health and Human Services shall periodically review and, as appropriate, update the regulations under section 420(b) of the Federal Food, Drug, and Cosmetic Act, as added by subsection (a), and the guidance documents under subsection (b).

(d) Prohibited Acts.--Section 301 (21 U.S.C. 331 et seq.), as amended by section 105, is amended by adding at the end the following:

"(ww) The failure to comply with section 420.".

SEC. 107. AUTHORITY TO COLLECT FEES.

(a) Fees for Reinspection, Recall, and Importation Activities.--Subchapter C of chapter VII (21 U.S.C. 379f et seq.) is amended by adding at the end the following:

"PART 6--FEES RELATED TO FOOD

"SEC. 743. AUTHORITY TO COLLECT AND USE FEES.

"(a) In General.--

"(1) PURPOSE AND AUTHORITY.--For fiscal year 2010 and each subsequent fiscal year, the Secretary shall, in accordance with this section, assess and collect fees from--

"(A) the responsible party for each domestic facility (as defined in section 415(b)) and the United States agent for each foreign facility subject to a reinspection in such fiscal year, to cover reinspection-related costs for such year;

"(B) the responsible party for a domestic facility (as defined in section 415(b)) and an importer who does not comply with a recall order under section 423 or under section 412(f) in such fiscal year, to cover food recall activities associated with such order performed by the Secretary, including technical assistance, follow-up effectiveness checks, and public notifications, for such year;

"(C) each importer participating in the voluntary qualified importer program under section 806 in such year, to cover the administrative costs of such program for such year; and

"(D) each importer subject to a reinspection in such fiscal year, to cover reinspection-related costs for such year.

"(2) DEFINITIONS.--For purposes of this section--

"(A) the term 'reinspection' means--

"(i) with respect to domestic facilities (as defined in section 415(b)), 1 or more inspections conducted under section 704 subsequent to an inspection conducted under such provision which identified noncompliance materially related to a food safety requirement of this Act, specifically to determine whether compliance has been achieved to the Secretary's satisfaction; and

"(ii) with respect to importers, 1 or more examinations conducted under section 801 subsequent to an examination conducted under such provision which identified noncompliance materially related to a food safety requirement of this Act, specifically to determine whether compliance has been achieved to the Secretary's satisfaction;

"(B) the term 'reinspection-related costs' means all expenses, including administrative expenses, incurred in connection with--

"(i) arranging, conducting, and evaluating the results of reinspections; and "(ii) assessing and collecting reinspection fees under this section; and

"(C) the term 'responsible party' has the meaning given such term in section 417(a)(1).

"(b) Establishment of Fees.--

"(1) IN GENERAL.--Subject to subsections (c) and (d), the Secretary shall establish the fees to be collected under this section for each fiscal year specified in subsection (a)(1), based on the methodology described under paragraph (2), and shall publish such fees in a Federal Register notice not later than 60 days before the start of each such year.

"(2) FEE METHODOLOGY.--

"(A) FEES.--Fees amounts established for collection--

"(i) under subparagraph (A) of subsection (a)(1) for a fiscal year shall be based on the Secretary's estimate of 100 percent of the costs of the reinspection-related activities (including by type or level of reinspection activity, as the Secretary determines applicable) described in such subparagraph (A) for such year;

"(ii) under subparagraph (B) of subsection (a)(1) for a fiscal year shall be based on the Secretary's estimate of 100 percent of the costs of the activities described in such subparagraph (B) for such year;

"(iii) under subparagraph (C) of subsection (a)(1) for a fiscal year shall be based on the Secretary's estimate of 100 percent of the costs of the activities described in such subparagraph (C) for such year; and

"(iv) under subparagraph (D) of subsection (a)(1) for a fiscal year shall be based on the Secretary's estimate of 100 percent of the costs of the activities described in such subparagraph (D) for such year.

"(B) OTHER CONSIDERATIONS.--

"(i) VOLUNTARY QUALIFIED IMPORTER PROGRAM.--

"(I) PARTICIPATION.--In establishing the fee amounts under subparagraph (A)(iii) for a fiscal year, the Secretary shall provide for the number of importers who have submitted to the Secretary a notice under section 806(c) informing the Secretary of the intent of such importer to participate in the program under section 806 in such fiscal year.

"(II) RECOUPMENT.--In establishing the fee amounts under subparagraph (A)(iii) for the first 5 fiscal years after the date of enactment of this section, the Secretary shall include in such fee a reasonable surcharge that provides a recoupment of the costs expended by the Secretary to establish and implement the first year of the program under section 806.

"(ii) CREDITING OF FEES.--In establishing the fee amounts under subparagraph (A) for a fiscal year, the Secretary shall provide for the crediting of fees from the previous year to the next year if the Secretary overestimated the amount of fees needed to carry out such activities, and consider the need to account for any adjustment of fees and such other factors as the Secretary determines appropriate.

"(iii) PUBLISHED GUIDELINES.--Not later than 180 days after the date of enactment of the FDA Food Safety Modernization Act, the Secretary shall publish in the Federal Register a proposed set of guidelines in consideration of the burden of fee amounts on small business. Such consideration may include reduced fee amounts for small businesses. The Secretary shall provide for a period of public comment on such guidelines. The Secretary shall adjust the fee schedule for small businesses subject to such fees only through notice and comment rulemaking.

"(3) USE OF FEES.--The Secretary shall make all of the fees collected pursuant to clause (i), (ii), (iii), and (iv) of paragraph (2)(A) available solely to pay for the costs referred to in such clause (i), (ii), (iii), and (iv) of paragraph (2)(A), respectively.

"(c) Limitations.--

"(1) IN GENERAL.--Fees under subsection (a) shall be refunded for a fiscal year beginning after fiscal year 2010 unless the amount of the total appropriations for food safety activities at the Food and Drug Administration for such fiscal year (excluding the amount of fees appropriated for such fiscal year) is equal to or greater than the amount of appropriations for food safety activities at the Food and Drug Administration for fiscal year 2009 (excluding the amount of fees appropriated for such fiscal year), multiplied by the adjustment factor under paragraph (3).

"(2) AUTHORITY.--If--

"(A) the Secretary does not assess fees under subsection (a) for a portion of a fiscal year because paragraph (1) applies; and

"(B) at a later date in such fiscal year, such paragraph (1) ceases to apply,

the Secretary may assess and collect such fees under subsection (a), without any modification to the rate of such fees, notwithstanding the provisions of subsection (a) relating to the date fees are to be paid.

"(3) ADJUSTMENT FACTOR.--

"(A) IN GENERAL.--The adjustment factor described in paragraph (1) shall be the total percentage change that occurred in the Consumer Price Index for all urban consumers (all items; United States city average) for the 12-month period ending June 30 preceding the fiscal year, but in no case shall such adjustment factor be negative.

"(B) COMPOUNDED BASIS.--The adjustment under subparagraph (A) made each fiscal year shall be added on a compounded basis to the sum of all adjustments made each fiscal year after fiscal year 2009.

"(4) LIMITATION ON AMOUNT OF CERTAIN FEES.--

"(A) IN GENERAL.--Notwithstanding any other provision of this section and subject to subparagraph (B), the Secretary may not collect fees in a fiscal year such that the amount collected--

"(i) under subparagraph (B) of subsection (a)(1) exceeds $20,000,000; and

"(ii) under subparagraphs (A) and (D) of subsection (a)(1) exceeds $25,000,000 combined.

"(B) EXCEPTION.--If a domestic facility (as defined in section 415(b)) or an importer becomes subject to a fee described in subparagraph (A), (B), or (D) of subsection (a)(1) after the maximum amount of fees has been collected by the Secretary under subparagraph (A), the Secretary may collect a fee from such facility or importer.

"(d) Crediting and Availability of Fees.--Fees authorized under subsection (a) shall be collected and available for obligation only to the extent and in the amount provided in appropriations Acts. Such fees are authorized to remain available until expended. Such sums as may be necessary may be transferred from the Food and Drug Administration salaries and expenses account without fiscal year limitation to such appropriation account for salaries and expenses with such fiscal year limitation. The sums transferred shall be available solely for the purpose of paying the operating expenses of the Food and Drug Administration employees and contractors performing activities associated with these food safety fees.

"(e) Collection of Fees.--

"(1) IN GENERAL.--The Secretary shall specify in the Federal Register notice described in subsection (b)(1) the time and manner in which fees assessed under this section shall be collected.

"(2) COLLECTION OF UNPAID FEES.--In any case where the Secretary does not receive payment of a fee assessed under this section within 30 days after it is due, such fee shall be treated as a claim of the United States Government subject to provisions of subchapter II of chapter 37 of title 31, United States Code.

"(f) Annual Report to Congress.--Not later than 120 days after each fiscal year for which fees are assessed under this section, the Secretary shall submit a report to the Committee on Health, Education, Labor, and Pensions of the Senate and the Committee on Energy and Commerce of the House of Representatives, to include a description of fees assessed and collected for each such year and a summary description of the entities paying such fees and the types of business in which such entities engage.

"(g) Authorization of Appropriations.--For fiscal year 2010 and each fiscal year thereafter, there is authorized to be appropriated for fees under this section an amount equal to the total revenue amount determined under subsection (b) for the fiscal year, as adjusted or otherwise affected under the other provisions of this section.".

(b) Export Certification Fees for Foods and Animal Feed.--

(1) AUTHORITY FOR EXPORT CERTIFICATIONS FOR FOOD, INCLUDING ANIMAL FEED.--Section 801(e)(4)(A) (21 U.S.C. 381(e)(4)(A)) is amended--

(A) in the matter preceding clause (i), by striking "a drug" and inserting "a food, drug";

(B) in clause (i) by striking "exported drug" and inserting "exported food, drug"; and

(C) in clause (ii) by striking "the drug" each place it appears and inserting "the food, drug".

(2) CLARIFICATION OF CERTIFICATION.--Section 801(e)(4) (21 U.S.C. 381(e)(4)) is amended by inserting after subparagraph (B) the following new subparagraph:

"(C) For purposes of this paragraph, a certification by the Secretary shall be made on such basis, and in such form (including a publicly available listing) as the Secretary determines appropriate.".

SEC. 108. NATIONAL AGRICULTURE AND FOOD DEFENSE STRATEGY.

(a) Development and Submission of Strategy.--

(1) IN GENERAL.--Not later than 1 year after the date of enactment of this Act, the Secretary of Health and Human Services and the Secretary of Agriculture, in coordination with the Secretary of Homeland Security, shall prepare and transmit to the relevant committees of Congress, and make publicly available on the Internet Web sites of the Department of Health and Human Services and the Department of Agriculture, the National Agriculture and Food Defense Strategy.

(2) IMPLEMENTATION PLAN.--The strategy shall include an implementation plan for use by the Secretaries described under paragraph (1) in carrying out the strategy.

(3) RESEARCH.--The strategy shall include a coordinated research agenda for use by the Secretaries described under paragraph (1) in

conducting research to support the goals and activities described in paragraphs (1) and (2) of subsection (b).

(4) REVISIONS.--Not later than 4 years after the date on which the strategy is submitted to the relevant committees of Congress under paragraph (1), and not less frequently than every 4 years thereafter, the Secretary of Health and Human Services and the Secretary of Agriculture, in coordination with the Secretary of Homeland Security, shall revise and submit to the relevant committees of Congress the strategy.

(5) CONSISTENCY WITH EXISTING PLANS.--The strategy described in paragraph (1) shall be consistent with--

(A) the National Incident Management System;

(B) the National Response Framework;

(C) the National Infrastructure Protection Plan;

(D) the National Preparedness Goals; and

(E) other relevant national strategies.

(b) Components.--

(1) IN GENERAL.--The strategy shall include a description of the process to be used by the Department of Health and Human Services, the Department of Agriculture, and the Department of Homeland Security--

(A) to achieve each goal described in paragraph (2); and

(B) to evaluate the progress made by Federal, State, local, and tribal governments towards the achievement of each goal described in paragraph (2).

(2) GOALS.--The strategy shall include a description of the process to be used by the Department of Health and Human Services, the Department of Agriculture, and the Department of Homeland Security to achieve the following goals:

(A) PREPAREDNESS GOAL.--Enhance the preparedness of the agriculture and food system by--

(i) conducting vulnerability assessments of the agriculture and food system;

(ii) mitigating vulnerabilities of the system;

(iii) improving communication and training relating to the system;

(iv) developing and conducting exercises to test decontamination and disposal plans;

(v) developing modeling tools to improve event consequence assessment and decision support; and

(vi) preparing risk communication tools and enhancing public awareness through outreach.

(B) DETECTION GOAL.--Improve agriculture and food system detection capabilities by--

(i) identifying contamination in food products at the earliest possible time; and

(ii) conducting surveillance to prevent the spread of diseases.

(C) EMERGENCY RESPONSE GOAL.--Ensure an efficient response to agriculture and food emergencies by--

(i) immediately investigating animal disease outbreaks and suspected food contamination;

(ii) preventing additional human illnesses;

(iii) organizing, training, and equipping animal, plant, and food emergency response teams of--

(I) the Federal Government; and

(II) State, local, and tribal governments;

(iv) designing, developing, and evaluating training and exercises carried out under agriculture and food defense plans; and

(v) ensuring consistent and organized risk communication to the public by--

(I) the Federal Government;

(II) State, local, and tribal governments; and

(III) the private sector.

(D) RECOVERY GOAL.--Secure agriculture and food production after an agriculture or food emergency by--

(i) working with the private sector to develop business recovery plans to rapidly resume agriculture, food production, and international trade;

(ii) conducting exercises of the plans described in subparagraph (C) with the goal of long-term recovery results;

(iii) rapidly removing, and effectively disposing of--

(I) contaminated agriculture and food products; and

(II) infected plants and animals; and

(iv) decontaminating and restoring areas affected by an agriculture or food emergency.

(3) EVALUATION.--The Secretary, in coordination with the Secretary of Agriculture and the Secretary of Homeland Security, shall--

(A) develop metrics to measure progress for the evaluation process described in paragraph (1)(B); and

(B) report on the progress measured in subparagraph (A) as part of the National Agriculture and Food Defense strategy described in subsection (a)(1).

(c) Limited Distribution.--In the interest of national security, the Secretary of Health and Human Services and the Secretary of Agriculture, in coordination with the Secretary of Homeland Security, may determine the manner and format in which the National Agriculture and Food Defense strategy established under this section is made publicly available on the Internet Web sites of the Department of Health and Human Services, the Department of Homeland Security, and the Department of Agriculture, as described in subsection (a)(1).

SEC. 109. FOOD AND AGRICULTURE COORDINATING COUNCILS.

The Secretary of Homeland Security, in coordination with the Secretary of Health and Human Services and the Secretary of Agriculture, shall within 180 days of enactment of this Act, and annually thereafter, submit to the relevant committees of Congress, and make publicly available on the Internet Web site of the Department of Homeland Security, a report on the activities of the Food and Agriculture Government Coordinating Council and the Food and Agriculture Sector Coordinating Council, including the progress of such Councils on--

(1) facilitating partnerships between public and private entities to help coordinate and enhance the protection of the agriculture and food system of the United States;

(2) providing for the regular and timely interchange of information between each council relating to the security of the agriculture and food system (including intelligence information);

(3) identifying best practices and methods for improving the coordination among Federal, State, local, and private sector preparedness and response plans for agriculture and food defense; and

(4) recommending methods by which to protect the economy and the public health of the United States from the effects of--

(A) animal or plant disease outbreaks;

(B) food contamination; and

(C) natural disasters affecting agriculture and food.

SEC. 110. BUILDING DOMESTIC CAPACITY.

(a) In General.--

(1) INITIAL REPORT.--The Secretary, in coordination with the Secretary of Agriculture and the Secretary of Homeland Security, shall, not later than 2 years after the date of enactment of this Act, submit to Congress a comprehensive report that identifies programs and practices that are intended to promote the safety and supply chain security of food and to prevent outbreaks of foodborne illness and other food-related hazards that can be

addressed through preventive activities. Such report shall include a description of the following:

(A) Analysis of the need for further regulations or guidance to industry.

(B) Outreach to food industry sectors, including through the Food and Agriculture Coordinating Councils referred to in section 109, to identify potential sources of emerging threats to the safety and security of the food supply and preventive strategies to address those threats.

(C) Systems to ensure the prompt distribution to the food industry of information and technical assistance concerning preventive strategies.

(D) Communication systems to ensure that information about specific threats to the safety and security of the food supply are rapidly and effectively disseminated.

(E) Surveillance systems and laboratory networks to rapidly detect and respond to foodborne illness outbreaks and other food-related hazards, including how such systems and networks are integrated.

(F) Outreach, education, and training provided to States and local governments to build State and local food safety and food defense capabilities, including progress implementing strategies developed under sections 108 and 205.

(G) The estimated resources needed to effectively implement the programs and practices identified in the report developed in this section over a 5-year period.

(H) The impact of requirements under this Act (including amendments made by this Act) on certified organic farms and facilities (as defined in section 415 (21 U.S.C. 350d).

(I) Specific efforts taken pursuant to the agreements authorized under section 421(c) of the Federal Food, Drug, and Cosmetic Act (as added by section 201), together with, as necessary, a description of any additional authorities necessary to improve seafood safety.

(2) BIENNIAL REPORTS.--On a biennial basis following the submission of the report under paragraph (1), the Secretary shall submit to Congress a report that--

(A) reviews previous food safety programs and practices;

(B) outlines the success of those programs and practices;

(C) identifies future programs and practices; and

(D) includes information related to any matter described in subparagraphs (A) through (H) of paragraph (1), as necessary.

(b) Risk-based Activities.--The report developed under subsection (a)(1) shall describe methods that seek to ensure that resources available to the Secretary for food safety-related activities are directed at those actions most likely to reduce risks from food, including the use of preventive strategies and allocation of inspection resources. The Secretary shall promptly undertake those risk-based actions that are identified during the development of the report as likely to contribute to the safety and security of the food supply.

(c) Capability for Laboratory Analyses; Research.--The report developed under subsection (a)(1) shall provide a description of methods to increase capacity to undertake analyses of food samples promptly after collection, to identify new and rapid analytical techniques, including commercially-available techniques that can be employed at ports of entry and by Food Emergency Response Network laboratories, and to provide for well-equipped and staffed laboratory facilities and progress toward laboratory accreditation under section 422 of the Federal Food, Drug, and Cosmetic Act (as added by section 202).

(d) Information Technology.--The report developed under subsection (a)(1) shall include a description of such information technology systems as may be needed to identify risks and receive data from multiple sources, including foreign governments, State, local, and tribal governments, other Federal agencies, the food industry, laboratories, laboratory networks, and consumers. The information technology systems that the Secretary describes shall also provide for the integration of the facility registration system under section 415 of the Federal Food, Drug, and Cosmetic Act (21 U.S.C. 350d), and the prior notice system under section 801(m) of such Act (21 U.S.C. 381(m)) with other information technology systems that are used by the Federal Government for the processing of food offered for import into the United States.

(e) Automated Risk Assessment.--The report developed under subsection (a)(1) shall include a description of progress toward developing and improving an automated risk assessment system for food safety surveillance and allocation of resources.

(f) Traceback and Surveillance Report.--The Secretary shall include in the report developed under subsection (a)(1) an analysis of the Food and Drug Administration's performance in foodborne illness outbreaks during the 5-year period preceding the date of enactment of this Act involving fruits and vegetables that are raw agricultural commodities (as defined in section 201(r) (21 U.S.C. 321(r)) and recommendations for enhanced surveillance, outbreak response, and traceability. Such findings and recommendations shall address communication and coordination with the public, industry, and State and local governments, as such communication and coordination relates to outbreak identification and traceback.

(g) Biennial Food Safety and Food Defense Research Plan.--The Secretary, the Secretary of Agriculture, and the Secretary of Homeland Security shall, on a biennial basis, submit to Congress a joint food safety and food defense research plan which may include studying the long-term health effects of foodborne illness. Such biennial plan shall include a list and description of projects conducted during the previous 2-year period and the plan for projects to be conducted during the subsequent 2-year period.

(h) Effectiveness of Programs Administered by the Department of Health and Human Services.--

(1) IN GENERAL.--To determine whether existing Federal programs administered by the Department of Health and Human Services are effective in achieving the stated goals of such programs, the Secretary shall, beginning not later than 1 year after the date of enactment of this Act--

(A) conduct an annual evaluation of each program of such Department to determine the effectiveness of each such program in achieving legislated intent, purposes, and objectives; and

(B) submit to Congress a report concerning such evaluation.

(2) CONTENT.--The report described under paragraph (1)(B) shall--

(A) include conclusions concerning the reasons that such existing programs have proven successful or not successful and what factors contributed to such conclusions;

(B) include recommendations for consolidation and elimination to reduce duplication and inefficiencies in such programs at such Department as identified during the evaluation conduct under this subsection; and

(C) be made publicly available in a publication entitled "Guide to the U.S. Department of Health and Human Services Programs".

(i) Unique Identification Numbers.--

(1) IN GENERAL.--Not later than 1 year after the date of enactment of this Act, the Secretary, acting through the Commissioner of Food and Drugs, shall conduct a study regarding the need for, and challenges associated with, development and

implementation of a program that requires a unique identification number for each food facility registered with the Secretary and, as appropriate, each broker that imports food into the United States. Such study shall include an evaluation of the costs associated with development and implementation of such a system, and make recommendations about what new authorities, if any, would be necessary to develop and implement such a system.

(2) REPORT.--Not later than 15 months after the date of enactment of this Act, the Secretary shall submit to Congress a report that describes the findings of the study conducted under paragraph (1) and that includes any recommendations determined appropriate by the Secretary.

SEC. 111. SANITARY TRANSPORTATION OF FOOD.

(a) In General.--Not later than 18 months after the date of enactment of this Act, the Secretary shall promulgate regulations described in section 416(b) of the Federal Food, Drug, and Cosmetic Act (21 U.S.C. 350e(b)).

(b) Food Transportation Study.--The Secretary, acting through the Commissioner of Food and Drugs, shall conduct a study of the transportation of food for consumption in the United States, including transportation by air, that includes an examination of the unique needs of rural and frontier areas with regard to the delivery of safe food.

SEC. 112. FOOD ALLERGY AND ANAPHYLAXIS MANAGEMENT.

(a) Definitions.--In this section:

(1) EARLY CHILDHOOD EDUCATION PROGRAM.--The term "early childhood education program" means--

(A) a Head Start program or an Early Head Start program carried out under the Head Start Act (42 U.S.C. 9831 et seq.);

(B) a State licensed or regulated child care program or school; or

(C) a State prekindergarten program that serves children from birth through kindergarten.

(2) ESEA DEFINITIONS.--The terms "local educational agency", "secondary school", "elementary school", and "parent" have the meanings given the terms in section 9101 of the Elementary and Secondary Education Act of 1965 (20 U.S.C. 7801).

(3) SCHOOL.--The term "school" includes public--

(A) kindergartens;

(B) elementary schools; and

(C) secondary schools.

(4) SECRETARY.--The term "Secretary" means the Secretary of Health and Human Services.

(b) Establishment of Voluntary Food Allergy and Anaphylaxis Management Guidelines.--

(1) ESTABLISHMENT.--

(A) IN GENERAL.--Not later than 1 year after the date of enactment of this Act, the Secretary, in consultation with the Secretary of Education, shall--

(i) develop guidelines to be used on a voluntary basis to develop plans for individuals to manage the risk of food allergy and anaphylaxis in schools and early childhood education programs; and

(ii) make such guidelines available to local educational agencies, schools, early childhood education programs, and other interested entities and individuals to be implemented on a voluntary basis only.

(B) APPLICABILITY OF FERPA.--Each plan described in subparagraph (A) that is developed for an individual shall be considered an education record for the purpose of section 444 of the General Education Provisions Act (commonly referred to as the "Family Educational Rights and Privacy Act of 1974") (20 U.S.C. 1232g).

(2) CONTENTS.--The voluntary guidelines developed by the Secretary under paragraph (1) shall address each of the following and may be updated as the Secretary determines necessary:

(A) Parental obligation to provide the school or early childhood education program, prior to the start of every school year, with--

(i) documentation from their child's physician or nurse--

(I) supporting a diagnosis of food allergy, and any risk of anaphylaxis, if applicable;

(II) identifying any food to which the child is allergic;

(III) describing, if appropriate, any prior history of anaphylaxis;

(IV) listing any medication prescribed for the child for the treatment of anaphylaxis;

(V) detailing emergency treatment procedures in the event of a reaction;

(VI) listing the signs and symptoms of a reaction; and

(VII) assessing the child's readiness for self-administration of prescription medication; and

(ii) a list of substitute meals that may be offered to the child by school or early childhood education program food service personnel.

(B) The creation and maintenance of an individual plan for food allergy management, in consultation with the parent, tailored to the needs of each child with a documented risk for anaphylaxis, including any procedures for the self-administration of medication by such children in instances where--

(i) the children are capable of self-administering medication; and

(ii) such administration is not prohibited by State law.

(C) Communication strategies between individual schools or early childhood education programs and providers of emergency medical services, including appropriate instructions for emergency medical response.

(D) Strategies to reduce the risk of exposure to anaphylactic causative agents in classrooms and common school or early childhood education program areas such as cafeterias.

(E) The dissemination of general information on life-threatening food allergies to school or early childhood education program staff, parents, and children.

(F) Food allergy management training of school or early childhood education program personnel who regularly come into contact with children with life-threatening food allergies.

(G) The authorization and training of school or early childhood education program personnel to administer epinephrine when the nurse is not immediately available.

(H) The timely accessibility of epinephrine by school or early childhood education program personnel when the nurse is not immediately available.

(I) The creation of a plan contained in each individual plan for food allergy management that addresses the appropriate response to an incident of anaphylaxis of a child while such child is engaged in extracurricular programs of a school or early childhood education program, such as non-academic outings and field trips, before- and after-school programs or before- and after-early child education program programs, and school-sponsored or early childhood education program-sponsored programs held on weekends.

(J) Maintenance of information for each administration of epinephrine to a child at risk for anaphylaxis and prompt notification to parents.

(K) Other elements the Secretary determines necessary for the management of food allergies and anaphylaxis in schools and early childhood education programs.

(3) RELATION TO STATE LAW.--Nothing in this section or the guidelines developed by the Secretary under paragraph (1) shall be construed to preempt State law, including any State law regarding whether students at risk for anaphylaxis may self-administer medication.

(c) School-based Food Allergy Management Grants.--

(1) IN GENERAL.--The Secretary may award grants to local educational agencies to assist such agencies with implementing

voluntary food allergy and anaphylaxis management guidelines described in subsection (b).

(2) APPLICATION.--

(A) IN GENERAL.--To be eligible to receive a grant under this subsection, a local educational agency shall submit an application to the Secretary at such time, in such manner, and including such information as the Secretary may reasonably require.

(B) CONTENTS.--Each application submitted under subparagraph (A) shall include--

(i) an assurance that the local educational agency has developed plans in accordance with the food allergy and anaphylaxis management guidelines described in subsection (b);

(ii) a description of the activities to be funded by the grant in carrying out the food allergy and anaphylaxis management guidelines, including--

(I) how the guidelines will be carried out at individual schools served by the local educational agency;

(II) how the local educational agency will inform parents and students of the guidelines in place;

(III) how school nurses, teachers, administrators, and other school-based staff will be made aware of, and given training on, when applicable, the guidelines in place; and

(IV) any other activities that the Secretary determines appropriate;

(iii) an itemization of how grant funds received under this subsection will be expended;

(iv) a description of how adoption of the guidelines and implementation of grant activities will be monitored; and

(v) an agreement by the local educational agency to report information required by the Secretary to conduct evaluations under this subsection.

(3) USE OF FUNDS.--Each local educational agency that receives a grant under this subsection may use the grant funds for the following:

(A) Purchase of materials and supplies, including limited medical supplies such as epinephrine and disposable wet wipes, to support carrying out the food allergy and anaphylaxis management guidelines described in subsection (b).

(B) In partnership with local health departments, school nurse, teacher, and personnel training for food allergy management.

(C) Programs that educate students as to the presence of, and policies and procedures in place related to, food allergies and anaphylactic shock.

(D) Outreach to parents.

(E) Any other activities consistent with the guidelines described in subsection (b).

(4) DURATION OF AWARDS.--The Secretary may award grants under this subsection for a period of not more than 2 years. In the event the Secretary conducts a program evaluation under this subsection, funding in the second year of the grant, where applicable, shall be contingent on a successful program evaluation by the Secretary after the first year.

(5) LIMITATION ON GRANT FUNDING.--The Secretary may not provide grant funding to a local educational agency under this subsection after such local educational agency has received 2 years of grant funding under this subsection.

(6) MAXIMUM AMOUNT OF ANNUAL AWARDS.--A grant awarded under this subsection may not be made in an amount that is more than $50,000 annually.

(7) PRIORITY.--In awarding grants under this subsection, the Secretary shall give priority to local educational agencies with the highest percentages of children who are counted under section 1124(c) of the Elementary and Secondary Education Act of 1965 (20 U.S.C. 6333(c)).

(8) MATCHING FUNDS.--

> (A) IN GENERAL.--The Secretary may not award a grant under this subsection unless the local educational agency agrees that, with respect to the costs to be incurred by such local educational agency in carrying out the grant activities, the local educational agency shall make available (directly or through donations from public or private entities) non-Federal funds toward such costs in an amount equal to not less than 25 percent of the amount of the grant.

> (B) DETERMINATION OF AMOUNT OF NON-FEDERAL CONTRIBUTION.--Non-Federal funds required under subparagraph (A) may be cash or in kind, including plant, equipment, or services. Amounts provided

by the Federal Government, and any portion of any service subsidized by the Federal Government, may not be included in determining the amount of such non-Federal funds.

(9) ADMINISTRATIVE FUNDS.--A local educational agency that receives a grant under this subsection may use not more than 2 percent of the grant amount for administrative costs related to carrying out this subsection.

(10) PROGRESS AND EVALUATIONS.--At the completion of the grant period referred to in paragraph (4), a local educational agency shall provide the Secretary with information on how grant funds were spent and the status of implementation of the food allergy and anaphylaxis management guidelines described in subsection (b).

(11) SUPPLEMENT, NOT SUPPLANT.--Grant funds received under this subsection shall be used to supplement, and not supplant, non-Federal funds and any other Federal funds available to carry out the activities described in this subsection.

(12) AUTHORIZATION OF APPROPRIATIONS.--There is authorized to be appropriated to carry out this subsection $30,000,000 for fiscal year 2011 and such sums as may be necessary for each of the 4 succeeding fiscal years.

(d) Voluntary Nature of Guidelines.--

(1) IN GENERAL.--The food allergy and anaphylaxis management guidelines developed by the Secretary under subsection (b) are voluntary. Nothing in this section or the guidelines developed by the Secretary under subsection (b) shall be construed to require a local educational agency to implement such guidelines.

(2) EXCEPTION.--Notwithstanding paragraph (1), the Secretary may enforce an agreement by a local educational agency to

implement food allergy and anaphylaxis management guidelines as a condition of the receipt of a grant under subsection (c).

SEC. 113. NEW DIETARY INGREDIENTS.

(a) In General.--Section 413 of the Federal Food, Drug, and Cosmetic Act (21 U.S.C. 350b) is amended--

    (1) by redesignating subsection (c) as subsection (d); and

    (2) by inserting after subsection (b) the following:

        "(c) Notification.--

            "(1) IN GENERAL.--If the Secretary determines that the information in a new dietary ingredient notification submitted under this section for an article purported to be a new dietary ingredient is inadequate to establish that a dietary supplement containing such article will reasonably be expected to be safe because the article may be, or may contain, an anabolic steroid or an analogue of an anabolic steroid, the Secretary shall notify the Drug Enforcement Administration of such determination. Such notification by the Secretary shall include, at a minimum, the name of the dietary supplement or article, the name of the person or persons who marketed the product or made the submission of information regarding the article to the Secretary under this section, and any contact information for such person or persons that the Secretary has.

            "(2) DEFINITIONS.--For purposes of this subsection--

                "(A) the term 'anabolic steroid' has the meaning given such term in section 102(41) of the Controlled Substances Act; and

"(B) the term 'analogue of an anabolic steroid' means a substance whose chemical structure is substantially similar to the chemical structure of an anabolic steroid.".

(b) Guidance.--Not later than 180 days after the date of enactment of this Act, the Secretary shall publish guidance that clarifies when a dietary supplement ingredient is a new dietary ingredient, when the manufacturer or distributor of a dietary ingredient or dietary supplement should provide the Secretary with information as described in section 413(a)(2) of the Federal Food, Drug, and Cosmetic Act, the evidence needed to document the safety of new dietary ingredients, and appropriate methods for establishing the identify of a new dietary ingredient.

SEC. 114. REQUIREMENT FOR GUIDANCE RELATING TO POST HARVEST PROCESSING OF RAW OYSTERS.

(a) In General.--Not later than 90 days prior to the issuance of any guidance, regulation, or suggested amendment by the Food and Drug Administration to the National Shellfish Sanitation Program's Model Ordinance, or the issuance of any guidance or regulation by the Food and Drug Administration relating to the Seafood Hazard Analysis Critical Control Points Program of the Food and Drug Administration (parts 123 and 1240 of title 21, Code of Federal Regulations (or any successor regulations), where such guidance, regulation or suggested amendment relates to post harvest processing for raw oysters, the Secretary shall prepare and submit to the Committee on Health, Education, Labor, and Pensions of the Senate and the Committee on Energy and Commerce of the House of Representatives a report which shall include--

(1) an assessment of how post harvest processing or other equivalent controls feasibly may be implemented in the fastest, safest, and most economical manner;

(2) the projected public health benefits of any proposed post harvest processing;

(3) the projected costs of compliance with such post harvest processing measures;

(4) the impact post harvest processing is expected to have on the sales, cost, and availability of raw oysters;

(5) criteria for ensuring post harvest processing standards will be applied equally to shellfish imported from all nations of origin;

(6) an evaluation of alternative measures to prevent, eliminate, or reduce to an acceptable level the occurrence of foodborne illness; and

(7) the extent to which the Food and Drug Administration has consulted with the States and other regulatory agencies, as appropriate, with regard to post harvest processing measures.

(b) Limitation.--Subsection (a) shall not apply to the guidance described in section 103(h).

(c) Review and Evaluation.--Not later than 30 days after the Secretary issues a proposed regulation or guidance described in subsection (a), the Comptroller General of the United States shall--

(1) review and evaluate the report described in (a) and report to Congress on the findings of the estimates and analysis in the report;

(2) compare such proposed regulation or guidance to similar regulations or guidance with respect to other regulated foods, including a comparison of risks the Secretary may find associated with seafood and the instances of those risks in such other regulated foods; and

(3) evaluate the impact of post harvest processing on the competitiveness of the domestic oyster industry in the United States and in international markets.

(d) Waiver.--The requirement of preparing a report under subsection (a) shall be waived if the Secretary issues a guidance that is adopted as a consensus agreement between Federal and State regulators and the oyster industry, acting through the Interstate Shellfish Sanitation Conference.

(e) Public Access.--Any report prepared under this section shall be made available to the public.

SEC. 115. PORT SHOPPING.

Until the date on which the Secretary promulgates a final rule that implements the amendments made by section 308 of the Public Health Security and Bioterrorism Preparedness and Response Act of 2002, (Public Law 107-188), the Secretary shall notify the Secretary of Homeland Security of all instances in which the Secretary refuses to admit a food into the United States under section 801(a) of the Federal Food, Drug, and Cosmetic Act (21 U.S.C. 381(a)) so that the Secretary of Homeland Security, acting through the Commissioner of Customs and Border Protection, may prevent food refused admittance into the United States by a United States port of entry from being admitted by another United States port of entry, through the notification of other such United States ports of entry.

SEC. 116. ALCOHOL-RELATED FACILITIES.

(a) In General.--Except as provided by sections 102, 206, 207, 302, 304, 402, 403, and 404 of this Act, and the amendments made by such sections, nothing in this Act, or the amendments made by this Act, shall be construed to apply to a facility that--

(1) under the Federal Alcohol Administration Act (27 U.S.C. 201 et seq.) or chapter 51 of subtitle E of the Internal Revenue Code of 1986 (26 U.S.C. 5001 et seq.) is required to obtain a permit or to register with the Secretary of the Treasury as a condition of doing business in the United States; and

(2) under section 415 of the Federal Food, Drug, and Cosmetic Act (21 U.S.C. 350d) is required to register as a facility because such facility is engaged in manufacturing, processing, packing, or holding

1 or more alcoholic beverages, with respect to the activities of such facility that relate to the manufacturing, processing, packing, or holding of alcoholic beverages.

(b) Limited Receipt and Distribution of Non-alcohol Food.--Subsection (a) shall not apply to a facility engaged in the receipt and distribution of any non-alcohol food, except that such paragraph shall apply to a facility described in such paragraph that receives and distributes non-alcohol food, provided such food is received and distributed--

(1) in a prepackaged form that prevents any direct human contact with such food; and

(2) in amounts that constitute not more than 5 percent of the overall sales of such facility, as determined by the Secretary of the Treasury.

(c) Rule of Construction.--Except as provided in subsections (a) and (b), this section shall not be construed to exempt any food, other than alcoholic beverages, as defined in section 214 of the Federal Alcohol Administration Act (27 U.S.C. 214), from the requirements of this Act (including the amendments made by this Act).

TITLE II--IMPROVING CAPACITY TO DETECT AND RESPOND TO FOOD SAFETY PROBLEMS

SEC. 201. TARGETING OF INSPECTION RESOURCES FOR DOMESTIC FACILITIES, FOREIGN FACILITIES, AND PORTS OF ENTRY; ANNUAL REPORT.

(a) Targeting of Inspection Resources for Domestic Facilities, Foreign Facilities, and Ports of Entry.--Chapter IV (21 U.S.C. 341 et seq.), as amended by section 106, is amended by adding at the end the following:

"SEC. 421. TARGETING OF INSPECTION RESOURCES FOR DOMESTIC FACILITIES, FOREIGN FACILITIES, AND PORTS OF ENTRY; ANNUAL REPORT.

"(a) Identification and Inspection of Facilities.--

"(1) IDENTIFICATION.--The Secretary shall identify high-risk facilities and shall allocate resources to inspect facilities according to the known safety risks of the facilities, which shall be based on the following factors:

"(A) The known safety risks of the food manufactured, processed, packed, or held at the facility.

"(B) The compliance history of a facility, including with regard to food recalls, outbreaks of foodborne illness, and violations of food safety standards.

"(C) The rigor and effectiveness of the facility's hazard analysis and risk-based preventive controls.

"(D) Whether the food manufactured, processed, packed, or held at the facility meets the criteria for priority under section 801(h)(1).

"(E) Whether the food or the facility that manufactured, processed, packed, or held such food has received a certification as described in section 801(q) or 806, as appropriate.

"(F) Any other criteria deemed necessary and appropriate by the Secretary for purposes of allocating inspection resources.

"(2) INSPECTIONS.--

"(A) IN GENERAL.--Beginning on the date of enactment of the FDA Food Safety Modernization Act, the Secretary shall increase the frequency of inspection of all facilities.

"(B) DOMESTIC HIGH-RISK FACILITIES.--* The Secretary shall increase the frequency of inspection of domestic facilities identified under paragraph (1) as high-risk facilities such that each such facility is inspected--

"(i) not less often than once in the 5-year period following the date of enactment of the FDA Food Safety Modernization Act; and

"(ii) not less often than once every 3 years thereafter.

"(C) DOMESTIC NON-HIGH-RISK FACILITIES.--The Secretary shall ensure that each domestic facility that is not identified under paragraph (1) as a high-risk facility is inspected--

"(i) not less often than once in the 7-year period following the date of enactment of the FDA Food Safety Modernization Act; and

"(ii) not less often than once every 5 years thereafter.

"(D) FOREIGN FACILITIES.--

"(i) YEAR 1.--In the 1-year period following the date of enactment of the

FDA Food Safety Modernization Act, the Secretary shall inspect not fewer than 600 foreign facilities.

"(ii) SUBSEQUENT YEARS.--In each of the 5 years following the 1-year period described in clause (i), the Secretary shall inspect not fewer than twice the number of foreign facilities inspected by the Secretary during the previous year.

"(E) RELIANCE ON FEDERAL, STATE, OR LOCAL INSPECTIONS.--In meeting the inspection requirements under this subsection for domestic facilities, the Secretary may rely on inspections conducted by other Federal, State, or local agencies under interagency agreement, contract, memoranda of understanding, or other obligation.

"(b) Identification and Inspection at Ports of Entry.--The Secretary, in consultation with the Secretary of Homeland Security, shall allocate resources to inspect any article of food imported into the United States according to the known safety risks of the article of food, which shall be based on the following factors:

"(1) The known safety risks of the food imported.

"(2) The known safety risks of the countries or regions of origin and countries through which such article of food is transported.

"(3) The compliance history of the importer, including with regard to food recalls, outbreaks of foodborne illness, and violations of food safety standards.

"(4) The rigor and effectiveness of the activities conducted by the importer of such article of food to satisfy the requirements of the foreign supplier verification program under section 805.

"(5) Whether the food importer participates in the voluntary qualified importer program under section 806.

"(6) Whether the food meets the criteria for priority under section 801(h)(1).

"(7) Whether the food or the facility that manufactured, processed, packed, or held such food received a certification as described in section 801(q) or 806.

"(8) Any other criteria deemed necessary and appropriate by the Secretary for purposes of allocating inspection resources.

"(c) Interagency Agreements With Respect to Seafood.--

"(1) IN GENERAL.--The Secretary of Health and Human Services, the Secretary of Commerce, the Secretary of Homeland Security, the Chairman of the Federal Trade Commission, and the heads of other appropriate agencies may enter into such agreements as may be necessary or appropriate to improve seafood safety.

"(2) SCOPE OF AGREEMENTS.--The agreements under paragraph (1) may include--

"(A) cooperative arrangements for examining and testing seafood imports that leverage the resources, capabilities, and authorities of each party to the agreement;

"(B) coordination of inspections of foreign facilities to increase the percentage of imported seafood and seafood facilities inspected;

"(C) standardization of data on seafood names, inspection records, and laboratory testing to improve interagency coordination;

"(D) coordination to detect and investigate violations under applicable Federal law;

"(E) a process, including the use or modification of existing processes, by which officers and employees of the National Oceanic and Atmospheric Administration may be duly designated by the Secretary to carry out seafood examinations and investigations under section 801 of this Act or section 203 of the Food Allergen Labeling and Consumer Protection Act of 2004;

"(F) the sharing of information concerning observed non-compliance with United States food requirements domestically and in foreign nations and new regulatory decisions and policies that may affect the safety of food imported into the United States;

"(G) conducting joint training on subjects that affect and strengthen seafood inspection effectiveness by Federal authorities; and

"(H) outreach on Federal efforts to enhance seafood safety and compliance with Federal food safety requirements.

"(d) Coordination.--The Secretary shall improve coordination and cooperation with the Secretary of Agriculture and the Secretary of Homeland Security to target food inspection resources.

"(e) Facility.--For purposes of this section, the term 'facility' means a domestic facility or a foreign facility that is required to register under section 415.".

(b) Annual Report.--Section 1003 (21 U.S.C. 393) is amended by adding at the end the following:

"(h) Annual Report Regarding Food.--Not later than February 1 of each year, the Secretary shall submit to Congress a report, including efforts to coordinate and cooperate with other Federal agencies with responsibilities for food inspections, regarding--

"(1) information about food facilities including--

"(A) the appropriations used to inspect facilities registered pursuant to section 415 in the previous fiscal year;

"(B) the average cost of both a non-high-risk food facility inspection and a high-risk food facility inspection, if such a difference exists, in the previous fiscal year;

"(C) the number of domestic facilities and the number of foreign facilities registered pursuant to section 415 that the Secretary inspected in the previous fiscal year;

"(D) the number of domestic facilities and the number of foreign facilities registered pursuant to section 415 that were scheduled for inspection in the previous fiscal year and which the Secretary did not inspect in such year;

"(E) the number of high-risk facilities identified pursuant to section 421 that the Secretary inspected in the previous fiscal year; and

"(F) the number of high-risk facilities identified pursuant to section 421 that were scheduled for inspection in the previous fiscal year and which the Secretary did not inspect in such year.

"(2) information about food imports including--

"(A) the number of lines of food imported into the United States that the Secretary physically inspected or sampled in the previous fiscal year;

"(B) the number of lines of food imported into the United States that the Secretary did not physically inspect or sample in the previous fiscal year; and

"(C) the average cost of physically inspecting or sampling a line of food subject to this Act that is imported or offered for import into the United States; and

"(3) information on the foreign offices of the Food and Drug Administration including--

"(A) the number of foreign offices established; and

"(B) the number of personnel permanently stationed in each foreign office.

"(i) Public Availability of Annual Food Reports.--The Secretary shall make the reports required under subsection (h) available to the public on the Internet Web site of the Food and Drug Administration.".

(c) Advisory Committee Consultation.--In allocating inspection resources as described in section 421 of the Federal Food, Drug, and Cosmetic Act (as added by subsection (a)), the Secretary may, as appropriate, consult with any relevant advisory committee within the Department of Health and Human Services.

SEC. 202. LABORATORY ACCREDITATION FOR ANALYSES OF FOODS.

(a) In General.--Chapter IV (21 U.S.C. 341 et seq.), as amended by section 201, is amended by adding at the end the following:

"SEC. 422. LABORATORY ACCREDITATION FOR ANALYSES OF FOODS.

"(a) Recognition of Laboratory Accreditation.--

"(1) IN GENERAL.--Not later than 2 years after the date of enactment of the FDA Food Safety Modernization Act, the Secretary shall--

"(A) establish a program for the testing of food by accredited laboratories;

"(B) establish a publicly available registry of accreditation bodies recognized by the Secretary and laboratories accredited by a recognized accreditation body, including the name of, contact information for, and other information deemed appropriate by the Secretary about such bodies and laboratories; and

"(C) require, as a condition of recognition or accreditation, as appropriate, that recognized accreditation bodies and accredited laboratories report to the Secretary any changes that would affect the recognition of such accreditation body or the accreditation of such laboratory.

"(2) PROGRAM REQUIREMENTS.--The program established under paragraph (1)(A) shall provide for the recognition of laboratory accreditation bodies that meet criteria established by the Secretary for accreditation of laboratories, including independent private laboratories and laboratories run and operated by a Federal agency (including the Department of Commerce), State, or locality with a demonstrated capability to conduct 1 or more sampling and analytical testing methodologies for food.

"(3) INCREASING THE NUMBER OF QUALIFIED LABORATORIES.--The Secretary shall work with the laboratory accreditation bodies recognized under paragraph (1), as appropriate, to increase the number of qualified laboratories that are eligible to perform testing under subparagraph (b) beyond the number so qualified on the date of enactment of the FDA Food Safety Modernization Act.

"(4) LIMITED DISTRIBUTION.--In the interest of national security, the Secretary, in coordination with the Secretary of Homeland Security, may determine the time, manner, and form in which the registry established under paragraph (1)(B) is made publicly available.

"(5) FOREIGN LABORATORIES.--Accreditation bodies recognized by the Secretary under paragraph (1) may accredit laboratories that operate outside the United States, so long as such laboratories meet the accreditation standards applicable to domestic laboratories accredited under this section.

"(6) MODEL LABORATORY STANDARDS.--The Secretary shall develop model standards that a laboratory shall meet to be accredited by a recognized accreditation body for a specified sampling or analytical testing methodology and included in the registry provided for under paragraph (1). In developing the model standards, the Secretary shall consult existing standards for guidance. The model standards shall include--

"(A) methods to ensure that--

"(i) appropriate sampling, analytical procedures (including rapid analytical procedures), and commercially available techniques are followed and reports of analyses are certified as true and accurate;

"(ii) internal quality systems are established and maintained;

"(iii) procedures exist to evaluate and respond promptly to complaints regarding analyses and other activities for which the laboratory is accredited; and

"(iv) individuals who conduct the sampling and analyses are qualified by training and experience to do so; and

"(B) any other criteria determined appropriate by the Secretary.

"(7) REVIEW OF RECOGNITION.--To ensure compliance with the requirements of this section, the Secretary--

"(A) shall periodically, and in no case less than once every 5 years, reevaluate accreditation bodies recognized under paragraph (1) and may accompany auditors from an accreditation body to assess whether the accreditation body meets the criteria for recognition; and

"(B) shall promptly revoke the recognition of any accreditation body found not to be in compliance with the requirements of this section, specifying, as appropriate, any terms and conditions necessary for laboratories accredited by such body to continue to perform testing as described in this section.

"(b) Testing Procedures.--

"(1) IN GENERAL.--Not later than 30 months after the date of enactment of the FDA Food Safety Modernization Act, food testing shall be conducted by Federal laboratories or non-Federal laboratories that have been accredited for the appropriate sampling or analytical testing methodology or methodologies by a recognized accreditation body on the registry established by the Secretary under subsection (a)(1)(B) whenever such testing is conducted--

"(A) by or on behalf of an owner or consignee--

"(i) in response to a specific testing requirement under this Act or implementing regulations, when applied to address an identified or suspected food safety problem; and

"(ii) as required by the Secretary, as the Secretary deems appropriate, to address an identified or suspected food safety problem; or

"(B) on behalf of an owner or consignee--

"(i) in support of admission of an article of food under section 801(a); and

"(ii) under an Import Alert that requires successful consecutive tests.

"(2) RESULTS OF TESTING.--The results of any such testing shall be sent directly to the Food and Drug Administration, except the Secretary may by regulation exempt test results from such submission requirement if the Secretary determines that such results do not contribute to the protection of public health. Test results required to be submitted may be submitted to the Food and Drug Administration through electronic means.

"(3) EXCEPTION.--The Secretary may waive requirements under this subsection if--

"(A) a new methodology or methodologies have been developed and validated but a laboratory has not yet been accredited to perform such methodology or methodologies; and

"(B) the use of such methodology or methodologies are necessary to prevent, control, or mitigate a food emergency or foodborne illness outbreak.

"(c) Review by Secretary.--If food sampling and testing performed by a laboratory run and operated by a State or locality that is accredited by a recognized accreditation body on the registry established by the Secretary under subsection (a) result in a State recalling a food, the Secretary shall review the sampling and testing results for the purpose of determining the need for a national recall or other compliance and enforcement activities.

"(d) No Limit on Secretarial Authority.--Nothing in this section shall be construed to limit the ability of the Secretary to review and act upon information from food testing, including determining the sufficiency of such information and testing.".

(b) Food Emergency Response Network.--The Secretary, in coordination with the Secretary of Agriculture, the Secretary of Homeland Security, and State, local, and tribal governments shall, not later than 180 days after the date of enactment of this Act, and biennially thereafter, submit to the relevant committees of Congress, and make publicly available on the Internet Web site of the Department of Health and Human Services, a report on the progress in implementing a national food emergency response laboratory network that--

(1) provides ongoing surveillance, rapid detection, and surge capacity for large-scale food-related emergencies, including intentional adulteration of the food supply;

(2) coordinates the food laboratory capacities of State, local, and tribal food laboratories, including the adoption of novel surveillance and identification technologies and the sharing of data between Federal agencies and State laboratories to develop national situational awareness;

(3) provides accessible, timely, accurate, and consistent food laboratory services throughout the United States;

(4) develops and implements a methods repository for use by Federal, State, and local officials;

(5) responds to food-related emergencies; and

(6) is integrated with relevant laboratory networks administered by other Federal agencies.

SEC. 203. INTEGRATED CONSORTIUM OF LABORATORY NETWORKS.

(a) In General.--The Secretary of Homeland Security, in coordination with the Secretary of Health and Human Services, the Secretary of Agriculture, the Secretary of Commerce, and the Administrator of the Environmental Protection Agency, shall maintain an agreement through which relevant laboratory network members, as determined by the Secretary of Homeland Security, shall--

(1) agree on common laboratory methods in order to reduce the time required to detect and respond to foodborne illness outbreaks and facilitate the sharing of knowledge and information relating to animal health, agriculture, and human health;

(2) identify means by which laboratory network members could work cooperatively--

    (A) to optimize national laboratory preparedness; and

    (B) to provide surge capacity during emergencies; and

(3) engage in ongoing dialogue and build relationships that will support a more effective and integrated response during emergencies.

(b) Reporting Requirement.--The Secretary of Homeland Security shall, on a biennial basis, submit to the relevant committees of Congress, and make publicly available on the Internet Web site of the Department of Homeland Security, a report on the progress of the integrated consortium of laboratory networks, as established under subsection (a), in carrying out this section.

SEC. 204. ENHANCING TRACKING AND TRACING OF FOOD AND RECORDKEEPING.

(a) Pilot Projects.--

(1) IN GENERAL.--Not later than 270 days after the date of enactment of this Act, the Secretary of Health and Human Services (referred to in this section as the "Secretary"), taking into account recommendations from the Secretary of Agriculture and representatives of State departments of health and agriculture, shall establish pilot projects in coordination with the food industry to explore and evaluate methods to rapidly and effectively identify recipients of food to prevent or mitigate a foodborne illness outbreak and to address credible threats of serious adverse health consequences or death to humans or animals as a result of such

food being adulterated under section 402 of the Federal Food, Drug, and Cosmetic Act (21 U.S.C. 342) or misbranded under section 403(w) of such Act (21 U.S.C. 343(w)).

(2) CONTENT.--The Secretary shall conduct 1 or more pilot projects under paragraph (1) in coordination with the processed food sector and 1 or more such pilot projects in coordination with processors or distributors of fruits and vegetables that are raw agricultural commodities. The Secretary shall ensure that the pilot projects under paragraph (1) reflect the diversity of the food supply and include at least 3 different types of foods that have been the subject of significant outbreaks during the 5-year period preceding the date of enactment of this Act, and are selected in order to--

> (A) develop and demonstrate methods for rapid and effective tracking and tracing of foods in a manner that is practicable for facilities of varying sizes, including small businesses;

> (B) develop and demonstrate appropriate technologies, including technologies existing on the date of enactment of this Act, that enhance the tracking and tracing of food; and

> (C) inform the promulgation of regulations under subsection (d).

(3) REPORT.--Not later than 18 months after the date of enactment of this Act, the Secretary shall report to Congress on the findings of the pilot projects under this subsection together with recommendations for improving the tracking and tracing of food.

(b) Additional Data Gathering.--

> (1) IN GENERAL.--The Secretary, in coordination with the Secretary of Agriculture and multiple representatives of State departments of health and agriculture, shall assess--

(A) the costs and benefits associated with the adoption and use of several product tracing technologies, including technologies used in the pilot projects under subsection (a);

(B) the feasibility of such technologies for different sectors of the food industry, including small businesses; and

(C) whether such technologies are compatible with the requirements of this subsection.

(2) REQUIREMENTS.--To the extent practicable, in carrying out paragraph (1), the Secretary shall--

(A) evaluate domestic and international product tracing practices in commercial use;

(B) consider international efforts, including an assessment of whether product tracing requirements developed under this section are compatible with global tracing systems, as appropriate; and

(C) consult with a diverse and broad range of experts and stakeholders, including representatives of the food industry, agricultural producers, and nongovernmental organizations that represent the interests of consumers.

(c) Product Tracing System.--The Secretary, in consultation with the Secretary of Agriculture, shall, as appropriate, establish within the Food and Drug Administration a product tracing system to receive information that improves the capacity of the Secretary to effectively and rapidly track and trace food that is in the United States or offered for import into the United States. Prior to the establishment of such product tracing system, the Secretary shall examine the results of applicable pilot projects and shall ensure that the activities of such system are adequately supported by the results of such pilot projects.

(d) Additional Recordkeeping Requirements for High Risk Foods.--

(1) IN GENERAL.--In order to rapidly and effectively identify recipients of a food to prevent or mitigate a foodborne illness outbreak and to address credible threats of serious adverse health consequences or death to humans or animals as a result of such food being adulterated under section 402 of the Federal Food, Drug, and Cosmetic Act or misbranded under section 403(w) of such Act, not later than 2 years after the date of enactment of this Act, the Secretary shall publish a notice of proposed rulemaking to establish recordkeeping requirements, in addition to the requirements under section 414 of the Federal Food, Drug, and Cosmetic Act (21 U.S.C. 350c) and subpart J of part 1 of title 21, Code of Federal Regulations (or any successor regulations), for facilities that manufacture, process, pack, or hold foods that the Secretary designates under paragraph (2) as high-risk foods. The Secretary shall set an appropriate effective date of such additional requirements for foods designated as high risk that takes into account the length of time necessary to comply with such requirements. Such requirements shall--

(A) relate only to information that is reasonably available and appropriate;

(B) be science-based;

(C) not prescribe specific technologies for the maintenance of records;

(D) ensure that the public health benefits of imposing additional recordkeeping requirements outweigh the cost of compliance with such requirements;

(E) be scale-appropriate and practicable for facilities of varying sizes and capabilities with respect to costs and recordkeeping burdens, and not require the creation and maintenance of duplicate records where the information is contained in other company records kept in the normal course of business;

(F) minimize the number of different recordkeeping requirements for facilities that handle more than 1 type of food;

(G) to the extent practicable, not require a facility to change business systems to comply with such requirements;

(H) allow any person subject to this subsection to maintain records required under this subsection at a central or reasonably accessible location provided that such records can be made available to the Secretary not later than 24 hours after the Secretary requests such records;

(I) include a process by which the Secretary may issue a waiver of the requirements under this subsection if the Secretary determines that such requirements would result in an economic hardship for an individual facility or a type of facility;

(J) be commensurate with the known safety risks of the designated food;

(K) take into account international trade obligations;

(L) not require--

> (i) a full pedigree, or a record of the complete previous distribution history of the food from the point of origin of such food;

> (ii) records of recipients of a food beyond the immediate subsequent recipient of such food; or

(iii) product tracking to the case level by persons subject to such requirements; and

(M) include a process by which the Secretary may remove a high-risk food designation developed under paragraph (2) for a food or type of food.

(2) DESIGNATION OF HIGH-RISK FOODS.--

(A) IN GENERAL.--Not later than 1 year after the date of enactment of this Act, and thereafter as the Secretary determines necessary, the Secretary shall designate high-risk foods for which the additional recordkeeping requirements described in paragraph (1) are appropriate and necessary to protect the public health. Each such designation shall be based on--

(i) the known safety risks of a particular food, including the history and severity of foodborne illness outbreaks attributed to such food, taking into consideration foodborne illness data collected by the Centers for Disease Control and Prevention;

(ii) the likelihood that a particular food has a high potential risk for microbiological or chemical contamination or would support the growth of pathogenic microorganisms due to the nature of the food or the processes used to produce such food;

(iii) the point in the manufacturing process of the food where contamination is most likely to occur;

(iv) the likelihood of contamination and steps taken during the manufacturing process to reduce the possibility of contamination;

(v) the likelihood that consuming a particular food will result in a foodborne illness due to contamination of the food; and

(vi) the likely or known severity, including health and economic impacts, of a foodborne illness attributed to a particular food.

(B) LIST OF HIGH-RISK FOODS.--At the time the Secretary promulgates the final rules under paragraph (1), the Secretary shall publish the list of the foods designated under subparagraph (A) as high-risk foods on the Internet website of the Food and Drug Administration. The Secretary may update the list to designate new high-risk foods and to remove foods that are no longer deemed to be high-risk foods, provided that each such update to the list is consistent with the requirements of this subsection and notice of such update is published in the Federal Register.

(3) PROTECTION OF SENSITIVE INFORMATION.--In promulgating regulations under this subsection, the Secretary shall take appropriate measures to ensure that there are effective procedures to prevent the unauthorized disclosure of any trade secret or confidential information that is obtained by the Secretary pursuant to this section, including periodic risk assessment and planning to prevent unauthorized release and controls to--

(A) prevent unauthorized reproduction of trade secret or confidential information;

(B) prevent unauthorized access to trade secret or confidential information; and

(C) maintain records with respect to access by any person to trade secret or confidential information maintained by the agency.

(4) PUBLIC INPUT.--During the comment period in the notice of proposed rulemaking under paragraph (1), the Secretary shall conduct not less than 3 public meetings in diverse geographical areas of the United States to provide persons in different regions an opportunity to comment.

(5) RETENTION OF RECORDS.--Except as otherwise provided in this subsection, the Secretary may require that a facility retain records under this subsection for not more than 2 years, taking into consideration the risk of spoilage, loss of value, or loss of palatability of the applicable food when determining the appropriate timeframes.

(6) LIMITATIONS.--

(A) FARM TO SCHOOL PROGRAMS.--In establishing requirements under this subsection, the Secretary shall, in consultation with the Secretary of Agriculture, consider the impact of requirements on farm to school or farm to institution programs of the Department of Agriculture and other farm to school and farm to institution programs outside such agency, and shall modify the requirements under this subsection, as appropriate, with respect to such programs so that the requirements do not place undue burdens on farm to school or farm to institution programs.

(B) IDENTITY-PRESERVED LABELS WITH RESPECT TO FARM SALES OF FOOD THAT IS PRODUCED AND PACKAGED ON A FARM.--The requirements under this subsection shall not apply to a food that is produced and packaged on a farm if--

(i) the packaging of the food maintains the integrity of the product and prevents subsequent contamination or alteration of the product; and

(ii) the labeling of the food includes the name, complete address (street address, town, State, country, and zip or other postal code), and business phone number of the farm, unless the Secretary waives the requirement to include a business phone number of the farm, as appropriate, in order to accommodate a religious belief of the individual in charge of such farm.

(C) FISHING VESSELS.--The requirements under this subsection with respect to a food that is produced through the use of a fishing vessel (as defined in section 3(18) of the Magnuson-Stevens Fishery Conservation and Management Act (16 U.S.C. 1802(18))) shall be limited to the requirements under subparagraph (F) until such time as the food is sold by the owner, operator, or agent in charge of such fishing vessel.

(D) COMMINGLED RAW AGRICULTURAL COMMODITIES.--

(i) LIMITATION ON EXTENT OF TRACING.--Recordkeeping requirements under this subsection with regard to any commingled raw agricultural commodity shall be limited to the requirements under subparagraph (F).

(ii) DEFINITIONS.--For the purposes of this subparagraph--

(I) the term "commingled raw agricultural commodity" means any commodity that is combined or mixed after harvesting, but before processing;

(II) the term "commingled raw agricultural commodity" shall not include types of fruits and vegetables that are raw agricultural commodities for which the Secretary has determined that standards promulgated under section 419 of the Federal Food, Drug, and Cosmetic Act (as added by section 105) would minimize the risk of serious adverse health consequences or death; and

(III) the term "processing" means operations that alter the general state of the commodity, such as canning, cooking, freezing, dehydration, milling, grinding, pasteurization, or homogenization.

(E) EXEMPTION OF OTHER FOODS.--The Secretary may, by notice in the Federal Register, modify the requirements under this subsection with respect to, or exempt a food or a type of facility from, the requirements of this subsection (other than the requirements under subparagraph (F), if applicable) if the Secretary determines that product tracing requirements for such food (such as bulk or commingled ingredients that are intended to be processed to destroy pathogens) or type of facility is not necessary to protect the public health.

(F) RECORDKEEPING REGARDING PREVIOUS SOURCES AND SUBSEQUENT RECIPIENTS.--In the case of a person or food to which a limitation or exemption under subparagraph (C), (D), or (E) applies, if such person, or a person who manufactures, processes, packs, or holds such food, is required to register with the Secretary under section 415 of the Federal Food, Drug, and Cosmetic Act (21 U.S.C. 350d) with respect to the manufacturing, processing, packing, or holding of the applicable food, the Secretary shall require such person to maintain records that identify the immediate previous source of such food and the immediate subsequent recipient of such food.

(G) GROCERY STORES.--With respect to a sale of a food described in subparagraph (H) to a grocery store, the Secretary shall not require such grocery store to maintain records under this subsection other than records documenting the farm that was the source of such food. The Secretary shall not require that such records be kept for more than 180 days.

(H) FARM SALES TO CONSUMERS.--The Secretary shall not require a farm to maintain any distribution records under this subsection with respect to a sale of a food described in subparagraph (I) (including a sale of a food that is produced and packaged on such farm), if such sale is made by the farm directly to a consumer.

(I) SALE OF A FOOD.--A sale of a food described in this subparagraph is a sale of a food in which--

(i) the food is produced on a farm; and

(ii) the sale is made by the owner, operator, or agent in charge of such farm directly to a consumer or grocery store.

(7) NO IMPACT ON NON-HIGH-RISK FOODS.--The recordkeeping requirements established under paragraph (1) shall have no effect on foods that are not designated by the Secretary under paragraph (2) as high-risk foods. Foods described in the preceding sentence shall be subject solely to the recordkeeping requirements under section 414 of the Federal Food, Drug, and Cosmetic Act (21 U.S.C. 350c) and subpart J of part 1 of title 21, Code of Federal Regulations (or any successor regulations).

(e) Evaluation and Recommendations.--

(1) REPORT.--Not later than 1 year after the effective date of the final rule promulgated under subsection (d)(1), the Comptroller General of the United States shall submit to Congress a report,

taking into consideration the costs of compliance and other regulatory burdens on small businesses and Federal, State, and local food safety practices and requirements, that evaluates the public health benefits and risks, if any, of limiting--

(A) the product tracing requirements under subsection (d) to foods identified under paragraph (2) of such subsection, including whether such requirements provide adequate assurance of traceability in the event of intentional adulteration, including by acts of terrorism; and

(B) the participation of restaurants in the recordkeeping requirements.

(2) DETERMINATION AND RECOMMENDATIONS.--In conducting the evaluation and report under paragraph (1), if the Comptroller General of the United States determines that the limitations described in such paragraph do not adequately protect the public health, the Comptroller General shall submit to Congress recommendations, if appropriate, regarding recordkeeping requirements for restaurants and additional foods, in order to protect the public health.

(f) Farms.--

(1) REQUEST FOR INFORMATION.--Notwithstanding subsection (d), during an active investigation of a foodborne illness outbreak, or if the Secretary determines it is necessary to protect the public health and prevent or mitigate a foodborne illness outbreak, the Secretary, in consultation and coordination with State and local agencies responsible for food safety, as appropriate, may request that the owner, operator, or agent of a farm identify potential immediate recipients, other than consumers, of an article of the food that is the subject of such investigation if the Secretary reasonably believes such article of food--

(A) is adulterated under section 402 of the Federal Food, Drug, and Cosmetic Act;

(B) presents a threat of serious adverse health consequences or death to humans or animals; and

(C) was adulterated as described in subparagraph (A) on a particular farm (as defined in section 1.227 of chapter 21, Code of Federal Regulations (or any successor regulation)).

(2) MANNER OF REQUEST.--In making a request under paragraph (1), the Secretary, in consultation and coordination with State and local agencies responsible for food safety, as appropriate, shall issue a written notice to the owner, operator, or agent of the farm to which the article of food has been traced. The individual providing such notice shall present to such owner, operator, or agent appropriate credentials and shall deliver such notice at reasonable times and within reasonable limits and in a reasonable manner.

(3) DELIVERY OF INFORMATION REQUESTED.--The owner, operator, or agent of a farm shall deliver the information requested under paragraph (1) in a prompt and reasonable manner. Such information may consist of records kept in the normal course of business, and may be in electronic or non-electronic format.

(4) LIMITATION.--A request made under paragraph (1) shall not include a request for information relating to the finances, pricing of commodities produced, personnel, research, sales (other than information relating to shipping), or other disclosures that may reveal trade secrets or confidential information from the farm to which the article of food has been traced, other than information necessary to identify potential immediate recipients of such food. Section 301(j) of the Federal Food, Drug, and Cosmetic Act and the Freedom of Information Act shall apply with respect to any confidential commercial information that is disclosed to the Food and Drug Administration in the course of responding to a request under paragraph (1).

(5) RECORDS.--Except with respect to identifying potential immediate recipients in response to a request under this subsection,

nothing in this subsection shall require the establishment or maintenance by farms of new records.

(g) No Limitation on Commingling of Food.--Nothing in this section shall be construed to authorize the Secretary to impose any limitation on the commingling of food.

(h) Small Entity Compliance Guide.--Not later than 180 days after promulgation of a final rule under subsection (d), the Secretary shall issue a small entity compliance guide setting forth in plain language the requirements of the regulations under such subsection in order to assist small entities, including farms and small businesses, in complying with the recordkeeping requirements under such subsection.

(i) Flexibility for Small Businesses.--Notwithstanding any other provision of law, the regulations promulgated under subsection (d) shall apply--

> (1) to small businesses (as defined by the Secretary in section 103, not later than 90 days after the date of enactment of this Act) beginning on the date that is 1 year after the effective date of the final regulations promulgated under subsection (d); and

> (2) to very small businesses (as defined by the Secretary in section 103, not later than 90 days after the date of enactment of this Act) beginning on the date that is 2 years after the effective date of the final regulations promulgated under subsection (d).

(j) Enforcement.--

> (1) PROHIBITED ACTS.--Section 301(e) (21 U.S.C. 331(e)) is amended by inserting "; or the violation of any recordkeeping requirement under section 204 of the FDA Food Safety Modernization Act (except when such violation is committed by a farm)" before the period at the end.

> (2) IMPORTS.--Section 801(a) (21 U.S.C. 381(a)) is amended by inserting "or (4) the recordkeeping requirements under section 204 of the FDA Food Safety Modernization Act (other than the

requirements under subsection (f) of such section) have not been complied with regarding such article," in the third sentence before "then such article shall be refused admission".

SEC. 205. SURVEILLANCE.

(a) Definition of Foodborne Illness Outbreak.--In this Act, the term "foodborne illness outbreak" means the occurrence of 2 or more cases of a similar illness resulting from the ingestion of a certain food.

(b) Foodborne Illness Surveillance Systems.--

> (1) IN GENERAL.--The Secretary, acting through the Director of the Centers for Disease Control and Prevention, shall enhance foodborne illness surveillance systems to improve the collection, analysis, reporting, and usefulness of data on foodborne illnesses by--

>> (A) coordinating Federal, State and local foodborne illness surveillance systems, including complaint systems, and increasing participation in national networks of public health and food regulatory agencies and laboratories;

>> (B) facilitating sharing of surveillance information on a more timely basis among governmental agencies, including the Food and Drug Administration, the Department of Agriculture, the Department of Homeland Security, and State and local agencies, and with the public;

>> (C) developing improved epidemiological tools for obtaining quality exposure data and microbiological methods for classifying cases;

>> (D) augmenting such systems to improve attribution of a foodborne illness outbreak to a specific food;

>> (E) expanding capacity of such systems, including working toward automatic electronic searches, for implementation

of identification practices, including fingerprinting strategies, for foodborne infectious agents, in order to identify new or rarely documented causes of foodborne illness and submit standardized information to a centralized database;

(F) allowing timely public access to aggregated, de-identified surveillance data;

(G) at least annually, publishing current reports on findings from such systems;

(H) establishing a flexible mechanism for rapidly initiating scientific research by academic institutions;

(I) integrating foodborne illness surveillance systems and data with other biosurveillance and public health situational awareness capabilities at the Federal, State, and local levels, including by sharing foodborne illness surveillance data with the National Biosurveillance Integration Center; and

(J) other activities as determined appropriate by the Secretary.

(2) WORKING GROUP.--The Secretary shall support and maintain a diverse working group of experts and stakeholders from Federal, State, and local food safety and health agencies, the food and food testing industries, consumer organizations, and academia. Such working group shall provide the Secretary, through at least annual meetings of the working group and an annual public report, advice and recommendations on an ongoing and regular basis regarding the improvement of foodborne illness surveillance and implementation of this section, including advice and recommendations on--

(A) the priority needs of regulatory agencies, the food industry, and consumers for information and analysis on foodborne illness and its causes;

(B) opportunities to improve the effectiveness of initiatives at the Federal, State, and local levels, including coordination and integration of activities among Federal agencies, and between the Federal, State, and local levels of government;

(C) improvement in the timeliness and depth of access by regulatory and health agencies, the food industry, academic researchers, and consumers to foodborne illness aggregated, de-identified surveillance data collected by government agencies at all levels, including data compiled by the Centers for Disease Control and Prevention;

(D) key barriers at Federal, State, and local levels to improving foodborne illness surveillance and the utility of such surveillance for preventing foodborne illness;

(E) the capabilities needed for establishing automatic electronic searches of surveillance data; and

(F) specific actions to reduce barriers to improvement, implement the working group's recommendations, and achieve the purposes of this section, with measurable objectives and timelines, and identification of resource and staffing needs.

(3) AUTHORIZATION OF APPROPRIATIONS.--To carry out the activities described in paragraph (1), there is authorized to be appropriated $24,000,000 for each fiscal years 2011 through 2015.

(c) Improving Food Safety and Defense Capacity at the State and Local Level.--

(1) IN GENERAL.--The Secretary shall develop and implement strategies to leverage and enhance the food safety and defense

capacities of State and local agencies in order to achieve the following goals:

(A) Improve foodborne illness outbreak response and containment.

(B) Accelerate foodborne illness surveillance and outbreak investigation, including rapid shipment of clinical isolates from clinical laboratories to appropriate State laboratories, and conducting more standardized illness outbreak interviews.

(C) Strengthen the capacity of State and local agencies to carry out inspections and enforce safety standards.

(D) Improve the effectiveness of Federal, State, and local partnerships to coordinate food safety and defense resources and reduce the incidence of foodborne illness.

(E) Share information on a timely basis among public health and food regulatory agencies, with the food industry, with health care providers, and with the public.

(F) Strengthen the capacity of State and local agencies to achieve the goals described in section 108.

(2) REVIEW.--In developing of the strategies required by paragraph (1), the Secretary shall, not later than 1 year after the date of enactment of the FDA Food Safety Modernization Act, complete a review of State and local capacities, and needs for enhancement, which may include a survey with respect to--

(A) staffing levels and expertise available to perform food safety and defense functions;

(B) laboratory capacity to support surveillance, outbreak response, inspection, and enforcement activities;

(C) information systems to support data management and sharing of food safety and defense information among State and local agencies and with counterparts at the Federal level; and

(D) other State and local activities and needs as determined appropriate by the Secretary.

(d) Food Safety Capacity Building Grants.--Section 317R(b) of the Public Health Service Act (42 U.S.C. 247b-20(b)) is amended--

(1) by striking "2002" and inserting "2010"; and

(2) by striking "2003 through 2006" and inserting "2011 through 2015".

SEC. 206. MANDATORY RECALL AUTHORITY.

(a) In General.--Chapter IV (21 U.S.C. 341 et seq.), as amended by section 202, is amended by adding at the end the following:

"SEC. 423. MANDATORY RECALL AUTHORITY.

"(a) Voluntary Procedures.--If the Secretary determines, based on information gathered through the reportable food registry under section 417 or through any other means, that there is a reasonable probability that an article of food (other than infant formula) is adulterated under section 402 or misbranded under section 403(w) and the use of or exposure to such article will cause serious adverse health consequences or death to humans or animals, the Secretary shall provide the responsible party (as defined in section 417) with an opportunity to cease distribution and recall such article.

"(b) Prehearing Order To Cease Distribution and Give Notice.--

"(1) IN GENERAL.--If the responsible party refuses to or does not voluntarily cease distribution or recall such article within the time and in the manner prescribed by the

Secretary (if so prescribed), the Secretary may, by order require, as the Secretary deems necessary, such person to--

"(A) immediately cease distribution of such article; and

"(B) as applicable, immediately notify all persons--

"(i) manufacturing, processing, packing, transporting, distributing, receiving, holding, or importing and selling such article; and

"(ii) to which such article has been distributed, transported, or sold, to immediately cease distribution of such article.

"(2) REQUIRED ADDITIONAL INFORMATION.--

"(A) IN GENERAL.--If an article of food covered by a recall order issued under paragraph (1)(B) has been distributed to a warehouse-based third party logistics provider without providing such provider sufficient information to know or reasonably determine the precise identity of the article of food covered by a recall order that is in its possession, the notice provided by the responsible party subject to the order issued under paragraph (1)(B) shall include such information as is necessary for the warehouse-based third party logistics provider to identify the food.

"(B) RULES OF CONSTRUCTION.--Nothing in this paragraph shall be construed--

"(i) to exempt a warehouse-based third party logistics provider from the requirements of this Act, including the requirements in this section and section 414; or

"(ii) to exempt a warehouse-based third party logistics provider from being the subject of a mandatory recall order.

"(3) DETERMINATION TO LIMIT AREAS AFFECTED.--If the Secretary requires a responsible party to cease distribution under paragraph (1)(A) of an article of food identified in subsection (a), the Secretary may limit the size of the geographic area and the markets affected by such cessation if such limitation would not compromise the public health.

"(c) Hearing on Order.--The Secretary shall provide the responsible party subject to an order under subsection (b) with an opportunity for an informal hearing, to be held as soon as possible, but not later than 2 days after the issuance of the order, on the actions required by the order and on why the article that is the subject of the order should not be recalled.

"(d) Post-hearing Recall Order and Modification of Order.--

"(1) AMENDMENT OF ORDER.--If, after providing opportunity for an informal hearing under subsection (c), the Secretary determines that removal of the article from commerce is necessary, the Secretary shall, as appropriate--

"(A) amend the order to require recall of such article or other appropriate action;

"(B) specify a timetable in which the recall shall occur;

"(C) require periodic reports to the Secretary describing the progress of the recall; and

"(D) provide notice to consumers to whom such article was, or may have been, distributed.

"(2) VACATING OF ORDER.--If, after such hearing, the Secretary determines that adequate grounds do not exist to continue the actions required by the order, or that such actions should be modified, the Secretary shall vacate the order or modify the order.

"(e) Rule Regarding Alcoholic Beverages.--The Secretary shall not initiate a mandatory recall or take any other action under this section with respect to any alcohol beverage until the Secretary has provided the Alcohol and Tobacco Tax and Trade Bureau with a reasonable opportunity to cease distribution and recall such article under the Alcohol and Tobacco Tax and Trade Bureau authority.

"(f) Cooperation and Consultation.--The Secretary shall work with State and local public health officials in carrying out this section, as appropriate.

"(g) Public Notification.--In conducting a recall under this section, the Secretary shall--

"(1) ensure that a press release is published regarding the recall, as well as alerts and public notices, as appropriate, in order to provide notification--

"(A) of the recall to consumers and retailers to whom such article was, or may have been, distributed; and

"(B) that includes, at a minimum--

"(i) the name of the article of food subject to the recall;

"(ii) a description of the risk associated with such article; and "(iii) to the extent practicable, information for consumers about similar articles of food that are not affected by the recall;

"(2) consult the policies of the Department of Agriculture regarding providing to the public a list of retail consignees receiving products involved in a Class I recall and shall consider providing such a list to the public, as determined appropriate by the Secretary; and

"(3) if available, publish on the Internet Web site of the Food and Drug Administration an image of the article that is the subject of the press release described in (1).

"(h) No Delegation.--The authority conferred by this section to order a recall or vacate a recall order shall not be delegated to any officer or employee other than the Commissioner.

"(i) Effect.--Nothing in this section shall affect the authority of the Secretary to request or participate in a voluntary recall, or to issue an order to cease distribution or to recall under any other provision of this Act or under the Public Health Service Act.

"(j) Coordinated Communication.--

"(1) IN GENERAL.--To assist in carrying out the requirements of this subsection, the Secretary shall establish an incident command operation or a similar operation within the Department of Health and Human Services that will operate not later than 24 hours after the initiation of a mandatory recall or the recall of an article of food for which the use of, or exposure to, such article will cause serious adverse health consequences or death to humans or animals.

"(2) REQUIREMENTS.--To reduce the potential for miscommunication during recalls or regarding investigations of a food borne illness outbreak associated with a food that is subject to a recall, each incident command operation or similar operation under paragraph (1) shall use regular staff and resources of the Department of Health and Human Services to--

"(A) ensure timely and coordinated communication within the Department, including enhanced communication and coordination between different agencies and organizations within the Department;

"(B) ensure timely and coordinated communication from the Department, including public statements, throughout the duration of the investigation and related foodborne illness outbreak;

"(C) identify a single point of contact within the Department for public inquiries regarding any actions by the Secretary related to a recall;

"(D) coordinate with Federal, State, local, and tribal authorities, as appropriate, that have responsibilities related to the recall of a food or a foodborne illness outbreak associated with a food that is subject to the recall, including notification of the Secretary of Agriculture and the Secretary of Education in the event such recalled food is a commodity intended for use in a child nutrition program (as identified in section 25(b) of the Richard B. Russell National School Lunch Act (42 U.S.C. 1769f(b)); and

"(E) conclude operations at such time as the Secretary determines appropriate.

"(3) MULTIPLE RECALLS.--The Secretary may establish multiple or concurrent incident command operations or similar operations in the event of multiple recalls or foodborne illness outbreaks necessitating such action by the Department of Health and Human Services.".

(b) Search Engine.--Not later than 90 days after the date of enactment of this Act, the Secretary shall modify the Internet Web site of the Food and Drug Administration to include a search engine that--

(1) is consumer-friendly, as determined by the Secretary; and

(2) provides a means by which an individual may locate relevant information regarding each article of food subject to a recall under section 423 of the Federal Food, Drug, and Cosmetic Act and the status of such recall (such as whether a recall is ongoing or has been completed).

(c) Civil Penalty.--Section 303(f)(2)(A) (21 U.S.C. 333(f)(2)(A)) is amended by inserting "or any person who does not comply with a recall order under section 423" after "section 402(a)(2)(B)".

(d) Prohibited Acts.--Section 301 (21 U.S.C. 331 et seq.), as amended by section 106, is amended by adding at the end the following:

"(xx) The refusal or failure to follow an order under section 423.".

(e) GAO Review.--

(1) IN GENERAL.--Not later than 90 days after the date of enactment of this Act, the Comptroller General of the United States shall submit to Congress a report that--

(A) identifies State and local agencies with the authority to require the mandatory recall of food, and evaluates use of such authority with regard to frequency, effectiveness, and appropriateness, including consideration of any new or existing mechanisms available to compensate persons for general and specific recall-related costs when a recall is subsequently determined by the relevant authority to have been an error;

(B) identifies Federal agencies, other than the Department of Health and Human Services, with mandatory recall authority and examines use of that authority with regard to frequency, effectiveness, and appropriateness, including any new or existing mechanisms available to compensate persons for general and specific recall-related costs when a recall is subsequently determined by the relevant agency to have been an error;

(C) considers models for farmer restitution implemented in other nations in cases of erroneous recalls; and

(D) makes recommendations to the Secretary regarding use of the authority under section 423 of the Federal Food, Drug, and Cosmetic Act (as added by this section) to protect the public health while seeking to minimize unnecessary economic costs.

(2) EFFECT OF REVIEW.--If the Comptroller General of the United States finds, after the review conducted under paragraph (1), that the mechanisms described in such paragraph do not exist or are inadequate, then, not later than 90 days after the conclusion of such review, the Secretary of Agriculture shall conduct a study of the feasibility of implementing a farmer indemnification program to provide restitution to agricultural producers for losses sustained as a result of a mandatory recall of an agricultural commodity by a Federal or State regulatory agency that is subsequently determined to be in error. The Secretary of Agriculture shall submit to the Committee on Agriculture of the House of Representatives and the Committee on Agriculture, Nutrition, and Forestry of the Senate a report that describes the results of the study, including any recommendations.

(f) Annual Report to Congress.--

(1) IN GENERAL.--Not later than 2 years after the date of enactment of this Act and annually thereafter, the Secretary of Health and Human Services (referred to in this subsection as the

"Secretary") shall submit a report to the Committee on Health, Education, Labor, and Pensions of the Senate and the Committee on Energy and Commerce of the House of Representatives on the use of recall authority under section 423 of the Federal Food, Drug, and Cosmetic Act (as added by subsection (a)) and any public health advisories issued by the Secretary that advise against the consumption of an article of food on the ground that the article of food is adulterated and poses an imminent danger to health.

(2) CONTENT.--The report under paragraph (1) shall include, with respect to the report year--

> (A) the identity of each article of food that was the subject of a public health advisory described in paragraph (1), an opportunity to cease distribution and recall under subsection (a) of section 423 of the Federal Food, Drug, and Cosmetic Act, or a mandatory recall order under subsection (b) of such section;

> (B) the number of responsible parties, as defined in section 417 of the Federal Food, Drug, and Cosmetic Act, formally given the opportunity to cease distribution of an article of food and recall such article, as described in section 423(a) of such Act;

> (C) the number of responsible parties described in subparagraph (B) who did not cease distribution of or recall an article of food after given the opportunity to cease distribution or recall under section 423(a) of the Federal Food, Drug, and Cosmetic Act;

> (D) the number of recall orders issued under section 423(b) of the Federal Food, Drug, and Cosmetic Act; and

> (E) a description of any instances in which there was no testing that confirmed adulteration of an article of food that was the subject of a recall under section 423(b) of the

Federal Food, Drug, and Cosmetic Act or a public health advisory described in paragraph (1).

SEC. 207. ADMINISTRATIVE DETENTION OF FOOD.

(a) In General.--Section 304(h)(1)(A) (21 U.S.C. 334(h)(1)(A)) is amended by--

(1) striking "credible evidence or information indicating" and inserting "reason to believe"; and

(2) striking "presents a threat of serious adverse health consequences or death to humans or animals" and inserting "is adulterated or misbranded".

(b) Regulations.--Not later than 120 days after the date of enactment of this Act, the Secretary shall issue an interim final rule amending subpart K of part 1 of title 21, Code of Federal Regulations, to implement the amendment made by this section.

(c) Effective Date.--The amendment made by this section shall take effect 180 days after the date of enactment of this Act.

SEC. 208. DECONTAMINATION AND DISPOSAL STANDARDS AND PLANS.

(a) In General.--The Administrator of the Environmental Protection Agency (referred to in this section as the "Administrator"), in coordination with the Secretary of Health and Human Services, Secretary of Homeland Security, and Secretary of Agriculture, shall provide support for, and technical assistance to, State, local, and tribal governments in preparing for, assessing, decontaminating, and recovering from an agriculture or food emergency.

(b) Development of Standards.--In carrying out subsection (a), the Administrator, in coordination with the Secretary of Health and Human Services, Secretary of Homeland Security, Secretary of Agriculture, and State, local, and tribal governments, shall develop and disseminate specific standards and protocols to undertake clean-up, clearance, and recovery activities following the decontamination and disposal of specific threat agents and foreign animal diseases.

(c) Development of Model Plans.--In carrying out subsection (a), the Administrator, the Secretary of Health and Human Services, and the Secretary of Agriculture shall jointly develop and disseminate model plans for--

(1) the decontamination of individuals, equipment, and facilities following an intentional contamination of agriculture or food; and

(2) the disposal of large quantities of animals, plants, or food products that have been infected or contaminated by specific threat agents and foreign animal diseases.

(d) Exercises.--In carrying out subsection (a), the Administrator, in coordination with the entities described under subsection (b), shall conduct exercises at least annually to evaluate and identify weaknesses in the decontamination and disposal model plans described in subsection (c). Such exercises shall be carried out, to the maximum extent practicable, as part of the national exercise program under section 648(b)(1) of the Post-Katrina Emergency Management Reform Act of 2006 (6 U.S.C. 748(b)(1)).

(e) Modifications.--Based on the exercises described in subsection (d), the Administrator, in coordination with the entities described in subsection (b), shall review and modify as necessary the plans described in subsection (c) not less frequently than biennially.

(f) Prioritization.--The Administrator, in coordination with the entities described in subsection (b), shall develop standards and plans under subsections (b) and (c) in an identified order of priority that takes into account--

(1) highest-risk biological, chemical, and radiological threat agents;

(2) agents that could cause the greatest economic devastation to the agriculture and food system; and

(3) agents that are most difficult to clean or remediate.

SEC. 209. IMPROVING THE TRAINING OF STATE, LOCAL, TERRITORIAL, AND TRIBAL FOOD SAFETY OFFICIALS.

(a) Improving Training.--Chapter X (21 U.S.C.391 et seq.) is amended by adding at the end the following:

"SEC. 1011. IMPROVING THE TRAINING OF STATE, LOCAL, TERRITORIAL, AND TRIBAL FOOD SAFETY OFFICIALS.

"(a) Training.--The Secretary shall set standards and administer training and education programs for the employees of State, local, territorial, and tribal food safety officials relating to the regulatory responsibilities and policies established by this Act, including programs for--

"(1) scientific training;

"(2) training to improve the skill of officers and employees authorized to conduct inspections under sections 702 and 704;

"(3) training to achieve advanced product or process specialization in such inspections;

"(4) training that addresses best practices;

"(5) training in administrative process and procedure and integrity issues;

"(6) training in appropriate sampling and laboratory analysis methodology; and

"(7) training in building enforcement actions following inspections, examinations, testing, and investigations.

"(b) Partnerships With State and Local Officials.--

"(1) IN GENERAL.--The Secretary, pursuant to a contract or memorandum of understanding between the Secretary and the head of a State, local, territorial, or tribal department or agency, is authorized and encouraged to conduct examinations, testing, and investigations for the purposes of determining compliance with the food safety provisions of this Act through the officers and employees of such State, local, territorial, or tribal department or agency.

"(2) CONTENT.--A contract or memorandum described under paragraph (1) shall include provisions to ensure adequate training of such officers and employees to conduct such examinations, testing, and investigations. The contract or memorandum shall contain provisions regarding reimbursement. Such provisions may, at the sole discretion of the head of the other department or agency, require reimbursement, in whole or in part, from the Secretary for the examinations, testing, or investigations performed pursuant to this section by the officers or employees of the State, territorial, or tribal department or agency.

"(3) EFFECT.--Nothing in this subsection shall be construed to limit the authority of the Secretary under section 702.

"(c) Extension Service.--The Secretary shall ensure coordination with the extension activities of the National Institute of Food and Agriculture of the Department of Agriculture in advising producers and small processors transitioning into new practices required as a result of the enactment of the FDA Food Safety Modernization Act and assisting regulated industry with compliance with such Act.

"(d) National Food Safety Training, Education, Extension, Outreach and Technical Assistance Program.--

"(1) IN GENERAL.--In order to improve food safety and reduce the incidence of foodborne illness, the Secretary shall, not later than 180 days after the date of enactment of the FDA Food Safety Modernization Act, enter into one or more memoranda of understanding, or enter into other cooperative agreements, with the Secretary of Agriculture to establish a competitive grant program within the National Institute for Food and Agriculture to provide food safety training, education, extension, outreach, and technical assistance to--

"(A) owners and operators of farms;

"(B) small food processors; and

"(C) small fruit and vegetable merchant wholesalers.

"(2) IMPLEMENTATION.--The competitive grant program established under paragraph (1) shall be carried out in accordance with section 405 of the Agricultural Research, Extension, and Education Reform Act of 1998.

"(e) Authorization of Appropriations.--There are authorized to be appropriated such sums as may be necessary to carry out this section for fiscal years 2011 through 2015.".

(b) National Food Safety Training, Education, Extension, Outreach, and Technical Assistance Program.--Title IV of the Agricultural Research, Extension, and Education Reform Act of 1998 is amended by inserting after section 404 (7 U.S.C. 7624) the following:

"SEC. 405. NATIONAL FOOD SAFETY TRAINING, EDUCATION, EXTENSION, OUTREACH, AND TECHNICAL ASSISTANCE PROGRAM.

"(a) In General.--The Secretary shall award grants under this section to carry out the competitive grant program established under section 1011(d) of the Federal Food, Drug, and Cosmetic Act, pursuant to any memoranda of understanding entered into under such section.

"(b) Integrated Approach.--The grant program described under subsection (a) shall be carried out under this section in a manner that facilitates the integration of food safety standards and guidance with the variety of agricultural production systems, encompassing conventional, sustainable, organic, and conservation and environmental practices.

"(c) Priority.--In awarding grants under this section, the Secretary shall give priority to projects that target small and medium-sized farms, beginning farmers, socially disadvantaged farmers, small processors, or small fresh fruit and vegetable merchant wholesalers.

"(d) Program Coordination.--

"(1) IN GENERAL.--The Secretary shall coordinate implementation of the grant program under this section with the National Integrated Food Safety Initiative.

"(2) INTERACTION.--The Secretary shall--

"(A) in carrying out the grant program under this section, take into consideration applied research, education, and extension results obtained from the National Integrated Food Safety Initiative; and

"(B) in determining the applied research agenda for the National Integrated Food Safety Initiative, take into consideration the needs articulated by participants in projects funded by the program under this section.

"(e) Grants.--

"(1) IN GENERAL.--In carrying out this section, the Secretary shall make competitive grants to support training, education, extension, outreach, and technical assistance projects that will help improve public health by increasing the understanding and adoption of established food safety standards, guidance, and protocols.

"(2) ENCOURAGED FEATURES.--The Secretary shall encourage projects carried out using grant funds under this section to include co-management of food safety, conservation systems, and ecological health.

"(3) MAXIMUM TERM AND SIZE OF GRANT.--

"(A) IN GENERAL.--A grant under this section shall have a term that is not more than 3 years.

"(B) LIMITATION ON GRANT FUNDING.-- The Secretary may not provide grant funding to an entity under this section after such entity has received 3 years of grant funding under this section.

"(f) Grant Eligibility.--

"(1) IN GENERAL.--To be eligible for a grant under this section, an entity shall be--

"(A) a State cooperative extension service;

"(B) a Federal, State, local, or tribal agency, a nonprofit community-based or non-governmental organization, or an organization representing owners and operators of farms, small food processors, or small fruit and vegetable merchant wholesalers that has a commitment to public health and expertise in administering programs that contribute to food safety;

"(C) an institution of higher education (as defined in section 101(a) of the Higher Education Act of 1965 (20 U.S.C. 1001(a))) or a foundation maintained by an institution of higher education;

"(D) a collaboration of 2 of more eligible entities described in this subsection; or

"(E) such other appropriate entity, as determined by the Secretary.

"(2) MULTISTATE PARTNERSHIPS.--Grants under this section may be made for projects involving more than 1 State.

"(g) Regional Balance.--In making grants under this section, the Secretary shall, to the maximum extent practicable, ensure--

"(1) geographic diversity; and

"(2) diversity of types of agricultural production.

"(h) Technical Assistance.--The Secretary may use funds made available under this section to provide technical assistance to grant recipients to further the purposes of this section.

"(i) Best Practices and Model Programs.--Based on evaluations of, and responses arising from, projects funded under this section, the Secretary may issue a set of recommended best practices and models for food safety training programs for agricultural producers, small food processors, and small fresh fruit and vegetable merchant wholesalers.

"(j) Authorization of Appropriations.--For the purposes of making grants under this section, there are authorized to be appropriated such sums as may be necessary for fiscal years 2011 through 2015.".

SEC. 210. ENHANCING FOOD SAFETY.

(a) Grants to Enhance Food Safety.--Section 1009 of the Federal Food, Drug, and Cosmetic Act (21 U.S.C. 399) is amended to read as follows:

"SEC. 1009. GRANTS TO ENHANCE FOOD SAFETY.

"(a) In General.--The Secretary is authorized to make grants to eligible entities to--

> "(1) undertake examinations, inspections, and investigations, and related food safety activities under section 702;

> "(2) train to the standards of the Secretary for the examination, inspection, and investigation of food manufacturing, processing, packing, holding, distribution, and importation, including as such examination, inspection, and investigation relate to retail food establishments;

> "(3) build the food safety capacity of the laboratories of such eligible entity, including the detection of zoonotic diseases;

> "(4) build the infrastructure and capacity of the food safety programs of such eligible entity to meet the standards as outlined in the grant application; and

> "(5) take appropriate action to protect the public health in response to--

>> "(A) a notification under section 1008, including planning and otherwise preparing to take such action; or

>> "(B) a recall of food under this Act.

"(b) Eligible Entities; Application.--

"(1) IN GENERAL.--In this section, the term 'eligible entity' means an entity--

"(A) that is--

"(i) a State;

"(ii) a locality;

"(iii) a territory;

"(iv) an Indian tribe (as defined in section 4(e) of the Indian Self-Determination and Education Assistance Act); or

"(v) a nonprofit food safety training entity that collaborates with 1 or more institutions of higher education; and

"(B) that submits an application to the Secretary at such time, in such manner, and including such information as the Secretary may reasonably require.

"(2) CONTENTS.--Each application submitted under paragraph (1) shall include--

"(A) an assurance that the eligible entity has developed plans to engage in the types of activities described in subsection (a);

"(B) a description of the types of activities to be funded by the grant;

"(C) an itemization of how grant funds received under this section will be expended;

"(D) a description of how grant activities will be monitored; and

"(E) an agreement by the eligible entity to report information required by the Secretary to conduct evaluations under this section.

"(c) Limitations.--The funds provided under subsection (a) shall be available to an eligible entity that receives a grant under this section only to the extent such entity funds the food safety programs of such entity independently of any grant under this section in each year of the grant at a level equal to the level of such funding in the previous year, increased by the Consumer Price Index. Such non-Federal matching funds may be provided directly or through donations from public or private entities and may be in cash or in-kind, fairly evaluated, including plant, equipment, or services.

"(d) Additional Authority.--The Secretary may--

"(1) award a grant under this section in each subsequent fiscal year without reapplication for a period of not more than 3 years, provided the requirements of subsection (c) are met for the previous fiscal year; and

"(2) award a grant under this section in a fiscal year for which the requirement of subsection (c) has not been met only if such requirement was not met because such funding was diverted for response to 1 or more natural disasters or in other extenuating circumstances that the Secretary may determine appropriate.

"(e) Duration of Awards.--The Secretary may award grants to an individual grant recipient under this section for periods of not more than 3 years. In the event the Secretary conducts a program evaluation, funding in the second year or third year of the grant, where applicable, shall be contingent on a successful program evaluation by the Secretary after the first year.

"(f) Progress and Evaluation.--

"(1) IN GENERAL.--The Secretary shall measure the status and success of each grant program authorized under the FDA Food Safety Modernization Act (and any amendment made by such Act), including the grant program under this section. A recipient of a grant described in the preceding sentence shall, at the end of each grant year, provide the Secretary with information on how grant funds were spent and the status of the efforts by such recipient to enhance food safety. To the extent practicable, the Secretary shall take the performance of such a grant recipient into account when determining whether to continue funding for such recipient.

"(2) NO DUPLICATION.--In carrying out paragraph (1), the Secretary shall not duplicate the efforts of the Secretary under other provisions of this Act or the FDA Food Safety Modernization Act that require measurement and review of the activities of grant recipients under either such Act.

"(g) Supplement Not Supplant.--Grant funds received under this section shall be used to supplement, and not supplant, non-Federal funds and any other Federal funds available to carry out the activities described in this section.

"(h) Authorization of Appropriations.--For the purpose of making grants under this section, there are authorized to be appropriated such sums as may be necessary for fiscal years 2011 through 2015.".

(b) Centers of Excellence.--Part P of the Public Health Service Act (42 U.S.C. 280g et seq.) is amended by adding at the end the following:

"SEC. 399V-5. FOOD SAFETY INTEGRATED CENTERS OF EXCELLENCE.

"(a) In General.--Not later than 1 year after the date of enactment of the FDA Food Safety Modernization Act, the Secretary, acting through the Director of the Centers for Disease Control and Prevention and in consultation with the working group described in subsection (b)(2), shall designate 5 Integrated Food Safety Centers of Excellence (referred to in this section as the 'Centers of Excellence') to serve as resources for Federal, State, and local public health professionals to respond to foodborne illness outbreaks. The Centers of Excellence shall be headquartered at selected State health departments.

"(b) Selection of Centers of Excellence.--

"(1) ELIGIBLE ENTITIES.--To be eligible to be designated as a Center of Excellence under subsection (a), an entity shall--

"(A) be a State health department;

"(B) partner with 1 or more institutions of higher education that have demonstrated knowledge, expertise, and meaningful experience with regional or national food production, processing, and distribution, as well as leadership in the laboratory, epidemiological, and environmental detection and investigation of foodborne illness; and

"(C) provide to the Secretary such information, at such time, and in such manner, as the Secretary may require.

"(2) WORKING GROUP.--Not later than 180 days after the date of enactment of the FDA Food Safety Modernization Act, the Secretary shall establish a diverse working group of experts and stakeholders from Federal, State, and local food safety and health agencies, the food industry, including food retailers and food manufacturers, consumer organizations, and academia to make recommendations to the Secretary regarding designations of the Centers of Excellence.

"(3) ADDITIONAL CENTERS OF EXCELLENCE.-- The Secretary may designate eligible entities to be regional Food Safety Centers of Excellence, in addition to the 5 Centers designated under subsection (a).

"(c) Activities.--Under the leadership of the Director of the Centers for Disease Control and Prevention, each Center of Excellence shall be based out of a selected State health department, which shall provide assistance to other regional, State, and local departments of health through activities that include--

"(1) providing resources, including timely information concerning symptoms and tests, for frontline health professionals interviewing individuals as part of routine surveillance and outbreak investigations;

"(2) providing analysis of the timeliness and effectiveness of foodborne disease surveillance and outbreak response activities;

"(3) providing training for epidemiological and environmental investigation of foodborne illness, including suggestions for streamlining and standardizing the investigation process;

"(4) establishing fellowships, stipends, and scholarships to train future epidemiological and food-safety leaders and to address critical workforce shortages;

"(5) training and coordinating State and local personnel;

"(6) strengthening capacity to participate in existing or new foodborne illness surveillance and environmental assessment information systems; and

"(7) conducting research and outreach activities focused on increasing prevention, communication, and education regarding food safety.

"(d) Report to Congress.--Not later than 2 years after the date of enactment of the FDA Food Safety Modernization Act, the Secretary shall submit to Congress a report that--

"(1) describes the effectiveness of the Centers of Excellence; and

"(2) provides legislative recommendations or describes additional resources required by the Centers of Excellence.

"(e) Authorization of Appropriations.--There is authorized to be appropriated such sums as may be necessary to carry out this section.

"(f) No Duplication of Effort.--In carrying out activities of the Centers of Excellence or other programs under this section, the Secretary shall not duplicate other Federal foodborne illness response efforts.".

SEC. 211. IMPROVING THE REPORTABLE FOOD REGISTRY.

(a) In General.--Section 417 (21 U.S.C. 350f) is amended--

(1) by redesignating subsections (f) through (k) as subsections (i) through (n), respectively; and

(2) by inserting after subsection (e) the following:

"(f) Critical Information.--Except with respect to fruits and vegetables that are raw agricultural commodities, not more than 18 months after the date of enactment of the FDA Food Safety Modernization Act, the Secretary may require a responsible party to submit to the Secretary consumer-oriented information regarding a reportable food, which shall include--

"(1) a description of the article of food as provided in subsection (e)(3);

"(2) as provided in subsection (e)(7), affected product identification codes, such as UPC, SKU, or lot or batch numbers sufficient for the consumer to identify the article of food;

"(3) contact information for the responsible party as provided in subsection (e)(8); and

"(4) any other information the Secretary determines is necessary to enable a consumer to accurately identify whether such consumer is in possession of the reportable food.

"(g) Grocery Store Notification.--

"(1) ACTION BY SECRETARY.--The Secretary shall--

"(A) prepare the critical information described under subsection (f) for a reportable food as a standardized one-page summary;

"(B) publish such one-page summary on the Internet website of the Food and Drug Administration in a format that can be easily printed by a grocery store for purposes of consumer notification.

"(2) ACTION BY GROCERY STORE.--A notification described under paragraph (1)(B) shall include the date and time such summary was posted on the Internet website of the Food and Drug Administration.

"(h) Consumer Notification.--

"(1) IN GENERAL.--If a grocery store sold a reportable food that is the subject of the posting and such establishment is part of chain of establishments with 15 or more physical locations, then such establishment shall, not later than 24 hours after a one page summary described in subsection (g) is published, prominently display such summary or the information from such summary via at least one of the methods identified under paragraph (2) and maintain the display for 14 days.

"(2) LIST OF CONSPICUOUS LOCATIONS.-- Not more than 1 year after the date of enactment of the FDA Food Safety Modernization Act, the Secretary shall develop and publish a list of acceptable conspicuous locations and manners, from which grocery stores shall select at least one, for providing the notification required in paragraph (1). Such list shall include--

"(A) posting the notification at or near the register;

"(B) providing the location of the reportable food;

"(C) providing targeted recall information given to customers upon purchase of a food; and

"(D) other such prominent and conspicuous locations and manners utilized by grocery stores as of the date of the enactment of the FDA Food Safety Modernization Act to provide notice of such recalls to consumers as considered appropriate by the Secretary.".

(b) Prohibited Act.--Section 301 (21 U.S.C. 331), as amended by section 206, is amended by adding at the end the following:

"(yy) The knowing and willful failure to comply with the notification requirement under section 417(h).".

(c) Conforming Amendment.--Section 301(e) (21 U.S.C. 331(e)) is amended by striking "417(g)" and inserting "417(j)".

TITLE III--IMPROVING THE SAFETY OF IMPORTED FOOD

SEC. 301. FOREIGN SUPPLIER VERIFICATION PROGRAM.

(a) In General.--Chapter VIII (21 U.S.C. 381 et seq.) is amended by adding at the end the following:

> "**SEC. 805. FOREIGN SUPPLIER VERIFICATION PROGRAM.**
>
> "(a) In General.--
>
> > "(1) VERIFICATION REQUIREMENT.--Except as provided under subsections (e) and (f), each importer shall perform risk-based foreign supplier verification activities for the purpose of verifying that the food imported by the importer or agent of an importer is--
> >
> > > "(A) produced in compliance with the requirements of section 418 or section 419, as appropriate; and
> > >
> > > "(B) is not adulterated under section 402 or misbranded under section 403(w).
> >
> > "(2) IMPORTER DEFINED.--For purposes of this section, the term 'importer' means, with respect to an article of food

"(A) the United States owner or consignee of the article of food at the time of entry of such article into the United States; or

"(B) in the case when there is no United States owner or consignee as described in subparagraph (A), the United States agent or representative of a foreign owner or consignee of the article of food at the time of entry of such article into the United States.

"(b) Guidance.--Not later than 1 year after the date of enactment of the FDA Food Safety Modernization Act, the Secretary shall issue guidance to assist importers in developing foreign supplier verification programs.

"(c) Regulations.--

"(1) IN GENERAL.--Not later than 1 year after the date of enactment of the FDA Food Safety Modernization Act, the Secretary shall promulgate regulations to provide for the content of the foreign supplier verification program established under subsection (a).

"(2) REQUIREMENTS.--The regulations promulgated under paragraph (1)--

"(A) shall require that the foreign supplier verification program of each importer be adequate to provide <u>assurances that each foreign supplier to the importer produces the imported food in compliance with</u>--

"<u>(i) processes and procedures, including reasonably appropriate risk-based preventive controls, that provide the same level of public health protection</u> as those required under section 418 or section 419 (taking into consideration variances granted under section 419), as appropriate; and

"(ii) section 402 and section 403(w).

"(B) shall include such other requirements as the Secretary deems necessary and appropriate to verify that food imported into the United States is as safe as food produced and sold within the United States.

"(3) CONSIDERATIONS.--In promulgating regulations under this subsection, the Secretary shall, as appropriate, take into account differences among importers and types of imported foods, including based on the level of risk posed by the imported food.

"(4) ACTIVITIES.--Verification activities under a foreign supplier verification program under this section may include monitoring records for shipments, lot-by-lot certification of compliance, annual on-site inspections, checking the hazard analysis and risk-based preventive control plan of the foreign supplier, and periodically testing and sampling shipments.

"(d) Record Maintenance and Access.--Records of an importer related to a foreign supplier verification program shall be maintained for a period of not less than 2 years and shall be made available promptly to a duly authorized representative of the Secretary upon request.

"(e) Exemption of Seafood, Juice, and Low-acid Canned Food Facilities in Compliance With HACCP.--This section shall not apply to a facility if the owner, operator, or agent in charge of such facility is required to comply with, and is in compliance with, 1 of the following standards and regulations with respect to such facility:

"(1) The Seafood Hazard Analysis Critical Control Points Program of the Food and Drug Administration.

"(2) The Juice Hazard Analysis Critical Control Points Program of the Food and Drug Administration.

"(3) The Thermally Processed Low-Acid Foods Packaged in Hermetically Sealed Containers standards of the Food and Drug Administration (or any successor standards).

The exemption under paragraph (3) shall apply only with respect to microbiological hazards that are regulated under the standards for Thermally Processed Low-Acid Foods Packaged in Hermetically Sealed Containers under part 113 of chapter 21, Code of Federal Regulations (or any successor regulations).

"(f) Additional Exemptions.--The Secretary, by notice published in the Federal Register, shall establish an exemption from the requirements of this section for articles of food imported in small quantities for research and evaluation purposes or for personal consumption, provided that such foods are not intended for retail sale and are not sold or distributed to the public.

"(g) Publication of List of Participants.--The Secretary shall publish and maintain on the Internet Web site of the Food and Drug Administration a current list that includes the name of, location of, and other information deemed necessary by the Secretary about, importers participating under this section.".

(b) Prohibited Act.--Section 301 (21 U.S.C. 331), as amended by section 211, is amended by adding at the end the following:

"(zz) The importation or offering for importation of a food if the importer (as defined in section 805) does not have in place a foreign supplier verification program in compliance with such section 805.".

(c) Imports.--Section 801(a) (21 U.S.C. 381(a)) is amended by adding "or the importer (as defined in section 805) is in violation of such section 805" after "or in violation of section 505".

(d) Effective Date.--The amendments made by this section shall take effect 2 years after the date of enactment of this Act.

SEC. 302. VOLUNTARY QUALIFIED IMPORTER PROGRAM.

Chapter VIII (21 U.S.C. 381 et seq.), as amended by section 301, is amended by adding at the end the following:

"SEC. 806. VOLUNTARY QUALIFIED IMPORTER PROGRAM.

"(a) In General.--Beginning not later than 18 months after the date of enactment of the FDA Food Safety Modernization Act, the Secretary shall--

"(1) establish a program, in consultation with the Secretary of Homeland Security--

"(A) to provide for the expedited review and importation of food offered for importation by importers who have voluntarily agreed to participate in such program; and

"(B) consistent with section 808, establish a process for the issuance of a facility certification to accompany food offered for importation by importers who have voluntarily agreed to participate in such program; and

TEXT OF AMENDMENTS
(Senate - November 18, 2010)

"(2) issue a guidance document related to participation in, revocation of such participation in, reinstatement in, and compliance with, such program.

"(b) Voluntary Participation.--An importer may request the Secretary to provide for the expedited review and importation of designated foods in accordance with the program established by the Secretary under subsection (a).

"(c) Notice of Intent To Participate.--An importer that intends to participate in the program under this section in a fiscal year shall submit a notice and application to the Secretary of such intent at the time and in a manner established by the Secretary.

"(d) Eligibility.--Eligibility shall be limited to an importer offering food for importation from a facility that has a certification described in subsection (a). In reviewing the applications and making determinations on such applications, the Secretary shall consider the risk of the food to be imported based on factors, such as the following:

"(1) The known safety risks of the food to be imported.

"(2) The compliance history of foreign suppliers used by the importer, as appropriate.

"(3) The capability of the regulatory system of the country of export to ensure compliance with United States food safety standards for a designated food.

"(4) The compliance of the importer with the requirements of section 805.

"(5) The recordkeeping, testing, inspections and audits of facilities, traceability of articles of food, temperature controls, and sourcing practices of the importer.

"(6) The potential risk for intentional adulteration of the food.

"(7) Any other factor that the Secretary determines appropriate.

"(e) Review and Revocation.--Any importer qualified by the Secretary in accordance with the eligibility criteria set forth in this section shall be reevaluated not less often than once every 3 years and the Secretary shall promptly revoke the qualified importer status of any importer found not to be in compliance with such criteria.

"(f) False Statements.--Any statement or representation made by an importer to the Secretary shall be subject to section 1001 of title 18, United States Code.

"(g) Definition.--For purposes of this section, the term 'importer' means the person that brings food, or causes food to be brought, from a foreign country into the customs territory of the United States.".

SEC. 303. AUTHORITY TO REQUIRE IMPORT CERTIFICATIONS FOR FOOD.

(a) In General.--Section 801(a) (21 U.S.C. 381(a)) is amended by inserting after the third sentence the following: "With respect to an article of food, if importation of such food is subject to, but not compliant with, the requirement under subsection (q) that such food be accompanied by a certification or other assurance that the food meets applicable requirements of this Act, then such article shall be refused admission.".

(b) Addition of Certification Requirement.--Section 801 (21 U.S.C. 381) is amended by adding at the end the following new subsection:

"(q) Certifications Concerning Imported Foods.--

"(1) IN GENERAL.--The Secretary may require, as a condition of granting admission to an article of food imported or offered for import into the United States, that an entity described in paragraph (3) provide a <u>certification, or such other assurances as the Secretary determines appropriate, that the article of food complies with applicable requirements of this Act.</u> Such certification or assurances may be provided in the form of shipment-specific certificates, a listing of certified facilities that manufacture, process, pack, or hold such food, or in such other form as the Secretary may specify.

"(2) FACTORS TO BE CONSIDERED IN REQUIRING CERTIFICATION.--The Secretary shall base the determination that an article of food is required to have a certification described in paragraph (1) on the risk of the food, including--

"(A) known safety risks associated with the food;

"(B) known food safety risks associated with the country, territory, or region of origin of the food;

"(C) a finding by the Secretary, supported by scientific, risk-based evidence, that--

"(i) the food safety programs, systems, and standards in the country, territory, or region of origin of the food are inadequate to ensure that the article of food is as safe as a similar article of food that is manufactured, processed, packed, or held in the United States in accordance with the requirements of this Act; and

"(ii) the certification would assist the Secretary in determining whether to refuse or admit the article of food under subsection (a); and

"(D) information submitted to the Secretary in accordance with the process established in paragraph (7).

"(3) CERTIFYING ENTITIES.--For purposes of paragraph (1), entities that shall provide the certification or assurances described in such paragraph are--

"(A) an agency or a representative of the government of the country from which the article of food at issue originated, as designated by the Secretary; or

"(B) such other persons or entities accredited pursuant to section 808 to provide such certification or assurance.

"(4) RENEWAL AND REFUSAL OF CERTIFICATIONS.--The Secretary may--

"(A) require that any certification or other assurance provided by an entity specified in paragraph (2) be renewed by such entity at such times as the Secretary determines appropriate; and

"(B) refuse to accept any certification or assurance if the Secretary determines that such certification or assurance is not valid or reliable.

"(5) ELECTRONIC SUBMISSION.--The Secretary shall provide for the electronic submission of certifications under this subsection.

"(6) FALSE STATEMENTS.--Any statement or representation made by an entity described in paragraph (2) to the Secretary shall be subject to section 1001 of title 18, United States Code.

"(7) ASSESSMENT OF FOOD SAFETY PROGRAMS, SYSTEMS, AND STANDARDS.--If the Secretary determines that the food safety programs, systems, and standards in a foreign region, country, or territory are inadequate to ensure that an article of food is as safe as a similar article of food that is manufactured, processed, packed, or held in the United States in accordance with the requirements of this Act, the Secretary shall, to the extent practicable, identify such inadequacies and establish a process by which the foreign region, country, or territory may inform the Secretary of improvements made to such food safety program, system, or standard and demonstrate that those controls are adequate to ensure that an article of food is as safe as a similar article of food that is manufactured, processed, packed, or held in the United States in accordance with the requirements of this Act.".

(c) Conforming Technical Amendment.--Section 801(b) (21 U.S.C. 381(b)) is amended in the second sentence by striking "with respect to an article included within the provision of the fourth sentence of subsection (a)" and inserting "with respect to an article described in subsection (a) relating to the requirements of sections 760 or 761,".

(d) No Limit on Authority.--Nothing in the amendments made by this section shall limit the authority of the Secretary to conduct inspections of imported food or to take such other steps as the Secretary deems appropriate to determine the admissibility of imported food.

SEC. 304. PRIOR NOTICE OF IMPORTED FOOD SHIPMENTS.

(a) In General.--Section 801(m)(1) (21 U.S.C. 381(m)(1)) is amended by inserting "any country to which the article has been refused entry;" after "the country from which the article is shipped;".

(b) Regulations.--Not later than 120 days after the date of enactment of this Act, the Secretary shall issue an interim final rule amending subpart I of part 1 of title 21, Code of Federal Regulations, to implement the amendment made by this section.

(c) Effective Date.--The amendment made by this section shall take effect 180 days after the date of enactment of this Act.

SEC. 305. BUILDING CAPACITY OF FOREIGN GOVERNMENTS WITH RESPECT TO FOOD SAFETY.

(a) In General.--The Secretary shall, not later than 2 years of the date of enactment of this Act, develop a comprehensive plan to expand the technical, scientific, and regulatory food safety capacity of foreign governments, and their respective food industries, from which foods are exported to the United States.

(b) Consultation.--In developing the plan under subsection (a), the Secretary shall consult with the Secretary of Agriculture, Secretary of State, Secretary of the Treasury, the Secretary of Homeland Security, the United States Trade Representative, and the Secretary of Commerce, representatives of the food industry, appropriate foreign government officials, nongovernmental organizations that represent the interests of consumers, and other stakeholders.

(c) Plan.--The plan developed under subsection (a) shall include, as appropriate, the following:

(1) Recommendations for bilateral and multilateral arrangements and agreements, including provisions to provide for responsibility of exporting countries to ensure the safety of food.

(2) Provisions for secure electronic data sharing.

(3) Provisions for mutual recognition of inspection reports.

(4) Training of foreign governments and food producers on United States requirements for safe food.

(5) Recommendations on whether and how to harmonize requirements under the Codex Alimentarius.

(6) Provisions for the multilateral acceptance of laboratory methods and testing and detection techniques.

(d) Rule of Construction.--Nothing in this section shall be construed to affect the regulation of dietary supplements under the Dietary Supplement Health and Education Act of 1994 (Public Law 103-417).

SEC. 306. INSPECTION OF FOREIGN FOOD FACILITIES.

(a) In General.--Chapter VIII (21 U.S.C. 381 et seq.), as amended by section 302, is amended by inserting at the end the following:

> ### "SEC. 807. INSPECTION OF FOREIGN FOOD FACILITIES.
>
> "(a) Inspection.--The Secretary--
>
> > "(1) may enter into arrangements and agreements with foreign governments to facilitate the inspection of foreign facilities registered under section 415; and
> >
> > "(2) shall direct resources to inspections of foreign facilities, suppliers, and food types, especially such facilities, suppliers, and food types that present a high risk (as identified by the Secretary), to help ensure the safety and security of the food supply of the United States.
>
> "(b) Effect of Inability To Inspect.--Notwithstanding any other provision of law, food shall be refused admission into the United States if it is from a foreign factory, warehouse, or other establishment of which the owner, operator, or agent in charge, or the government of the foreign country, refuses to permit entry of United States inspectors or other individuals duly designated by the Secretary, upon request, to inspect such factory, warehouse, or other establishment. For purposes of this subsection, such an owner, operator, or agent in charge shall be considered to have refused an inspection if such owner, operator, or agent in charge does not permit an inspection of a factory, warehouse, or other establishment during the 24-hour period after such request is submitted, or after such other time period, as agreed upon by the Secretary and the foreign factory, warehouse, or other establishment.".

(b) Inspection by the Secretary of Commerce.--

(1) IN GENERAL.--The Secretary of Commerce, in coordination with the Secretary of Health and Human Services, may send 1 or more inspectors to a country or facility of an exporter from which seafood imported into the United States originates. The inspectors shall assess practices and processes used in connection with the farming, cultivation, harvesting, preparation for market, or transportation of such seafood and may provide technical assistance related to such activities.

(2) INSPECTION REPORT.--

(A) IN GENERAL.--The Secretary of Health and Human Services, in coordination with the Secretary of Commerce, shall--

(i) prepare an inspection report for each inspection conducted under paragraph (1);

(ii) provide the report to the country or exporter that is the subject of the report; and

(iii) provide a 30-day period during which the country or exporter may provide a rebuttal or other comments on the findings of the report to the Secretary of Health and Human Services.

(B) DISTRIBUTION AND USE OF REPORT.--The Secretary of Health and Human Services shall consider the inspection reports described in subparagraph (A) in distributing inspection resources under section 421 of the Federal Food, Drug, and Cosmetic Act, as added by section 201.

SEC. 307. ACCREDITATION OF THIRD-PARTY AUDITORS.

Chapter VIII (21 U.S.C. 381 et seq.), as amended by section 306, is amended by adding at the end the following:

"SEC. 808. ACCREDITATION OF THIRD-PARTY AUDITORS.

"(a) Definitions.--In this section:

> "(1) AUDIT AGENT.--The term 'audit agent' means an individual who is an employee or agent of an accredited third-party auditor and, although not individually accredited, is qualified to conduct food safety audits on behalf of an accredited third-party auditor.

> "(2) ACCREDITATION BODY.--The term 'accreditation body' means an authority that performs accreditation of third-party auditors.

> "(3) THIRD-PARTY AUDITOR.--The term 'third-party auditor' means a foreign government, agency of a foreign government, foreign cooperative, or any other third party, as the Secretary determines appropriate in accordance with the model standards described in subsection (b)(2), that is eligible to be considered for accreditation to conduct food safety audits to certify that eligible entities meet the applicable requirements of this section. A third-party auditor may be a single individual. A third-party auditor may employ or use audit agents to help conduct consultative and regulatory audits.

> "(4) ACCREDITED THIRD-PARTY AUDITOR.--The term 'accredited third-party auditor' means a third-party auditor accredited by an accreditation body to conduct audits of eligible entities to certify that such eligible entities meet the applicable requirements of this section. An accredited third-party auditor may be an individual who

conducts food safety audits to certify that eligible entities meet the applicable requirements of this section.

"(5) CONSULTATIVE AUDIT.--The term 'consultative audit' means an audit of an eligible entity--

> "(A) to determine whether such entity is in compliance with the provisions of this Act and with applicable industry standards and practices; and
>
> "(B) the results of which are for internal purposes only.

"(6) ELIGIBLE ENTITY.--The term 'eligible entity' means a foreign entity, including a foreign facility registered under section 415, in the food import supply chain that chooses to be audited by an accredited third-party auditor or the audit agent of such accredited third-party auditor.

"(7) REGULATORY AUDIT.--The term 'regulatory audit' means an audit of an eligible entity--

> "(A) to determine whether such entity is in compliance with the provisions of this Act; and
>
> "(B) the results of which determine--
>
> > "(i) whether an article of food manufactured, processed, packed, or held by such entity is eligible to receive a food certification under section 801(q); or
> >
> > "(ii) whether a facility is eligible to receive a facility certification under section 806(a) for purposes of participating in the program under section 806.

"(b) Accreditation System.--

"(1) ACCREDITATION BODIES.--

"(A) RECOGNITION OF ACCREDITATION BODIES.--

"(i) IN GENERAL.--Not later than 2 years after the date of enactment of the FDA Food Safety Modernization Act, the Secretary shall establish a system for the recognition of accreditation bodies that accredit third-party auditors to certify that eligible entities meet the applicable requirements of this section.

"(ii) DIRECT ACCREDITATION.--If, by the date that is 2 years after the date of establishment of the system described in clause (i), the Secretary has not identified and recognized an accreditation body to meet the requirements of this section, the Secretary may directly accredit third-party auditors.

"(B) NOTIFICATION.--Each accreditation body recognized by the Secretary shall submit to the Secretary a list of all accredited third-party auditors accredited by such body and the audit agents of such auditors.

"(C) REVOCATION OF RECOGNITION AS AN ACCREDITATION BODY.--The Secretary shall promptly revoke the recognition of any accreditation body found not to be in compliance with the requirements of this section.

"(D) REINSTATEMENT.--The Secretary shall establish procedures to reinstate recognition of an accreditation body if the Secretary determines, based on evidence presented by such accreditation body, that revocation was inappropriate or that the body meets the requirements for recognition under this section.

"(2) MODEL ACCREDITATION STANDARDS.--Not later than 18 months after the date of enactment of the FDA Food Safety Modernization Act, the Secretary shall develop model standards, including requirements for regulatory audit reports, and each recognized accreditation body shall ensure that third-party auditors and audit agents of such auditors meet such standards in order to qualify such third-party auditors as accredited third-party auditors under this section. In developing the model standards, the Secretary shall look to standards in place on the date of the enactment of this section for guidance, to avoid unnecessary duplication of efforts and costs.

"(c) Third-party Auditors.--

"(1) REQUIREMENTS FOR ACCREDITATION AS A THIRD-PARTY AUDITOR.--

"(A) FOREIGN GOVERNMENTS.--Prior to accrediting a foreign government or an agency of a foreign government as an accredited third-party auditor, the accreditation body (or, in the case of direct accreditation under subsection (b)(1)(A)(ii), the Secretary) shall perform such reviews and audits of food safety programs, systems, and standards of the government or agency of the government as the Secretary deems necessary, including requirements under the model standards developed under subsection (b)(2), to determine that the foreign government or agency of the foreign government is capable of adequately ensuring that eligible entities or foods certified by such government or agency meet the requirements of this Act with respect to food manufactured, processed, packed, or held for import into the United States.

"(B) FOREIGN COOPERATIVES AND OTHER THIRD PARTIES.--Prior to accrediting a foreign cooperative that aggregates the products of growers or processors, or any other third party to be an accredited third-party auditor, the accreditation body (or, in the case of direct accreditation under subsection (b)(1)(A)(ii), the Secretary) shall perform such reviews and audits of the training and qualifications of audit agents used by that cooperative or party and conduct such reviews of internal systems and such other investigation of the cooperative or party as the Secretary deems necessary, including requirements under the model standards developed under subsection (b)(2), to determine that each eligible entity certified by the cooperative or party has systems and standards in use to ensure that such entity or food meets the requirements of this Act.

"(2) REQUIREMENT TO ISSUE CERTIFICATION OF ELIGIBLE ENTITIES OR FOODS.--

"(A) IN GENERAL.--An accreditation body (or, in the case of direct accreditation under subsection (b)(1)(A)(ii), the Secretary) may not accredit a third-party auditor unless such third-party auditor agrees to issue a written and, as appropriate, electronic food certification, described in section 801(q), or facility certification under section 806(a), as appropriate, to accompany each food shipment for import into the United States from an eligible entity, subject to requirements set forth by the Secretary. Such written or electronic certification may be included with other documentation regarding such food shipment. The Secretary shall consider certifications under section 801(q) and participation in the voluntary qualified importer program described in section 806 when targeting inspection resources under section 421.

"(B) PURPOSE OF CERTIFICATION.--The Secretary shall use certification provided by accredited third-party auditors to--

"(i) determine, in conjunction with any other assurances the Secretary may require under section 801(q), whether a food satisfies the requirements of such section; and

"(ii) determine whether a facility is eligible to be a facility from which food may be offered for import under the voluntary qualified importer program under section 806.

"(C) REQUIREMENTS FOR ISSUING CERTIFICATION.--

"(i) IN GENERAL.--An accredited third-party auditor shall issue a food certification under section 801(q) or a facility certification described under subparagraph (B) only after conducting a regulatory audit and such other activities that may be necessary to establish compliance with the requirements of such sections.

"(ii)   PROVISION   OF CERTIFICATION.--Only an accredited third-party auditor or the Secretary may provide a facility certification under section 806(a). Only those parties described in 801(q)(3) or the Secretary may provide a food certification under 301(g).

"(3) AUDIT REPORT SUBMISSION REQUIREMENTS.--

"(A) REQUIREMENTS IN GENERAL.--As a condition of accreditation, not later than 45 days after conducting an audit, an accredited third-party auditor or audit agent of such auditor shall prepare, and, in the case of a regulatory audit, submit, the audit report for each audit conducted, in a form and manner designated by the Secretary, which shall include--

"(i) the identity of the persons at the audited eligible entity responsible for compliance with food safety requirements;

"(ii) the dates of the audit;

"(iii) the scope of the audit; and

"(iv) any other information required by the Secretary that relates to or may influence an assessment of compliance with this Act.

"(B) RECORDS.--Following any accreditation of a third-party auditor, the Secretary may, at any time, require the accredited third-party auditor to submit to the Secretary an onsite audit report and such other reports or documents required as part of the audit process, for any eligible entity certified by the third-party auditor or audit agent of such auditor. Such report may include documentation that the eligible entity is in compliance with any applicable registration requirements.

"(C) LIMITATION.--The requirement under subparagraph (B) shall not include any report or other documents resulting from a consultative audit by the accredited third-party auditor, except that the Secretary may access the results of a consultative audit in accordance with section 414.

"(4) REQUIREMENTS OF ACCREDITED THIRD-PARTY AUDITORS AND AUDIT AGENTS OF SUCH AUDITORS.--

"(A) RISKS TO PUBLIC HEALTH.--If, at any time during an audit, an accredited third-party auditor or audit agent of such auditor discovers a condition that could cause or contribute to a serious risk to the public health, such auditor shall immediately notify the Secretary of--

"(i) the identification of the eligible entity subject to the audit; and

"(ii) such condition.

"(B) TYPES OF AUDITS.--An accredited third-party auditor or audit agent of such auditor may perform consultative and regulatory audits of eligible entities.

"(C) LIMITATIONS.--

"(i) IN GENERAL.--An accredited third party auditor may not perform a regulatory audit of an eligible entity if such agent has performed a consultative audit or a regulatory audit of such eligible entity during the previous 13-month period.

"(ii) WAIVER.--The Secretary may waive the application of clause (i) if the Secretary determines that there is insufficient access to accredited third-party auditors in a country or region.

"(5) CONFLICTS OF INTEREST.--

"(A) THIRD-PARTY AUDITORS.--An accredited third-party auditor shall--

"(i) not be owned, managed, or controlled by any person that owns or operates an eligible entity to be certified by such auditor;

"(ii) in carrying out audits of eligible entities under this section, have procedures to ensure against the use of any officer or employee of such auditor that has a financial conflict of interest regarding an eligible entity to be certified by such auditor; and

"(iii) annually make available to the Secretary disclosures of the extent to which such auditor and the officers and employees of such auditor have maintained compliance with clauses (i) and (ii) relating to financial conflicts of interest.

"(B) AUDIT AGENTS.--An audit agent shall--

"(i) not own or operate an eligible entity to be audited by such agent;

"(ii) in carrying out audits of eligible entities under this section, have procedures to ensure that such agent does not have a financial conflict of interest regarding an eligible entity to be audited by such agent; and

"(iii) annually make available to the Secretary disclosures of the extent to which such agent has maintained compliance with clauses (i) and (ii) relating to financial conflicts of interest.

"(C) REGULATIONS.--The Secretary shall promulgate regulations not later than 18 months after the date of enactment of the FDA Food Safety Modernization Act to implement this section and to ensure that there are protections against conflicts of interest between an accredited third-party auditor and the eligible entity to be certified by such auditor or audited by such audit agent. Such regulations shall include--

"(i) requiring that audits performed under this section be unannounced;

"(ii) a structure to decrease the potential for conflicts of interest, including timing and public disclosure, for fees paid by eligible entities to accredited third-party auditors; and "(iii) appropriate limits on financial affiliations between an accredited third-party auditor or audit agents of such auditor and any person that owns or operates an eligible entity to be certified by such auditor, as described in subparagraphs (A) and (B).

"(6) WITHDRAWAL OF ACCREDITATION.--

"(A) IN GENERAL.--The Secretary shall withdraw accreditation from an accredited third-party auditor--

"(i) if food certified under section 801(q) or from a facility certified under paragraph (2)(B) by such third-party auditor is linked to an outbreak of foodborne illness that has a reasonable probability of causing serious adverse health consequences or death in humans or animals;

"(ii) following an evaluation and finding by the Secretary that the third-party auditor no longer meets the requirements for accreditation; or

"(iii) following a refusal to allow United States officials to conduct such audits and investigations as may be necessary to ensure continued compliance with the requirements set forth in this section.

"(B) ADDITIONAL BASIS FOR WITHDRAWAL OF ACCREDITATION.--The Secretary may withdraw accreditation from an accredited third-party auditor in the case that such third-party auditor is accredited by an accreditation body for which recognition as an accreditation body under subsection (b)(1)(C) is revoked, if the Secretary determines that there is good cause for the withdrawal.

"(C) EXCEPTION.--The Secretary may waive the application of subparagraph (A)(i) if the Secretary--

"(i) conducts an investigation of the material facts related to the outbreak of human or animal illness; and

"(ii) reviews the steps or actions taken by the third party auditor to justify the certification and determines that the accredited third-party auditor satisfied the requirements under section 801(q) of certifying the food, or the requirements under paragraph (2)(B) of certifying the entity.

"(7) REACCREDITATION.--The Secretary shall establish procedures to reinstate the accreditation of a third-party auditor for which accreditation has been withdrawn under paragraph (6)--

"(A) if the Secretary determines, based on evidence presented, that the third-party auditor satisfies the requirements of this section and adequate grounds for revocation no longer exist; and

"(B) in the case of a third-party auditor accredited by an accreditation body for which recognition as an accreditation body under subsection (b)(1)(C) is revoked--

"(i) if the third-party auditor becomes accredited not later than 1 year after revocation of accreditation under paragraph (6)(A), through direct accreditation under subsection (b)(1)(A)(ii) or by an accreditation body in good standing; or

"(ii) under such conditions as the Secretary may require for a third-party auditor under paragraph (6)(B).

"(8) NEUTRALIZING COSTS.--The Secretary shall establish by regulation a reimbursement (user fee) program, similar to the method described in section 203(h) of the Agriculture Marketing Act of 1946, by which the Secretary assesses fees and requires accredited third-party auditors and audit agents to reimburse the Food and Drug Administration for the work performed to establish and administer the accreditation system under this section. The Secretary shall make operating this program revenue-neutral and shall not generate surplus revenue from such a reimbursement mechanism. Fees authorized under this paragraph shall be collected and available for obligation only to the extent and in the amount provided in advance in appropriation Acts. Such fees are authorized to remain available until expended.

"(d) Recertification of Eligible Entities.--An eligible entity shall apply for annual recertification by an accredited third-party auditor if such entity--

"(1) intends to participate in voluntary qualified importer program under section 806; or

"(2) is required to provide to the Secretary a certification under section 801(q) for any food from such entity.

"(e) False Statements.--Any statement or representation made--

"(1) by an employee or agent of an eligible entity to an accredited third-party auditor or audit agent; or

"(2) by an accredited third-party auditor to the Secretary,

shall be subject to section 1001 of title 18, United States Code.

"(f) Monitoring.--To ensure compliance with the requirements of this section, the Secretary shall--

"(1) periodically, or at least once every 4 years, reevaluate the accreditation bodies described in subsection (b)(1);

"(2) periodically, or at least once every 4 years, evaluate the performance of each accredited third-party auditor, through the review of regulatory audit reports by such auditors, the compliance history as available of eligible entities certified by such auditors, and any other measures deemed necessary by the Secretary;

"(3) at any time, conduct an onsite audit of any eligible entity certified by an accredited third-party auditor, with or without the auditor present; and

"(4) take any other measures deemed necessary by the Secretary.

"(g) Publicly Available Registry.--The Secretary shall establish a publicly available registry of accreditation bodies and of accredited third-party auditors, including the name of, contact information for, and other information deemed necessary by the Secretary about such bodies and auditors.

"(h) Limitations.--

　　"(1) NO EFFECT ON SECTION 704 INSPECTIONS.-- The audits performed under this section shall not be considered inspections under section 704.

　　"(2) NO EFFECT ON INSPECTION AUTHORITY.-- Nothing in this section affects the authority of the Secretary to inspect any eligible entity pursuant to this Act.".

SEC. 308. FOREIGN OFFICES OF THE FOOD AND DRUG ADMINISTRATION.

(a) In General.--The Secretary shall establish offices of the Food and Drug Administration in foreign countries selected by the Secretary, to provide assistance to the appropriate governmental entities of such countries with respect to measures to provide for the safety of articles of food and other products regulated by the Food and Drug Administration exported by such country to the United States, including by directly conducting risk-based inspections of such articles and supporting such inspections by such governmental entity.

(b) Consultation.--In establishing the foreign offices described in subsection (a), the Secretary shall consult with the Secretary of State, the Secretary of Homeland Security, and the United States Trade Representative.

(c) Report.--Not later than October 1, 2011, the Secretary shall submit to Congress a report on the basis for the selection by the Secretary of the foreign countries in which the Secretary established offices, the progress which such offices have made with respect to assisting the governments of such countries in providing for the safety of articles of food and other products regulated by the Food and Drug Administration exported to the United States, and the plans of the Secretary for establishing additional foreign offices of the Food and Drug Administration, as appropriate.

SEC. 309. SMUGGLED FOOD.

(a) In General.--Not later than 180 days after the enactment of this Act, the Secretary shall, in coordination with the Secretary of Homeland Security, develop and implement a strategy to better identify smuggled food and prevent entry of such food into the United States.

(b) Notification to Homeland Security.--Not later than 10 days after the Secretary identifies a smuggled food that the Secretary believes would cause serious adverse health consequences or death to humans or animals, the Secretary shall provide to the Secretary of Homeland Security a notification under section 417(n) of the Federal Food, Drug, and Cosmetic Act (21 U.S.C. 350f(k)) describing the smuggled food and, if available, the names of the individuals or entities that attempted to import such food into the United States.

(c) Public Notification.--If the Secretary--

  (1) identifies a smuggled food;

  (2) reasonably believes exposure to the food would cause serious adverse health consequences or death to humans or animals; and

  (3) reasonably believes that the food has entered domestic commerce and is likely to be consumed,

the Secretary shall promptly issue a press release describing that food and shall use other emergency communication or recall networks, as appropriate, to warn consumers and vendors about the potential threat.

(d) Effect of Section.--Nothing in this section shall affect the authority of the Secretary to issue public notifications under other circumstances.

(e) Definition.--In this subsection, the term "smuggled food" means any food that a person introduces into the United States through fraudulent means or with the intent to defraud or mislead.

TITLE IV--MISCELLANEOUS PROVISIONS

SEC. 401. FUNDING FOR FOOD SAFETY.

(a) In General.--There are authorized to be appropriated to carry out the activities of the Center for Food Safety and Applied Nutrition, the Center for Veterinary Medicine, and related field activities in the Office of Regulatory Affairs of the Food and Drug Administration such sums as may be necessary for fiscal years 2011 through 2015.

(b) Increased Number of Field Staff.--

> (1) IN GENERAL.--To carry out the activities of the Center for Food Safety and Applied Nutrition, the Center for Veterinary Medicine, and related field activities of the Office of Regulatory Affairs of the Food and Drug Administration, the Secretary of Health and Human Services shall increase the field staff of such Centers and Office with a goal of not fewer than--

>> (A) 4,000 staff members in fiscal year 2011;

>> (B) 4,200 staff members in fiscal year 2012;

>> (C) 4,600 staff members in fiscal year 2013; and

>> (D) 5,000 staff members in fiscal year 2014.

> (2) FIELD STAFF FOR FOOD DEFENSE.--The goal under paragraph (1) shall include an increase of 150 employees by fiscal year 2011 to--

>> (A) provide additional detection of and response to food defense threats; and

>> (B) detect, track, and remove smuggled food (as defined in section 309) from commerce.

SEC. 402. EMPLOYEE PROTECTIONS.

Chapter X of the Federal Food, Drug, and Cosmetic Act (21 U.S.C. 391 et seq.), as amended by section 209, is further amended by adding at the end the following:

"SEC. 1012. EMPLOYEE PROTECTIONS.

"(a) In General.--No entity engaged in the manufacture, processing, packing, transporting, distribution, reception, holding, or importation of food may discharge an employee or otherwise discriminate against an employee with respect to compensation, terms, conditions, or privileges of employment because the employee, whether at the employee's initiative or in the ordinary course of the employee's duties (or any person acting pursuant to a request of the employee)--

"(1) provided, caused to be provided, or is about to provide or cause to be provided to the employer, the Federal Government, or the attorney general of a State information relating to any violation of, or any act or omission the employee reasonably believes to be a violation of any provision of this Act or any order, rule, regulation, standard, or ban under this Act, or any order, rule, regulation, standard, or ban under this Act;

"(2) testified or is about to testify in a proceeding concerning such violation;

"(3) assisted or participated or is about to assist or participate in such a proceeding; or

"(4) objected to, or refused to participate in, any activity, policy, practice, or assigned task that the employee (or other such person) reasonably believed to be in violation of any provision of this Act, or any order, rule, regulation, standard, or ban under this Act.

"(b) Process.--

"(1) IN GENERAL.--A person who believes that he or she has been discharged or otherwise discriminated against by any person in violation of subsection (a) may, not later than 180 days after the date on which such violation occurs, file (or have any person file on his or her behalf) a complaint with the Secretary of Labor (referred to in this section as the 'Secretary') alleging such discharge or discrimination and identifying the person responsible for such act. Upon receipt of such a complaint, the Secretary shall notify, in writing, the person named in the complaint of the filing of the complaint, of the allegations contained in the complaint, of the substance of evidence supporting the complaint, and of the opportunities that will be afforded to such person under paragraph (2).

"(2) INVESTIGATION.--

"(A) IN GENERAL.--Not later than 60 days after the date of receipt of a complaint filed under paragraph (1) and after affording the complainant and the person named in the complaint an opportunity to submit to the Secretary a written response to the complaint and an opportunity to meet with a representative of the Secretary to present statements from witnesses, the Secretary shall initiate an investigation and determine whether there is reasonable cause to believe that the complaint has merit and notify, in writing, the complainant and the person alleged to have committed a violation of subsection (a) of the Secretary's findings.

"(B) REASONABLE CAUSE FOUND; PRELIMINARY ORDER.--If the Secretary concludes that there is reasonable cause to believe that a violation of subsection (a) has occurred, the

Secretary shall accompany the Secretary's findings with a preliminary order providing the relief prescribed by paragraph (3)(B). Not later than 30 days after the date of notification of findings under this paragraph, the person alleged to have committed the violation or the complainant may file objections to the findings or preliminary order, or both, and request a hearing on the record. The filing of such objections shall not operate to stay any reinstatement remedy contained in the preliminary order. Any such hearing shall be conducted expeditiously. If a hearing is not requested in such 30-day period, the preliminary order shall be deemed a final order that is not subject to judicial review.

"(C) DISMISSAL OF COMPLAINT.--

"(i) STANDARD FOR COMPLAINANT.--The Secretary shall dismiss a complaint filed under this subsection and shall not conduct an investigation otherwise required under subparagraph (A) unless the complainant makes a prima facie showing that any behavior described in paragraphs (1) through (4) of subsection (a) was a contributing factor in the unfavorable personnel action alleged in the complaint.

"(ii) STANDARD FOR EMPLOYER.-- Notwithstanding a finding by the Secretary that the complainant has made the showing required under clause (i), no investigation otherwise required under subparagraph (A) shall be conducted if the employer demonstrates, by clear and convincing evidence, that the employer would have taken the same unfavorable personnel action in the absence of that behavior.

"(iii) VIOLATION STANDARD.--The Secretary may determine that a violation of subsection (a) has occurred only if the complainant demonstrates that any behavior described in paragraphs (1) through (4) of subsection (a) was a contributing factor in the unfavorable personnel action alleged in the complaint.

"(iv) RELIEF STANDARD.--Relief may not be ordered under subparagraph (A) if the employer demonstrates by clear and convincing evidence that the employer would have taken the same unfavorable personnel action in the absence of that behavior.

"(3) FINAL ORDER.--

"(A) IN GENERAL.--Not later than 120 days after the date of conclusion of any hearing under paragraph (2), the Secretary shall issue a final order providing the relief prescribed by this paragraph or denying the complaint. At any time before issuance of a final order, a proceeding under this subsection may be terminated on the basis of a settlement agreement entered into by the Secretary, the complainant, and the person alleged to have committed the violation.

"(B) CONTENT OF ORDER.--If, in response to a complaint filed under paragraph (1), the Secretary determines that a violation of subsection

(a) has occurred, the Secretary shall order the person who committed such violation--

"(i) to take affirmative action to abate the violation;

"(ii) to reinstate the complainant to his or her former position together with compensation (including back pay) and restore the terms, conditions, and privileges associated with his or her employment; and

"(iii) to provide compensatory damages to the complainant.

"(C) PENALTY.--If such an order is issued under this paragraph, the Secretary, at the request of the complainant, shall assess against the person against whom the order is issued a sum equal to the aggregate amount of all costs and expenses (including attorneys' and expert witness fees) reasonably incurred, as determined by the Secretary, by the complainant for, or in connection with, the bringing of the complaint upon which the order was issued.

"(D) BAD FAITH CLAIM.--If the Secretary finds that a complaint under paragraph (1) is frivolous or has been brought in bad faith, the Secretary may award to the prevailing employer a reasonable attorneys' fee, not exceeding $1,000, to be paid by the complainant.

"(4) ACTION IN COURT.--

"(A) IN GENERAL.--If the Secretary has not issued a final decision within 210 days after the filing of the complaint, or within 90 days after receiving a written determination, the complainant may bring an action at law or equity for de novo review in the appropriate district court of the United States with jurisdiction, which shall have jurisdiction over such an action without regard to the amount in controversy, and which action shall, at the request of either party to such action, be tried by the court with a jury. The proceedings shall be governed by the same legal burdens of proof specified in paragraph (2)(C).

"(B) RELIEF.--The court shall have jurisdiction to grant all relief necessary to make the employee whole, including injunctive relief and compensatory damages, including--

"(i) reinstatement with the same seniority status that the employee would have had, but for the discharge or discrimination;

"(ii) the amount of back pay, with interest; and

"(iii) compensation for any special damages sustained as a result of the discharge or discrimination, including litigation costs, expert witness fees, and reasonable attorney's fees.

"(5) REVIEW.--

"(A) IN GENERAL.--Unless the complainant brings an action under paragraph (4), any person adversely affected or aggrieved by a final order issued under paragraph (3) may obtain review of the order in the United States Court of Appeals for the circuit in which the violation, with respect to which the order was issued, allegedly occurred or the circuit in which the complainant resided on the date of such violation. The petition for review, must be filed not later than 60 days after the date of the issuance of the final order of the Secretary. Review shall conform to chapter 7 of title 5, United States Code. The commencement of proceedings under this subparagraph shall not, unless ordered by the court, operate as a stay of the order.

"(B) NO JUDICIAL REVIEW.--An order of the Secretary with respect to which review could have been obtained under subparagraph (A) shall not be subject to judicial review in any criminal or other civil proceeding.

"(6) FAILURE TO COMPLY WITH ORDER.-- Whenever any person has failed to comply with an order issued under paragraph (3), the Secretary may file a civil action in the United States district court for the district in which the violation was found to occur, or in the United States district court for the District of Columbia, to enforce such order. In actions brought under this paragraph, the district courts shall have jurisdiction to grant all appropriate relief including, but not limited to, injunctive relief and compensatory damages.

"(7) CIVIL ACTION TO REQUIRE COMPLIANCE.--

"(A) IN GENERAL.--A person on whose behalf an order was issued under paragraph (3) may commence a civil action against the person to whom such order was issued to require compliance with such order. The appropriate United States district court shall have jurisdiction, without regard to the amount in controversy or the citizenship of the parties, to enforce such order.

"(B) AWARD.--The court, in issuing any final order under this paragraph, may award costs of litigation (including reasonable attorneys' and expert witness fees) to any party whenever the court determines such award is appropriate.

"(c) Effect of Section.--

"(1) OTHER LAWS.--Nothing in this section preempts or diminishes any other safeguards against discrimination, demotion, discharge, suspension, threats, harassment, reprimand, retaliation, or any other manner of discrimination provided by Federal or State law.

"(2) RIGHTS OF EMPLOYEES.--Nothing in this section shall be construed to diminish the rights, privileges, or remedies of any employee under any Federal or State law or under any collective bargaining agreement. The rights and remedies in this section may not be waived by any agreement, policy, form, or condition of employment.

"(d) Enforcement.--Any nondiscretionary duty imposed by this section shall be enforceable in a mandamus proceeding brought under section 1361 of title 28, United States Code.

"(e) Limitation.--Subsection (a) shall not apply with respect to an employee of an entity engaged in the manufacture, processing, packing, transporting, distribution, reception, holding, or importation of food who, acting without direction from such entity (or such entity's agent), deliberately causes a violation of any requirement relating to any violation or alleged violation of any order, rule, regulation, standard, or ban under this Act.".

SEC. 403. JURISDICTION; AUTHORITIES.

Nothing in this Act, or an amendment made by this Act, shall be construed to--

(1) alter the jurisdiction between the Secretary of Agriculture and the Secretary of Health and Human Services, under applicable statutes, regulations, or agreements regarding voluntary inspection of non-amenable species under the Agricultural Marketing Act of 1946 (7 U.S.C. 1621 et seq.);

(2) alter the jurisdiction between the Alcohol and Tobacco Tax and Trade Bureau and the Secretary of Health and Human Services, under applicable statutes and regulations;

(3) limit the authority of the Secretary of Health and Human Services under--

(A) the Federal Food, Drug, and Cosmetic Act (21 U.S.C. 301 et seq.) as in effect on the day before the date of enactment of this Act; or

(B) the Public Health Service Act (42 U.S.C. 301 et seq.) as in effect on the day before the date of enactment of this Act;

(4) alter or limit the authority of the Secretary of Agriculture under the laws administered by such Secretary, including--

(A) the Federal Meat Inspection Act (21 U.S.C. 601 et seq.);

(B) the Poultry Products Inspection Act (21 U.S.C. 451 et seq.);

(C) the Egg Products Inspection Act (21 U.S.C. 1031 et seq.);

(D) the United States Grain Standards Act (7 U.S.C. 71 et seq.);

(E) the Packers and Stockyards Act, 1921 (7 U.S.C. 181 et seq.);

(F) the United States Warehouse Act (7 U.S.C. 241 et seq.);

(G) the Agricultural Marketing Act of 1946 (7 U.S.C. 1621 et seq.); and

(H) the Agricultural Adjustment Act (7 U.S.C. 601 et seq.), reenacted with the amendments made by the Agricultural Marketing Agreement Act of 1937; or

(5) alter, impede, or affect the authority of the Secretary of Homeland Security under the Homeland Security Act of 2002 (6 U.S.C. 101 et seq.) or any other statute, including any authority related to securing the borders of the United States, managing ports of entry, or agricultural import and entry inspection activities.

SEC. 404. COMPLIANCE WITH INTERNATIONAL AGREEMENTS.

Nothing in this Act (or an amendment made by this Act) shall be construed in a manner inconsistent with the agreement establishing the World Trade Organization or any other treaty or international agreement to which the United States is a party.

SEC. 405. DETERMINATION OF BUDGETARY EFFECTS.

The budgetary effects of this Act, for the purpose of complying with the Statutory Pay-As-You-Go-Act of 2010, shall be determined by reference to the latest statement titled "Budgetary Effects of PAYGO Legislation" for this Act, submitted for printing in the Congressional Record by the Chairman of the Senate Budget Committee, provided that such statement has been submitted prior to the vote on passage.

TOPICAL INDEX BY CHAPTER

2010 legislation
    Description of passage 1

Administrative detention
    Enforcement 10
    FDA statements 10
    Implementation 10

Certification of imports
    Accreditation of qualified certifying entities 5
    Accreditation of third-party auditors and audit agents 5
    Consumer group statements 5
    Electronic submissions 5
    Enforcement 5
    Exemptions 5
    Implementation 5
    International trade obligations 5
    Limitation on other FDA authority 5
    Qualified certifying entities 5
    Requirements 5
    Trade association statements 5

Codex Alimentarius 5

Compliance with 2010 legislation
    Contingency plans 13
    Role of board of directors 13
    Role of customs brokers 13
    Role of trade associations 13
    Training 13

Congressional intent
    Extraterritorial Jurisdiction 10
    Fees 11
    Inspection of food facilities 9
    Mandatory reporting 10
    Performance standards 3
    Produce and raw agricultural commodity safety standards 3
    Recall authority 10

Records access 9
Records access for farms 9
Tracing requirement 3

Consumer group statements
Penalties 10
Certification of imports 5
Enforcement 10
Hazard analysis 2
Inspection of food facilities 9
Mandatory reporting 10
Performance standards Recall authority 10
Produce and raw agricultural commodity safety standards 3

Customs Brokers
Registration requirement 5

Enforcement
Import entry filings 9
Administrative detention 10
Certification of imports 5
Consumer group statements 10
Finished product testing 3
Food defense plan 4
Foreign supplier verification program 6
Hazard analysis and food safety plan 2
Impact of 2010 legislation 10
Inspections 9
Performance standards 3
Pre-2010 law 10
Produce and raw agricultural commodity safety standards 3
Quarantine auhtority 10
Recall authority 10
Registration requirement .... 6 & 7
Subpoena authority 10
Tracing requirement 8

Extraterritorial Jurisdiction
FDA statements 10
Generally 10
Congressional intent 10

Farms

Jurisdictional Division between FDA and USDA 1
Records access exemption 9
Registration requirement exemption 7
Tracing requirement exemption 8

FDA foreign capacity

Required by 2010 legislation 5

FDA foreign offices

Required by 2010 legislation 5

FDA statements

2010 legislation generally 1
Administrative detention 10
Enforcement 10
Extraterritorial Jurisdiction 10
Fees 11
Foreign supplier verification program 6
Hazard analysis 2
Inspection of food facilities 9
International trade obligations 12
Produce and raw agricultural commodity safety standards 3
Quarantine authority 10
Recall authority 10
Records access 9
Registration requirement .... 6 & 7
Subpoena authority 10
Tracing requirement 8

Fees

Congressional intent 11
FDA statements 11
Importation fees 11
International trade obligations 11
Purpose 11
Recall fees 11
Registration requirement 11
Reinspection fees 10
Trade association statements 8

Finished product testing
Enforcement 3
Implementation 3
Requirements 3

Food defense plan
Coverage 4
Enforcement 4
Implementation 4
Interaction between FDA, USDA and Homeland Security 4
Public disclosure of plan 4
Requirements 4

Food safety plan
Consumer group statements 2
Enforcement 2
FDA access to food safety plan 9
FDA statements 2
Pre-2010 legislation 2
Requirements 2
Trade association statements 2

Foreign supplier verification program
Enforcement 6
FDA statements 6
Implementation 6
Records access 6
Trade association statements 6

Funding of 2010 legislation 11

Good agricultural practices 1

Grain or similarly handled commodity
Records access 9
Tracing requirement exemption 8

Hazard analysis
Consumer group statements 2
Enforcement FDA statements 2
Exemptions 2

Existing HACCP requirements 2
FDA statements 2
Food safety plan requirements.. 2
Implementation 2
Pre-2010 legislation.. 10
Requirements... 2
Trade association statements 2
Verification activities ....2 & 3

Import entry filings
Requirements...6 & 9

Importers
Good importer practices.. 6
Registration requirement.. 6

Imports
Statistics... 1

Inspections at ports of entry
Process.. 6
Trade association statements 9

Inspections of food faclities
Congressional attention 9
Consumer group statements 9
Dedicated foreign inspectorate.. 9
Enforcement... 9
FDA access to a facility and records... 9
FDA statements 9
Implementation... 9
Schedule... 9
Third-party certification... 9

International trade obligations
Certification of imports.. 5
Enforcement of fees... 11
Generally .... 12 & 13
Hazard analysis and preventive controls...................................... 12

Sanitary and Phytosanitary Agreement 12
Tracing requirement 8
Trade association statements 12

Jurisdiction
Interaction between FDA and Customs and Border Protection 1
Interaction between FDA and USDA 1

Laboratory certification program
Impact of 3
Implementation 3
Interaction between FDA and Customs and Border Protection 3
Requirements for accreditation 3
Requirements for laboratory certification 3
Requirements for testing 3

Laboratory testing
Emergency response laboratory network 3
Integrated Consortium of Laboratory Networks 3

Mandatory reporting
Congressional intent 10
Consumer group statements 10

Organic food
Impact of 2010 legislation 1
Produce and raw agricultural commodity safety standards 3

Penalties
Civil Penalties 10
Consumer group statements 10
Criminal penalties 10
Trade association statements 10

Performance standards
Congressional intent 3
Consumer group statements 3
Coverage 3
Enforcement 3

Food safety plan requirements.. 2
Implementation... 3

Preventive controls
Food safety plan requirements.. 3
Hazard analysis requirements.. 2

Pre-2010 law
Enforcement.. 10
FDA access to records... 9
FDA cooperation with foreign nations.. 9
FDA oversight of imports.. 9
Foodborne illness costs... 9
Hazard analysis and food safety plan.. 2
History of FDA oversight.. 1
Registration requirement.. 7
Tracing requirement... 8

Processed food
Tracing requirement... 8

Produce and raw agricultural commodity safety standards
Congressional intent.. 3
Consumer group statements... 3
Coverage.. 3
Enforcement... 3
Exemptions.. 3
Existing HACCP requirements... 3
FDA statements.. 3
Implementation.. 3
Interaction between FDA and USDA.. 3
Requirements.. 3
Trade association statements.. 3

Produce farms
Tracing requirement exemption... 8

Quarantine authority
Enforcement... 10

FDA statements 10
Implementation 10
Requirements 10
Restrictions 10
Standard 10
Trade association statements 10

Raw agricultural commodities
Safety plan requirements 2

Raw milk 1

Recall authority
Appealing a recall order 10
Enforcement 10
FDA statements 10
Implementation 10
Standard 10
Trade association statements 10

Records access
Congressional attention 9
Farm exemption 9
FDA statements 9
Food safety plan 9
Foreign supplier verification program 6
Generally 9
Hazard analysis requirements 2
Implementation 9
Registration requirement 6
Remote access 9
Small businesses 9
Trade association statements 9

Registration requirement
Customs Brokers 6
Enforcement .... 6 & 7
Facilities 7
FDA statements .... 6 & 7

Fee .... 7 & 11
Impact of 2010 legislation 7
Implementation .... 6 & 7
Importers 6
Pre-2010 law 7
Records access 6
Trade association statements .... 6 & 7
Unique facilitiy identifier .... 6 & 7

Reportable Food Registry
Relation to safety standards .... 3 & 13

Retail Food establishments
Registration requirement exemption 7

Restaurants and grocery stores
Tracing requirement exemption 8

Safe and Secure Import Food Program 8

Safety standards
Impact of 3

Sanitary and Phytosanitary Agreement 12

Seafood related industries
Tracing requirement exemption 8

Small businesses
Food safety plan preventive controls 2
Impact of 2010 legislation 1
Produce and raw agricultural commodity safety standards 3
Records access 9

Subpoena authority
Congressional intent 10
FDA statements 10

Tracing requirement

Congressional attention 8
Coverage 8
Enforcement 8
Farm exemption 8
FDA statements 8
Food safety plan requirements 2
Grain or similarly handled commodity exemption 8
International trade obligations 8
Other food exemption 8
Pre-2010 law 8
Processed food 8
Produce farm exemption 8
Raw agricultural commodities 8
Restaurants and grocery stores exemption 8
Trade association statements 8

Trade association statements

2010 legislation generally 1
Certification of imports 5
Fees 11
Foreign supplier verification program 6
Hazard analysis and food safety plan 2
International trade obligations 10
Penalties 10
Produce and raw agricultural commodity safety standards 3
Quarantine authority 10
Recall authority 7
Records access 9
Registration requirement .... 6 & 7
Tracing requirement 8
Voluntary Qualified Import Program 6

Unique facilitiy identifier .... 6 & 7

United States Trade Representative 12

Verification activities

Food safety plan requirements 2
Hazard analysis requirements .... 2 & 3

Voluntary Qualified Import Program
  Generally 6
  Trade association statements 6

World Trade Organization .... 12 & 13

ABOUT THE AUTHORS

Professor **James T. O'Reilly** has taught food and drug law among other courses for three decades at the University of Cincinnati College of Law. He is the chair of the American Bar Association FDA committee, former chair of the Programs Committee of the Food & Drug Law Institute, and is a board member of the Food & Drug Law Journal. He has been active in FDA issues since the early 1970s, formerly was chief FDA lawyer for a food company, and has lectured and consulted internationally on FDA matters. In March 2000, the US Supreme Court quoted his Thomson Reuters text on FDA with the words "The experts have written…" Prof. O'Reilly is a graduate of Boston College and the University of Virginia School of Law. This is his forty-third textbook.

Shannon G. May practices law in New York focusing on commercial litigation and published the lead article on food law in Volume 65 of the *Food & Drug Law Journal.* She is a graduate of Fordham Law School, where she was an editor of the *International Law Journal*, and Louisiana State University.

ASPATORE